A Retelling of a Classic

BRAVE

STORY

4

Art by:
Yoichiro Ono

Brave Story Volume 4
Story by: Miyuki Miyabe
Art by: Yoichiro Ono

Translation - Bruce Dorsey
English Adaptation - Alan Swayze
Copy Editor - Jessica Chavez
Retouch and Lettering - Star Print Brokers
Production Artist - Lauren O'Connell
Graphic Designer - Louis Csontos

Editor - Hyun Joo Kim
Digital Imaging Manager - Chris Buford
Pre-Production Supervisor - Erika Terriquez
Production Manager - Elisabeth Brizzi
Managing Editor - Vy Nguyen
Creative Director - Anne Marie Horne
Editor-in-Chief - Rob Tokar
Publisher - Mike Kiley
President and C.O.O. - John Parker
C.E.O. and Chief Creative Officer - Stuart Levy

A  Manga

TOKYOPOP and  are trademarks or registered trademarks of TOKYOPOP Inc.

TOKYOPOP Inc.
5900 Wilshire Blvd. Suite 2000
Los Angeles, CA 90036

E-mail: info@TOKYOPOP.com
Come visit us online at www.TOKYOPOP.com

ISBN: 978-1-4278-0492-1

First TOKYOPOP printing: May 2008
10 9 8 7 6 5 4 3 2 1
Printed in the USA

A Retelling of a Classic

BRAVE STORY

Volume 4

Story by:
Miyuki Miyabe

Art by:
Yoichiro Ono

HAMBURG // LONDON // LOS ANGELES // TOKYO

A Retelling of a Classic
BRAVE STORY

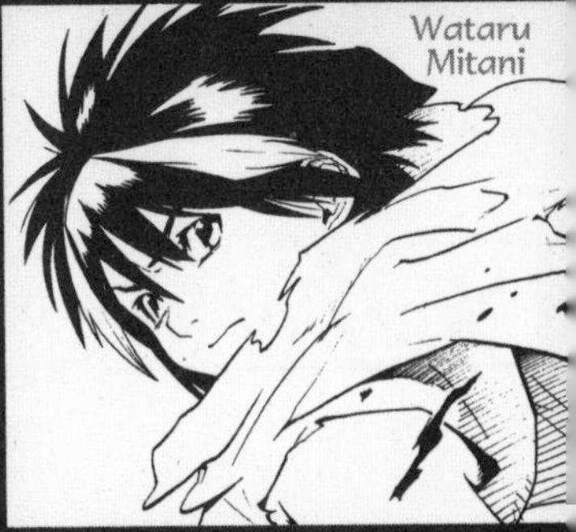
Wataru
Mitani

A TYPICAL MIDDLE SCHOOL STUDENT. HE JOURNEYED TO VISION IN ORDER TO MEND THE RIFT IN HIS SHATTERED FAMILY. HE'S A HERO IN TRAINING.

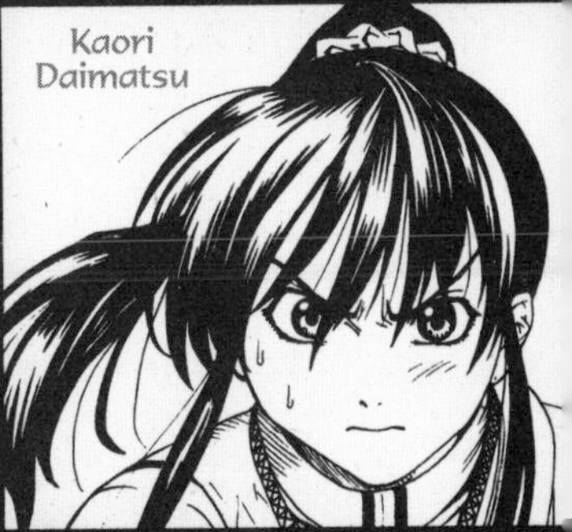
Kaori
Daimatsu

KAORI IS THE GIRL ON WHOM WATARU HAS A CRUSH--EVEN THOUGH SHE SEEMS TO BE INTERESTED IN ASHIKAWA. SHE CAME TO VISION IN THE HOPES OF SOLVING HER OWN FAMILY'S MOUNTING FINANCIAL PROBLEMS. SHE IS A CANON-LICENSE TRAVELER.

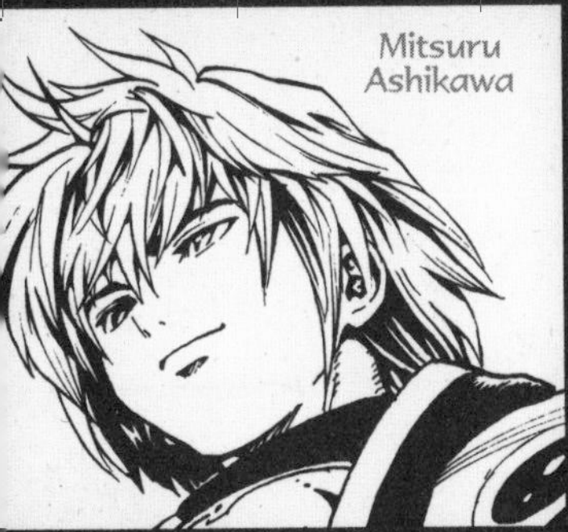
Mitsuru
Ashikawa

A BOY WITH A DARK PAST. HE TRAVELED TO VISION IN THE HOPES OF BRINGING HIS FAMILY BACK FROM THE GRAVE. HE IS A WIZARD-LICENSE TRAVELER.

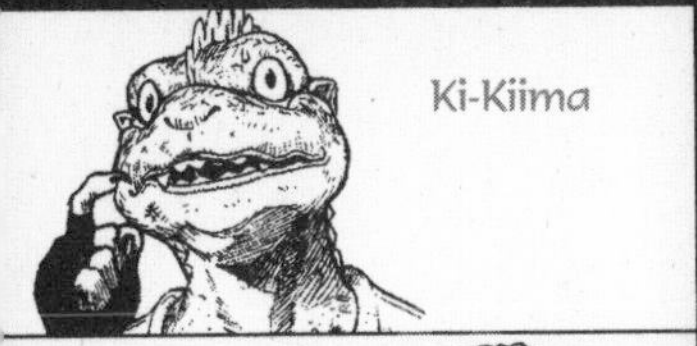
Ki-Kiima

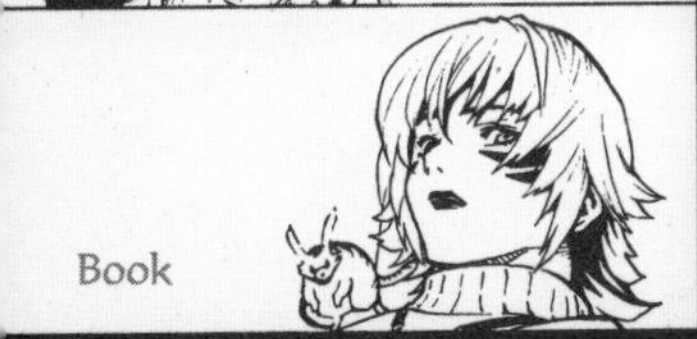
Book

CHARACTER INTRO & STORY

WATARU MITANI EXCELS IN PLAYING VIDEO GAMES OVER ALL ELSE--INCLUDING HIS STUDIES. EVER SINCE MITSURU ASHIKAWA TRANSFERRED TO HIS CLASS, HOWEVER, WATARU'S QUIET, NORMAL LIFE HAS BECOME A THING OF THE PAST. FIRST, WATARU'S FATHER ABANDONS HIS FAMILY TO GO AND LIVE WITH HIS LOVER. THEN HE LEARNS OF ASHIKAWA'S FAMILY TRAGEDY, WHICH EVENTUALLY LEADS TO HIS DISCOVERY OF THE EXISTENCE OF VISION. UPON FINDING OUT THAT IF YOU SUCCESSFULLY COMPLETE A CERTAIN QUEST IN VISION, YOUR FONDEST WISH WILL BE GRANTED, WATARU ACCEPTS THE CHALLENGE AND JOURNEYS TO VISION, HOT ON ASHIKAWA'S TRAIL AND COMPLETELY UNAWARE OF KAORI SECRETLY FOLLOWING HIM... KAORI IS LATER KIDNAPPED BY THE SHIGORA, AN ELITE GUARD WHO ARE DISCIPLES OF THE CHURCH OF THE ELDER GOD. WHILE TRYING TO INFILTRATE THE SHIGORA SAFE HOUSE, WATARU AND HIS ALLIES ARE SOUNDLY DEFEATED BY GRUSE OF THE SHIGORA. KAORI IS NOW REUNITED WITH ASHIKAWA IN THE NORTHERN EMPIRE, AND THE ONLY THING THAT'S MORE SHOCKING THAN HIS SUDDEN APPEARANCE THERE IS HIS NEW TITLE OF "LEFT SNAKE-TAIL" OF THE SHIGORA.

A Retelling of a Classic
BRAVE STORY

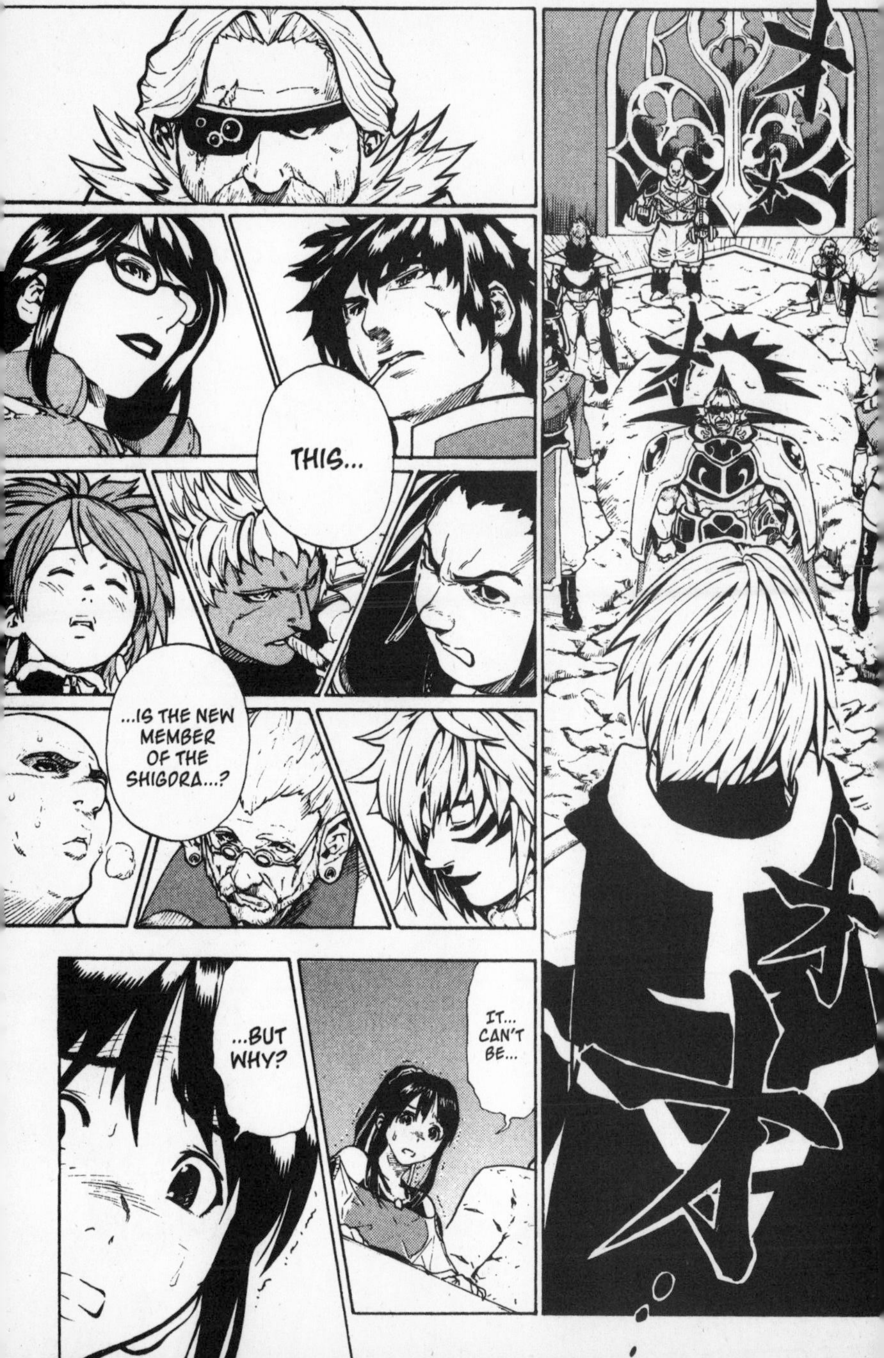
THIS...
...IS THE NEW MEMBER OF THE SHIGORA...?
IT... CAN'T BE...
...BUT WHY?

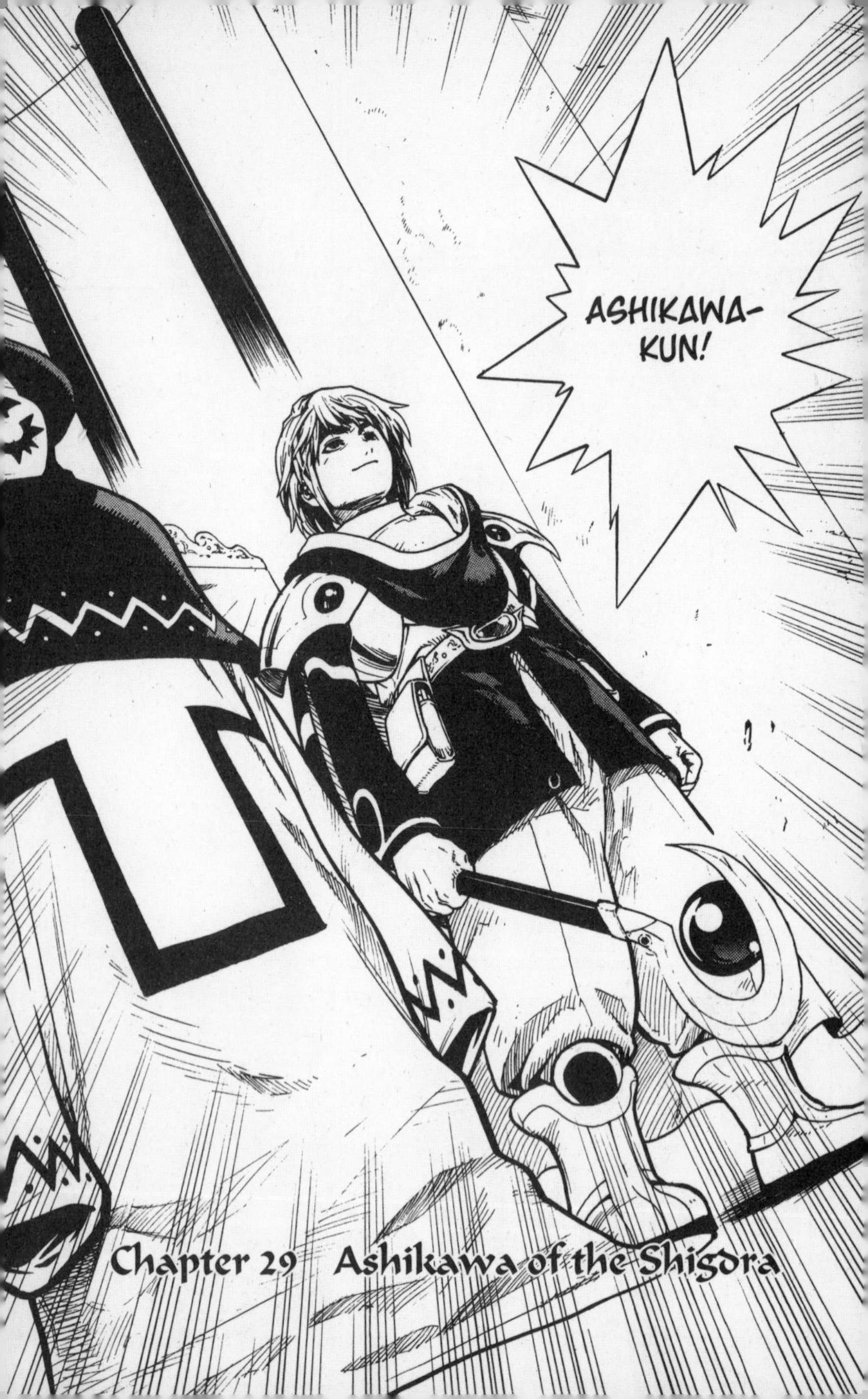
ASHIKAWA-KUN!
Chapter 29 Ashikawa of the Shigdra

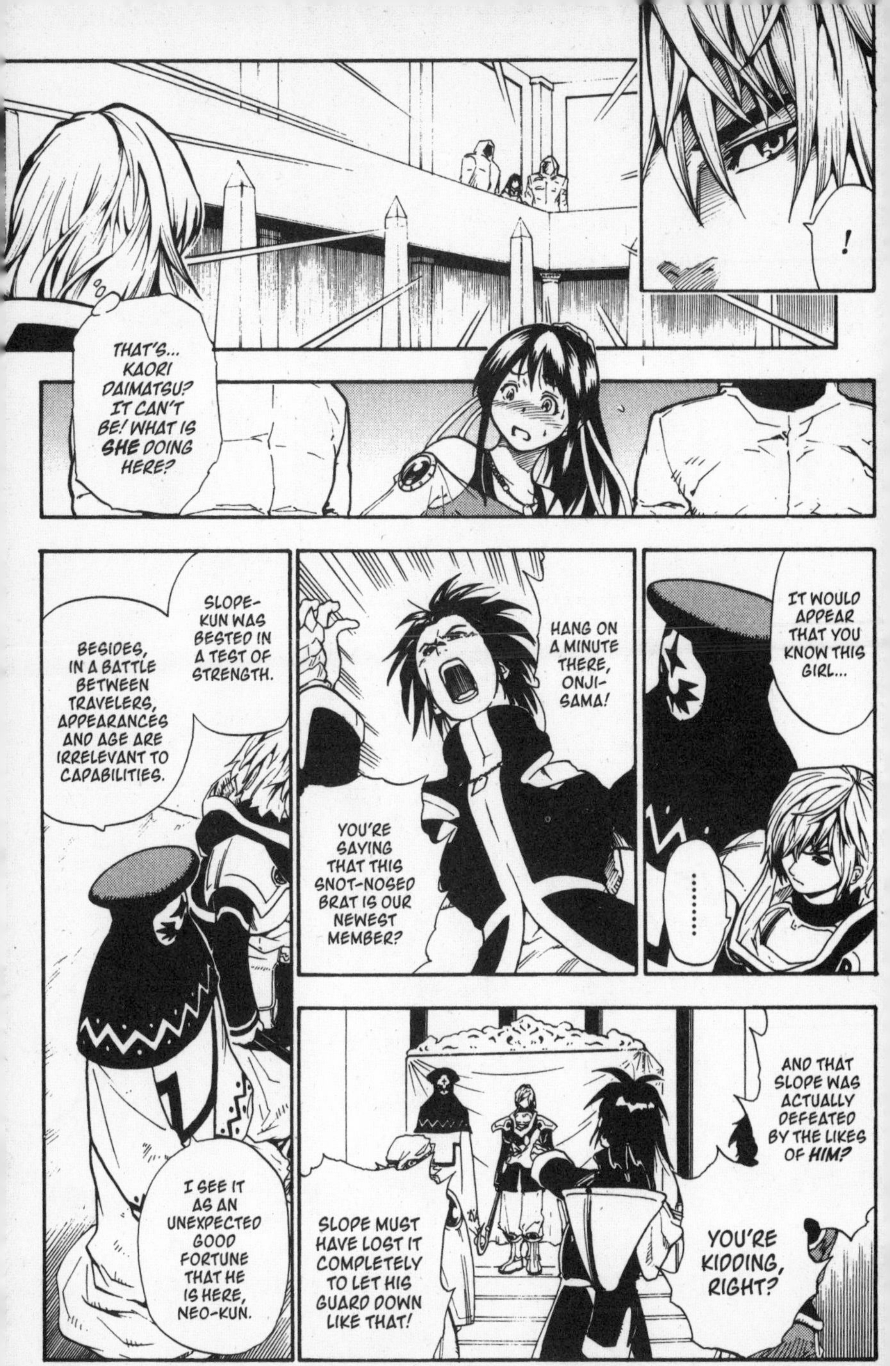
!
THAT'S... KAORI DAIMATSU? IT CAN'T BE! WHAT IS SHE DOING HERE?
IT WOULD APPEAR THAT YOU KNOW THIS GIRL...
......
HANG ON A MINUTE THERE, ONJI-SAMA!
YOU'RE SAYING THAT THIS SNOT-NOSED BRAT IS OUR NEWEST MEMBER?
SLOPE-KUN WAS BESTED IN A TEST OF STRENGTH.
BESIDES, IN A BATTLE BETWEEN TRAVELERS, APPEARANCES AND AGE ARE IRRELEVANT TO CAPABILITIES.
AND THAT SLOPE WAS ACTUALLY DEFEATED BY THE LIKES OF HIM?
YOU'RE KIDDING, RIGHT?
SLOPE MUST HAVE LOST IT COMPLETELY TO LET HIS GUARD DOWN LIKE THAT!
I SEE IT AS AN UNEXPECTED GOOD FORTUNE THAT HE IS HERE, NEO-KUN.

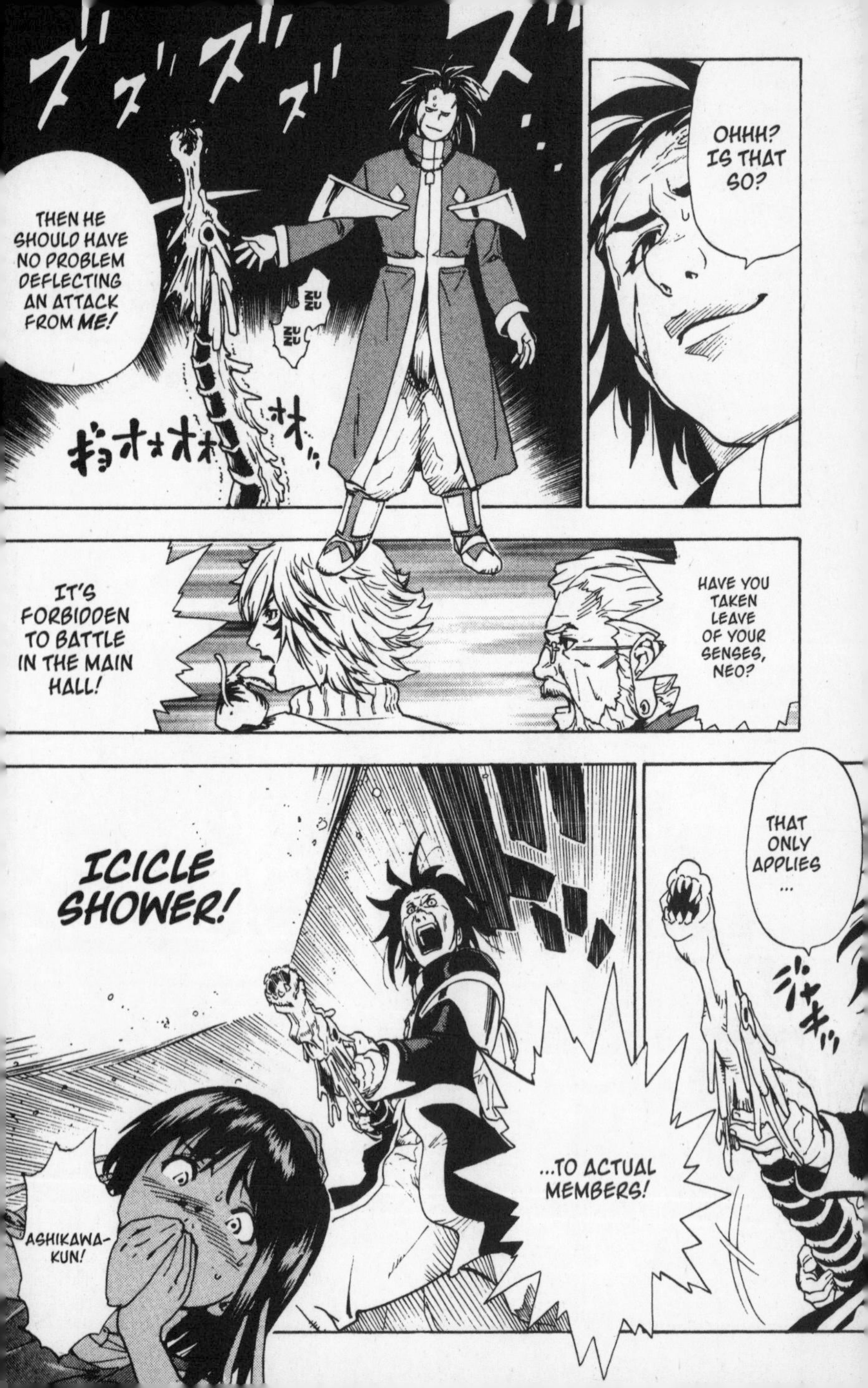
OHHH? IS THAT SO?
THEN HE SHOULD HAVE NO PROBLEM DEFLECTING AN ATTACK FROM ME!
ZU ZU
ZU ZU
HAVE YOU TAKEN LEAVE OF YOUR SENSES, NEO?
IT'S FORBIDDEN TO BATTLE IN THE MAIN HALL!
THAT ONLY APPLIES ...
ICICLE SHOWER!
...TO ACTUAL MEMBERS!
ASHIKAWA-KUN!

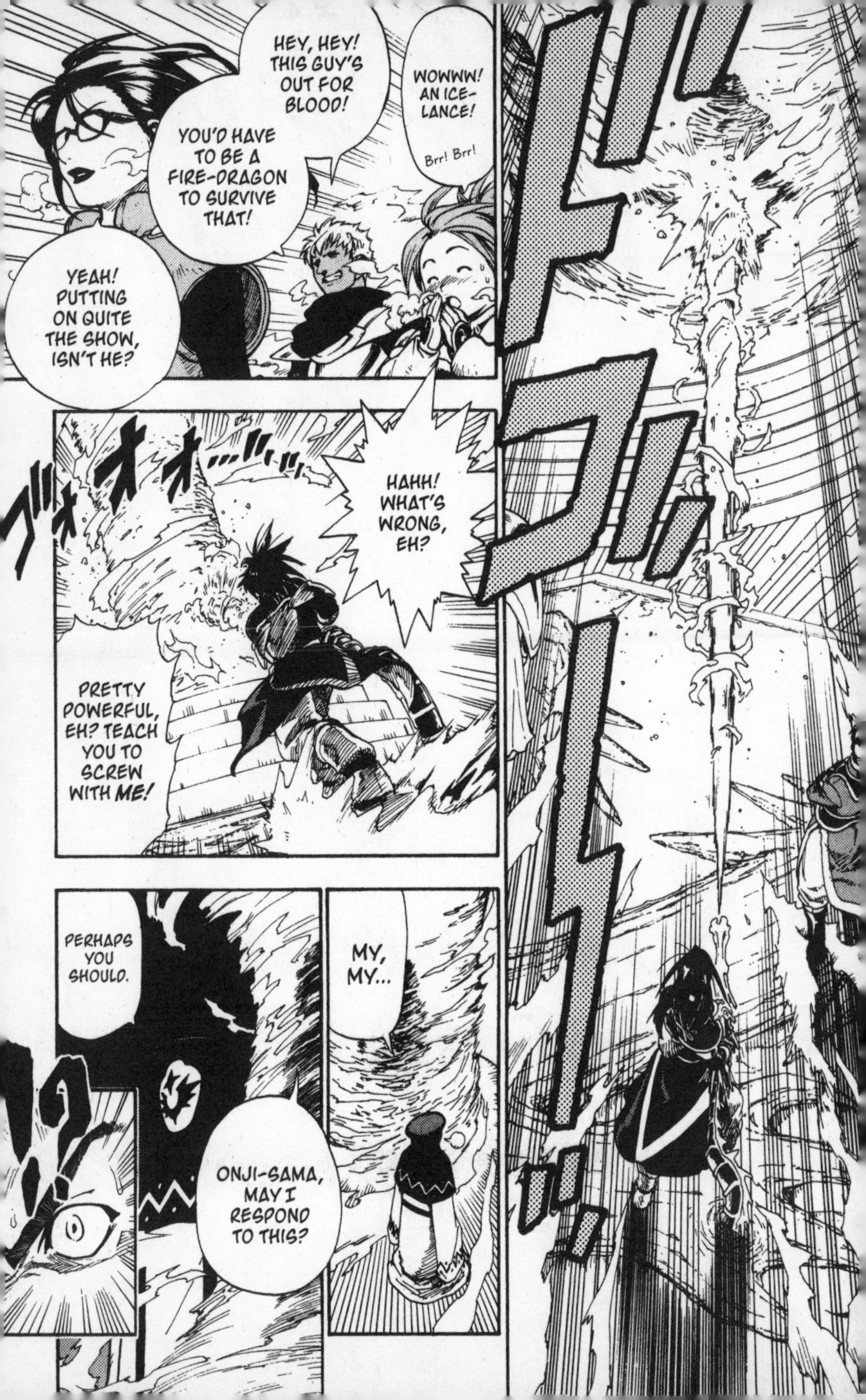
WOWWW! AN ICE-LANCE!
Brr! Brr!
HEY, HEY! THIS GUY'S OUT FOR BLOOD!
YOU'D HAVE TO BE A FIRE-DRAGON TO SURVIVE THAT!
YEAH! PUTTING ON QUITE THE SHOW, ISN'T HE?
HAHH! WHAT'S WRONG, EH?
PRETTY POWERFUL, EH? TEACH YOU TO SCREW WITH ME!
MY, MY...
ONJI-SAMA, MAY I RESPOND TO THIS?
PERHAPS YOU SHOULD.
!?

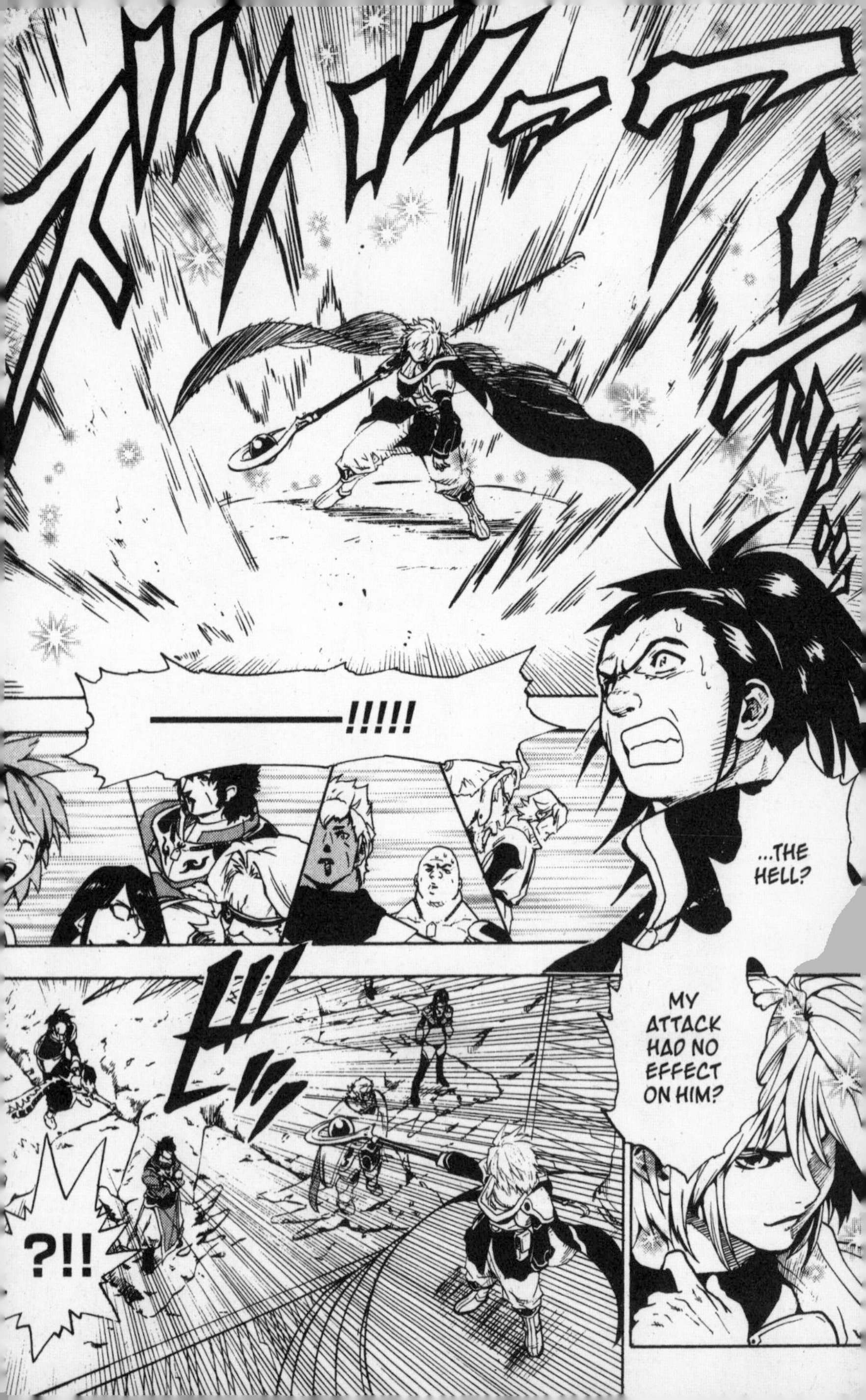
———————!!!!!
...THE HELL?
MY ATTACK HAD NO EFFECT ON HIM?
?!!

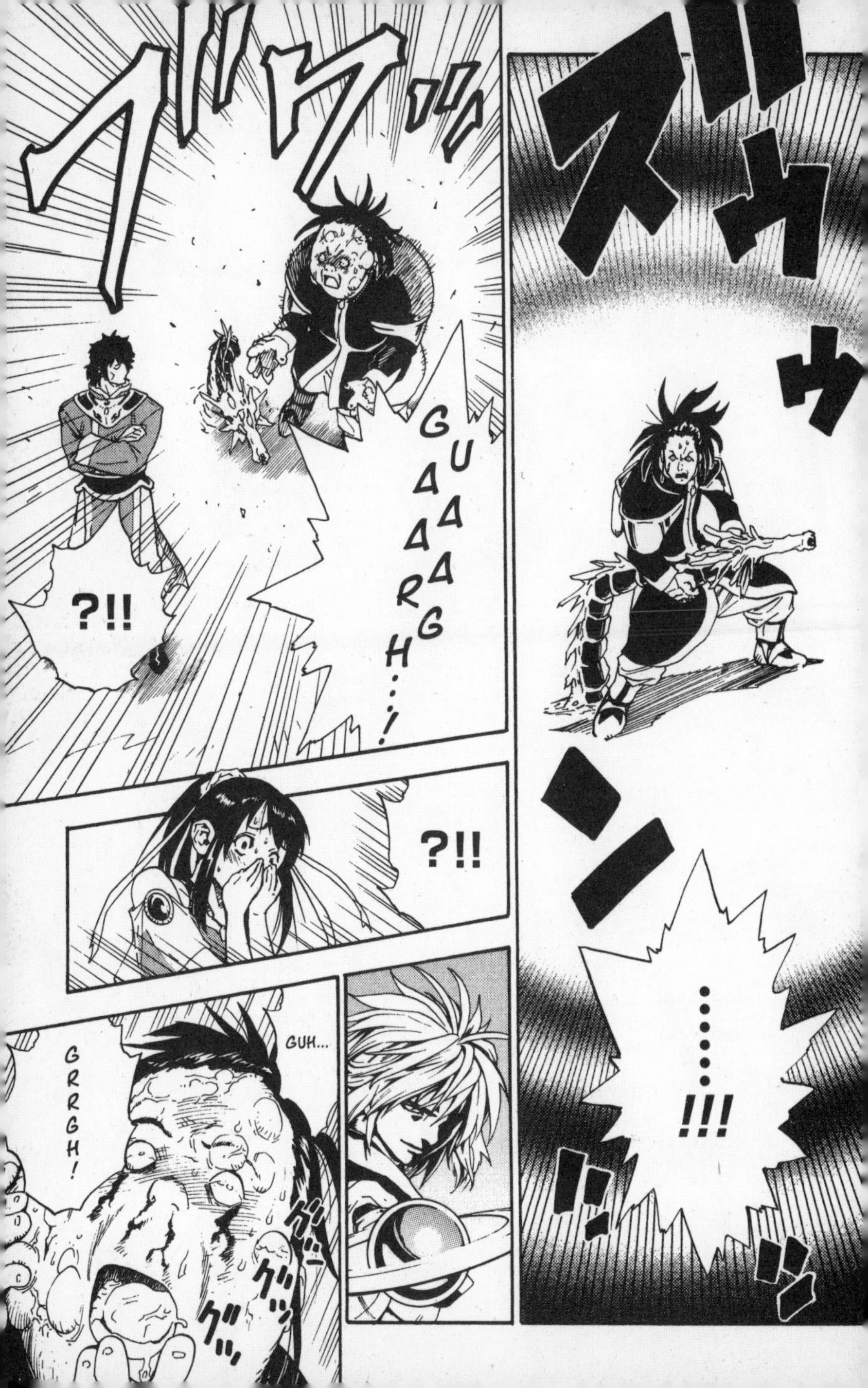
......!!!
GUAAAAARGH...!
?!!
?!!
GUH...
GRRGH!

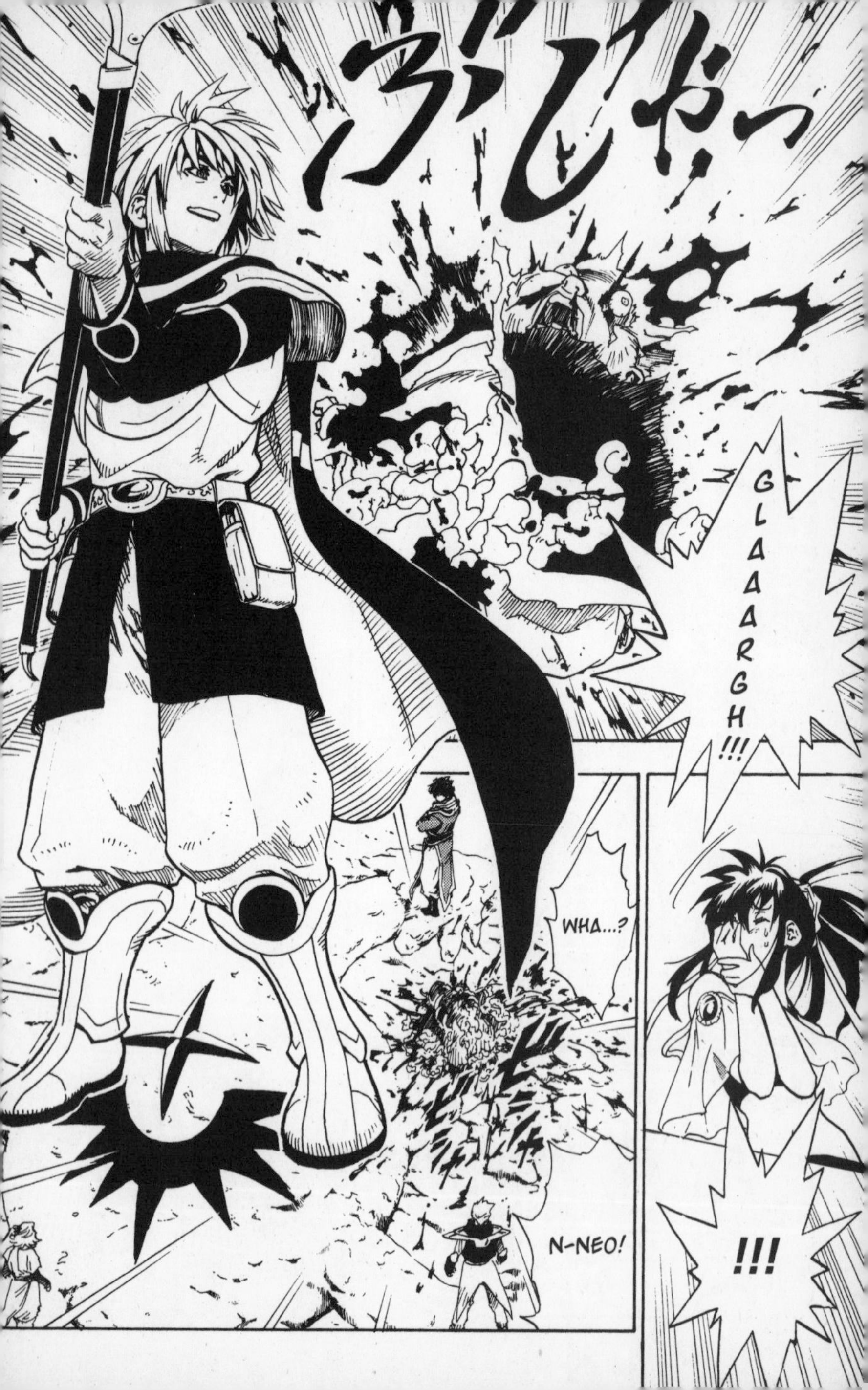
GLAAAARGH!!!
!!!
WHA...?
N-NEO!

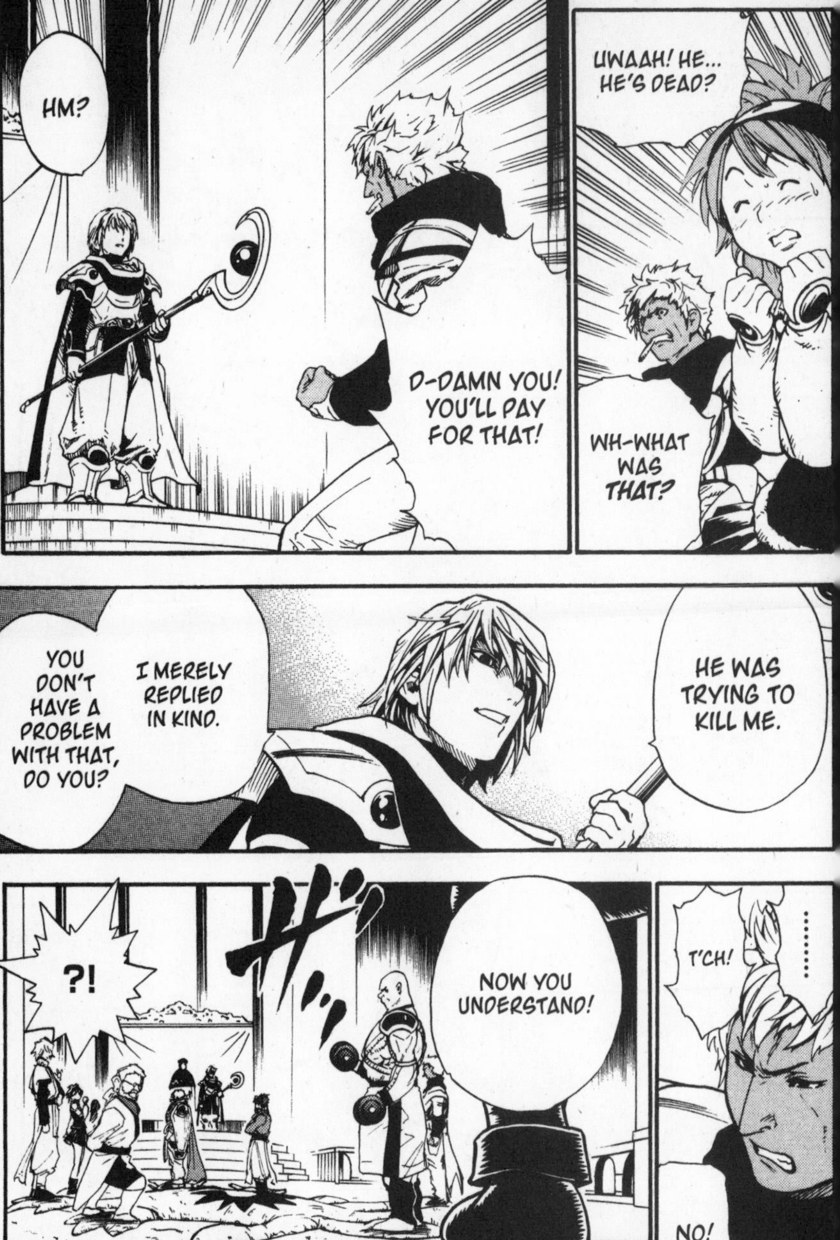
UWAAH! HE... HE'S DEAD?
WH-WHAT WAS THAT?
D-DAMN YOU! YOU'LL PAY FOR THAT!
HM?
HE WAS TRYING TO KILL ME.
I MERELY REPLIED IN KIND.
YOU DON'T HAVE A PROBLEM WITH THAT, DO YOU?
......
T'CH!
NO!
NOW YOU UNDERSTAND!
?!

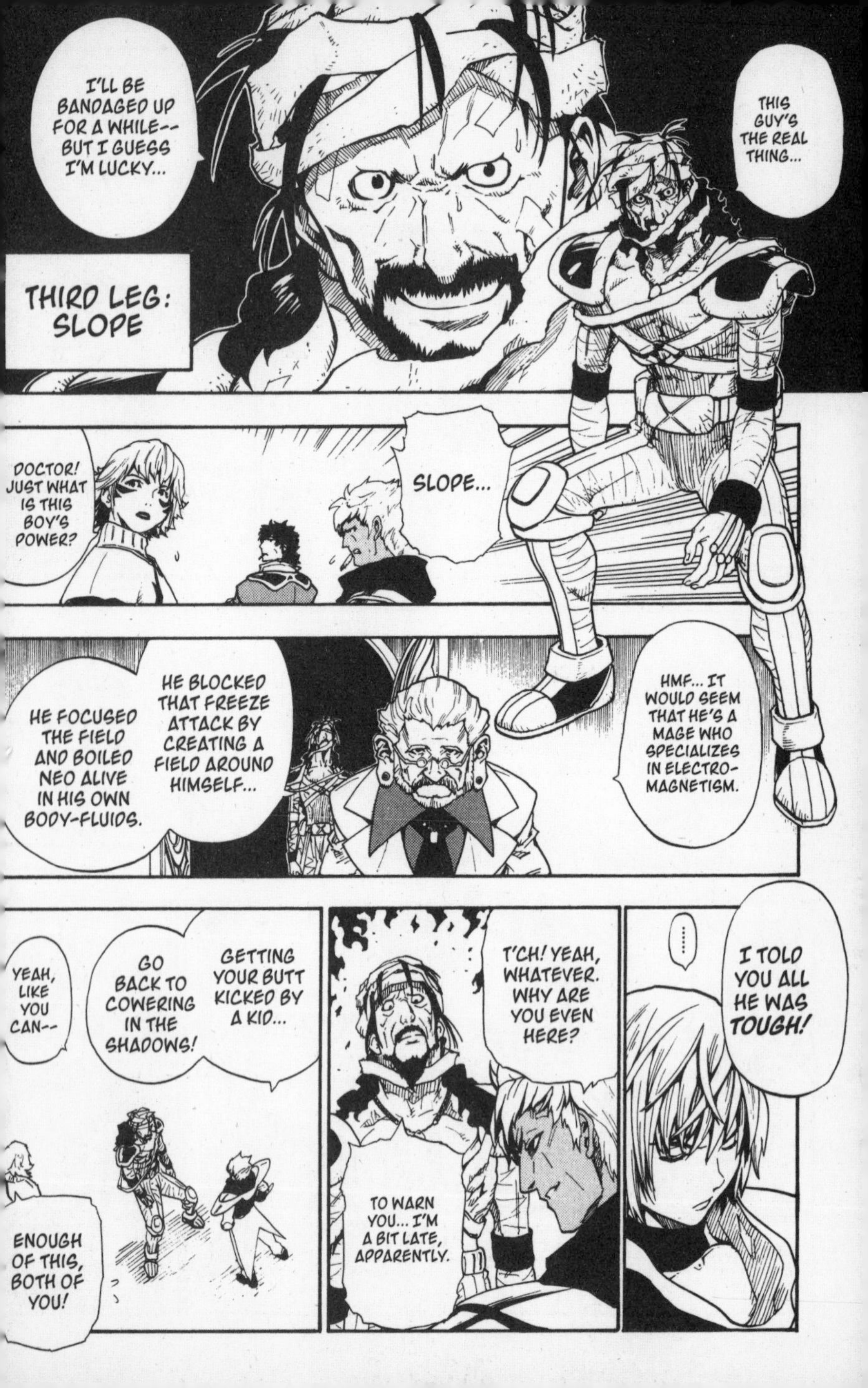
THIS GUY'S THE REAL THING...
I'LL BE BANDAGED UP FOR A WHILE-- BUT I GUESS I'M LUCKY...
THIRD LEG: SLOPE
SLOPE...
DOCTOR! JUST WHAT IS THIS BOY'S POWER?
HMF... IT WOULD SEEM THAT HE'S A MAGE WHO SPECIALIZES IN ELECTRO-MAGNETISM.
HE BLOCKED THAT FREEZE ATTACK BY CREATING A FIELD AROUND HIMSELF...
HE FOCUSED THE FIELD AND BOILED NEO ALIVE IN HIS OWN BODY-FLUIDS.
......
I TOLD YOU ALL HE WAS *TOUGH!*
T'CH! YEAH, WHATEVER. WHY ARE YOU EVEN HERE?
TO WARN YOU... I'M A BIT LATE, APPARENTLY.
GETTING YOUR BUTT KICKED BY A KID...
GO BACK TO COWERING IN THE SHADOWS!
YEAH, LIKE YOU CAN--
ENOUGH OF THIS, BOTH OF YOU!

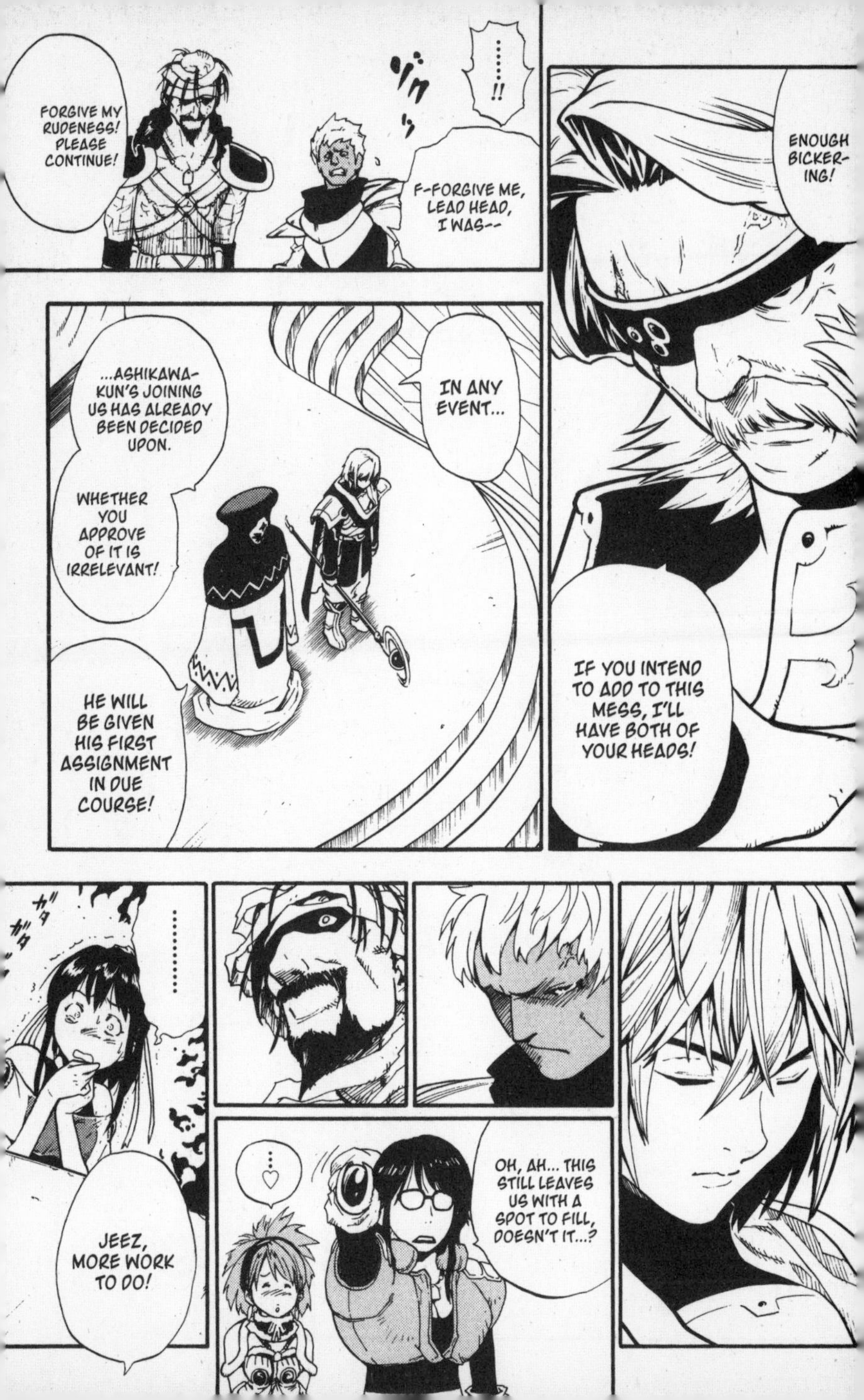

ENOUGH BICKER-ING!
IF YOU INTEND TO ADD TO THIS MESS, I'LL HAVE BOTH OF YOUR HEADS!
......!!
F-FORGIVE ME, LEAD HEAD, I WAS--
FORGIVE MY RUDENESS! PLEASE CONTINUE!
IN ANY EVENT...
...ASHIKAWA-KUN'S JOINING US HAS ALREADY BEEN DECIDED UPON.
WHETHER YOU APPROVE OF IT IS IRRELEVANT!
HE WILL BE GIVEN HIS FIRST ASSIGNMENT IN DUE COURSE!
OH, AH... THIS STILL LEAVES US WITH A SPOT TO FILL, DOESN'T IT...?
...♡
......
JEEZ, MORE WORK TO DO!

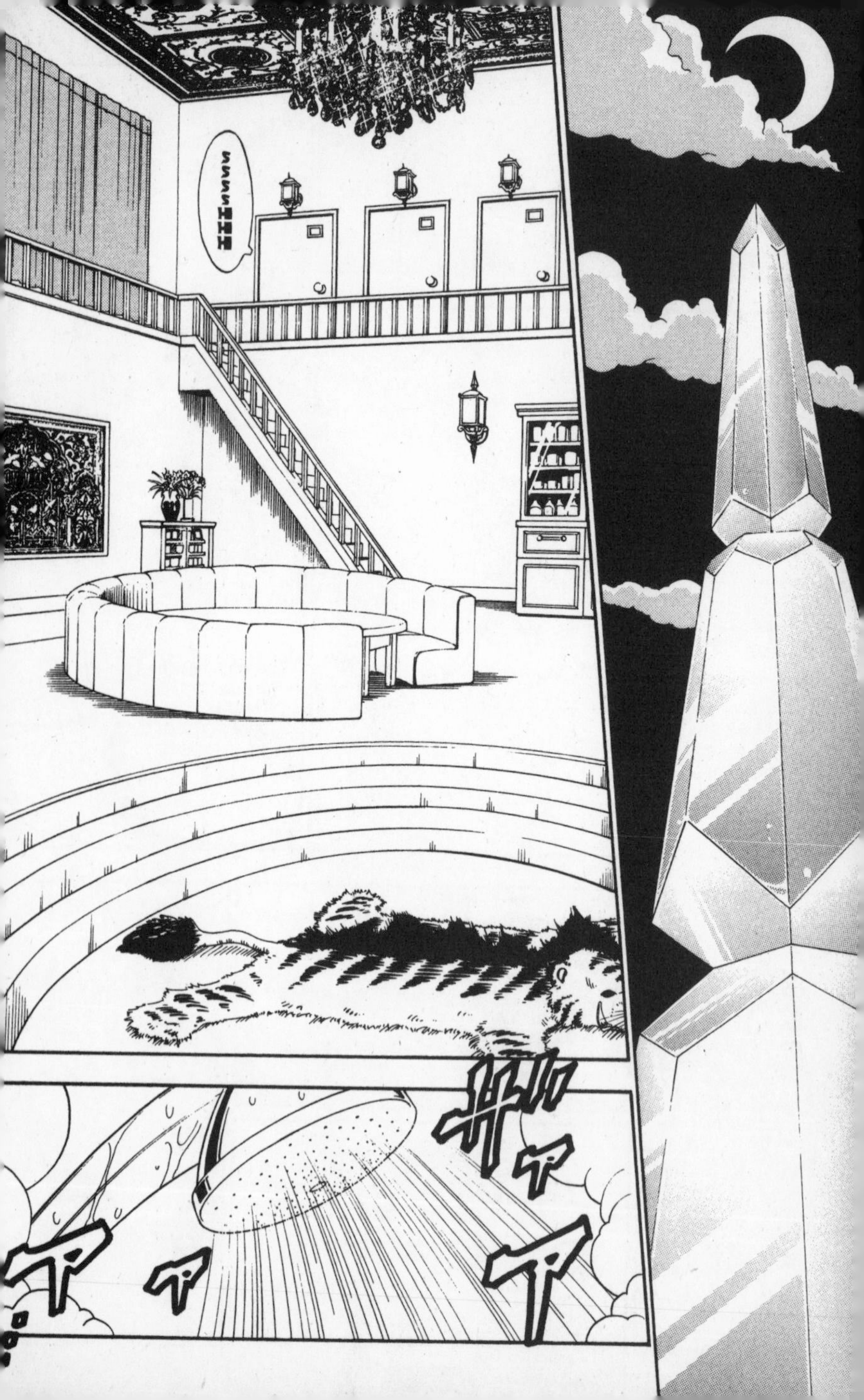
SSSSSHHH

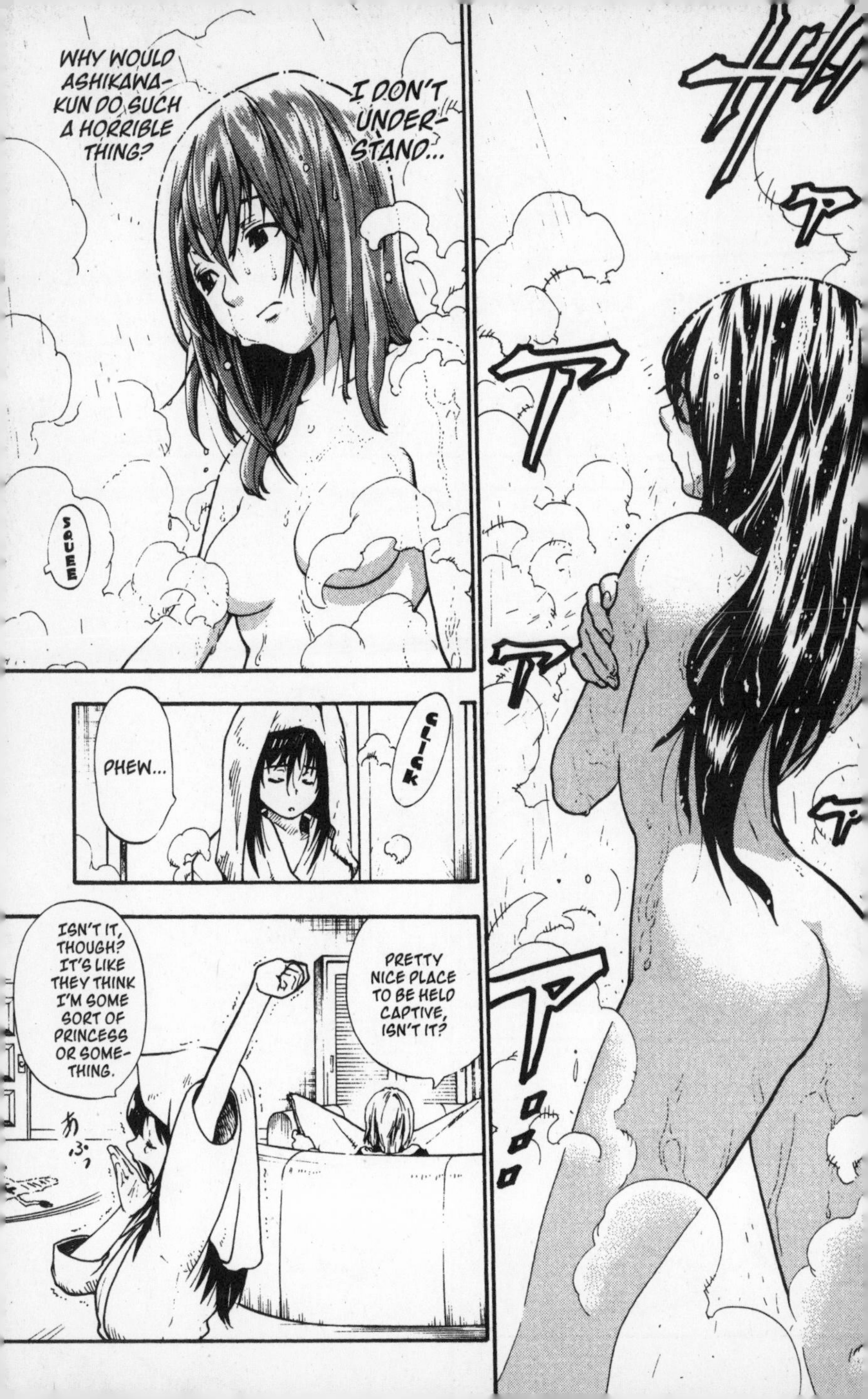

I DON'T UNDER-STAND...
WHY WOULD ASHIKAWA-KUN DO SUCH A HORRIBLE THING?
SQUEE
CLICK
PHEW...
PRETTY NICE PLACE TO BE HELD CAPTIVE, ISN'T IT?
ISN'T IT, THOUGH? IT'S LIKE THEY THINK I'M SOME SORT OF PRINCESS OR SOME-THING.
あふっ

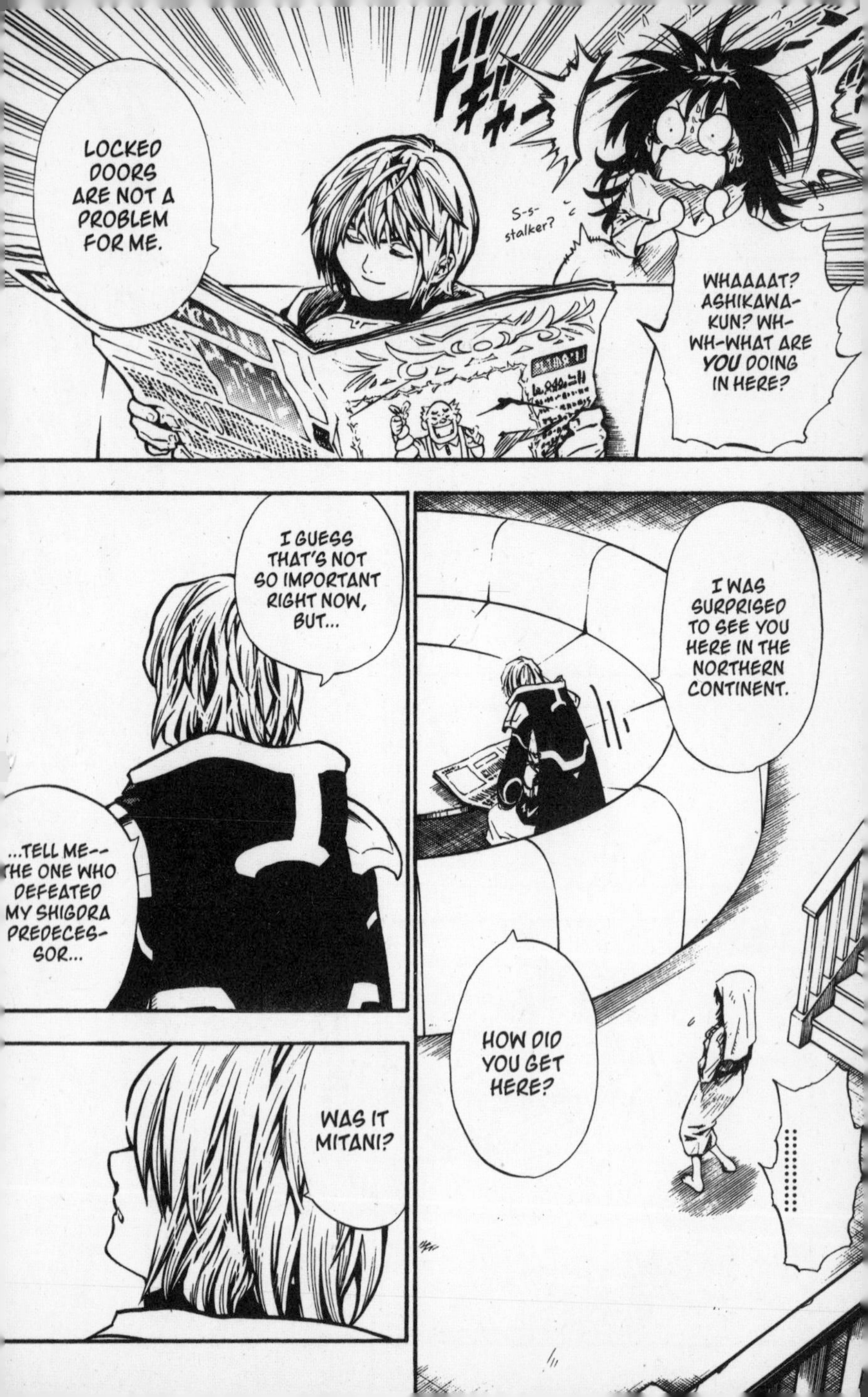
WHAAAAT? ASHIKAWA-KUN? WH-WH-WHAT ARE YOU DOING IN HERE?
S-s-stalker?
LOCKED DOORS ARE NOT A PROBLEM FOR ME.
I WAS SURPRISED TO SEE YOU HERE IN THE NORTHERN CONTINENT.
HOW DID YOU GET HERE?
I GUESS THAT'S NOT SO IMPORTANT RIGHT NOW, BUT...
...TELL ME-- THE ONE WHO DEFEATED MY SHIGORA PREDECES-SOR...
WAS IT MITANI?

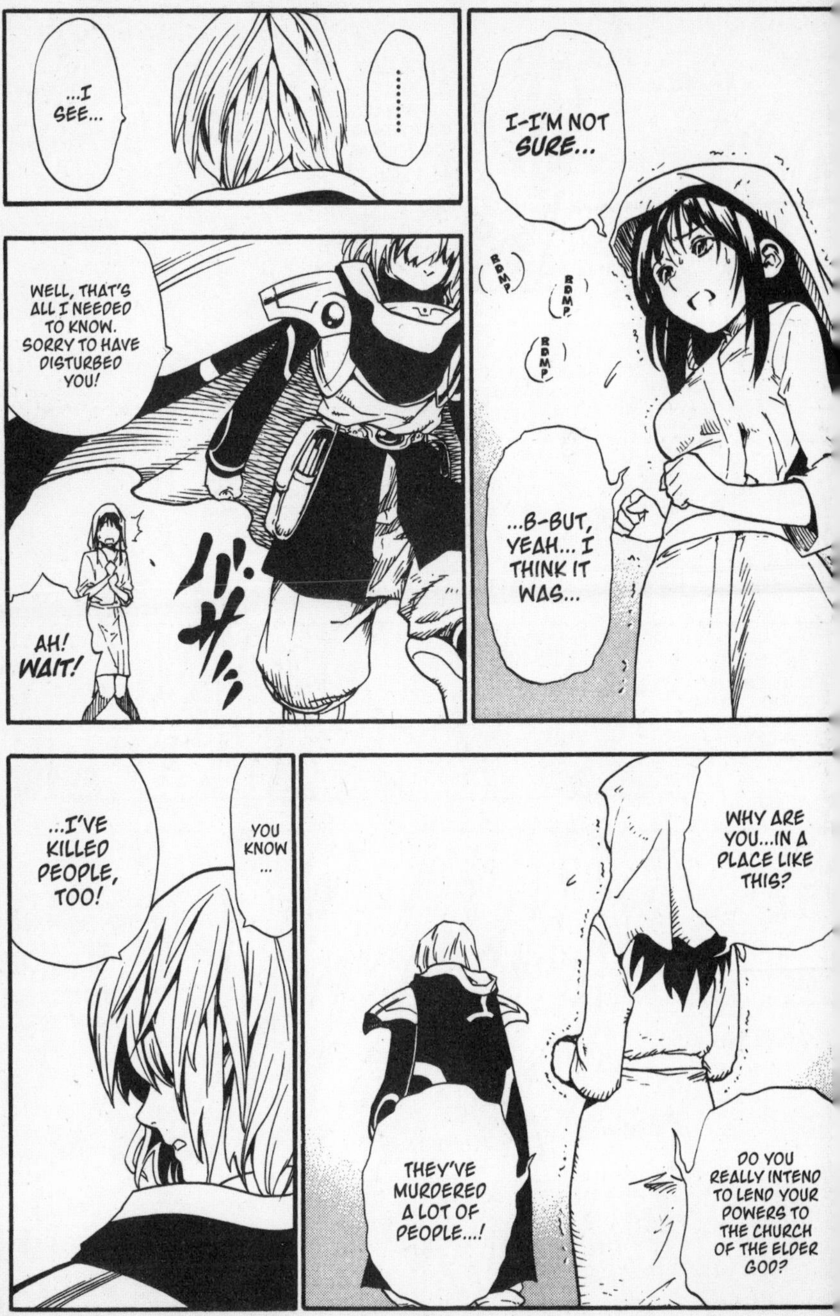
I-I'M NOT SURE...
BDMP
BDMP
BDMP
...B-BUT, YEAH... I THINK IT WAS...
....
...I SEE...
WELL, THAT'S ALL I NEEDED TO KNOW. SORRY TO HAVE DISTURBED YOU!
AH! WAIT!
WHY ARE YOU...IN A PLACE LIKE THIS?
DO YOU REALLY INTEND TO LEND YOUR POWERS TO THE CHURCH OF THE ELDER GOD?
THEY'VE MURDERED A LOT OF PEOPLE...!
YOU KNOW ...
...I'VE KILLED PEOPLE, TOO!

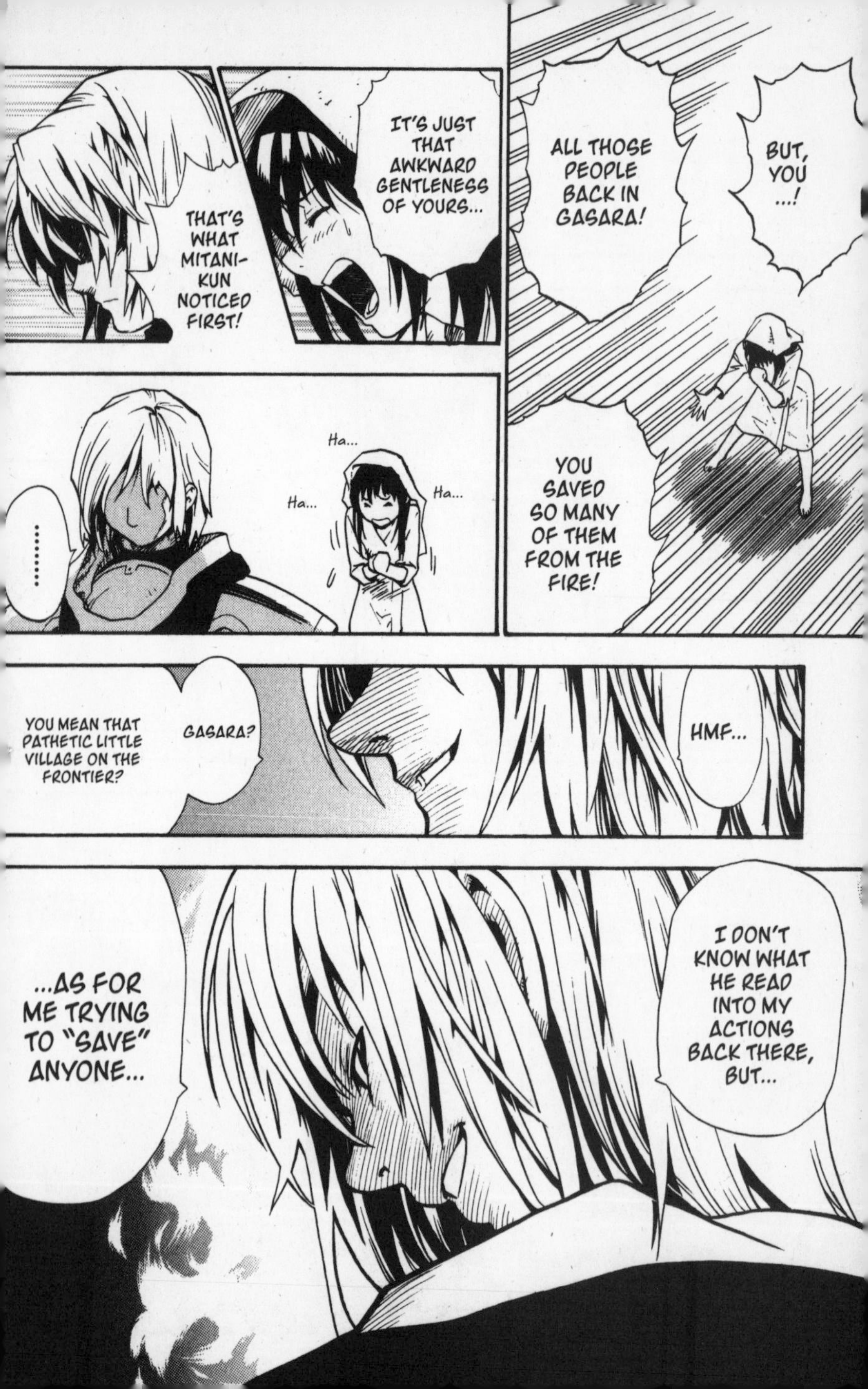
BUT, YOU ...!
ALL THOSE PEOPLE BACK IN GASARA!
YOU SAVED SO MANY OF THEM FROM THE FIRE!
IT'S JUST THAT AWKWARD GENTLENESS OF YOURS...
THAT'S WHAT MITANI-KUN NOTICED FIRST!
Ha...
Ha...
Ha...
....
HMF...
GASARA?
YOU MEAN THAT PATHETIC LITTLE VILLAGE ON THE FRONTIER?
I DON'T KNOW WHAT HE READ INTO MY ACTIONS BACK THERE, BUT...
...AS FOR ME TRYING TO "SAVE" ANYONE...

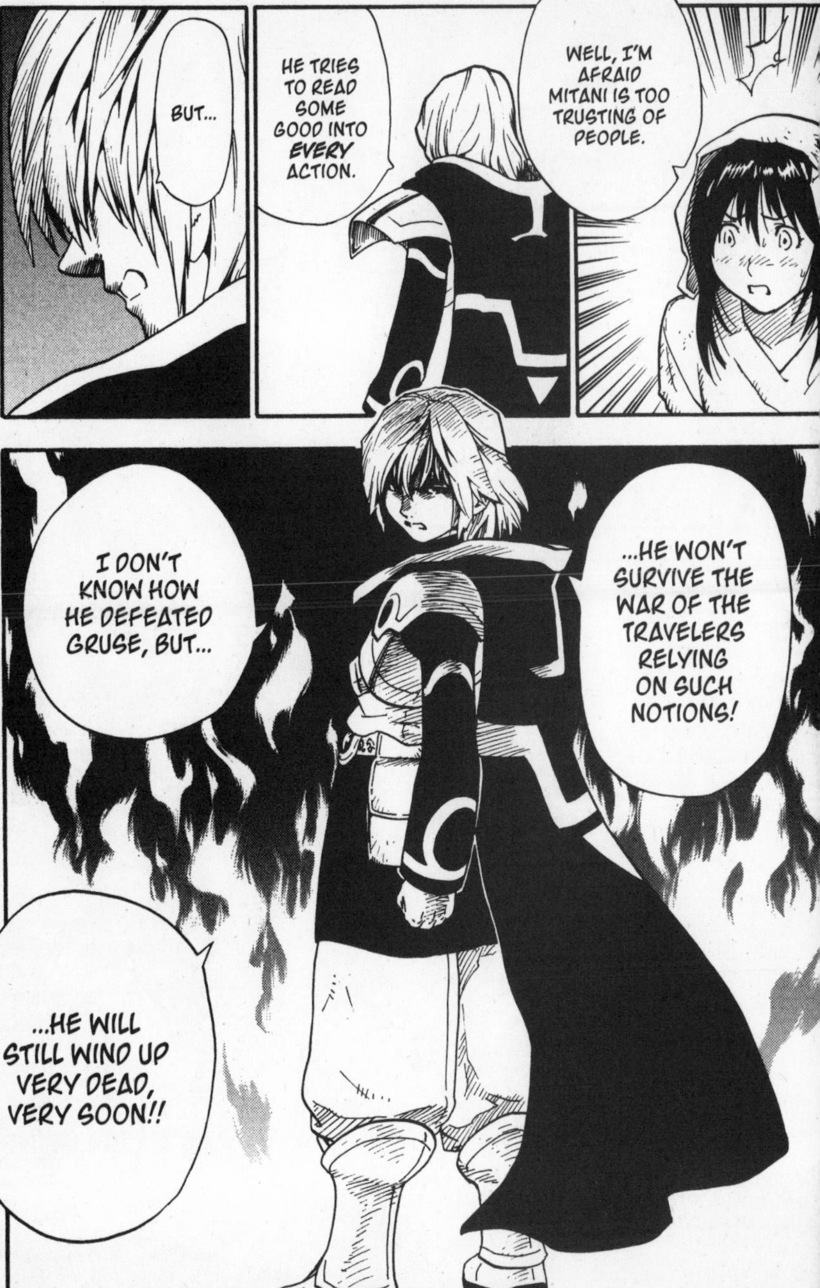
WELL, I'M AFRAID MITANI IS TOO TRUSTING OF PEOPLE.
HE TRIES TO READ SOME GOOD INTO **EVERY** ACTION.
BUT...
...HE WON'T SURVIVE THE WAR OF THE TRAVELERS RELYING ON SUCH NOTIONS!
I DON'T KNOW HOW HE DEFEATED GRUSE, BUT...
...HE WILL STILL WIND UP VERY DEAD, VERY SOON!!

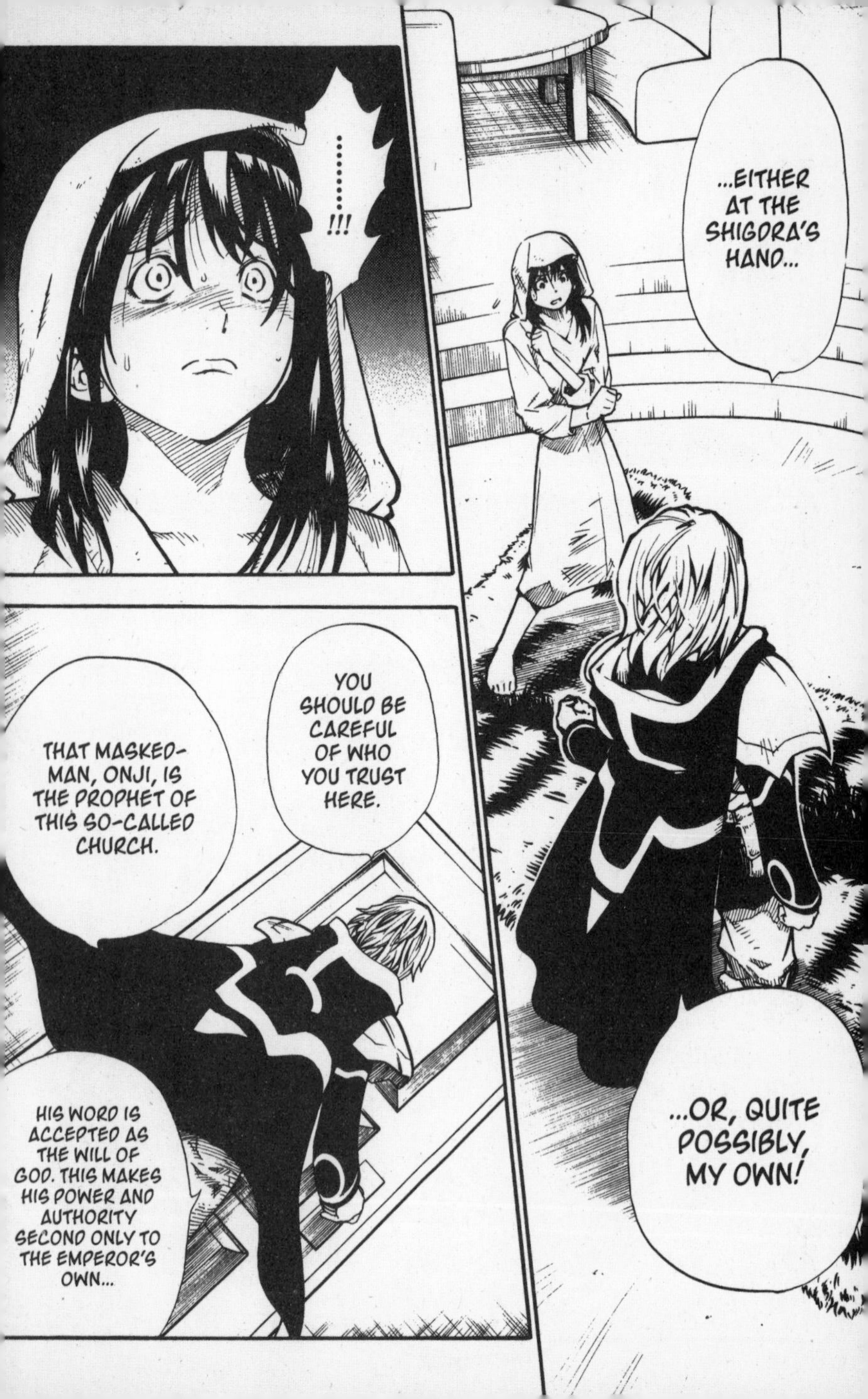
...EITHER AT THE SHIGORA'S HAND...
...OR, QUITE POSSIBLY, MY OWN!
......
!!!
YOU SHOULD BE CAREFUL OF WHO YOU TRUST HERE.
THAT MASKED-MAN, ONJI, IS THE PROPHET OF THIS SO-CALLED CHURCH.
HIS WORD IS ACCEPTED AS THE WILL OF GOD. THIS MAKES HIS POWER AND AUTHORITY SECOND ONLY TO THE EMPEROR'S OWN...

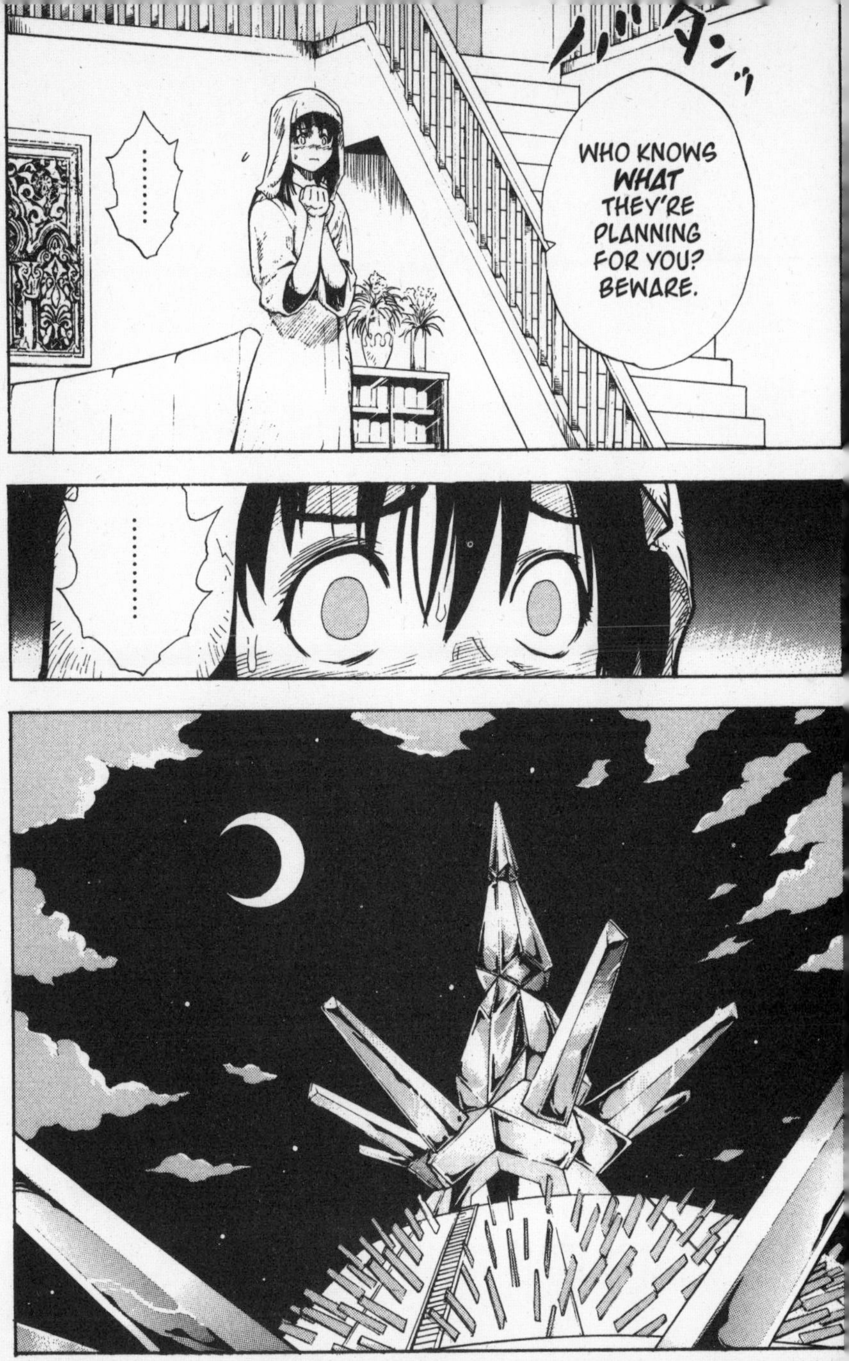
バタンッ
WHO KNOWS WHAT THEY'RE PLANNING FOR YOU? BEWARE.
......
......

A Retelling of a Classic
BRAVE STORY

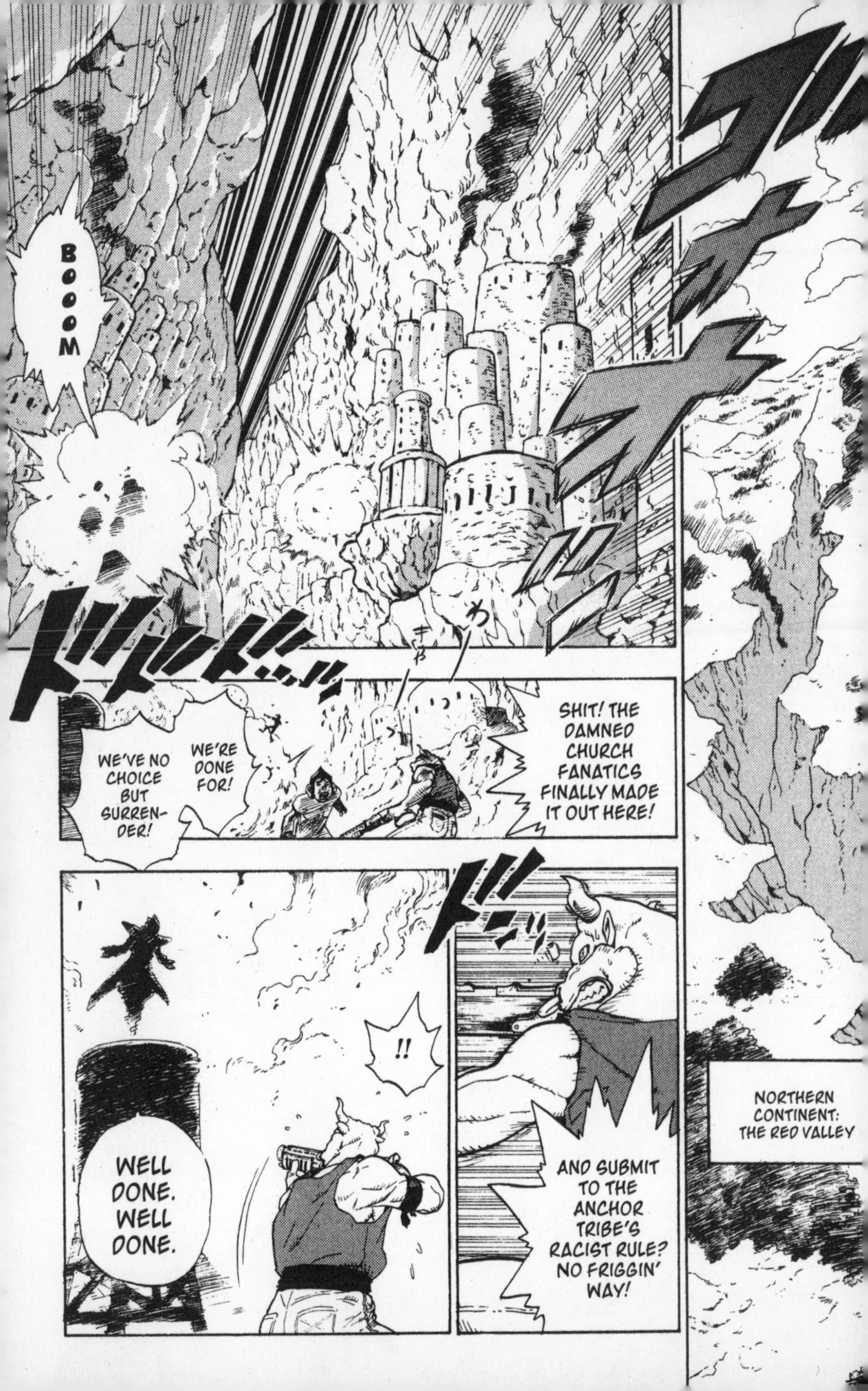
NORTHERN CONTINENT: THE RED VALLEY
BOOOM
SHIT! THE DAMNED CHURCH FANATICS FINALLY MADE IT OUT HERE!
WE'RE DONE FOR!
WE'VE NO CHOICE BUT SURRENDER!
AND SUBMIT TO THE ANCHOR TRIBE'S RACIST RULE? NO FRIGGIN' WAY!
!!
WELL DONE. WELL DONE.

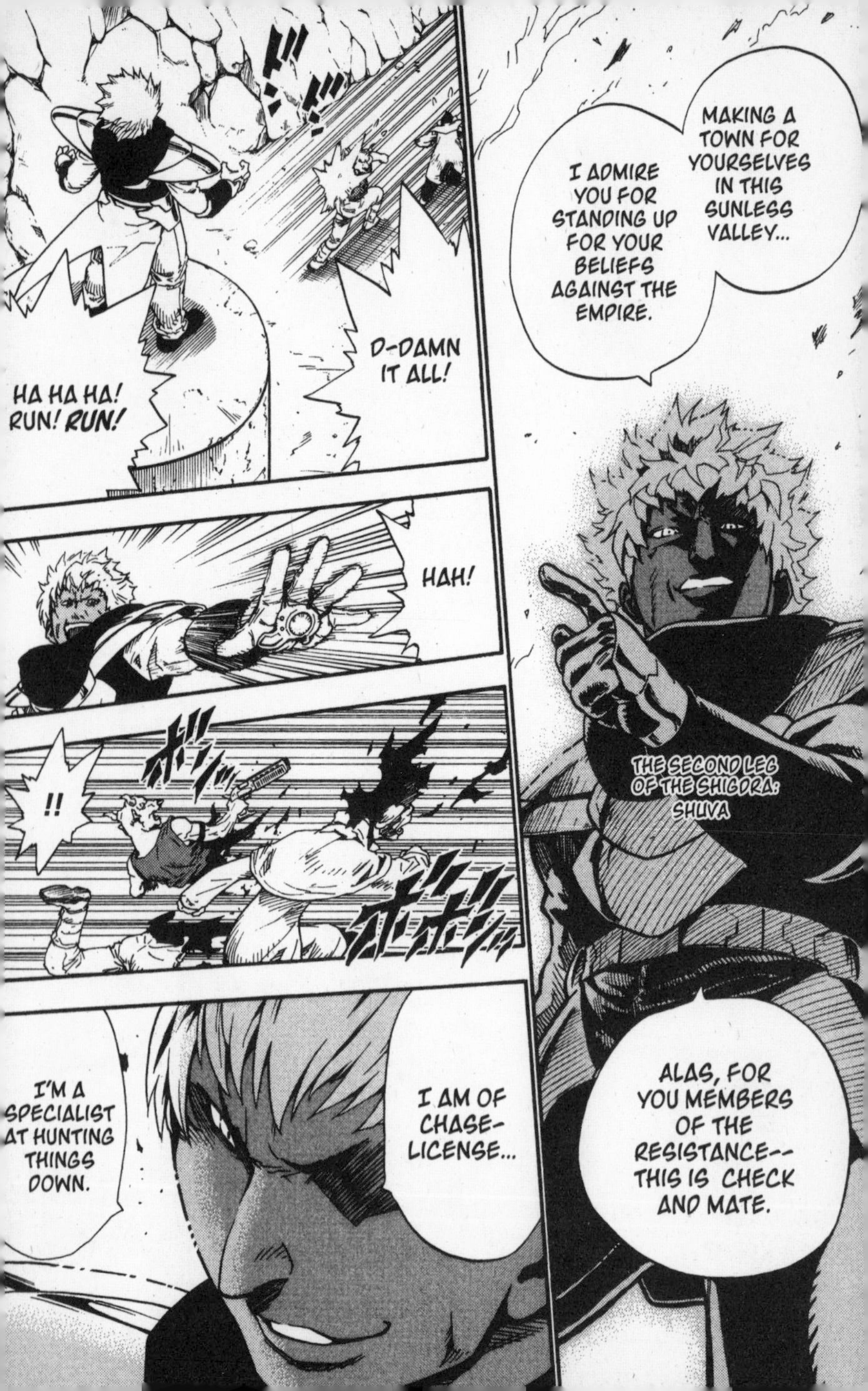
MAKING A TOWN FOR YOURSELVES IN THIS SUNLESS VALLEY...
I ADMIRE YOU FOR STANDING UP FOR YOUR BELIEFS AGAINST THE EMPIRE.
THE SECOND LEG OF THE SHIGORA: SHUVA
ALAS, FOR YOU MEMBERS OF THE RESISTANCE-- THIS IS CHECK AND MATE.
D-DAMN IT ALL!
HA HA HA! RUN! *RUN!*
HAH!
!!
I AM OF CHASE-LICENSE...
I'M A SPECIALIST AT HUNTING THINGS DOWN.

Chapter 30 The Fifth Orb

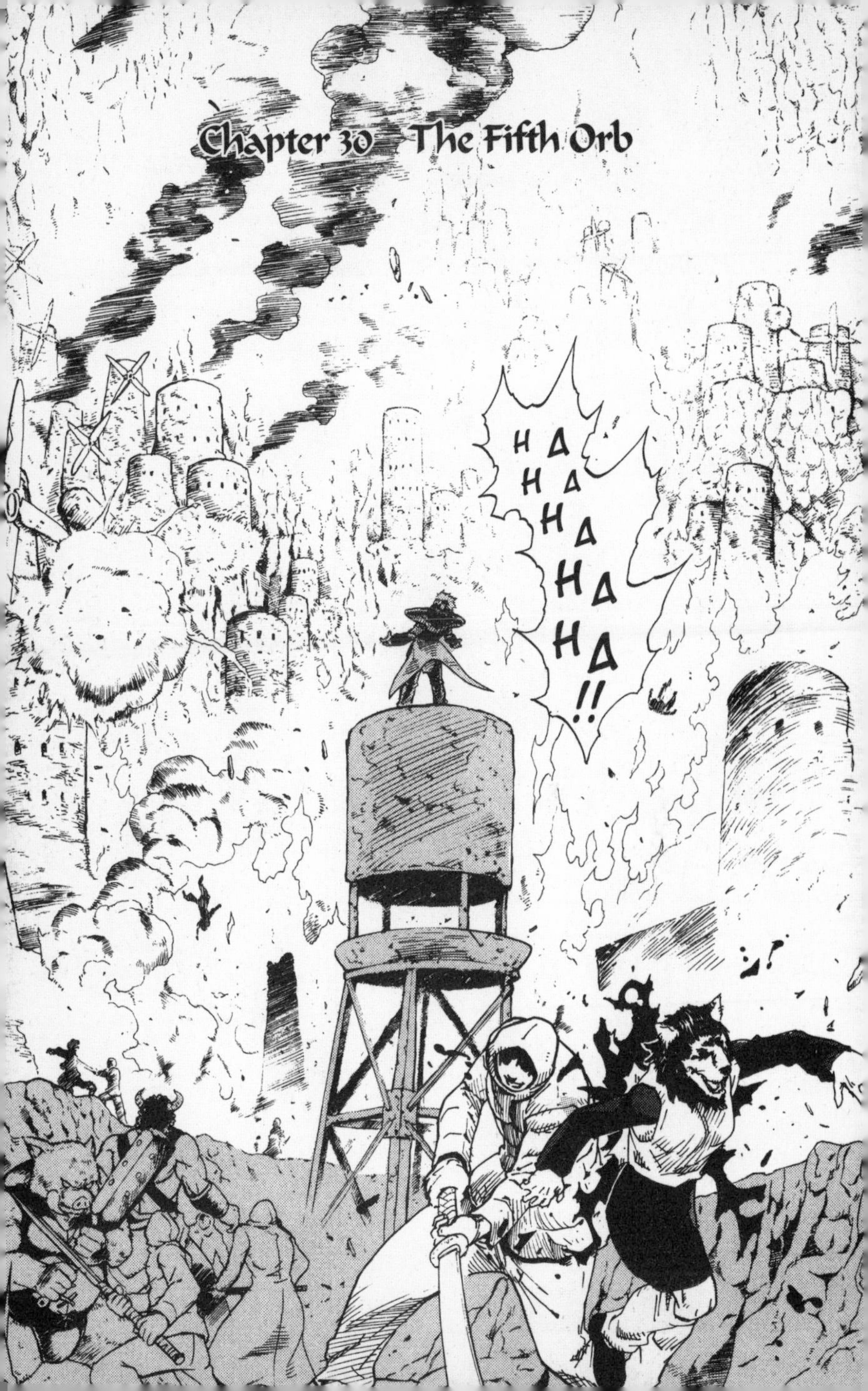
HA HA HA HA HA!!

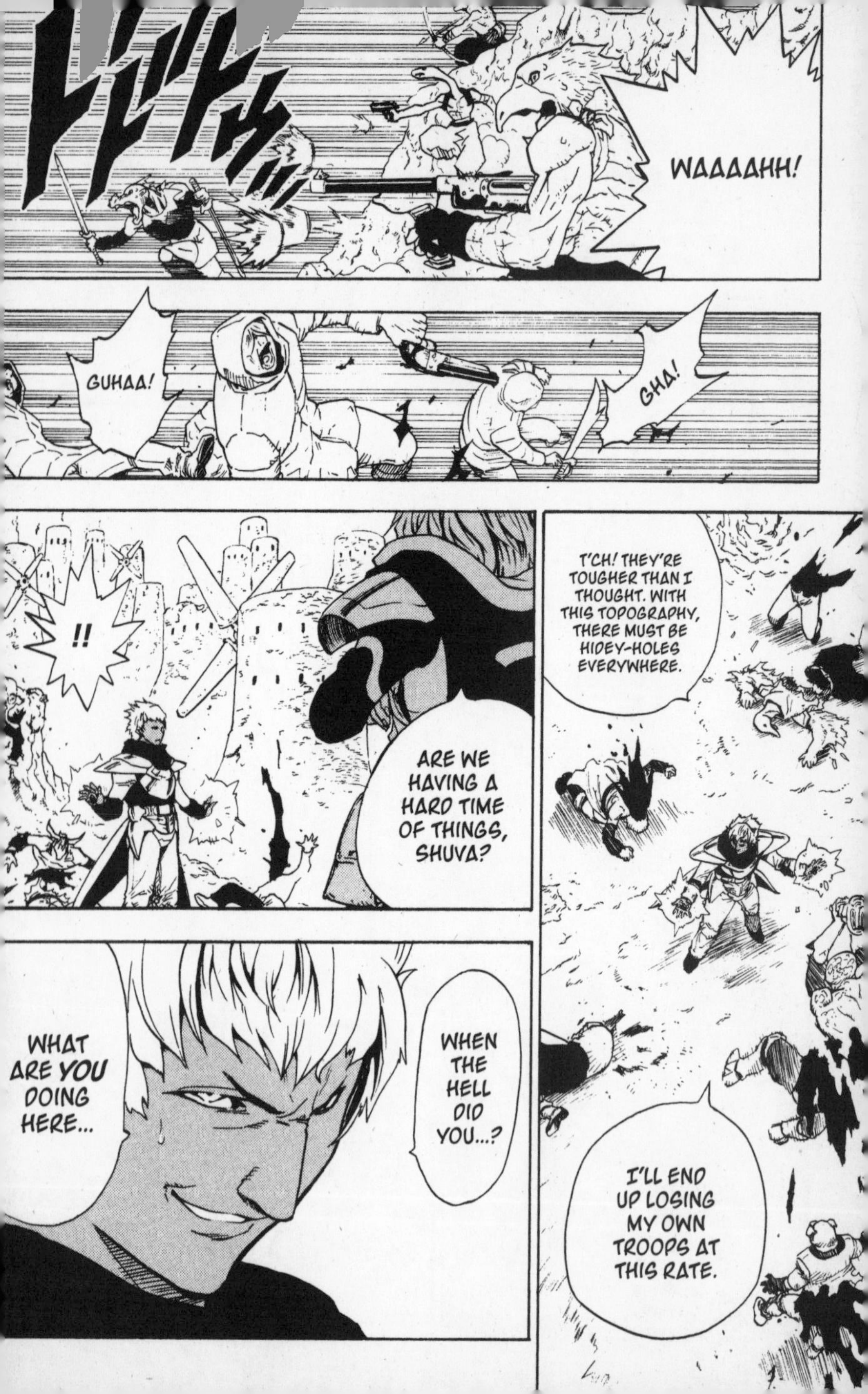
WAAAAHH!
GHA!
GUHAA!
T'CH! THEY'RE TOUGHER THAN I THOUGHT. WITH THIS TOPOGRAPHY, THERE MUST BE HIDEY-HOLES EVERYWHERE.
I'LL END UP LOSING MY OWN TROOPS AT THIS RATE.
ARE WE HAVING A HARD TIME OF THINGS, SHUVA?
!!
WHEN THE HELL DID YOU...?
WHAT ARE *YOU* DOING HERE...

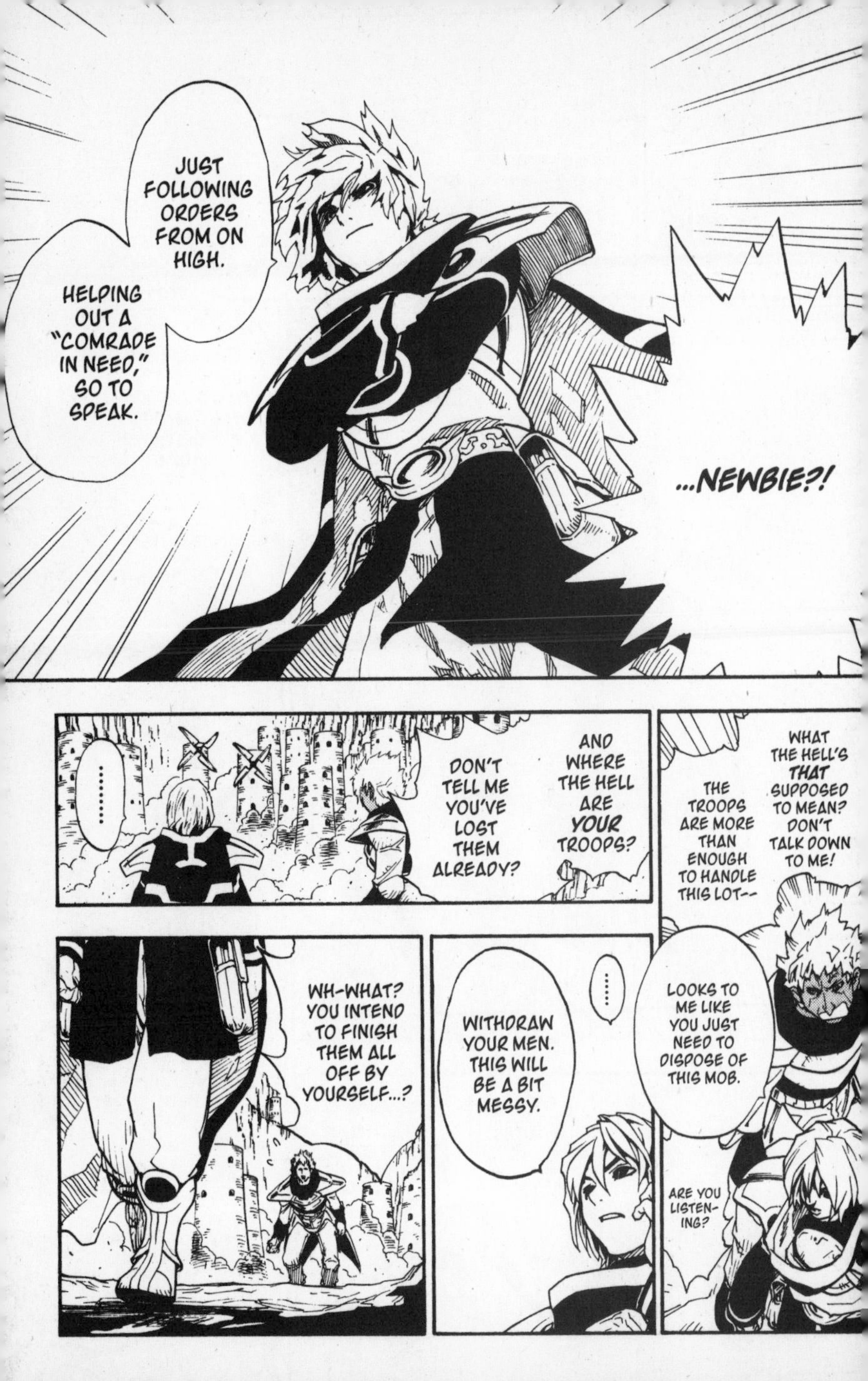
...NEWBIE?!
JUST FOLLOWING ORDERS FROM ON HIGH.
HELPING OUT A "COMRADE IN NEED," SO TO SPEAK.
WHAT THE HELL'S THAT SUPPOSED TO MEAN? DON'T TALK DOWN TO ME!
THE TROOPS ARE MORE THAN ENOUGH TO HANDLE THIS LOT--
LOOKS TO ME LIKE YOU JUST NEED TO DISPOSE OF THIS MOB.
ARE YOU LISTENING?
AND WHERE THE HELL ARE YOUR TROOPS?
DON'T TELL ME YOU'VE LOST THEM ALREADY?
....
......
WITHDRAW YOUR MEN. THIS WILL BE A BIT MESSY.
WH-WHAT? YOU INTEND TO FINISH THEM ALL OFF BY YOURSELF...?

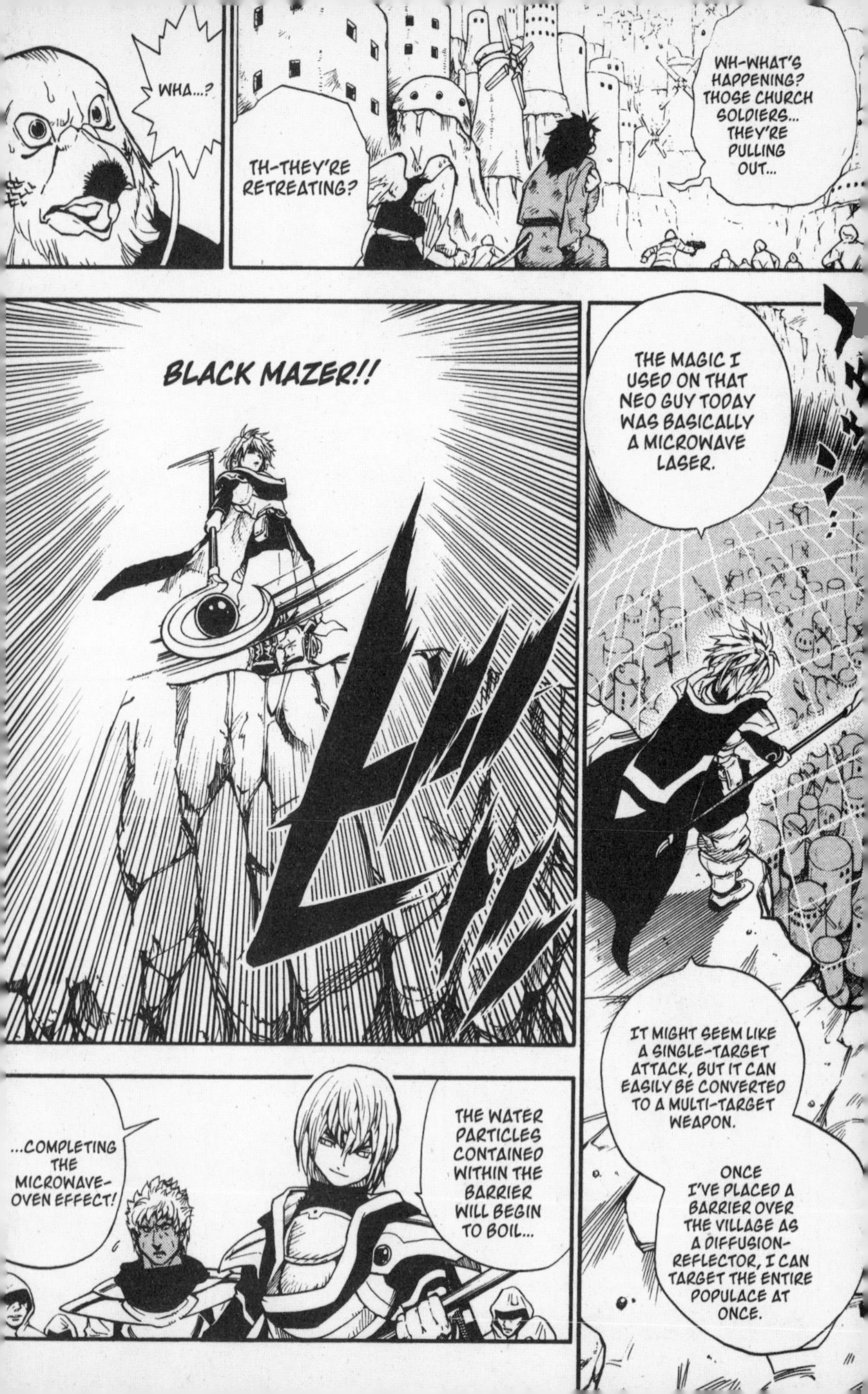
WH-WHAT'S HAPPENING? THOSE CHURCH SOLDIERS... THEY'RE PULLING OUT...
TH-THEY'RE RETREATING?
WHA...?
THE MAGIC I USED ON THAT NEO GUY TODAY WAS BASICALLY A MICROWAVE LASER.
IT MIGHT SEEM LIKE A SINGLE-TARGET ATTACK, BUT IT CAN EASILY BE CONVERTED TO A MULTI-TARGET WEAPON.
ONCE I'VE PLACED A BARRIER OVER THE VILLAGE AS A DIFFUSION-REFLECTOR, I CAN TARGET THE ENTIRE POPULACE AT ONCE.
BLACK MAZER!!
THE WATER PARTICLES CONTAINED WITHIN THE BARRIER WILL BEGIN TO BOIL...
...COMPLETING THE MICROWAVE-OVEN EFFECT!

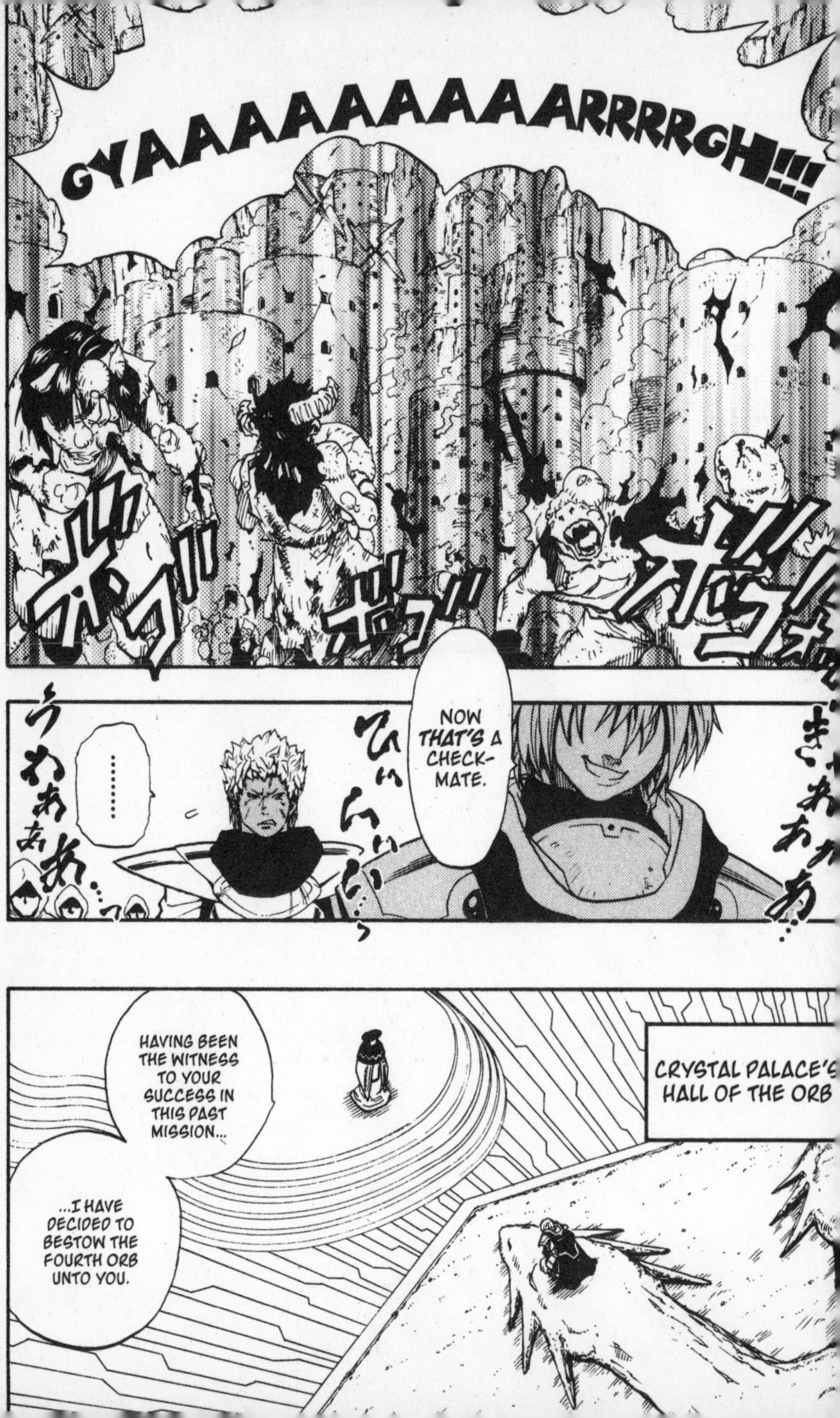
GYAAAAAAAAAAARRRRRGH!!!
NOW THAT'S A CHECK-MATE.
....
CRYSTAL PALACE'S HALL OF THE ORB
HAVING BEEN THE WITNESS TO YOUR SUCCESS IN THIS PAST MISSION...
...I HAVE DECIDED TO BESTOW THE FOURTH ORB UNTO YOU.

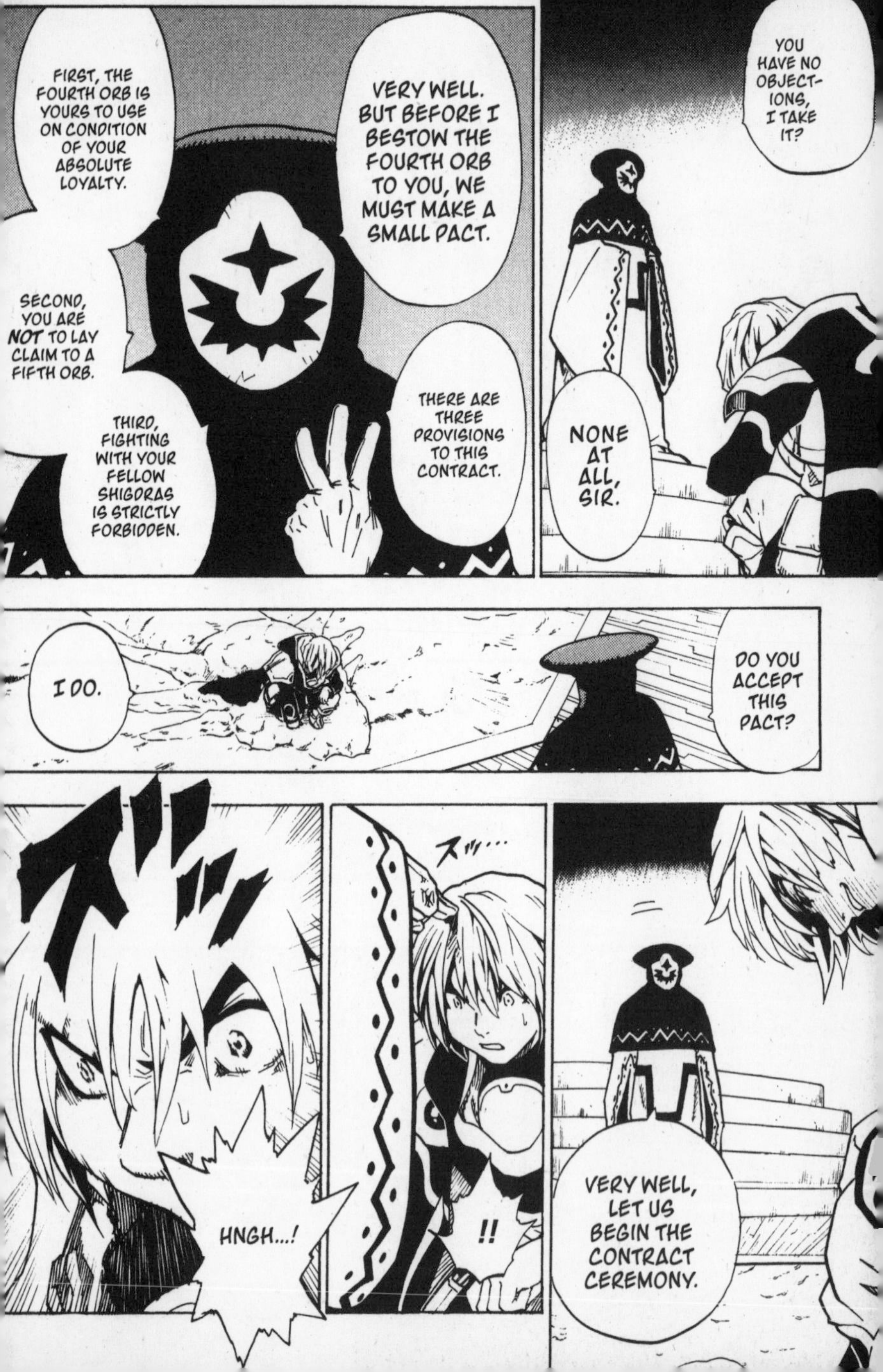
YOU HAVE NO OBJECTIONS, I TAKE IT?
NONE AT ALL, SIR.
VERY WELL. BUT BEFORE I BESTOW THE FOURTH ORB TO YOU, WE MUST MAKE A SMALL PACT.
THERE ARE THREE PROVISIONS TO THIS CONTRACT.
FIRST, THE FOURTH ORB IS YOURS TO USE ON CONDITION OF YOUR ABSOLUTE LOYALTY.
SECOND, YOU ARE **NOT** TO LAY CLAIM TO A FIFTH ORB.
THIRD, FIGHTING WITH YOUR FELLOW SHIGORAS IS STRICTLY FORBIDDEN.
DO YOU ACCEPT THIS PACT?
I DO.
VERY WELL, LET US BEGIN THE CONTRACT CEREMONY.
スッ…
!!
HNGH...!

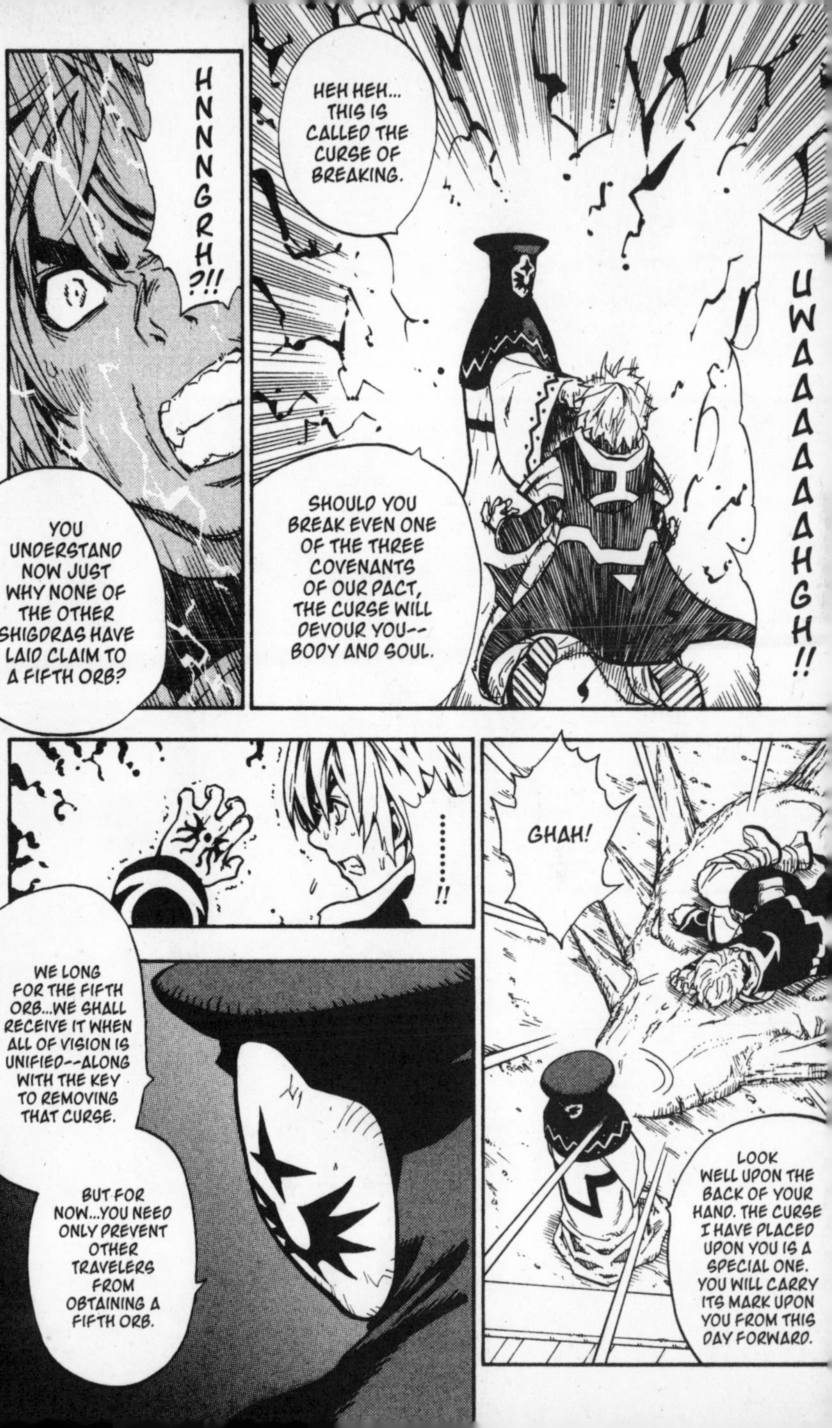
HEH HEH... THIS IS CALLED THE CURSE OF BREAKING.
UWAAAAAAAHGH!!
SHOULD YOU BREAK EVEN ONE OF THE THREE COVENANTS OF OUR PACT, THE CURSE WILL DEVOUR YOU--BODY AND SOUL.
HNNNGRH?!!
YOU UNDERSTAND NOW JUST WHY NONE OF THE OTHER SHIGDRAS HAVE LAID CLAIM TO A FIFTH ORB?
GHAH!
LOOK WELL UPON THE BACK OF YOUR HAND. THE CURSE I HAVE PLACED UPON YOU IS A SPECIAL ONE. YOU WILL CARRY ITS MARK UPON YOU FROM THIS DAY FORWARD.
......!!
WE LONG FOR THE FIFTH ORB...WE SHALL RECEIVE IT WHEN ALL OF VISION IS UNIFIED--ALONG WITH THE KEY TO REMOVING THAT CURSE.
BUT FOR NOW...YOU NEED ONLY PREVENT OTHER TRAVELERS FROM OBTAINING A FIFTH ORB.

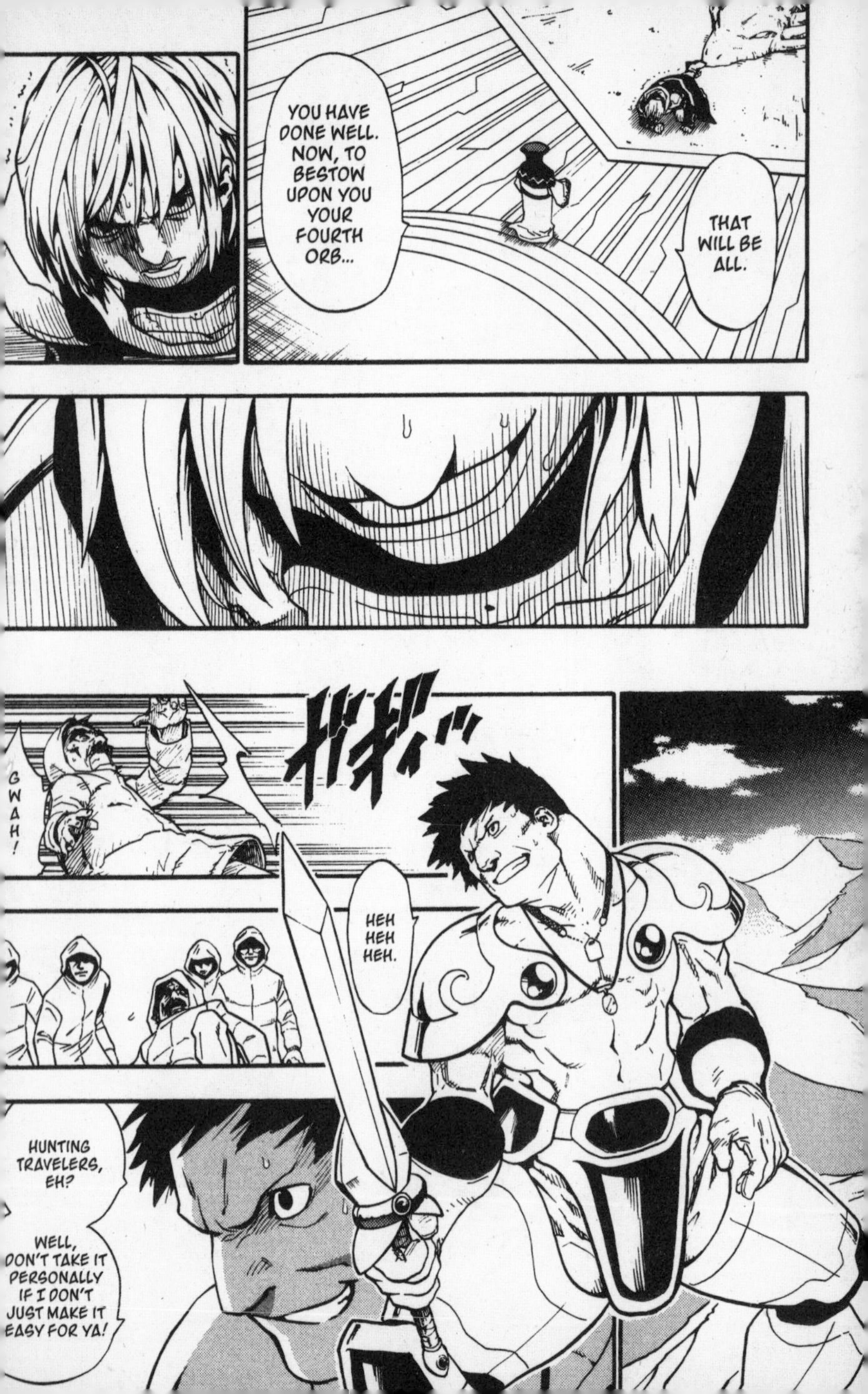
YOU HAVE DONE WELL. NOW, TO BESTOW UPON YOU YOUR FOURTH ORB...
THAT WILL BE ALL.
GWAH!
HEH HEH HEH.
HUNTING TRAVELERS, EH?
WELL, DON'T TAKE IT PERSONALLY IF I DON'T JUST MAKE IT EASY FOR YA!

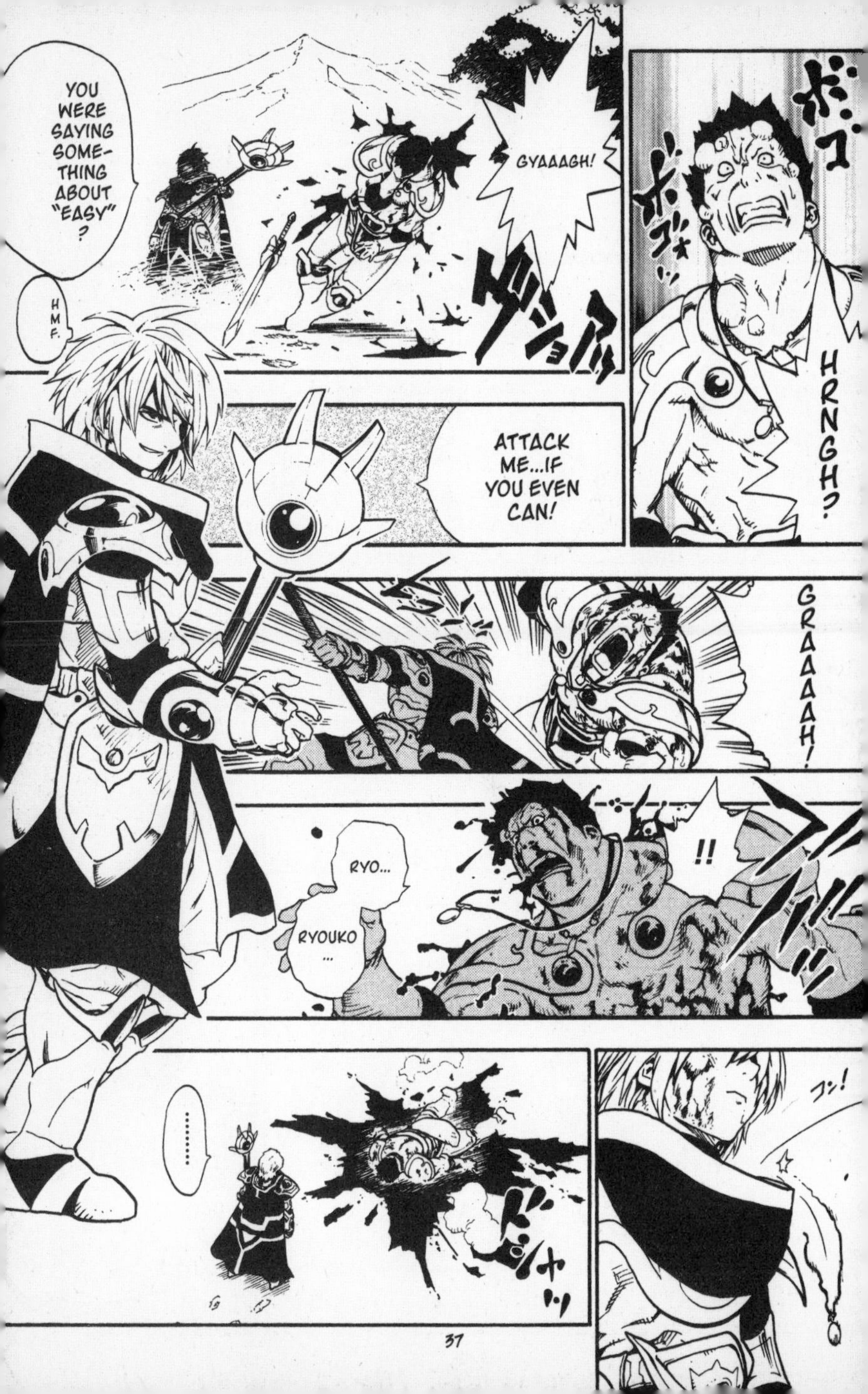
ボコ
ボコ
HRNGH?
GYAAAGH!
YOU WERE SAYING SOME-THING ABOUT "EASY"?
HMF.
ATTACK ME...IF YOU EVEN CAN!
GRAAAAAH!
!!
RYO...
RYOUKO...
コン!
....

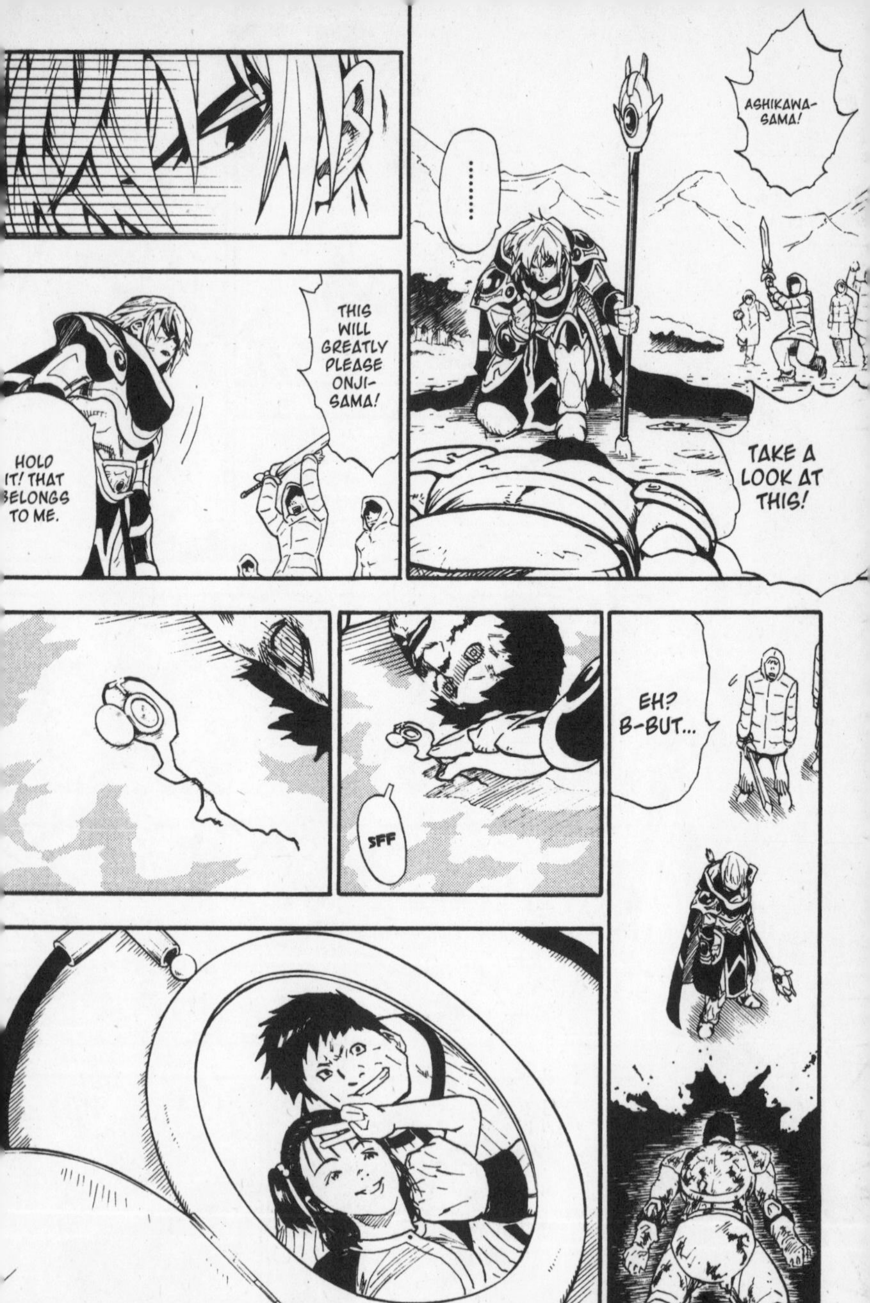
ASHIKAWA-SAMA!
......
TAKE A LOOK AT THIS!
THIS WILL GREATLY PLEASE ONJI-SAMA!
HOLD IT! THAT BELONGS TO ME.
EH? B-BUT...
SFF

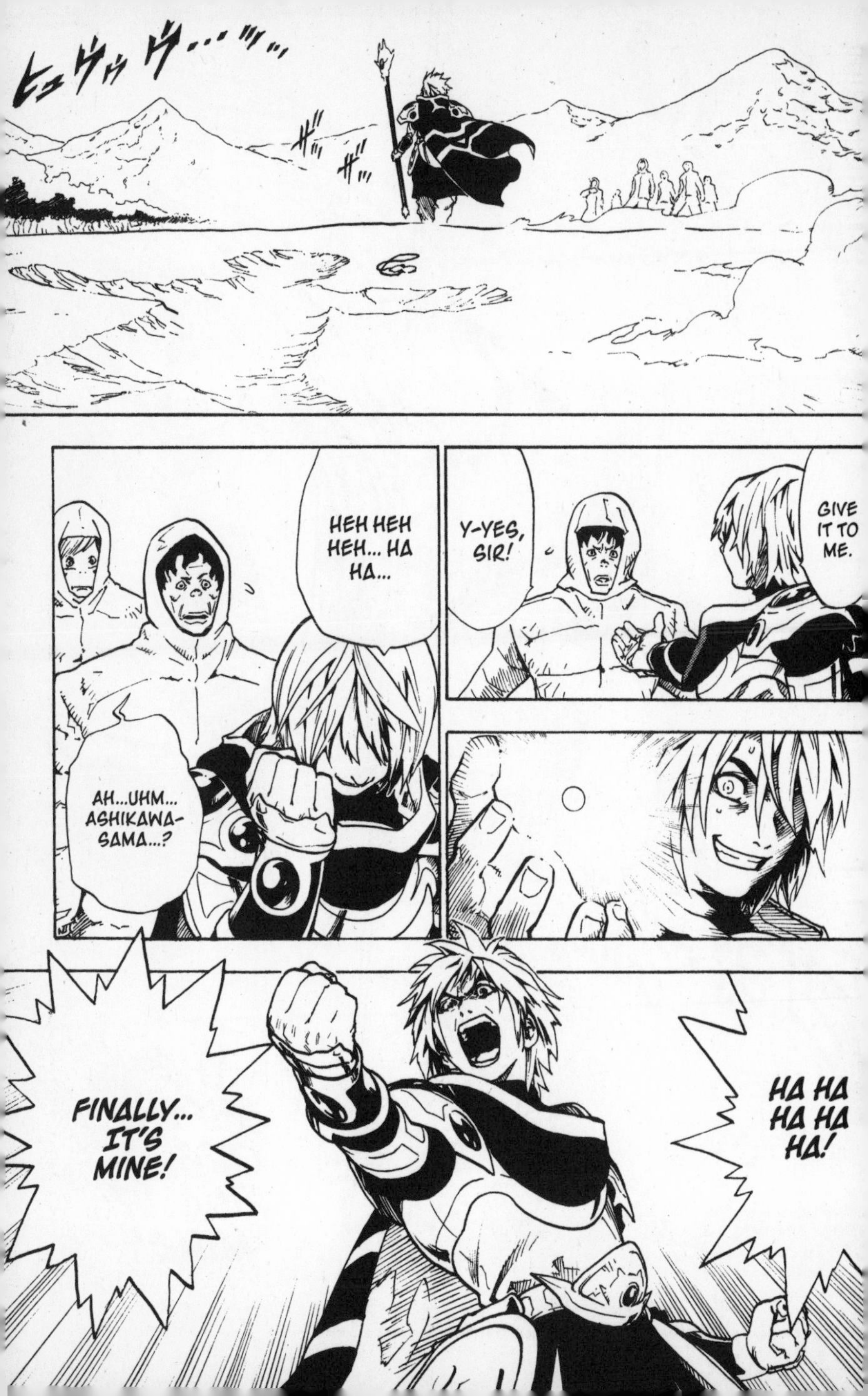
GIVE IT TO ME.
Y-YES, SIR!
HEH HEH HEH... HA HA...
AH...UHM... ASHIKAWA-SAMA...?
HA HA HA HA HA!
FINALLY... IT'S MINE!

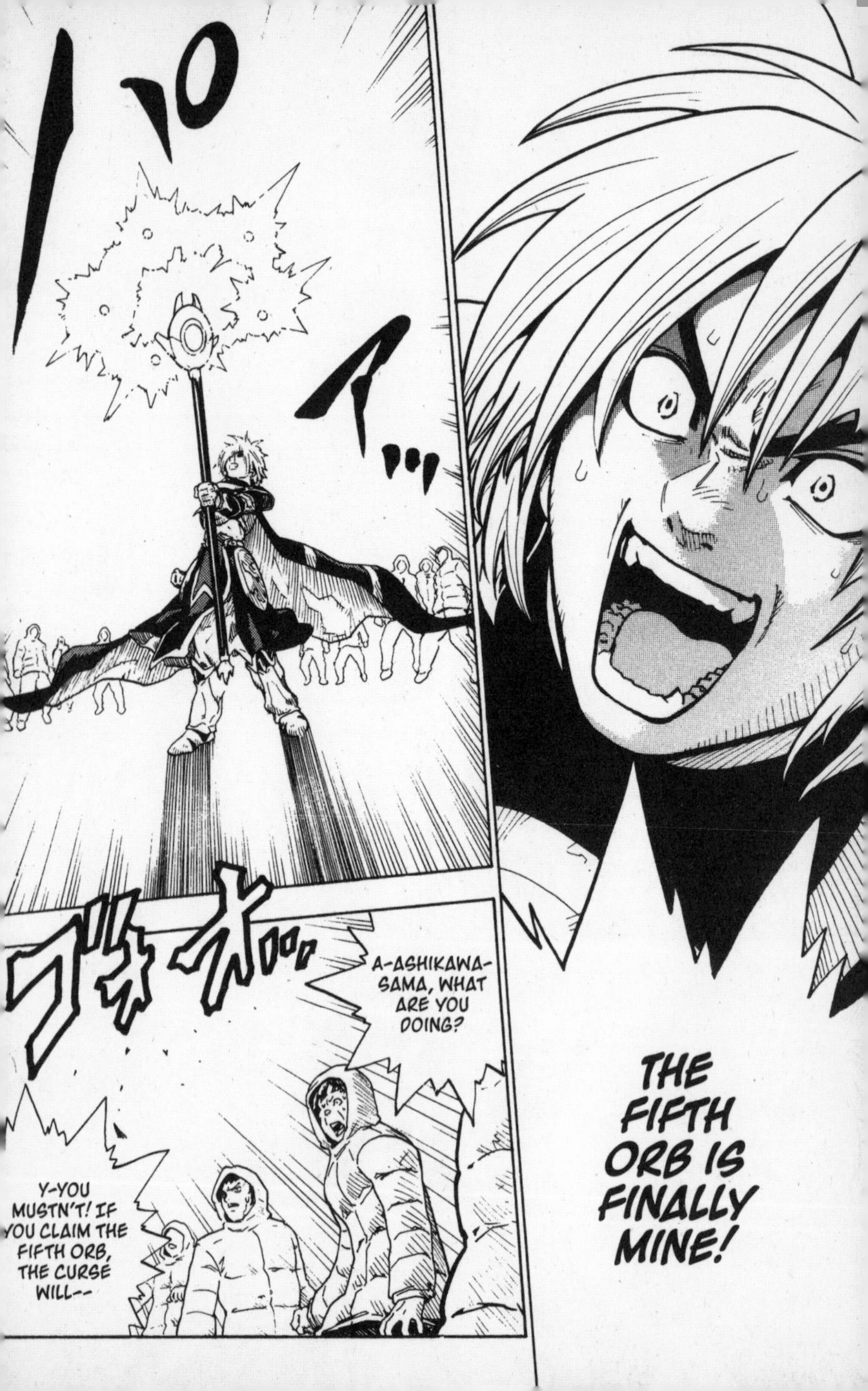
THE FIFTH ORB IS FINALLY MINE!
A-ASHIKAWA-SAMA, WHAT ARE YOU DOING?
Y-YOU MUSTN'T! IF YOU CLAIM THE FIFTH ORB, THE CURSE WILL--

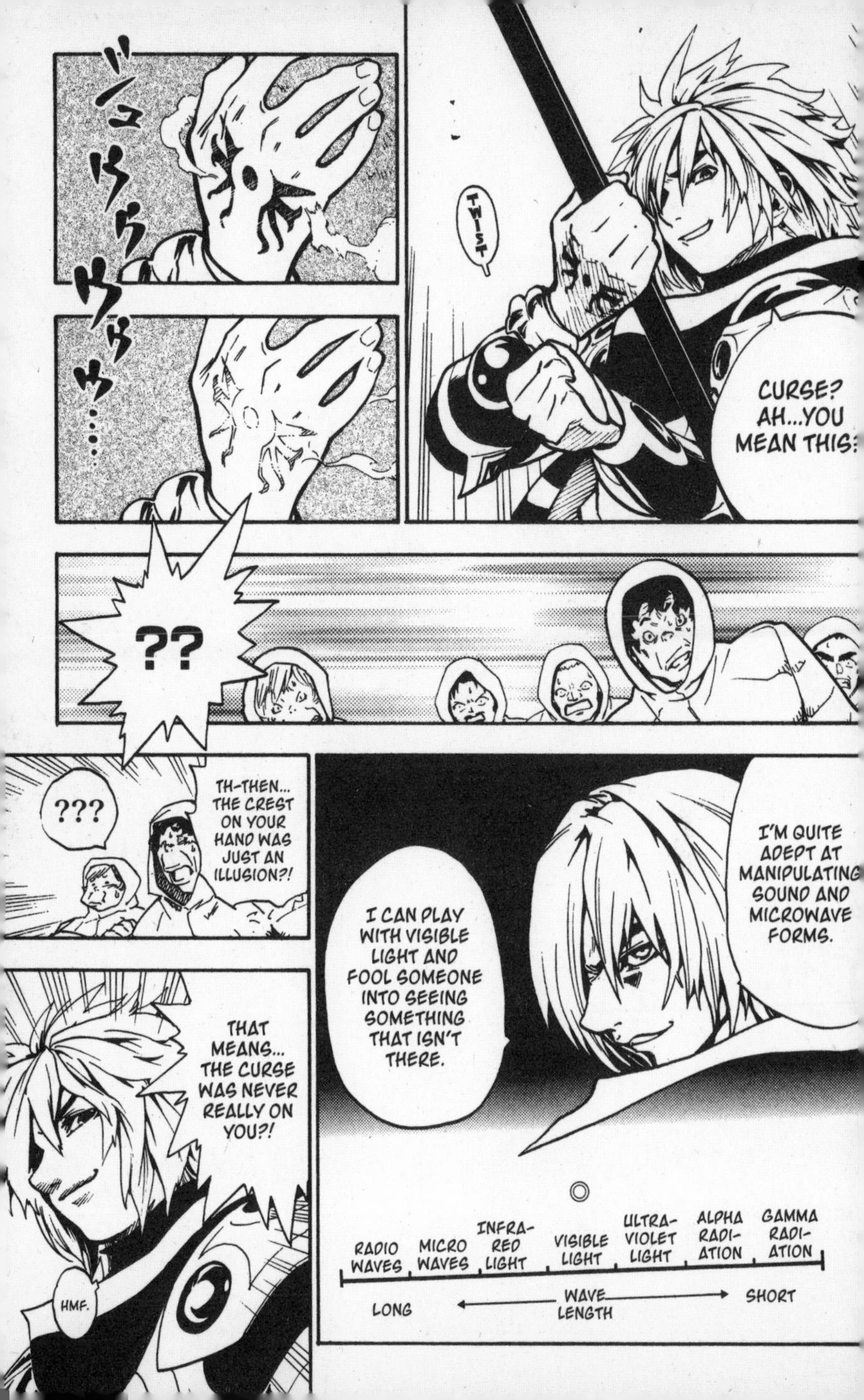
TWIST
CURSE? AH...YOU MEAN THIS?
??
I'M QUITE ADEPT AT MANIPULATING SOUND AND MICROWAVE FORMS.
I CAN PLAY WITH VISIBLE LIGHT AND FOOL SOMEONE INTO SEEING SOMETHING THAT ISN'T THERE.
◎
RADIO WAVES
MICRO WAVES
INFRA-RED LIGHT
VISIBLE LIGHT
ULTRA-VIOLET LIGHT
ALPHA RADI-ATION
GAMMA RADI-ATION
LONG
WAVE LENGTH
SHORT
TH-THEN... THE CREST ON YOUR HAND WAS JUST AN ILLUSION?!
???
THAT MEANS... THE CURSE WAS NEVER REALLY ON YOU?!
HMF.

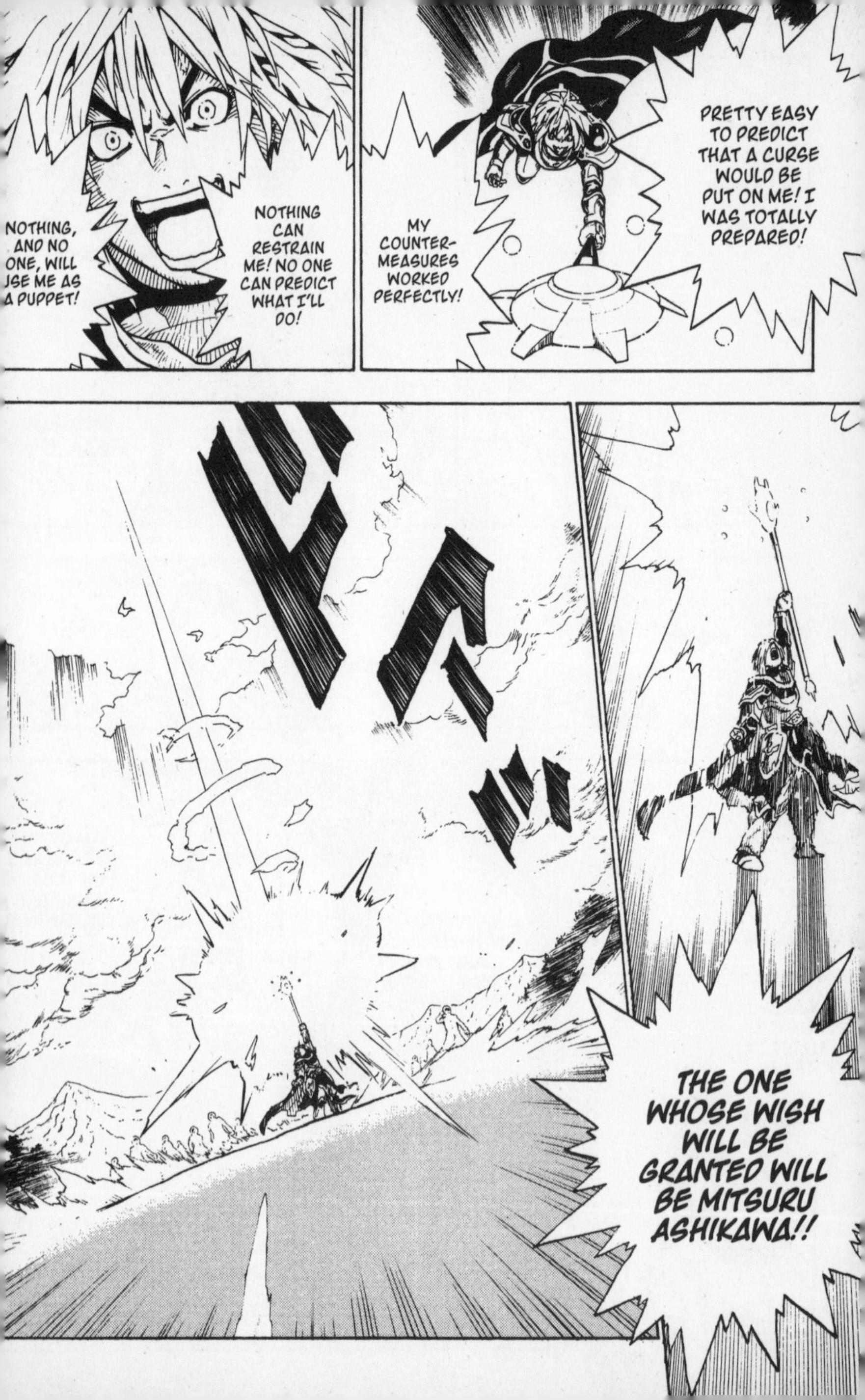
PRETTY EASY TO PREDICT THAT A CURSE WOULD BE PUT ON ME! I WAS TOTALLY PREPARED!
MY COUNTER-MEASURES WORKED PERFECTLY!
NOTHING CAN RESTRAIN ME! NO ONE CAN PREDICT WHAT I'LL DO!
NOTHING, AND NO ONE, WILL USE ME AS A PUPPET!
THE ONE WHOSE WISH WILL BE GRANTED WILL BE MITSURU ASHIKAWA!!

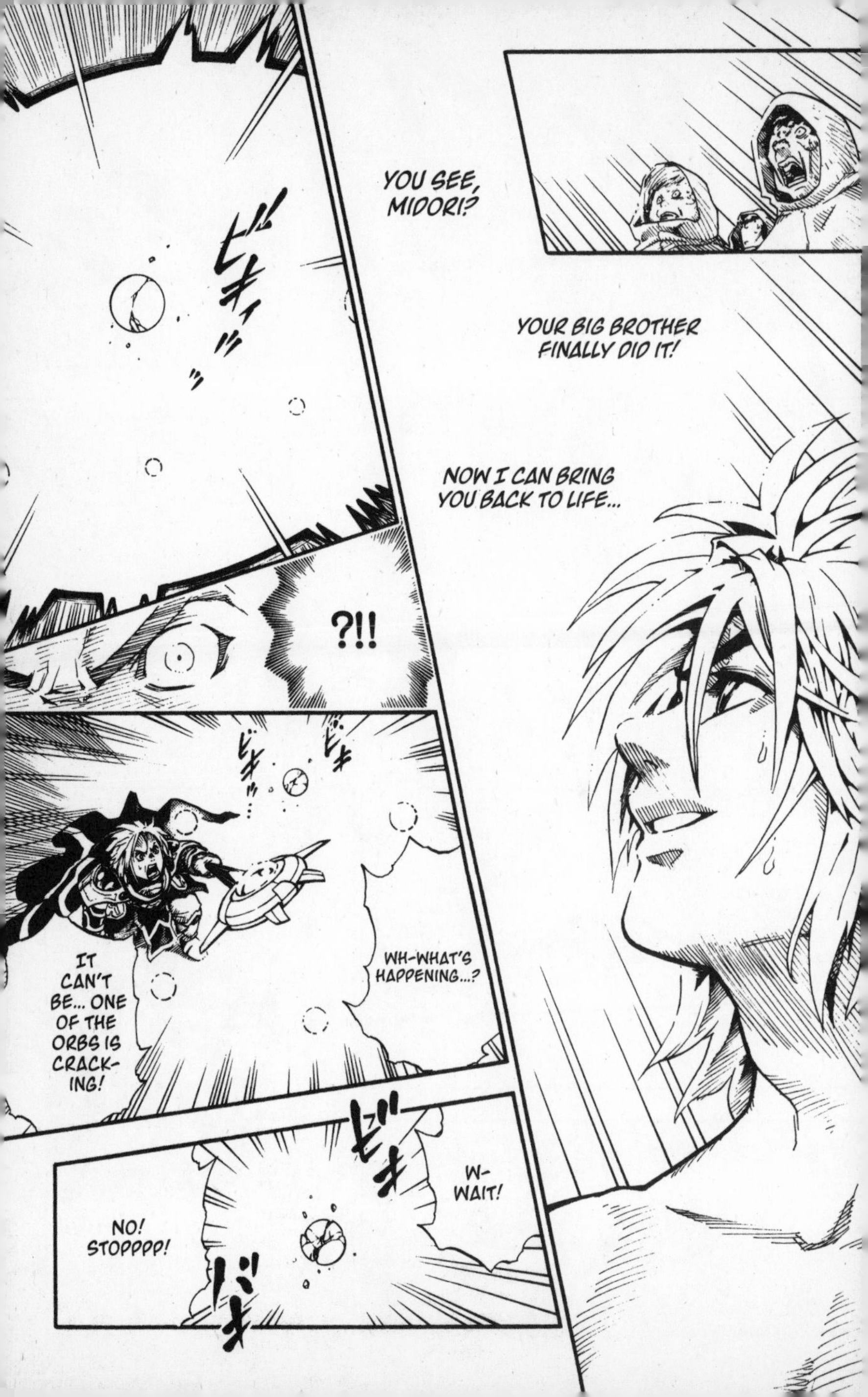
YOU SEE, MIDORI?
YOUR BIG BROTHER FINALLY DID IT!
NOW I CAN BRING YOU BACK TO LIFE...
?!!
WH-WHAT'S HAPPENING...?
IT CAN'T BE... ONE OF THE ORBS IS CRACKING!
W-WAIT!
NO! STOPPPP!

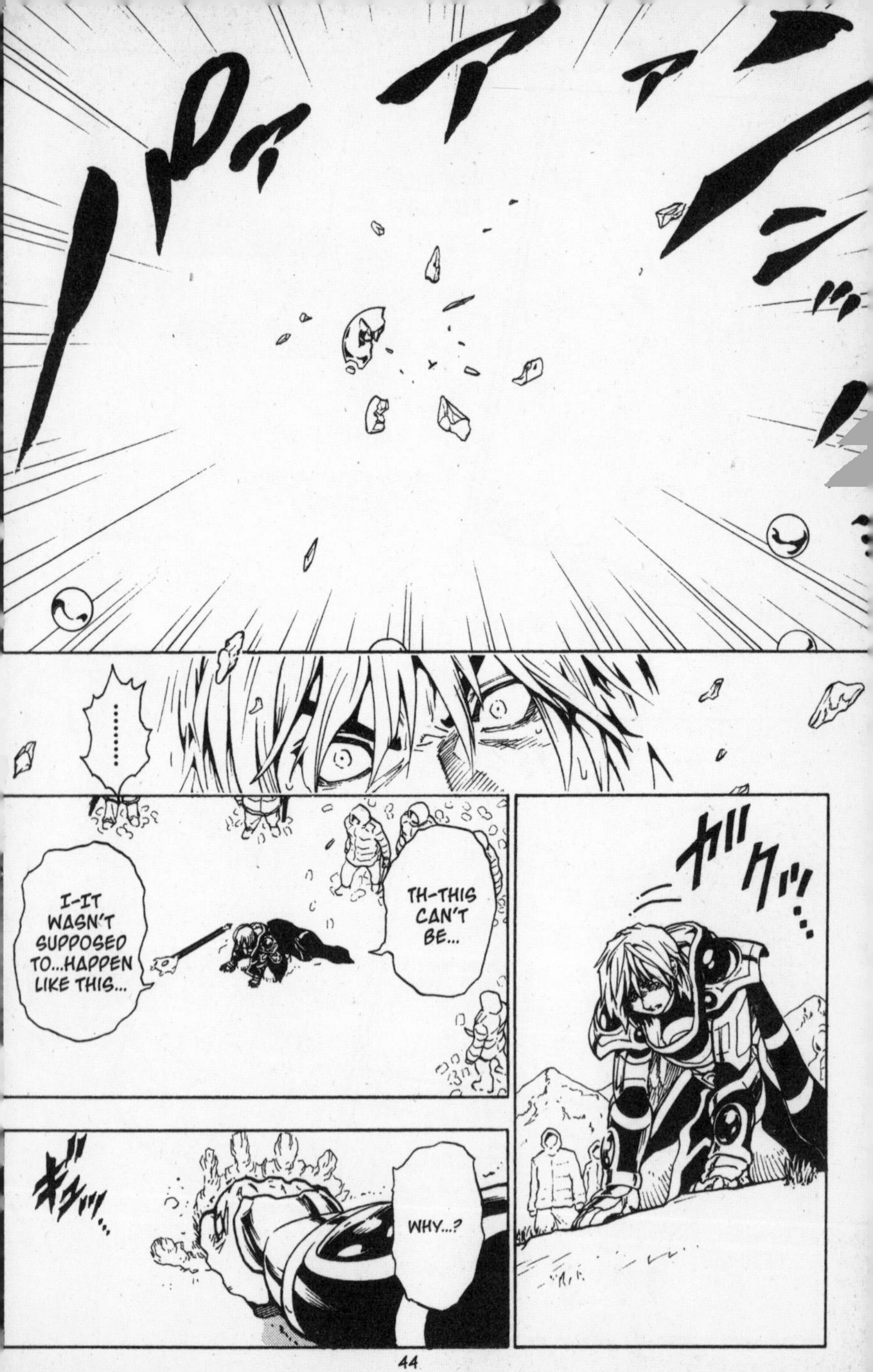
......
ガクッ...
TH-THIS CAN'T BE...
I-IT WASN'T SUPPOSED TO...HAPPEN LIKE THIS...
WHY...?

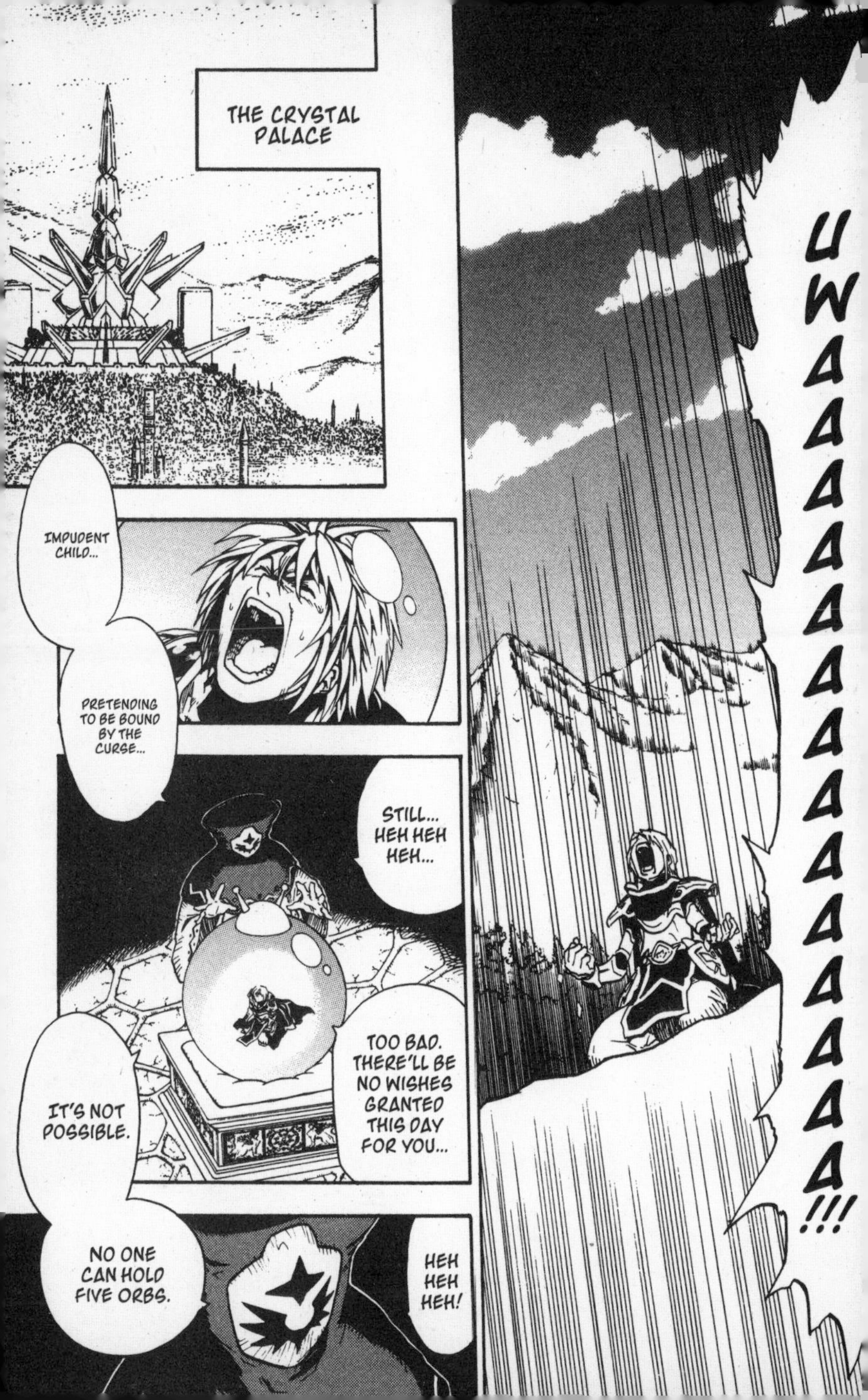

UWAAAAAAAAAAAAAAA!!!
THE CRYSTAL PALACE
IMPUDENT CHILD...
PRETENDING TO BE BOUND BY THE CURSE...
STILL... HEH HEH HEH...
TOO BAD. THERE'LL BE NO WISHES GRANTED THIS DAY FOR YOU...
IT'S NOT POSSIBLE.
HEH HEH HEH!
NO ONE CAN HOLD FIVE ORBS.

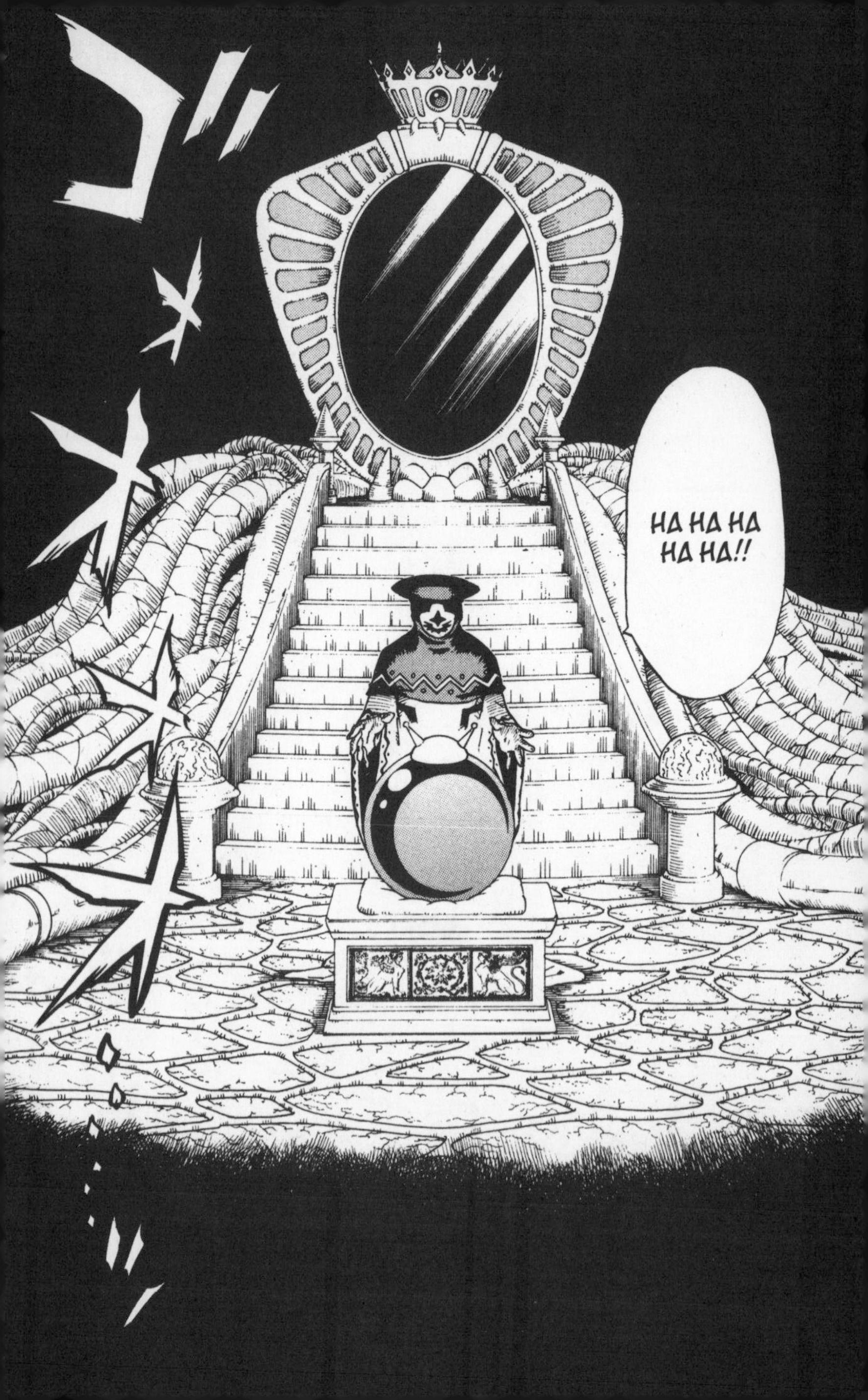
HA HA HA HA HA!!

A Retelling of a Classic
BRAVE STORY

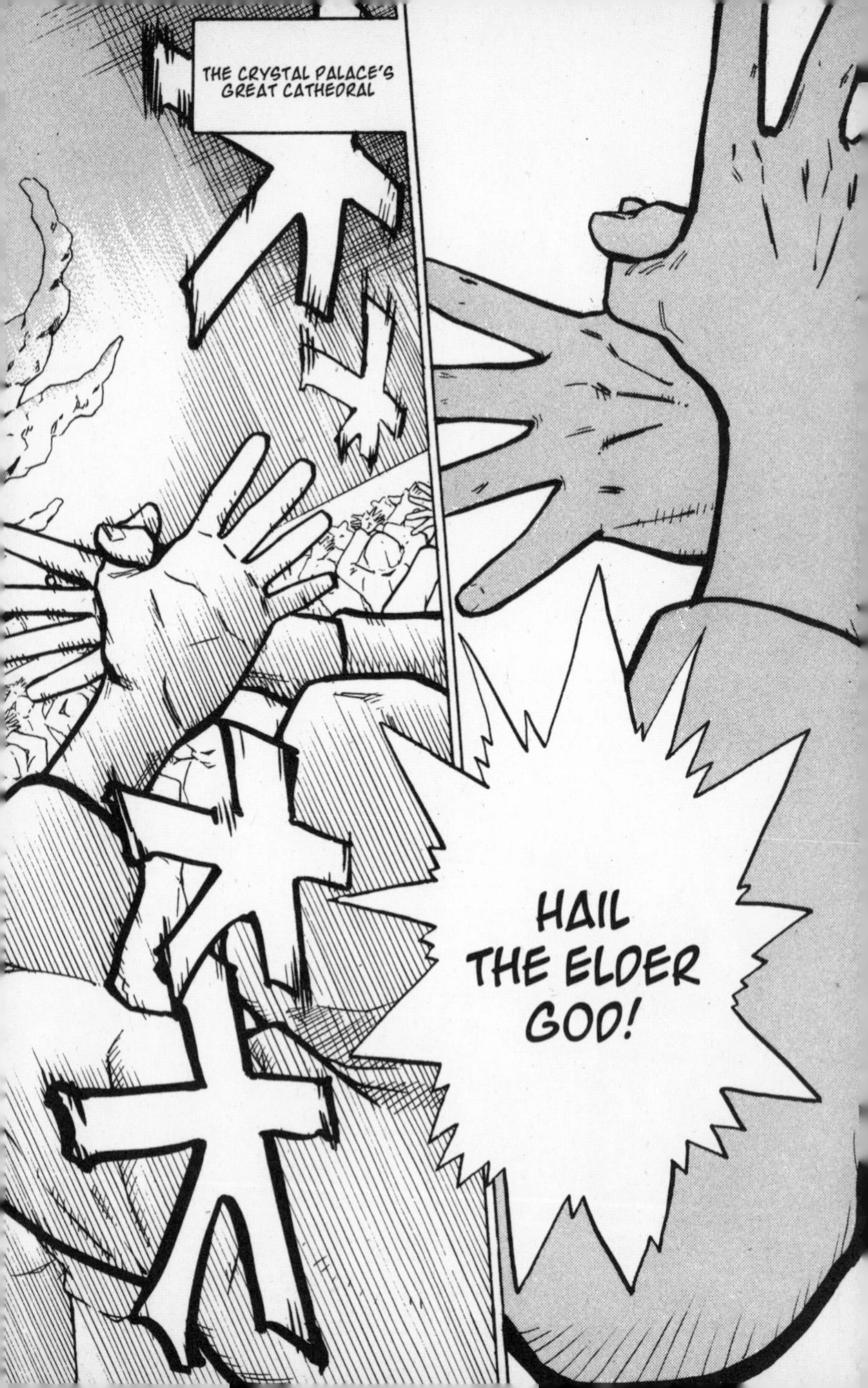
THE CRYSTAL PALACE'S GREAT CATHEDRAL
HAIL THE ELDER GOD!

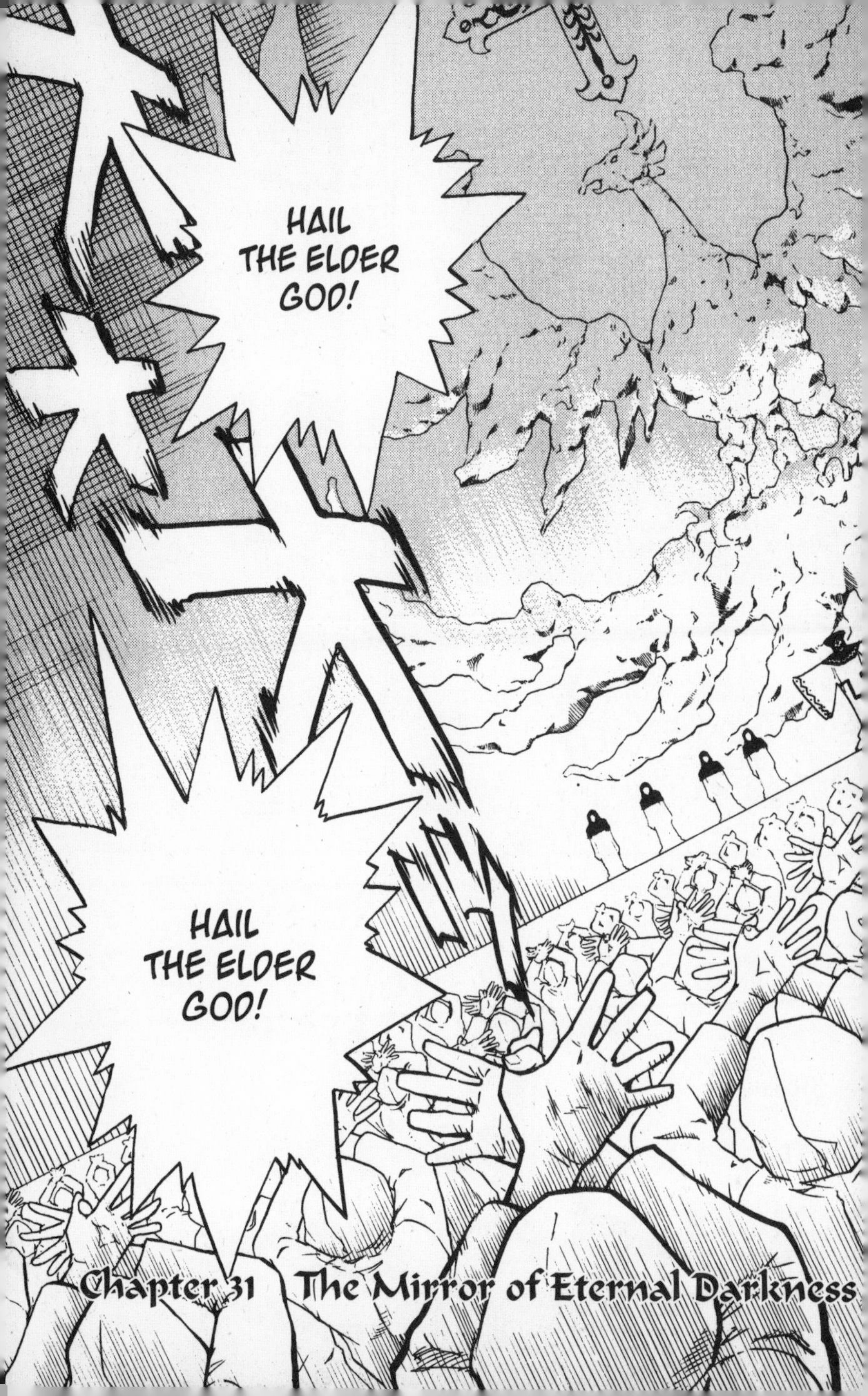
HAIL THE ELDER GOD!
HAIL THE ELDER GOD!
Chapter 31 The Mirror of Eternal Darkness

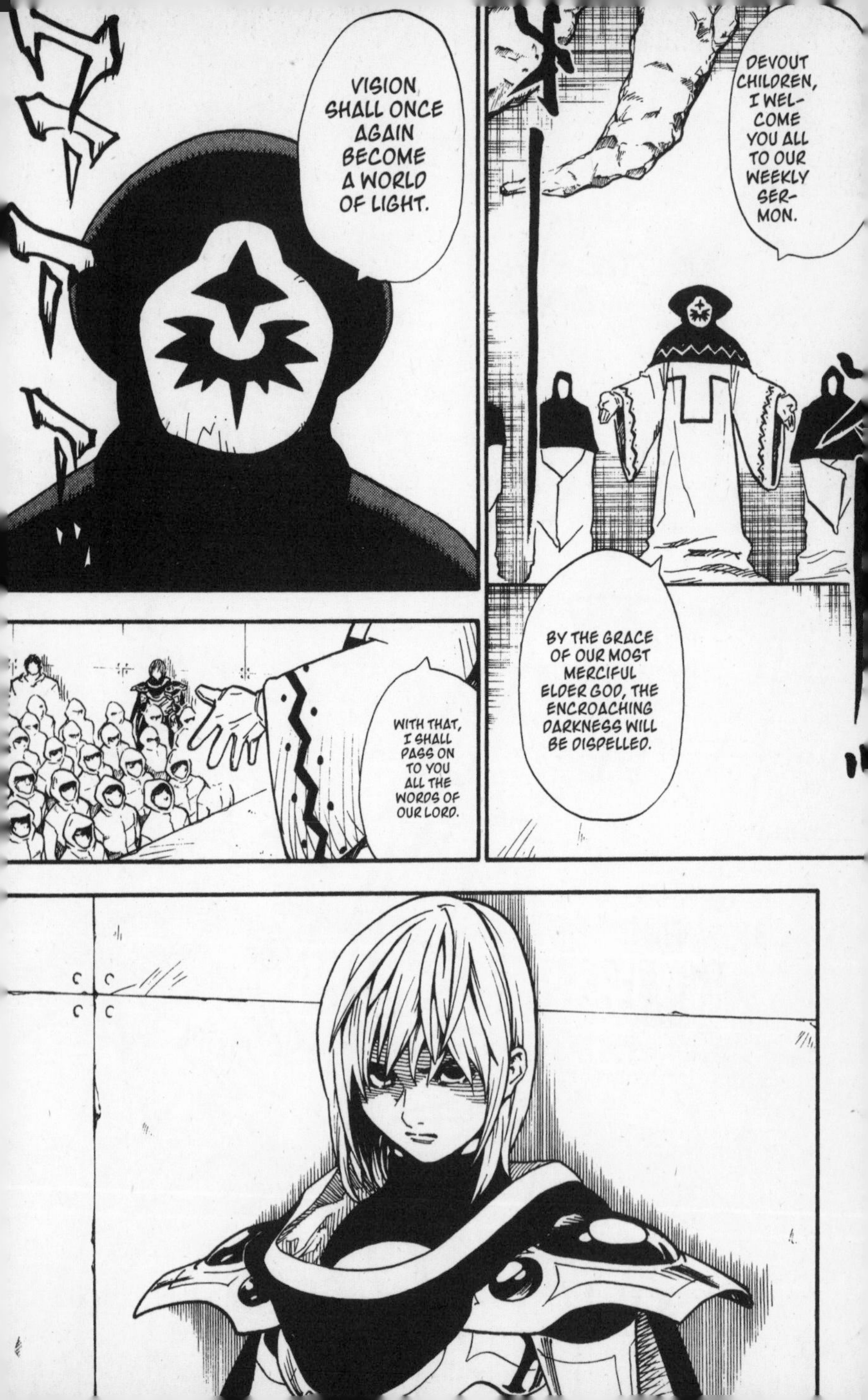
DEVOUT CHILDREN, I WELCOME YOU ALL TO OUR WEEKLY SERMON.
VISION SHALL ONCE AGAIN BECOME A WORLD OF LIGHT.
BY THE GRACE OF OUR MOST MERCIFUL ELDER GOD, THE ENCROACHING DARKNESS WILL BE DISPELLED.
WITH THAT, I SHALL PASS ON TO YOU ALL THE WORDS OF OUR LORD.

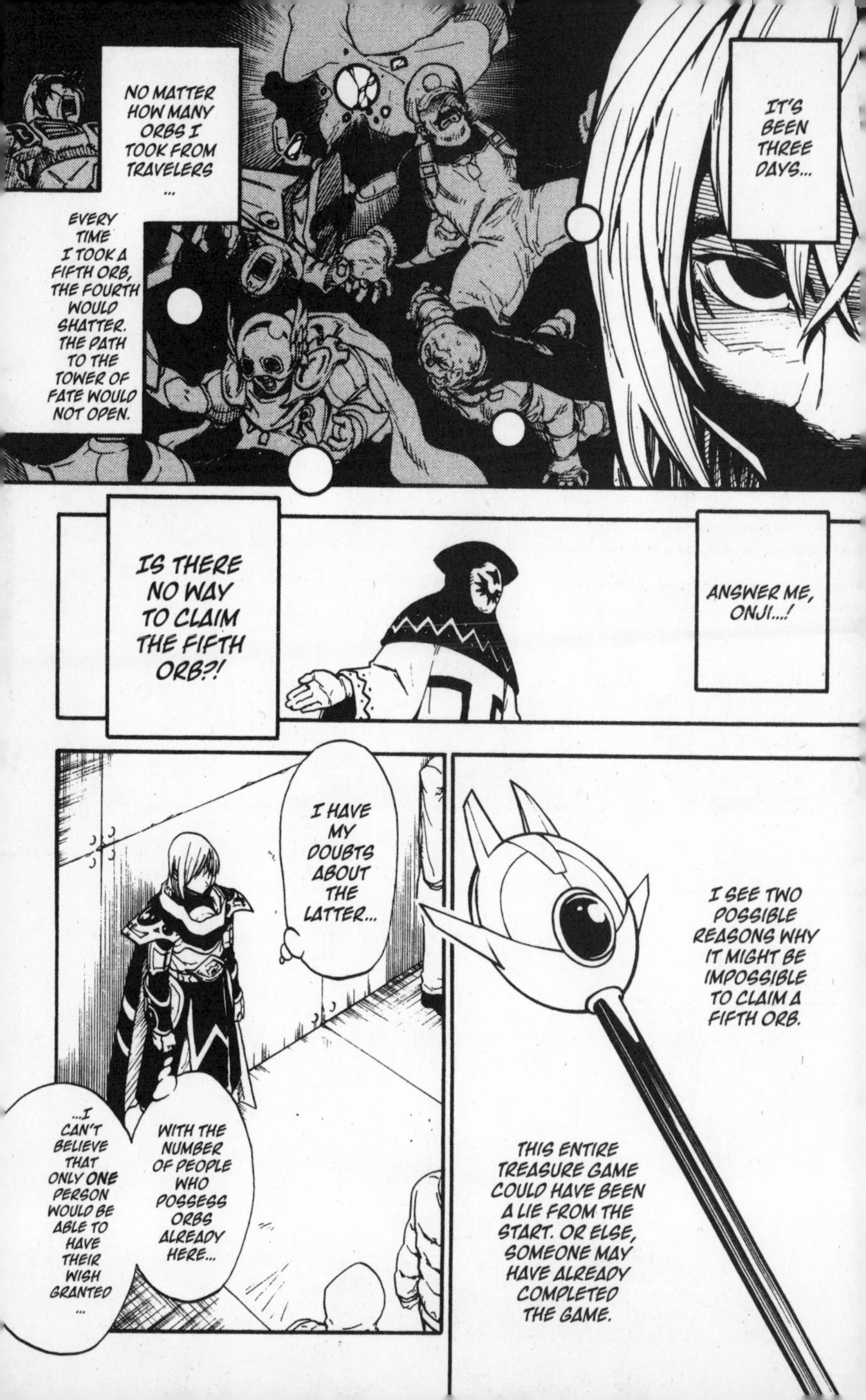
IT'S BEEN THREE DAYS...
NO MATTER HOW MANY ORBS I TOOK FROM TRAVELERS ...
EVERY TIME I TOOK A FIFTH ORB, THE FOURTH WOULD SHATTER. THE PATH TO THE TOWER OF FATE WOULD NOT OPEN.
ANSWER ME, ONJI...!
IS THERE NO WAY TO CLAIM THE FIFTH ORB?!
I SEE TWO POSSIBLE REASONS WHY IT MIGHT BE IMPOSSIBLE TO CLAIM A FIFTH ORB.
THIS ENTIRE TREASURE GAME COULD HAVE BEEN A LIE FROM THE START. OR ELSE, SOMEONE MAY HAVE ALREADY COMPLETED THE GAME.
I HAVE MY DOUBTS ABOUT THE LATTER...
WITH THE NUMBER OF PEOPLE WHO POSSESS ORBS ALREADY HERE...
...I CAN'T BELIEVE THAT ONLY ONE PERSON WOULD BE ABLE TO HAVE THEIR WISH GRANTED ...

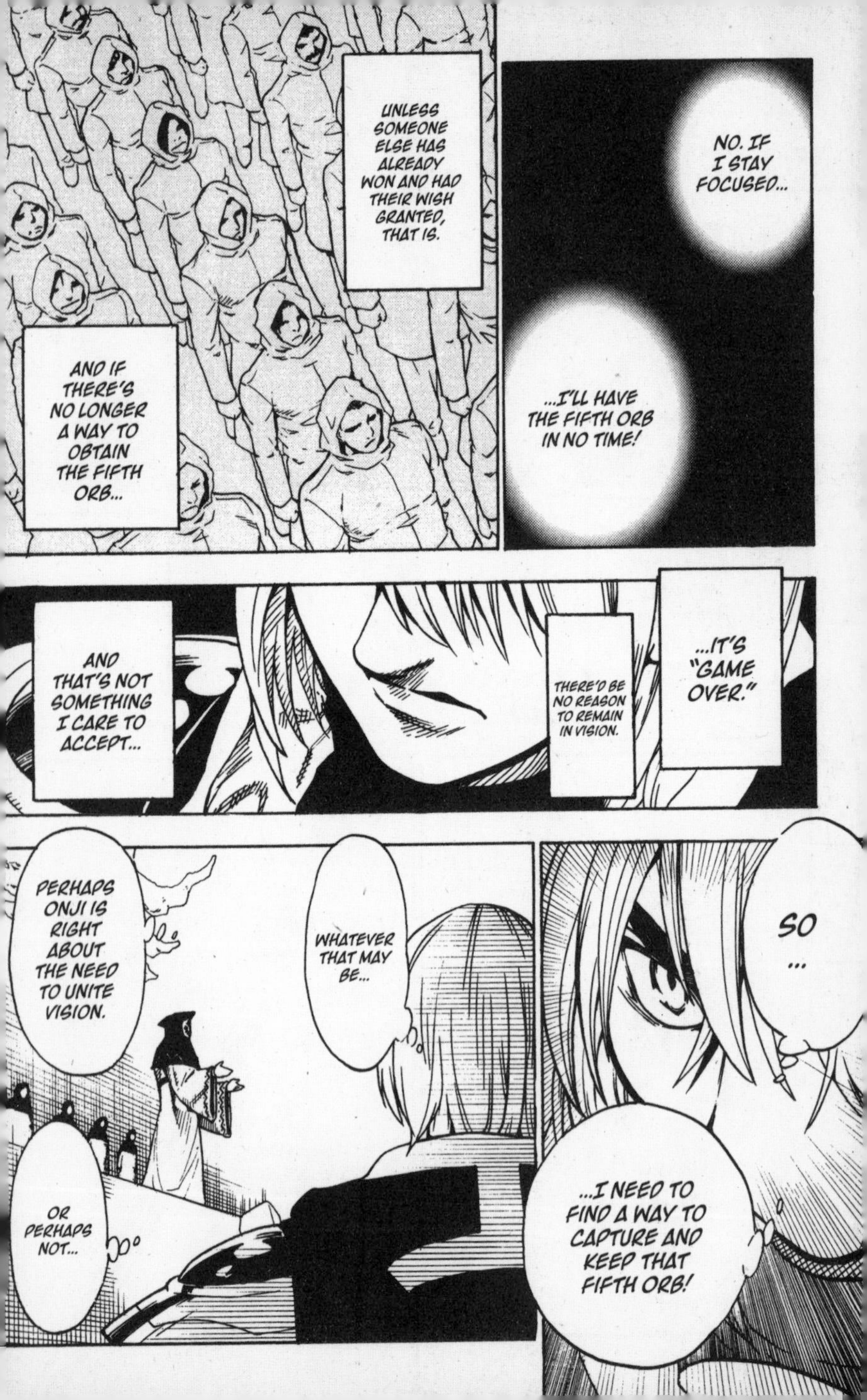
NO. IF I STAY FOCUSED...
...I'LL HAVE THE FIFTH ORB IN NO TIME!
UNLESS SOMEONE ELSE HAS ALREADY WON AND HAD THEIR WISH GRANTED, THAT IS.
AND IF THERE'S NO LONGER A WAY TO OBTAIN THE FIFTH ORB...
...IT'S "GAME OVER."
THERE'D BE NO REASON TO REMAIN IN VISION.
AND THAT'S NOT SOMETHING I CARE TO ACCEPT...
SO ...
...I NEED TO FIND A WAY TO CAPTURE AND KEEP THAT FIFTH ORB!
WHATEVER THAT MAY BE...
PERHAPS ONJI IS RIGHT ABOUT THE NEED TO UNITE VISION.
OR PERHAPS NOT...

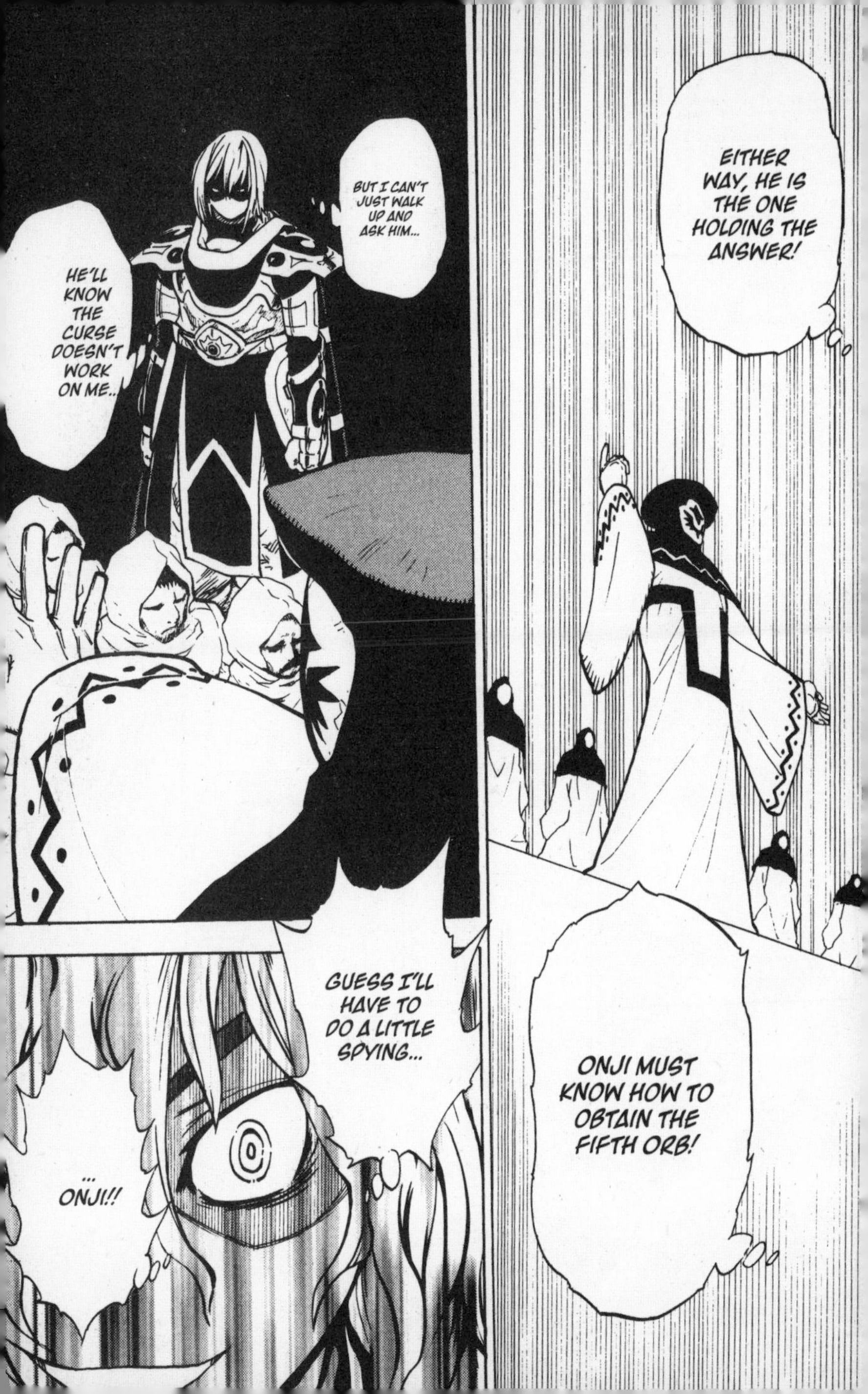
EITHER WAY, HE IS THE ONE HOLDING THE ANSWER!
ONJI MUST KNOW HOW TO OBTAIN THE FIFTH ORB!
BUT I CAN'T JUST WALK UP AND ASK HIM...
HE'LL KNOW THE CURSE DOESN'T WORK ON ME...
GUESS I'LL HAVE TO DO A LITTLE SPYING...
... ONJI!!

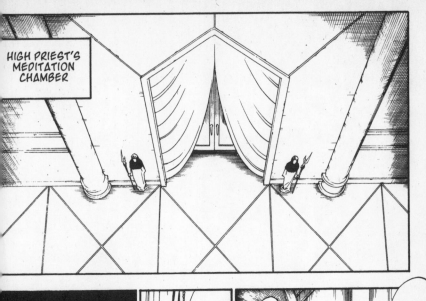

HIGH PRIEST'S MEDITATION CHAMBER
WE-COME BACK, LORD HIGH PRIEST.
HM.
YOU'VE RETURNED EARLY THIS DAY.
I FEEL SOMEWHAT UNDER THE WEATHER.
......
CREAK

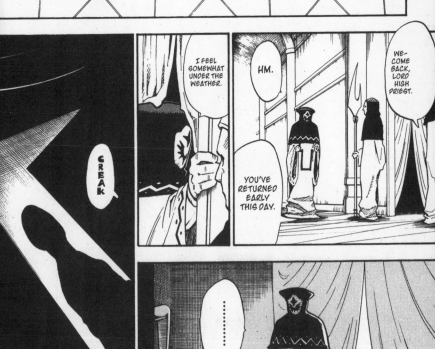

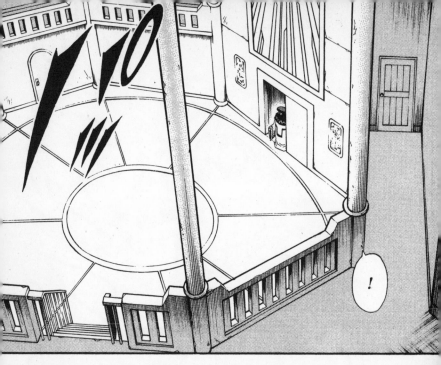

THIS IS...

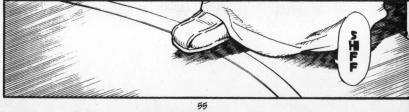

SHFF

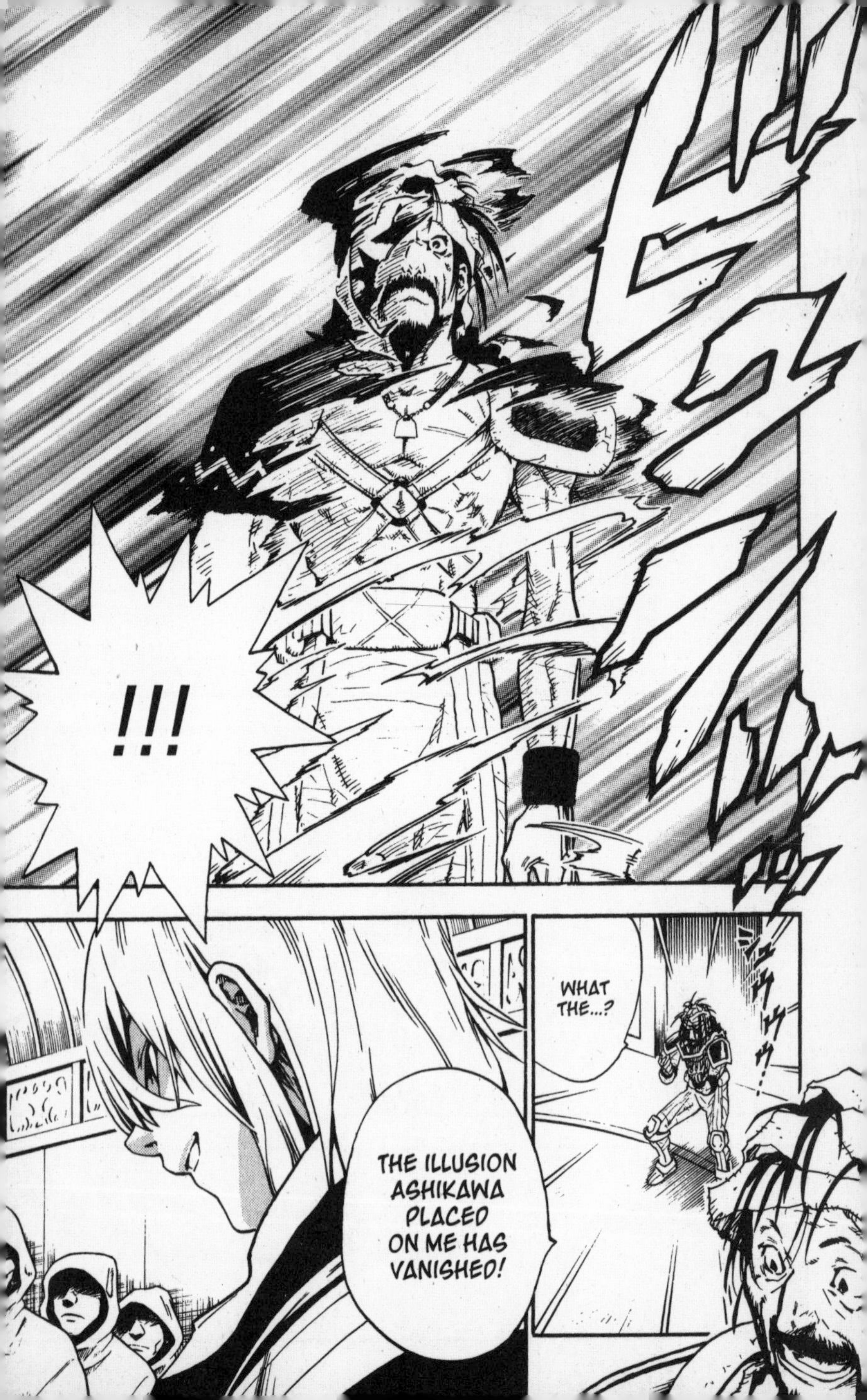
!!!
WHAT THE...?
THE ILLUSION ASHIKAWA PLACED ON ME HAS VANISHED!

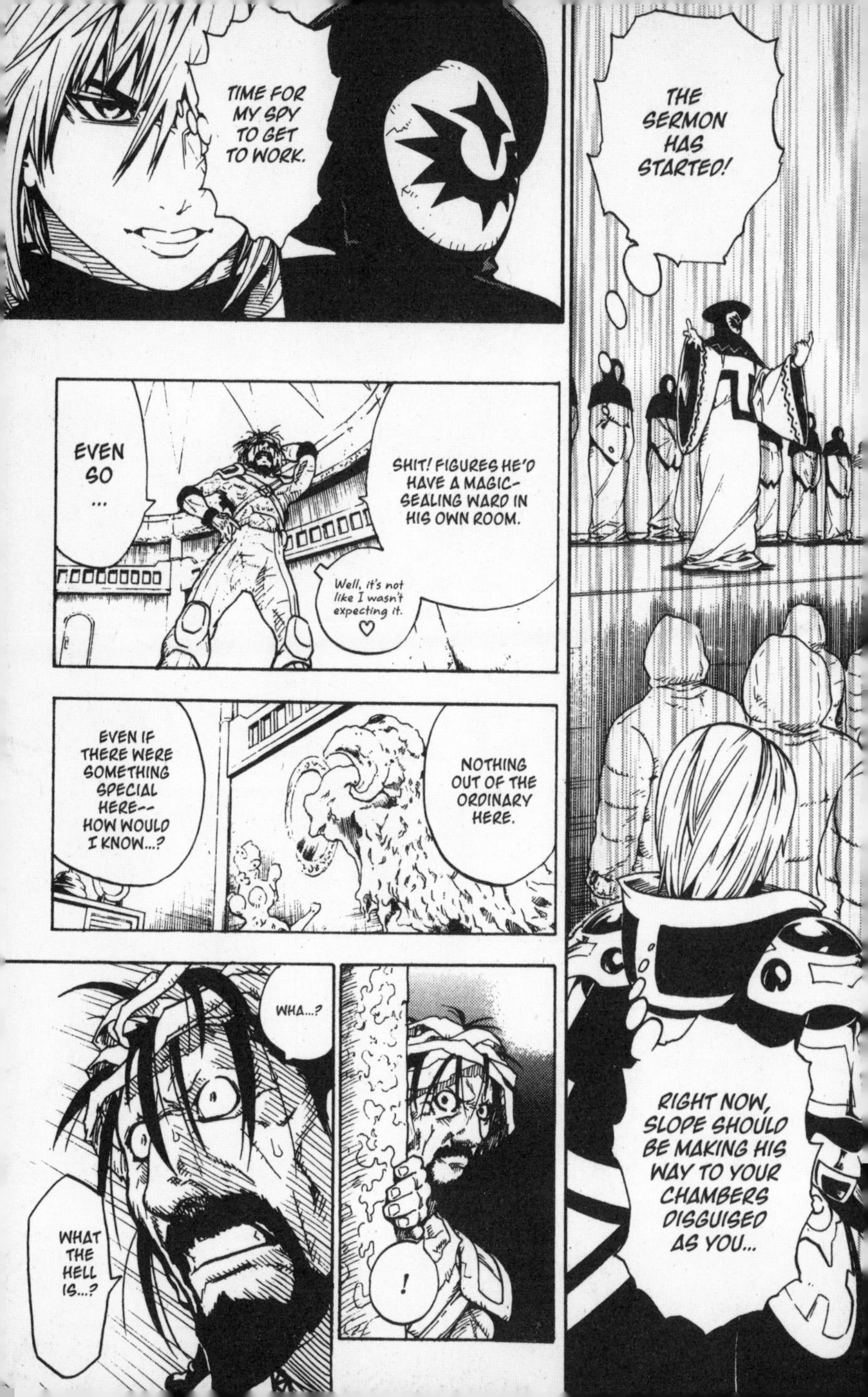
THE SERMON HAS STARTED!
RIGHT NOW, SLOPE SHOULD BE MAKING HIS WAY TO YOUR CHAMBERS DISGUISED AS YOU...
TIME FOR MY SPY TO GET TO WORK.
SHIT! FIGURES HE'D HAVE A MAGIC-SEALING WARD IN HIS OWN ROOM.
Well, it's not like I wasn't expecting it. ♡
EVEN SO ...
NOTHING OUT OF THE ORDINARY HERE.
EVEN IF THERE WERE SOMETHING SPECIAL HERE-- HOW WOULD I KNOW...?
WHA...?
!
WHAT THE HELL IS...?

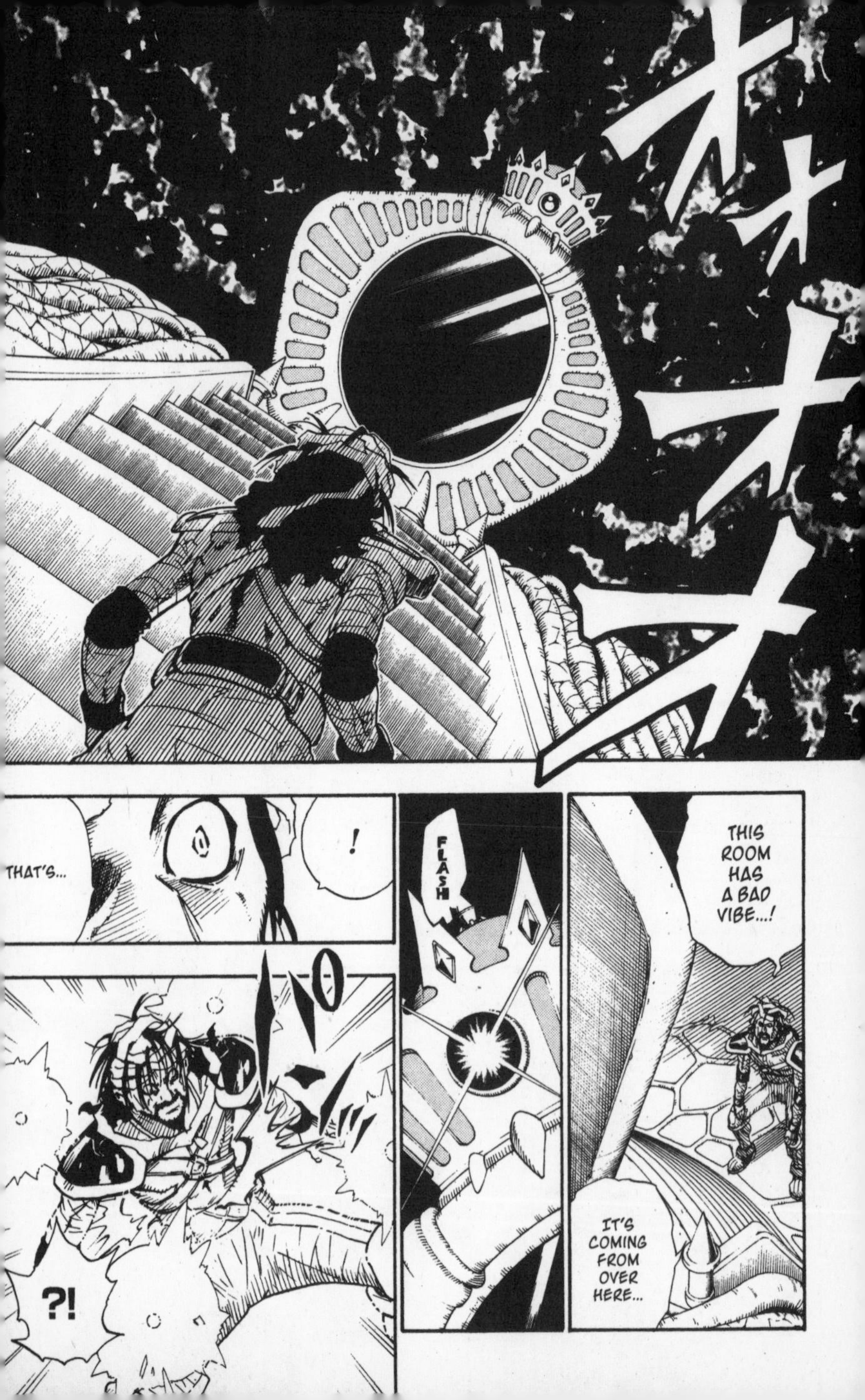
THIS ROOM HAS A BAD VIBE...!
IT'S COMING FROM OVER HERE...
FLASH
!
THAT'S...
?!

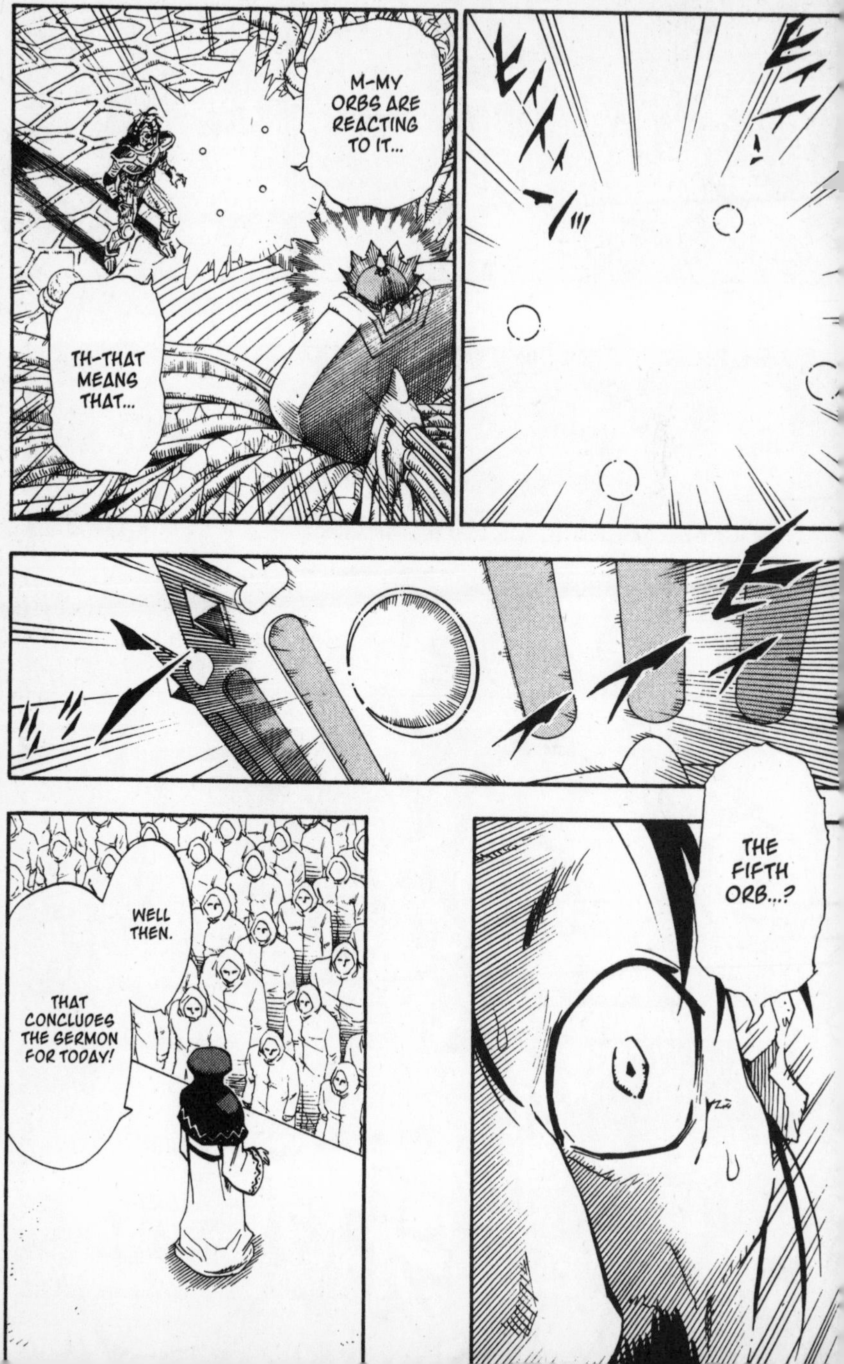
M-MY ORBS ARE REACTING TO IT...
TH-THAT MEANS THAT...
THE FIFTH ORB...?
WELL THEN.
THAT CONCLUDES THE SERMON FOR TODAY!

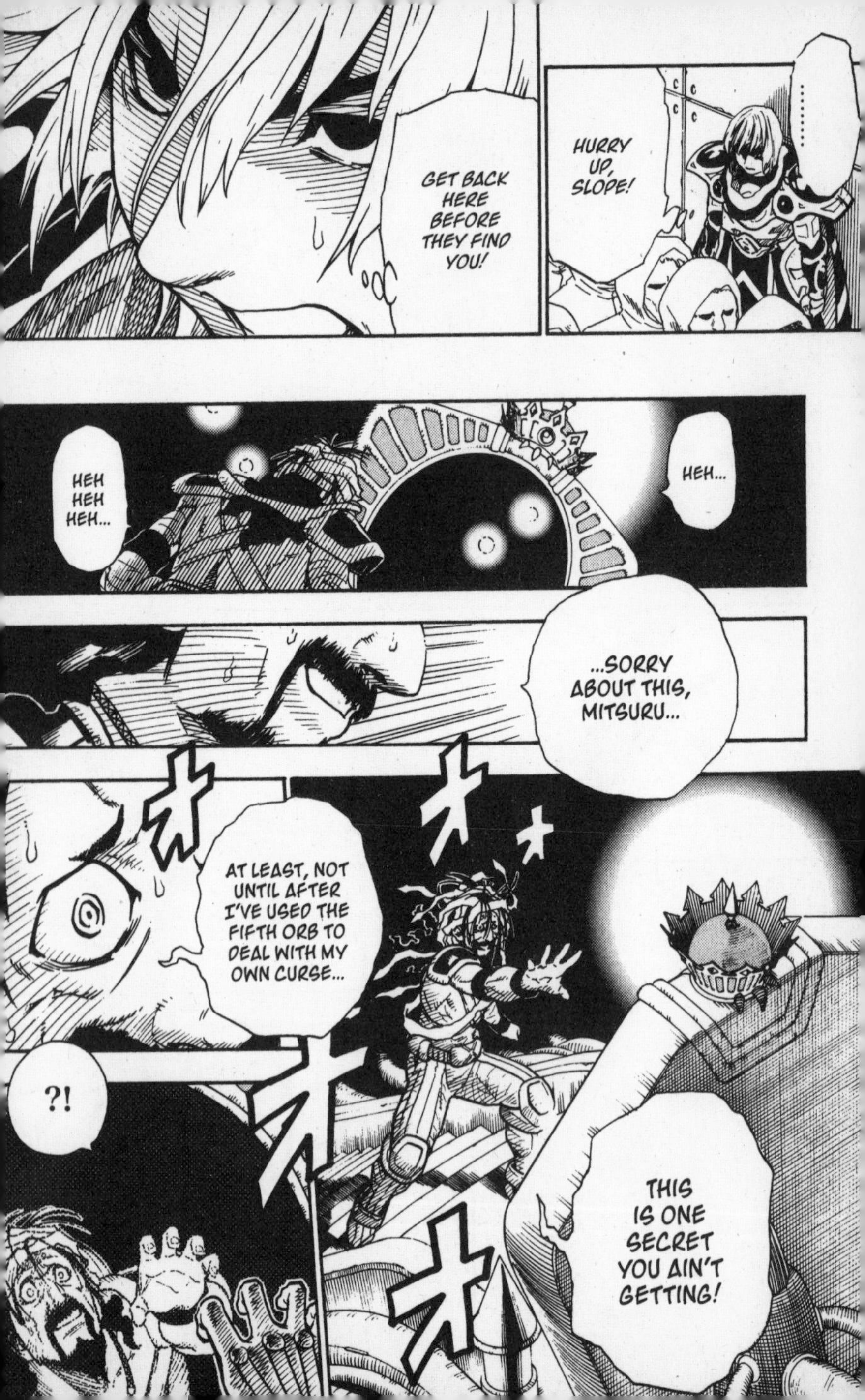
......
HURRY UP, SLOPE!
GET BACK HERE BEFORE THEY FIND YOU!
HEH...
HEH HEH HEH...
...SORRY ABOUT THIS, MITSURU...
THIS IS ONE SECRET YOU AIN'T GETTING!
AT LEAST, NOT UNTIL AFTER I'VE USED THE FIFTH ORB TO DEAL WITH MY OWN CURSE...
?!

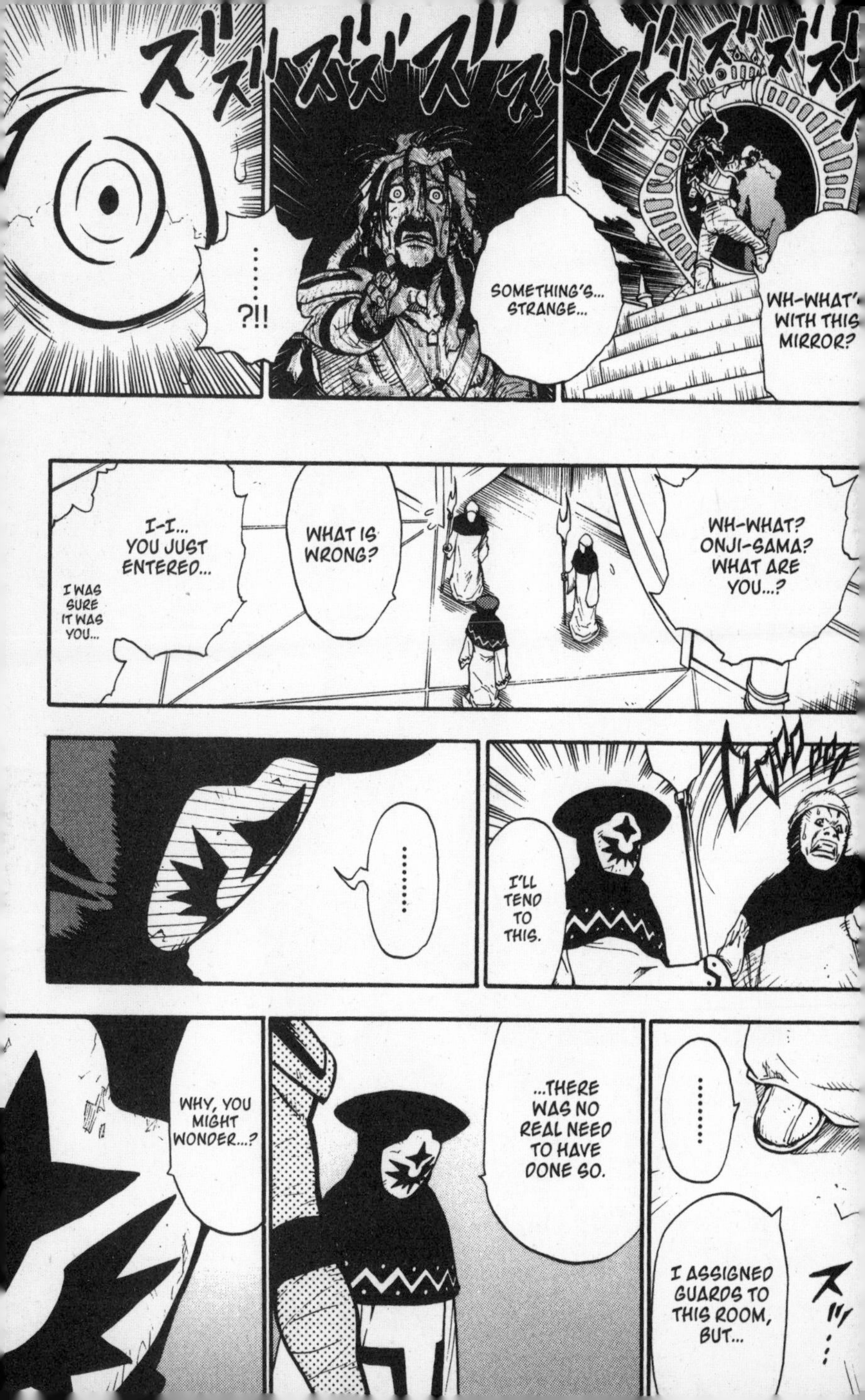

WH-WHAT' WITH THIS MIRROR?
SOMETHING'S... STRANGE...
......
?!!
WH-WHAT? ONJI-SAMA? WHAT ARE YOU...?
WHAT IS WRONG?
I-I... YOU JUST ENTERED...
I WAS SURE IT WAS YOU...
I'LL TEND TO THIS.
....
....
I ASSIGNED GUARDS TO THIS ROOM, BUT...
...THERE WAS NO REAL NEED TO HAVE DONE SO.
WHY, YOU MIGHT WONDER...?

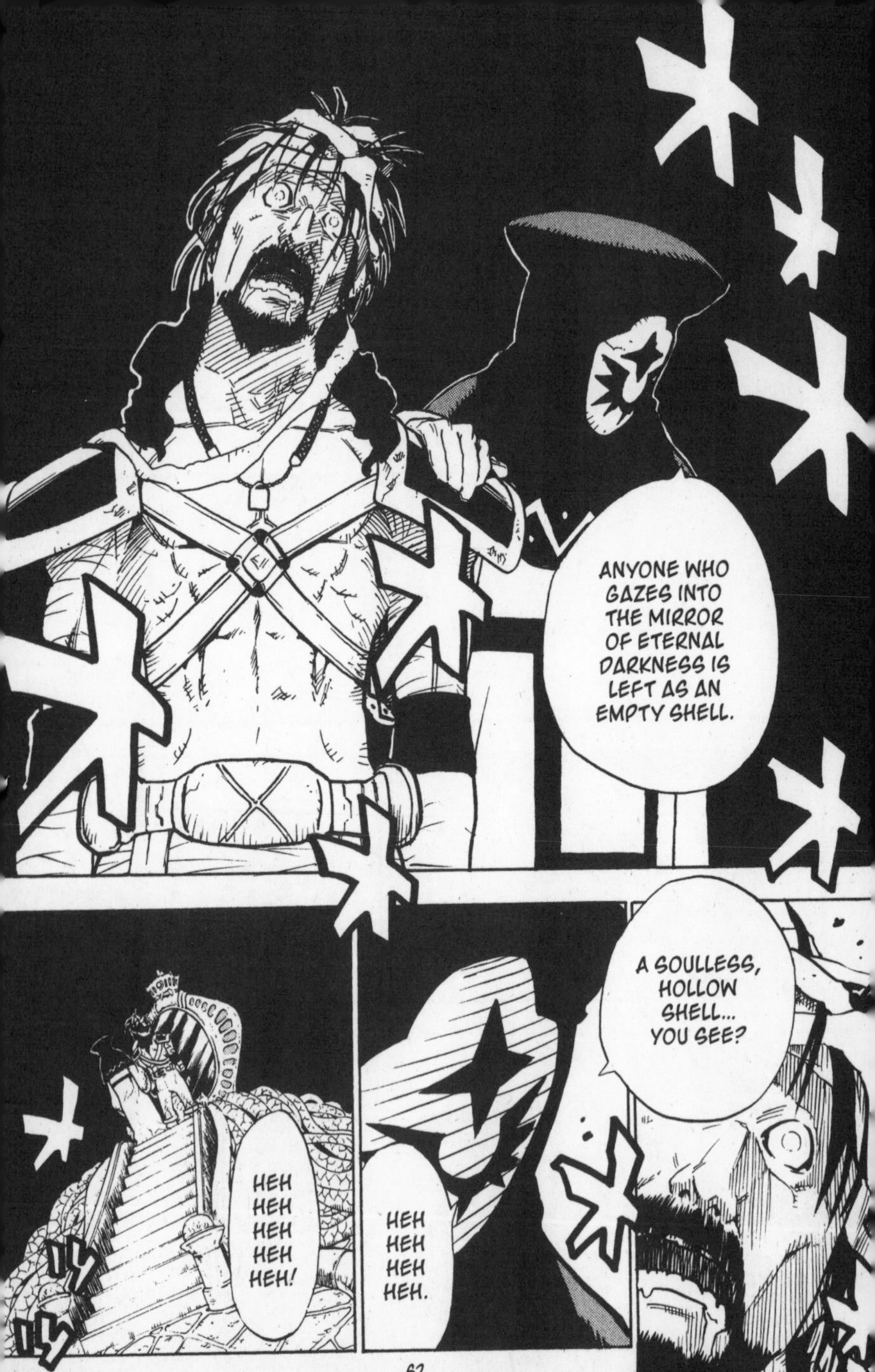
ANYONE WHO GAZES INTO THE MIRROR OF ETERNAL DARKNESS IS LEFT AS AN EMPTY SHELL.
A SOULLESS, HOLLOW SHELL... YOU SEE?
HEH HEH HEH HEH.
HEH HEH HEH HEH HEH!

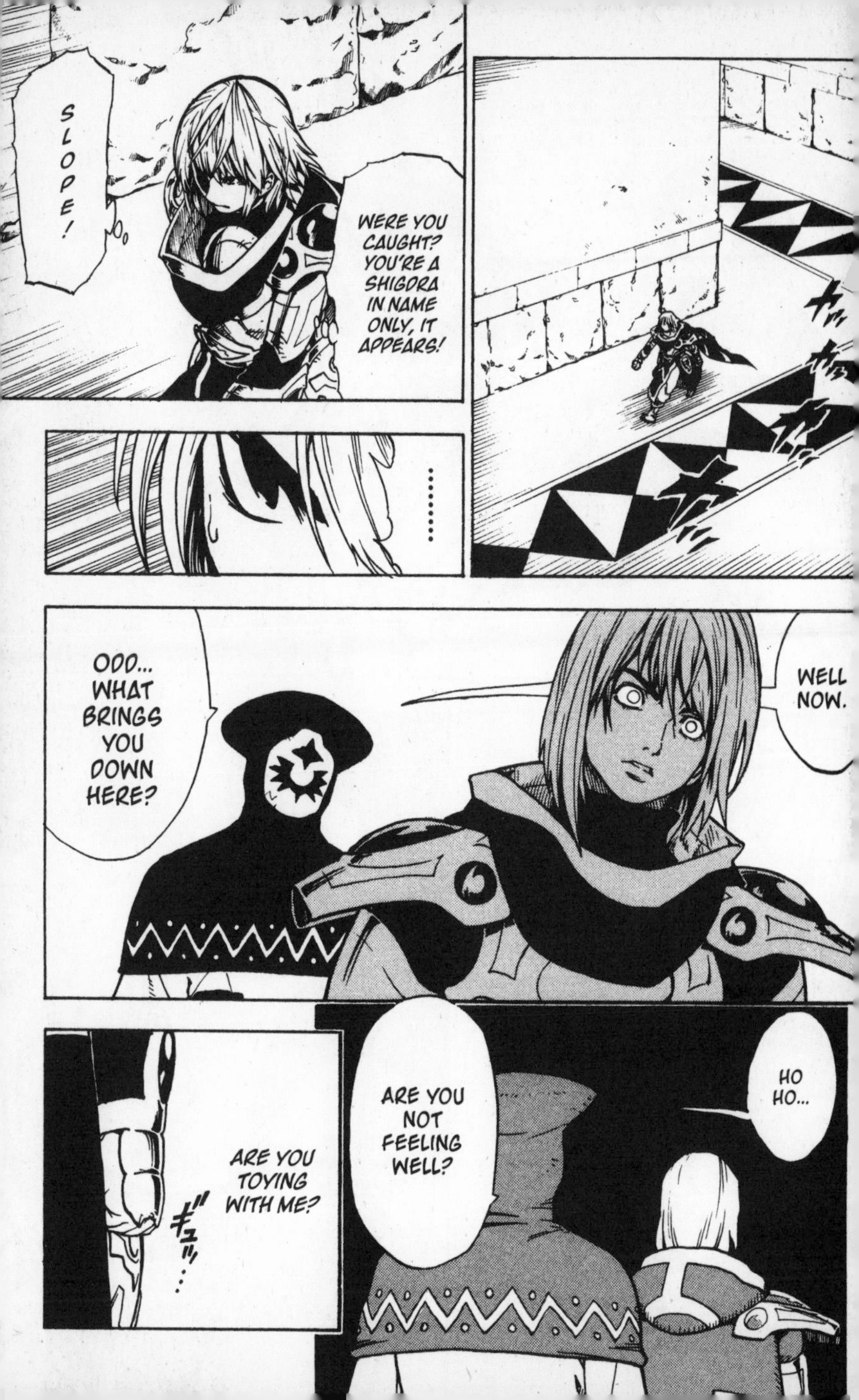

WERE YOU CAUGHT? YOU'RE A SHIGORA IN NAME ONLY, IT APPEARS!
SLOPE!
....
WELL NOW.
ODD... WHAT BRINGS YOU DOWN HERE?
HO HO...
ARE YOU NOT FEELING WELL?
ARE YOU TOYING WITH ME?

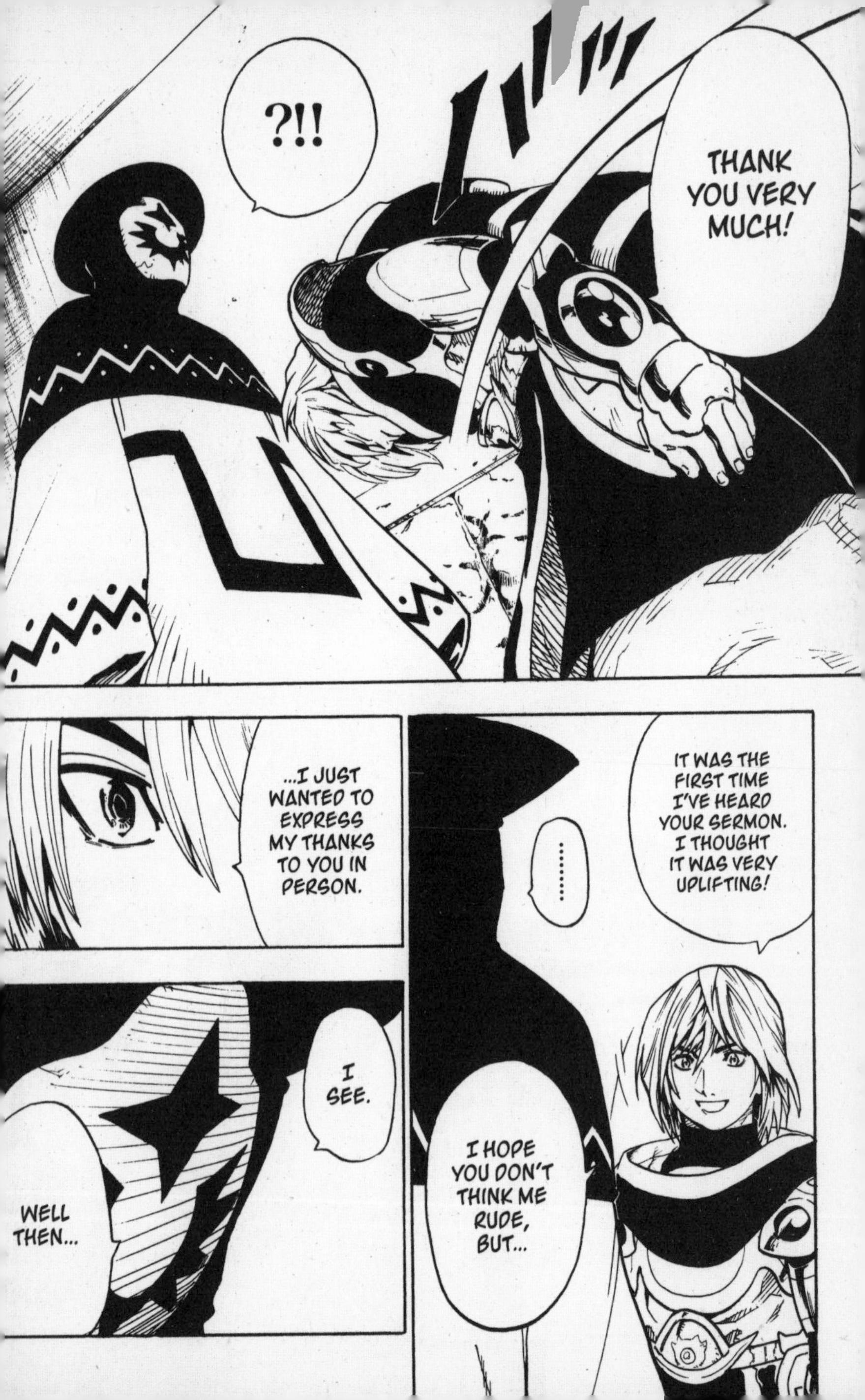
THANK YOU VERY MUCH!
?!!
IT WAS THE FIRST TIME I'VE HEARD YOUR SERMON. I THOUGHT IT WAS VERY UPLIFTING!
....
I HOPE YOU DON'T THINK ME RUDE, BUT...
...I JUST WANTED TO EXPRESS MY THANKS TO YOU IN PERSON.
I SEE.
WELL THEN...

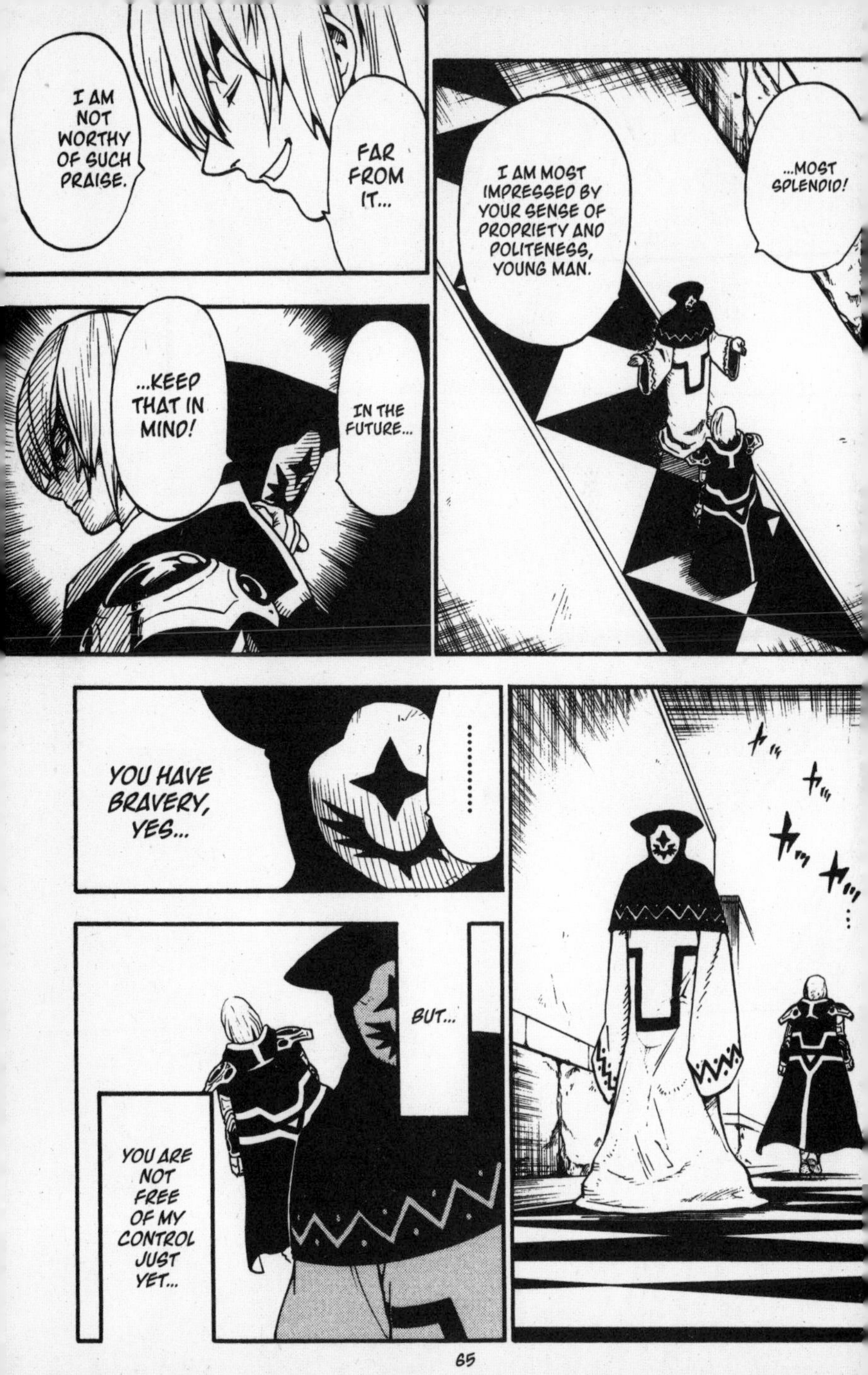
...MOST SPLENDID!
I AM MOST IMPRESSED BY YOUR SENSE OF PROPRIETY AND POLITENESS, YOUNG MAN.
FAR FROM IT...
I AM NOT WORTHY OF SUCH PRAISE.
IN THE FUTURE...
...KEEP THAT IN MIND!
......
YOU HAVE BRAVERY, YES...
BUT...
YOU ARE NOT FREE OF MY CONTROL JUST YET...

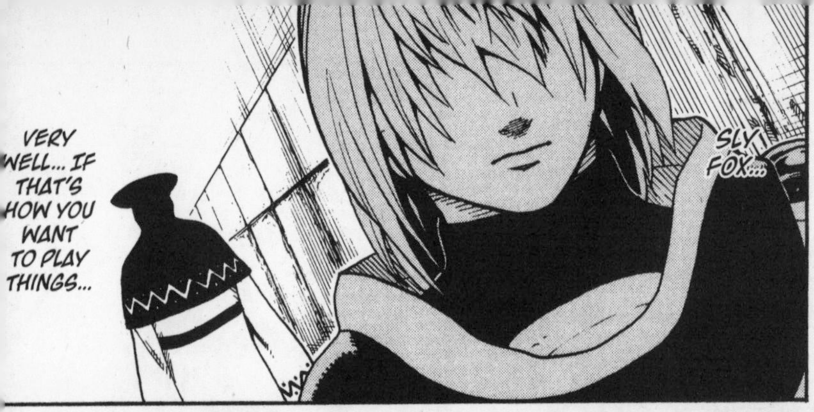
SLY FOX...
VERY WELL... IF THAT'S HOW YOU WANT TO PLAY THINGS...

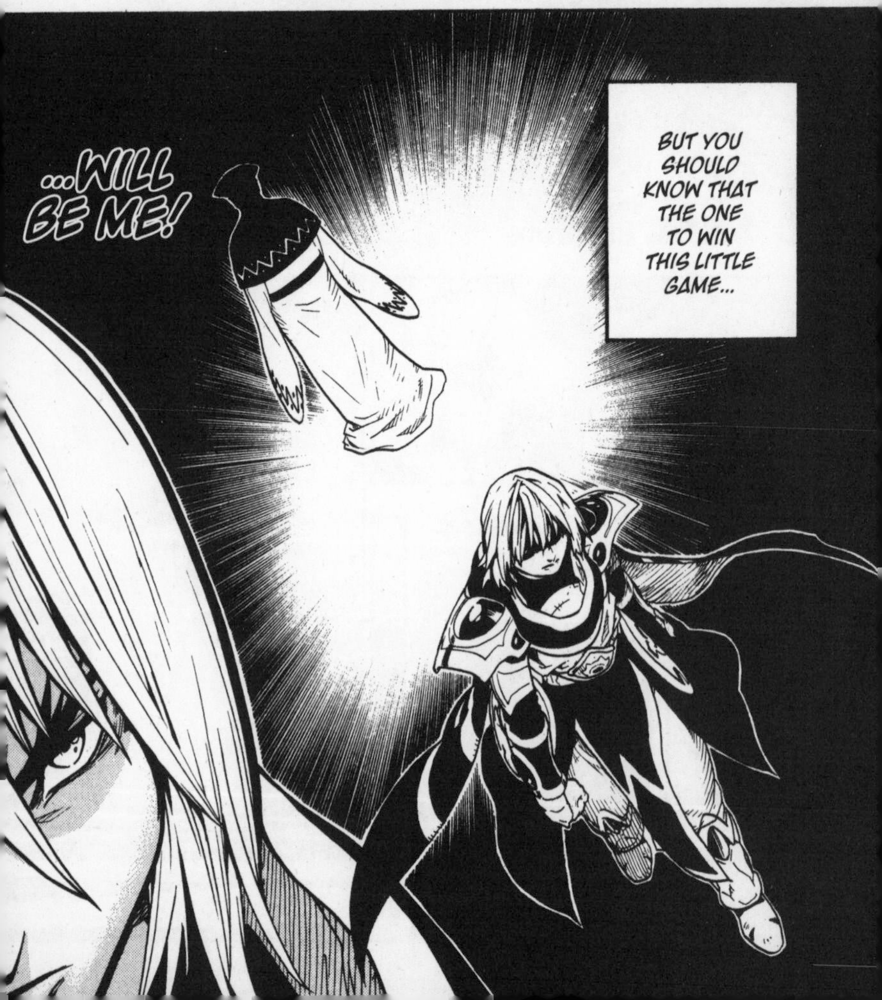
BUT YOU SHOULD KNOW THAT THE ONE TO WIN THIS LITTLE GAME...
...WILL BE ME!

A Retelling of a Classic

BRAVE STORY

Chapter 32 Not Alone

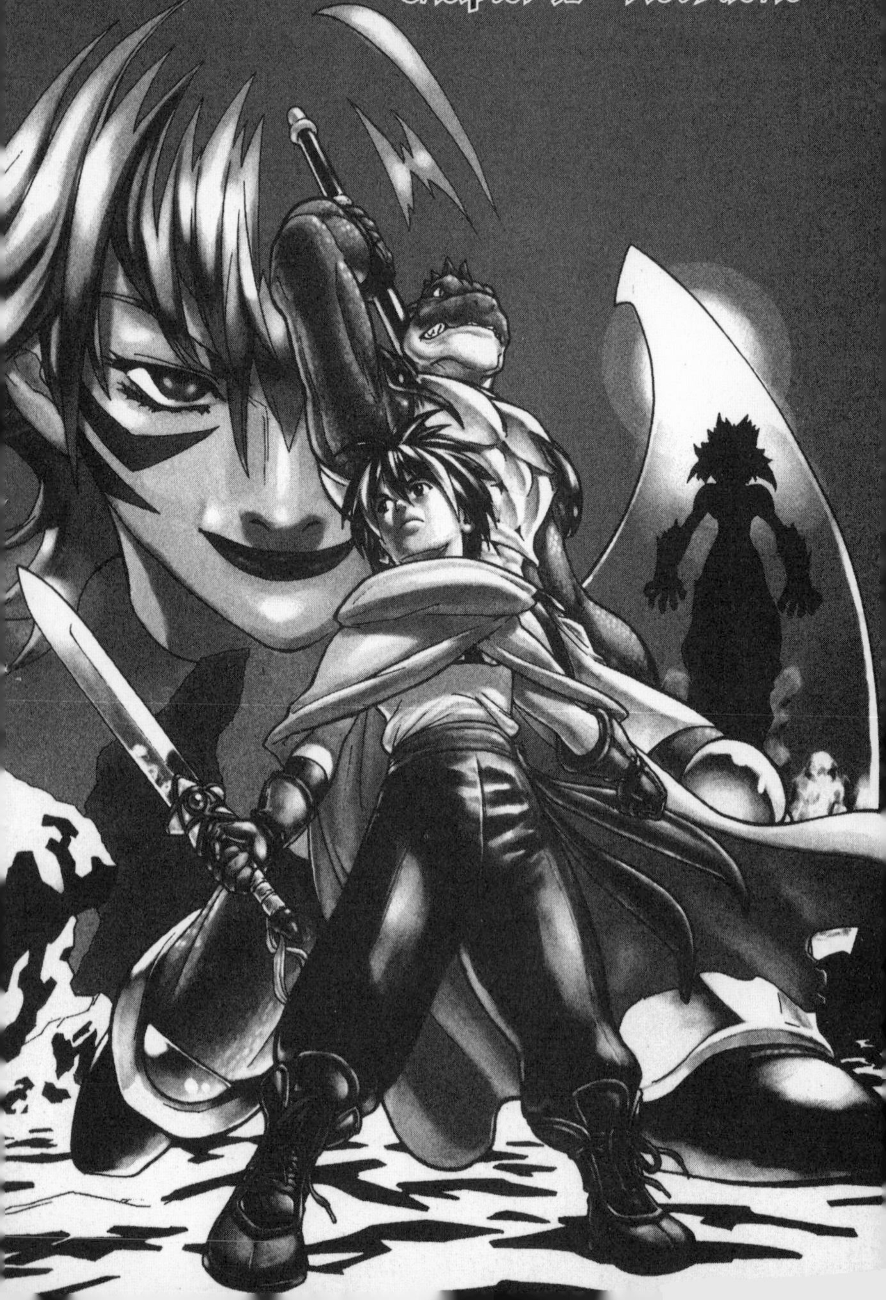

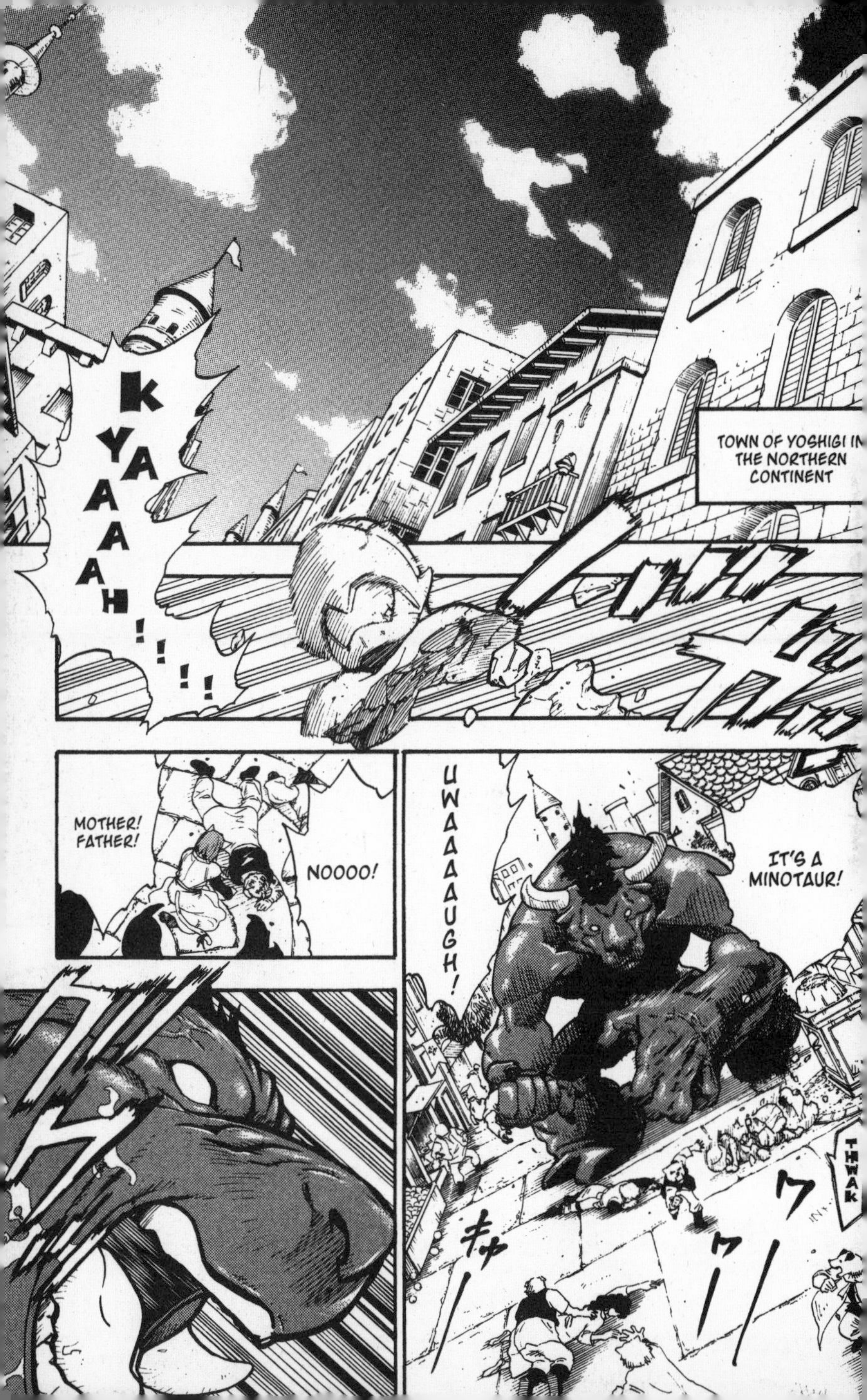
TOWN OF YOSHIGI IN THE NORTHERN CONTINENT
KYAAAAAH!!!!
IT'S A MINOTAUR!
UWAAAAAAUGH!
THWAK
MOTHER! FATHER!
NOOOO!

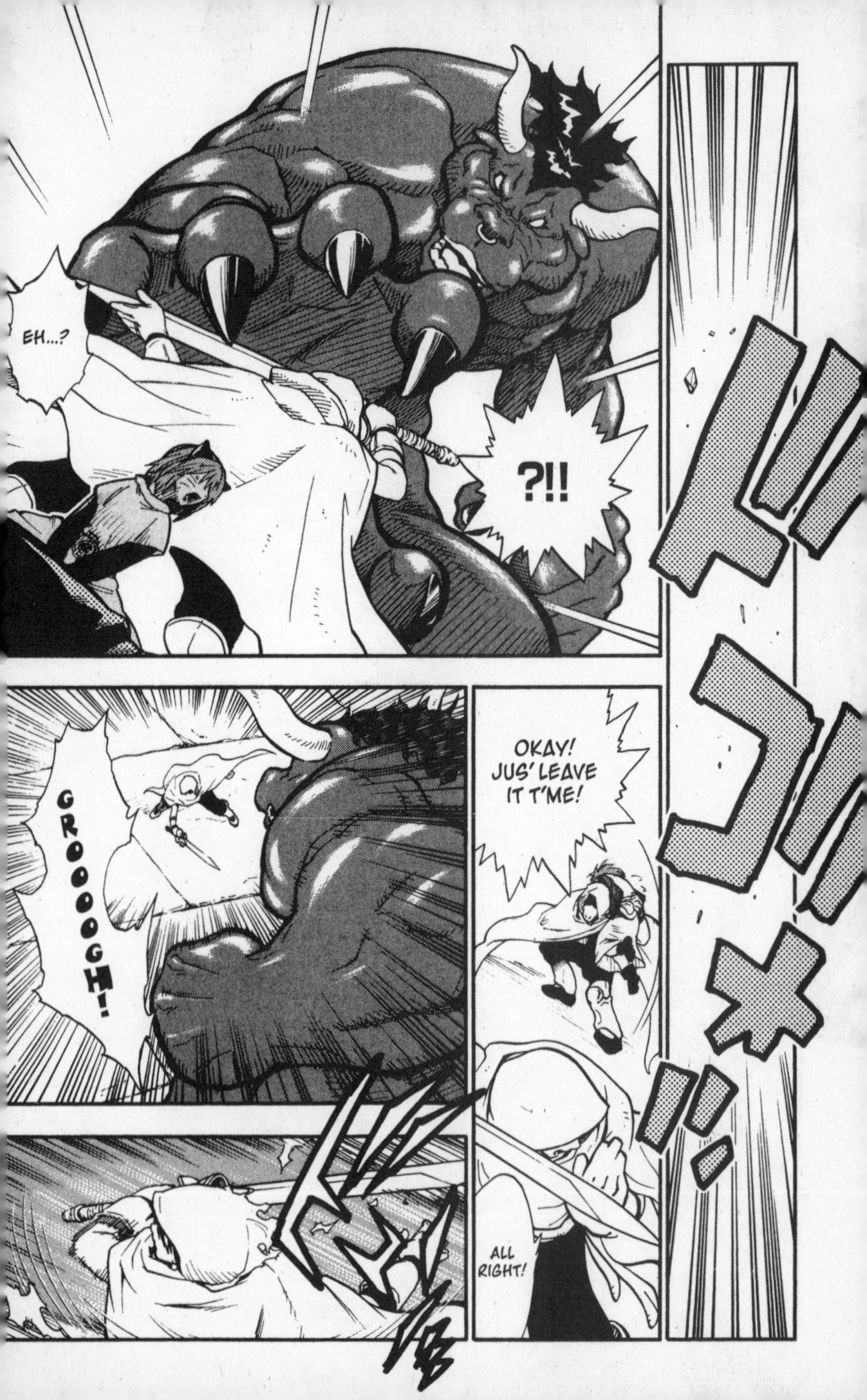
?!!
EH...?
OKAY! JUS' LEAVE IT T'ME!
GROOOOOGH!
ALL RIGHT!

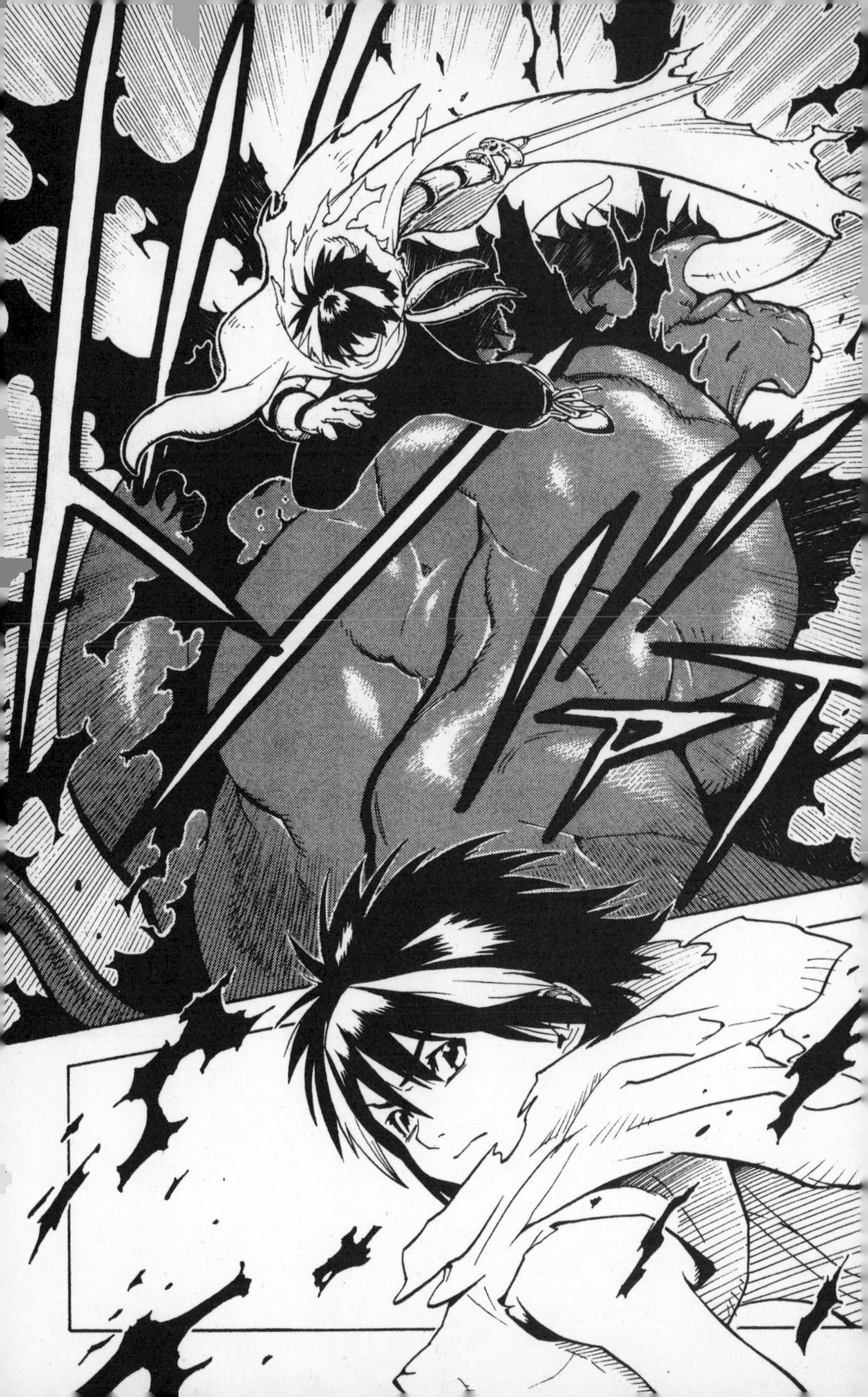

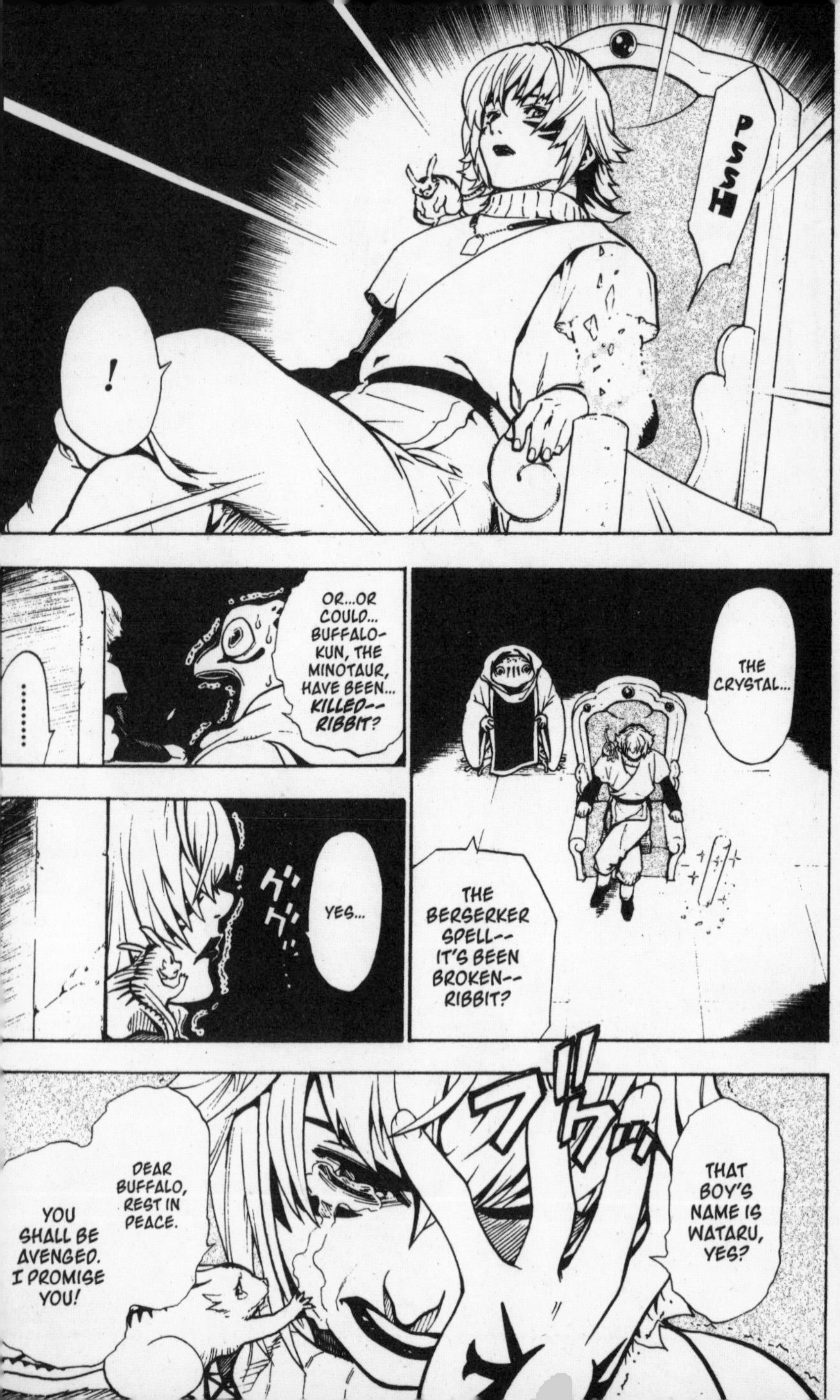
PSSH
!
THE CRYSTAL...
THE BERSERKER SPELL--IT'S BEEN BROKEN--RIBBIT?
OR...OR COULD... BUFFALO-KUN, THE MINOTAUR, HAVE BEEN... KILLED--RIBBIT?
......
YES...
THAT BOY'S NAME IS WATARU, YES?
DEAR BUFFALO, REST IN PEACE.
YOU SHALL BE AVENGED. I PROMISE YOU!

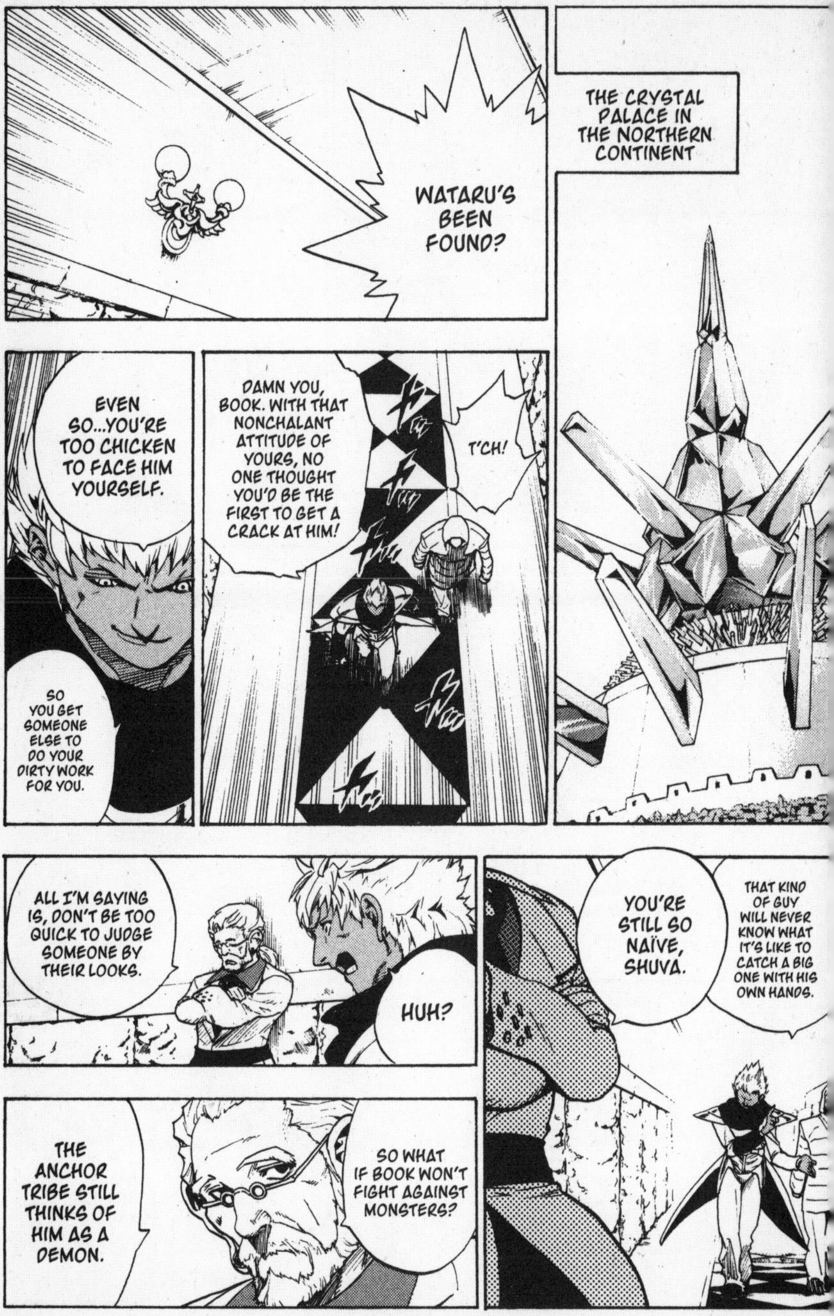
THE CRYSTAL PALACE IN THE NORTHERN CONTINENT
WATARU'S BEEN FOUND?
T'CH!
DAMN YOU, BOOK. WITH THAT NONCHALANT ATTITUDE OF YOURS, NO ONE THOUGHT YOU'D BE THE FIRST TO GET A CRACK AT HIM!
EVEN SO...YOU'RE TOO CHICKEN TO FACE HIM YOURSELF.
SO YOU GET SOMEONE ELSE TO DO YOUR DIRTY WORK FOR YOU.
THAT KIND OF GUY WILL NEVER KNOW WHAT IT'S LIKE TO CATCH A BIG ONE WITH HIS OWN HANDS.
YOU'RE STILL SO NAÏVE, SHUVA.
HUH?
ALL I'M SAYING IS, DON'T BE TOO QUICK TO JUDGE SOMEONE BY THEIR LOOKS.
SO WHAT IF BOOK WON'T FIGHT AGAINST MONSTERS?
THE ANCHOR TRIBE STILL THINKS OF HIM AS A DEMON.

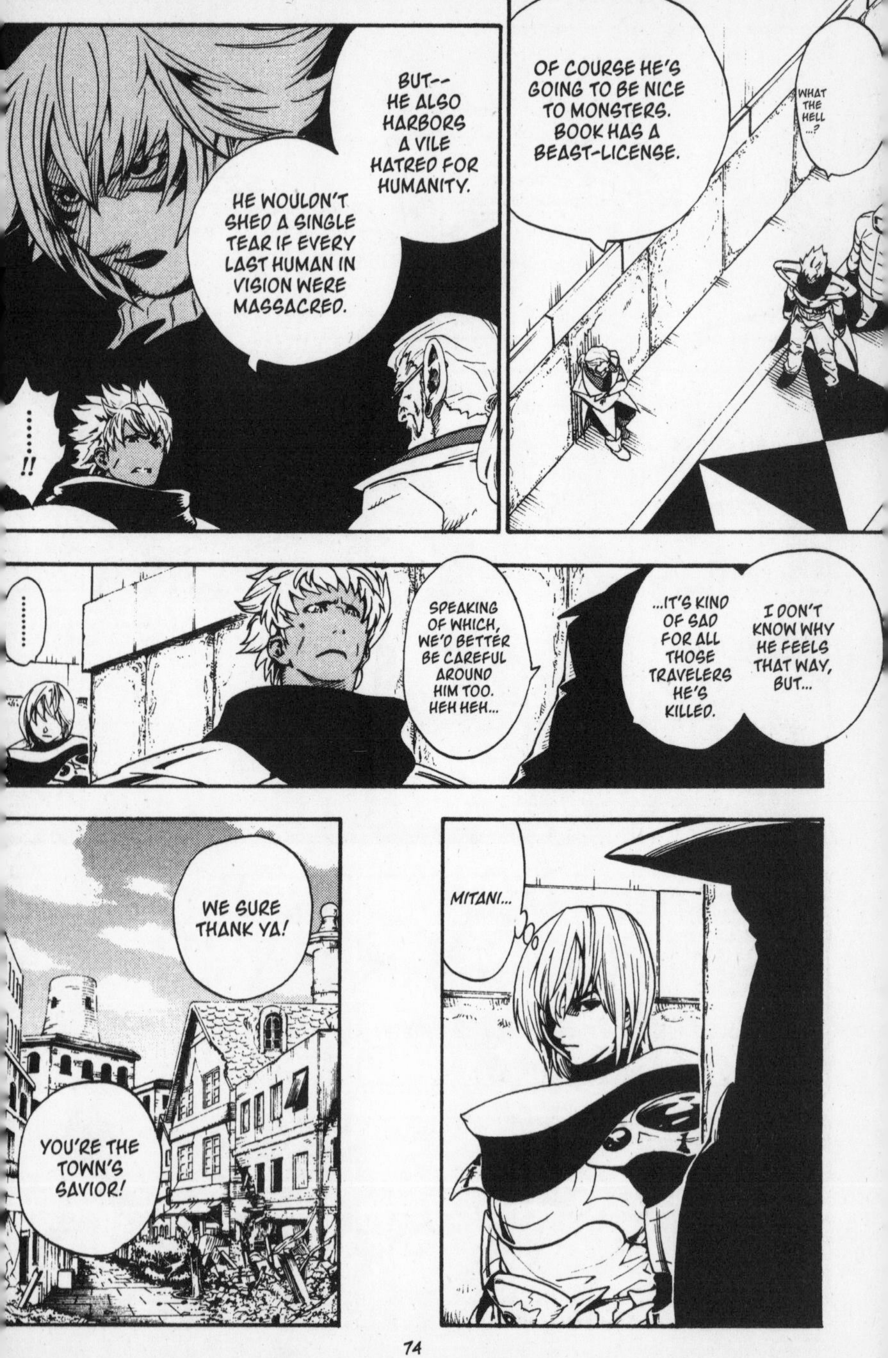
WHAT THE HELL ...?
OF COURSE HE'S GOING TO BE NICE TO MONSTERS. BOOK HAS A BEAST-LICENSE.
BUT-- HE ALSO HARBORS A VILE HATRED FOR HUMANITY.
HE WOULDN'T SHED A SINGLE TEAR IF EVERY LAST HUMAN IN VISION WERE MASSACRED.
......!!
I DON'T KNOW WHY HE FEELS THAT WAY, BUT...
...IT'S KIND OF SAD FOR ALL THOSE TRAVELERS HE'S KILLED.
SPEAKING OF WHICH, WE'D BETTER BE CAREFUL AROUND HIM TOO. HEH HEH...
......
MITANI...
WE SURE THANK YA!
YOU'RE THE TOWN'S SAVIOR!

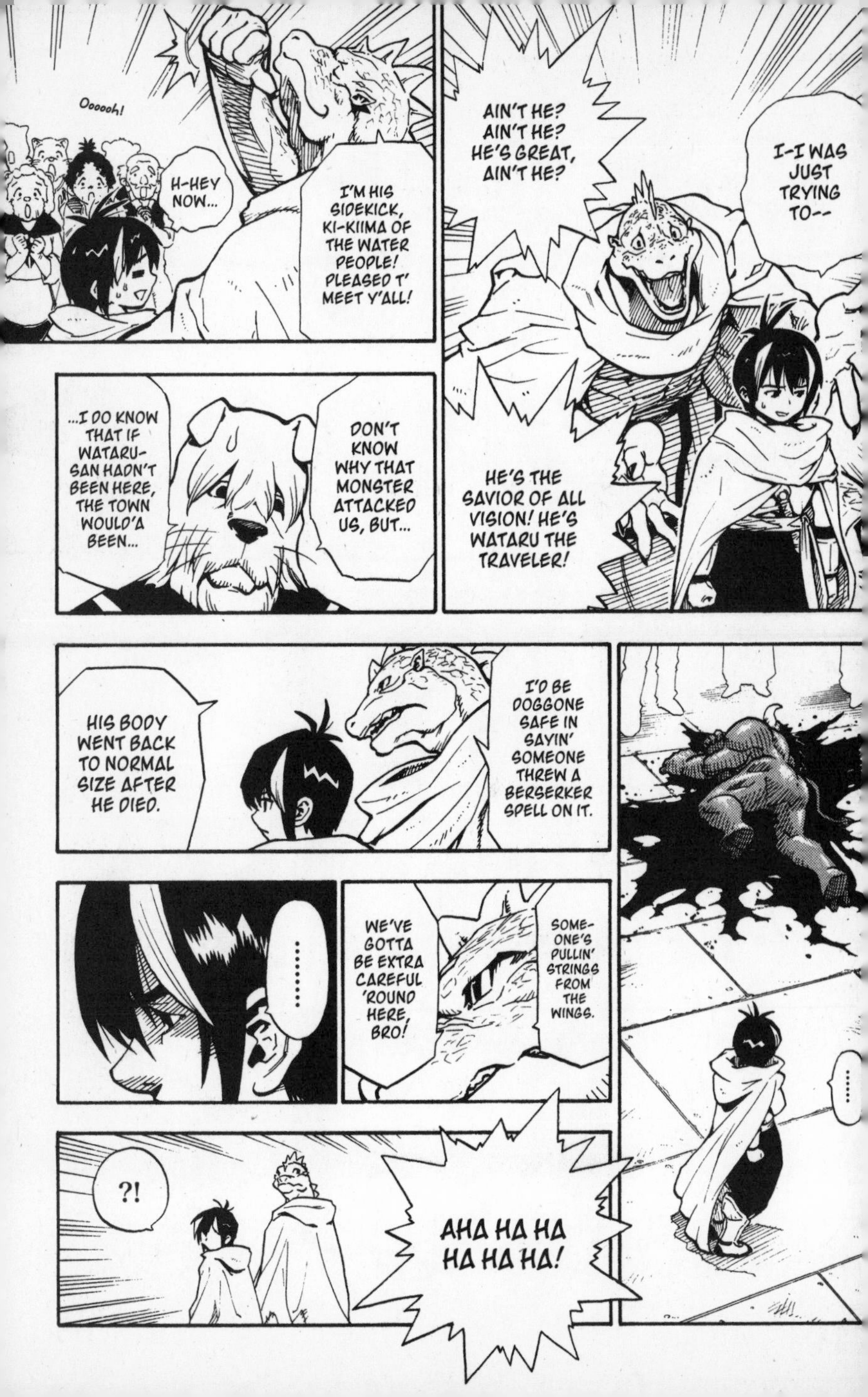
I-I WAS JUST TRYING TO--
AIN'T HE? AIN'T HE? HE'S GREAT, AIN'T HE?
HE'S THE SAVIOR OF ALL VISION! HE'S WATARU THE TRAVELER!
I'M HIS SIDEKICK, KI-KIIMA OF THE WATER PEOPLE! PLEASED T' MEET Y'ALL!
Oooooh!
H-HEY NOW...
DON'T KNOW WHY THAT MONSTER ATTACKED US, BUT...
...I DO KNOW THAT IF WATARU-SAN HADN'T BEEN HERE, THE TOWN WOULD'A BEEN...
......
I'D BE DOGGONE SAFE IN SAYIN' SOMEONE THREW A BERSERKER SPELL ON IT.
HIS BODY WENT BACK TO NORMAL SIZE AFTER HE DIED.
SOME-ONE'S PULLIN' STRINGS FROM THE WINGS.
WE'VE GOTTA BE EXTRA CAREFUL 'ROUND HERE, BRO!
......
AHA HA HA HA HA HA!
?!

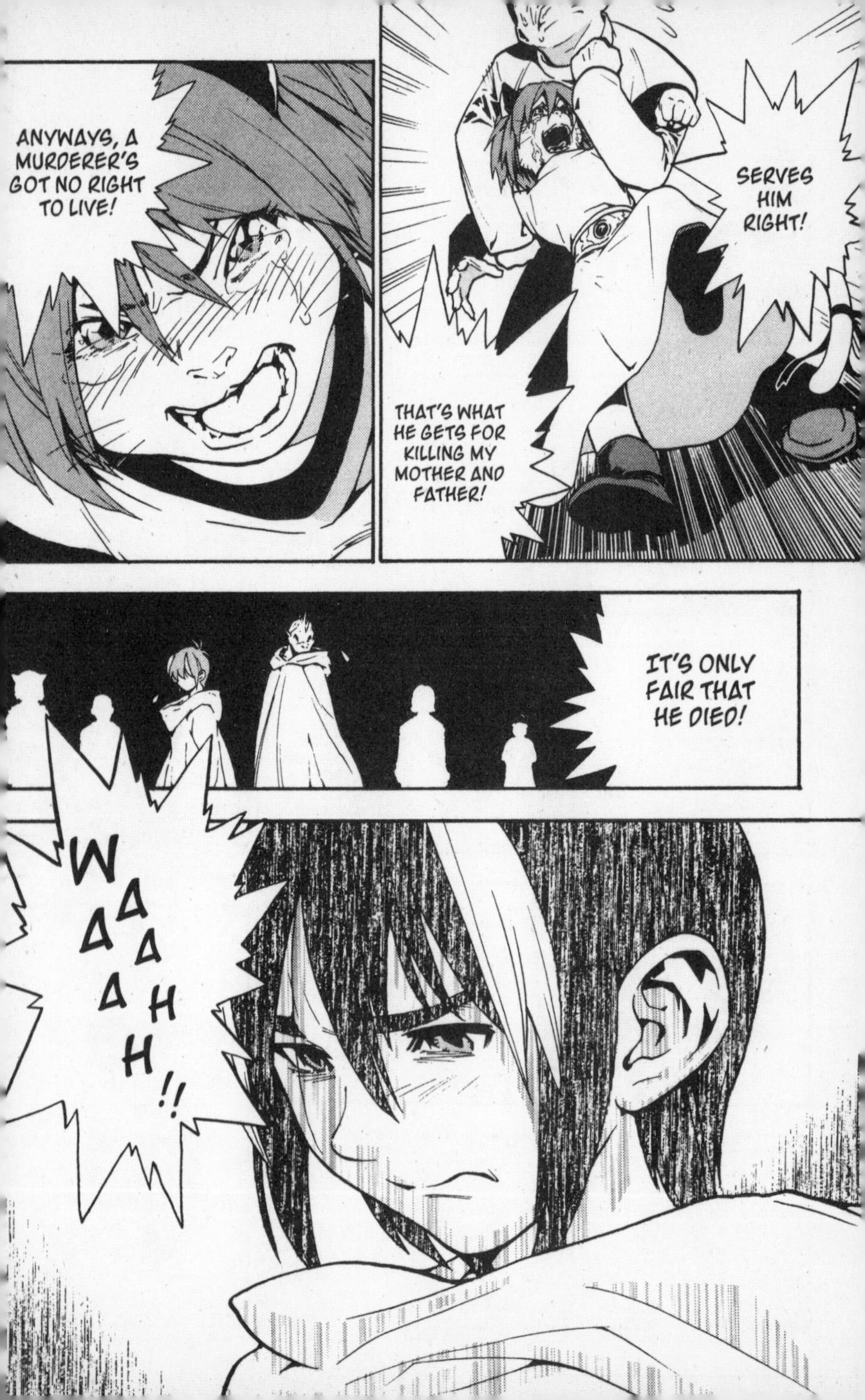
SERVES HIM RIGHT!
THAT'S WHAT HE GETS FOR KILLING MY MOTHER AND FATHER!
ANYWAYS, A MURDERER'S GOT NO RIGHT TO LIVE!
IT'S ONLY FAIR THAT HE DIED!
WAAAAHH!!

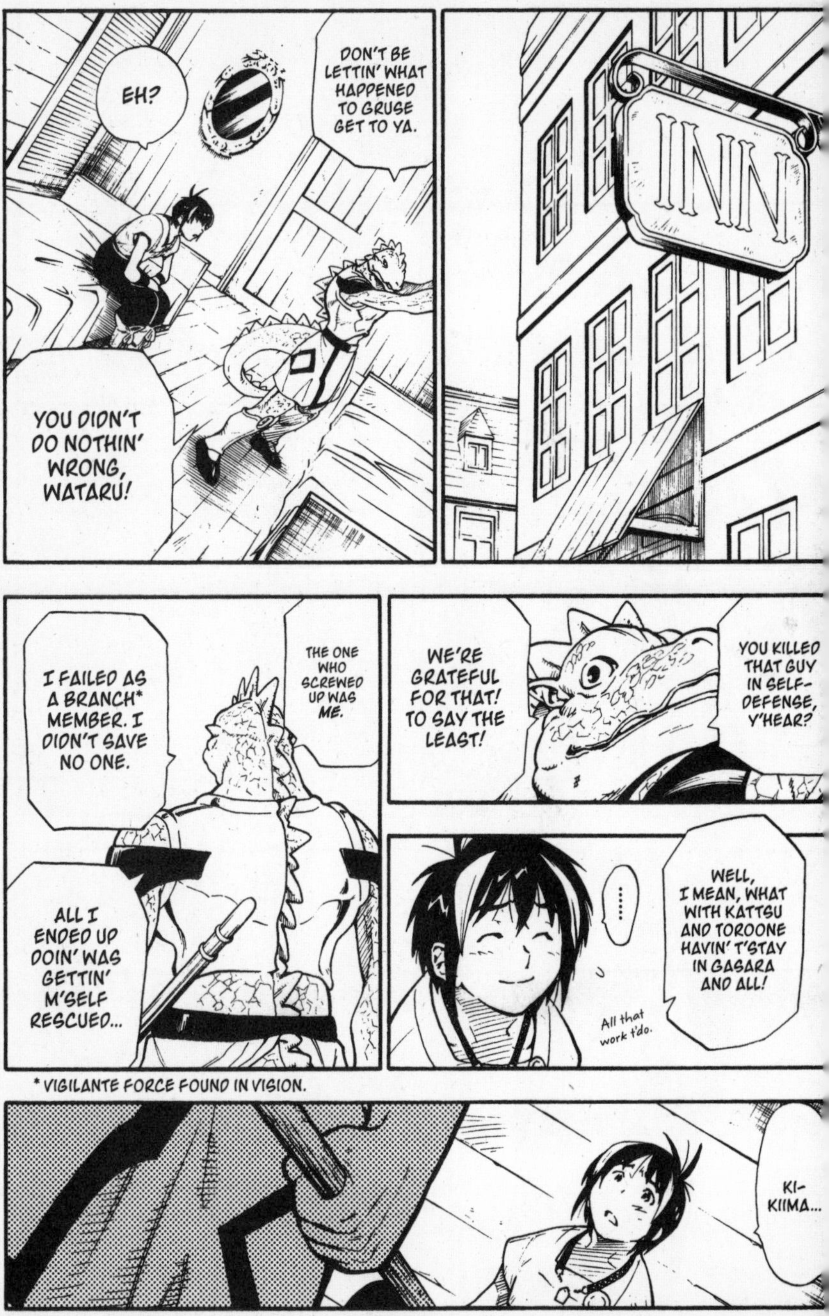
INN
DON'T BE LETTIN' WHAT HAPPENED TO GRUSE GET TO YA.
EH?
YOU DIDN'T DO NOTHIN' WRONG, WATARU!
YOU KILLED THAT GUY IN SELF-DEFENSE, Y'HEAR?
WE'RE GRATEFUL FOR THAT! TO SAY THE LEAST!
WELL, I MEAN, WHAT WITH KATTSU AND TOROONE HAVIN' T'STAY IN GASARA AND ALL!
All that work t'do.
......
THE ONE WHO SCREWED UP WAS ME.
I FAILED AS A BRANCH* MEMBER. I DIDN'T SAVE NO ONE.
ALL I ENDED UP DOIN' WAS GETTIN' M'SELF RESCUED...
KI-KIIMA...

* VIGILANTE FORCE FOUND IN VISION.

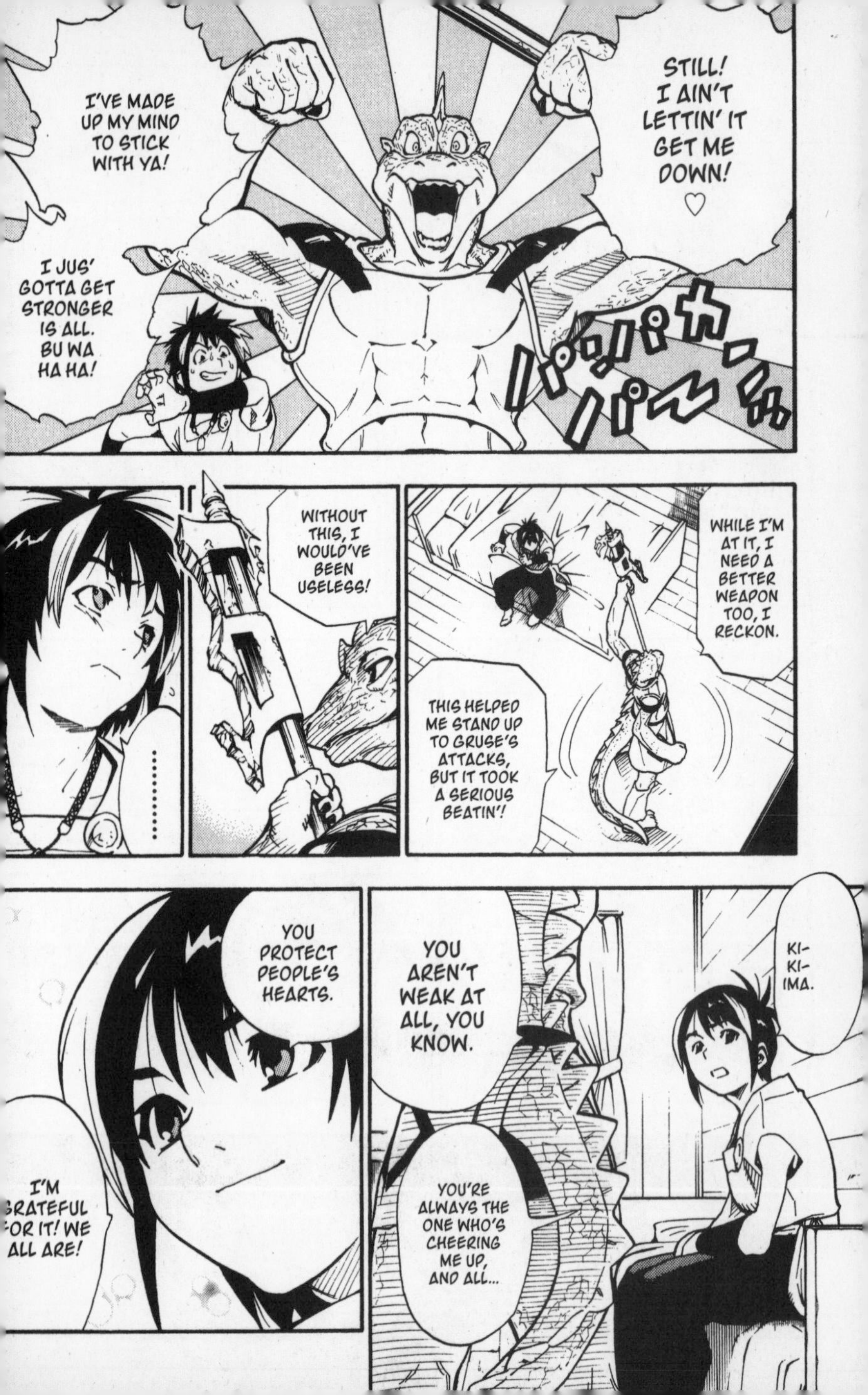
STILL! I AIN'T LETTIN' IT GET ME DOWN! ♡
I'VE MADE UP MY MIND TO STICK WITH YA!
I JUS' GOTTA GET STRONGER IS ALL. BU WA HA HA!
WHILE I'M AT IT, I NEED A BETTER WEAPON TOO, I RECKON.
THIS HELPED ME STAND UP TO GRUSE'S ATTACKS, BUT IT TOOK A SERIOUS BEATIN'!
WITHOUT THIS, I WOULD'VE BEEN USELESS!
....
KI-KI-IMA.
YOU AREN'T WEAK AT ALL, YOU KNOW.
YOU PROTECT PEOPLE'S HEARTS.
YOU'RE ALWAYS THE ONE WHO'S CHEERING ME UP, AND ALL...
I'M GRATEFUL FOR IT! WE ALL ARE!

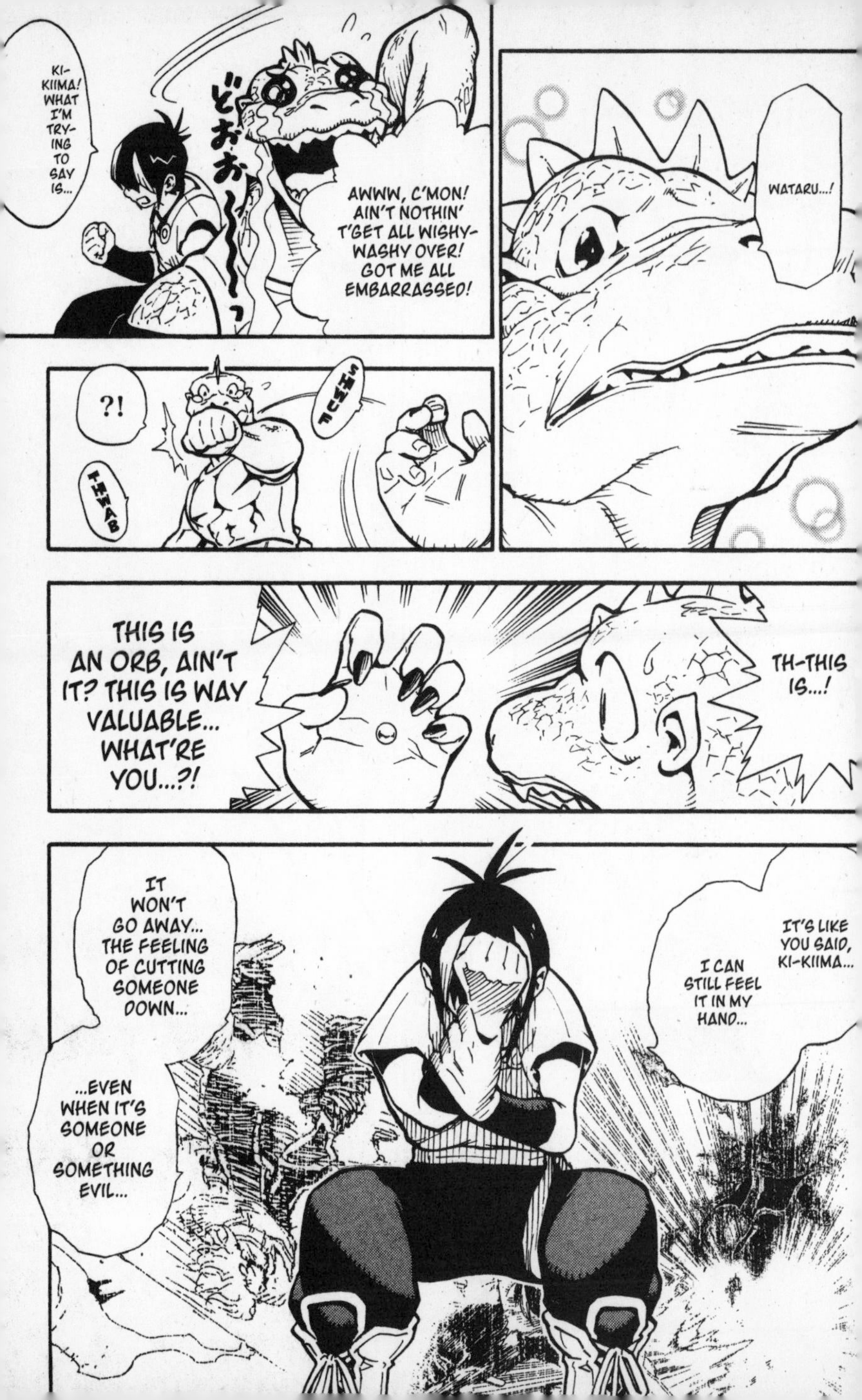
WATARU...!
AWWW, C'MON! AIN'T NOTHIN' T'GET ALL WISHY-WASHY OVER! GOT ME ALL EMBARRASSED!
どぉぉ～～っ
KI-KIIMA! WHAT I'M TRYING TO SAY IS...
SHUFF
?!
THWAB
TH-THIS IS...!
THIS IS AN ORB, AIN'T IT? THIS IS WAY VALUABLE... WHAT'RE YOU...?!
IT'S LIKE YOU SAID, KI-KIIMA...
I CAN STILL FEEL IT IN MY HAND...
IT WON'T GO AWAY... THE FEELING OF CUTTING SOMEONE DOWN...
...EVEN WHEN IT'S SOMEONE OR SOMETHING EVIL...

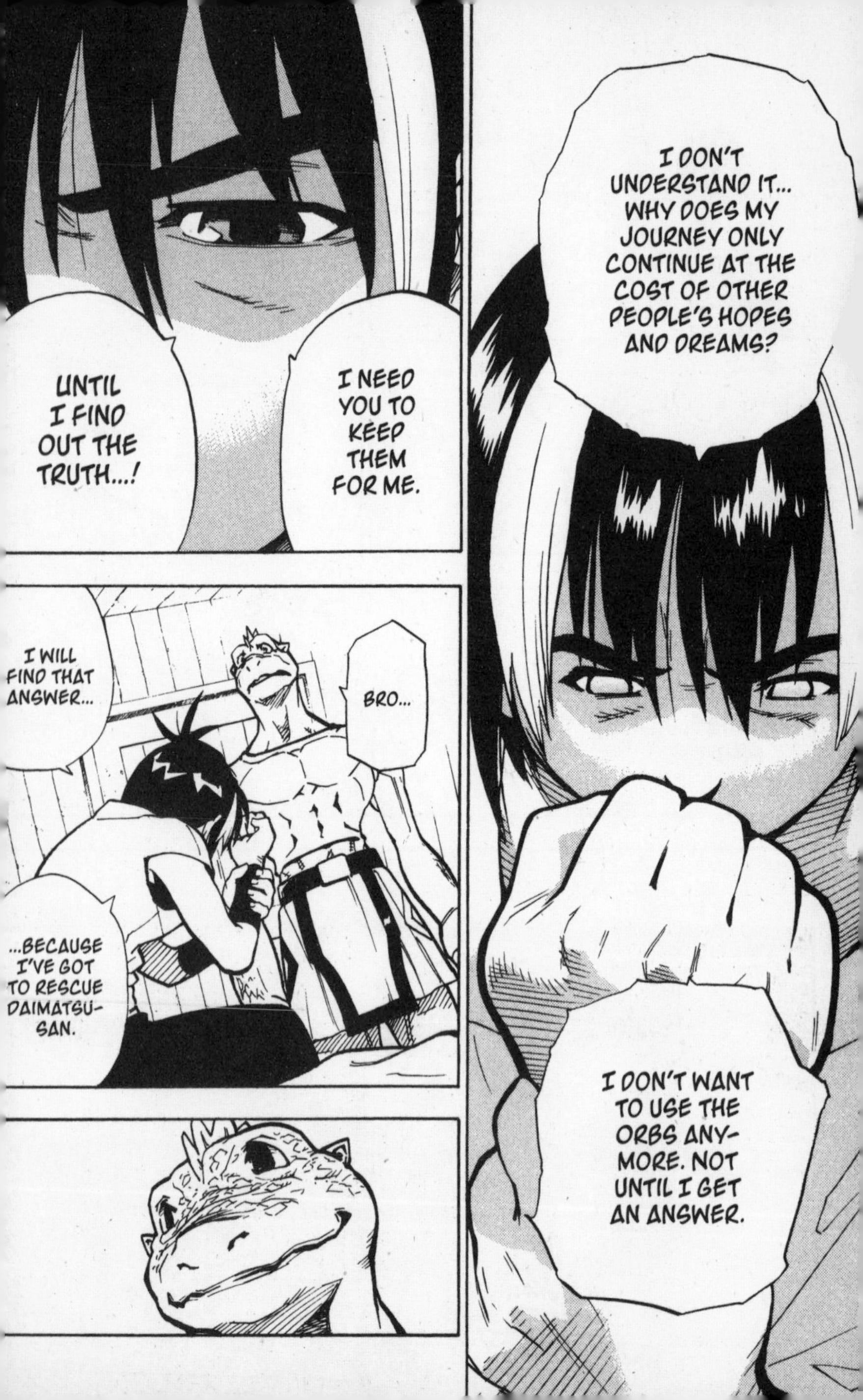
I DON'T UNDERSTAND IT... WHY DOES MY JOURNEY ONLY CONTINUE AT THE COST OF OTHER PEOPLE'S HOPES AND DREAMS?
I DON'T WANT TO USE THE ORBS ANY-MORE. NOT UNTIL I GET AN ANSWER.
I NEED YOU TO KEEP THEM FOR ME.
UNTIL I FIND OUT THE TRUTH...!
BRO...
I WILL FIND THAT ANSWER...
...BECAUSE I'VE GOT TO RESCUE DAIMATSU-SAN.

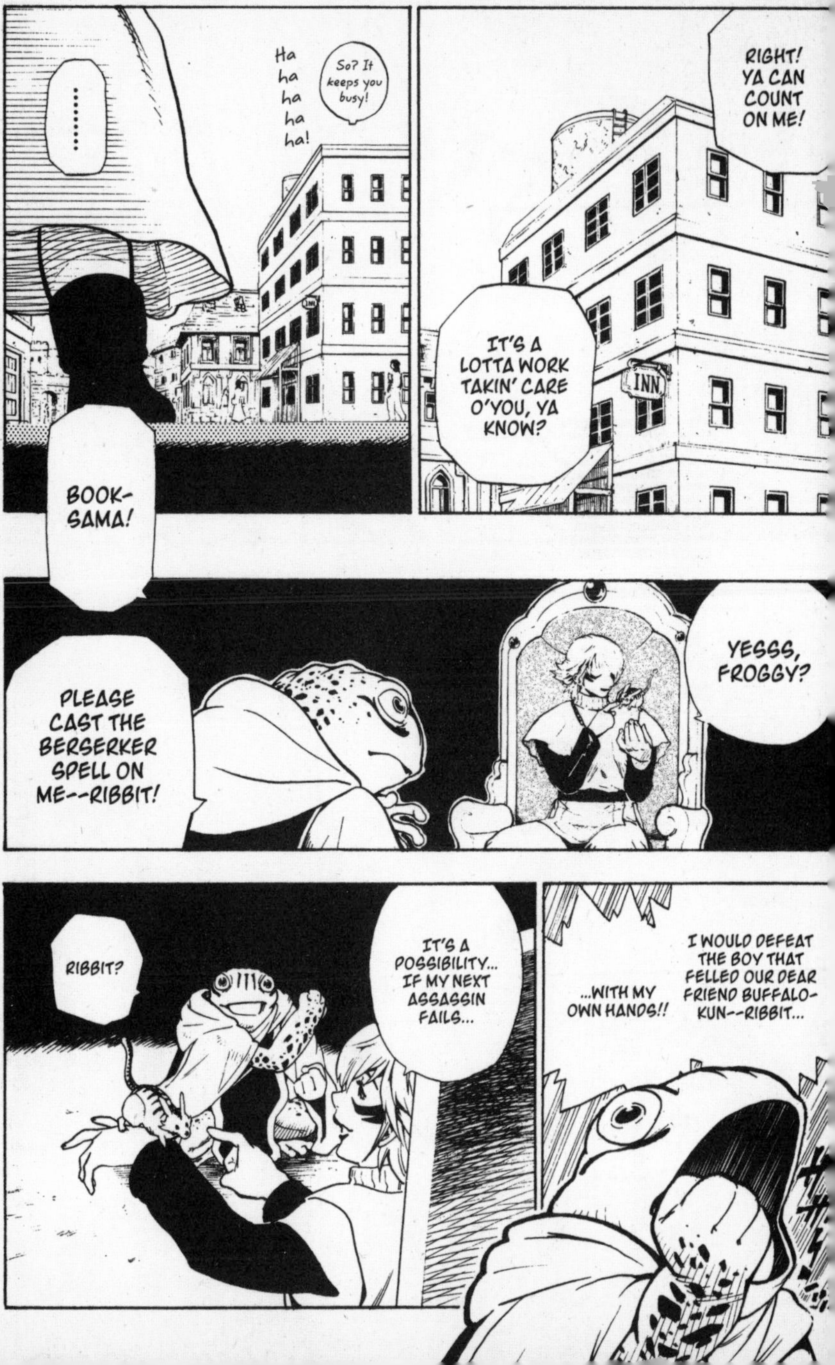
RIGHT! YA CAN COUNT ON ME!
IT'S A LOTTA WORK TAKIN' CARE O'YOU, YA KNOW?
So? It keeps you busy!
Ha ha ha ha ha!
......
BOOK-SAMA!
YESSS, FROGGY?
PLEASE CAST THE BERSERKER SPELL ON ME--RIBBIT!
I WOULD DEFEAT THE BOY THAT FELLED OUR DEAR FRIEND BUFFALO-KUN--RIBBIT...
...WITH MY OWN HANDS!!
IT'S A POSSIBILITY... IF MY NEXT ASSASSIN FAILS...
RIBBIT?

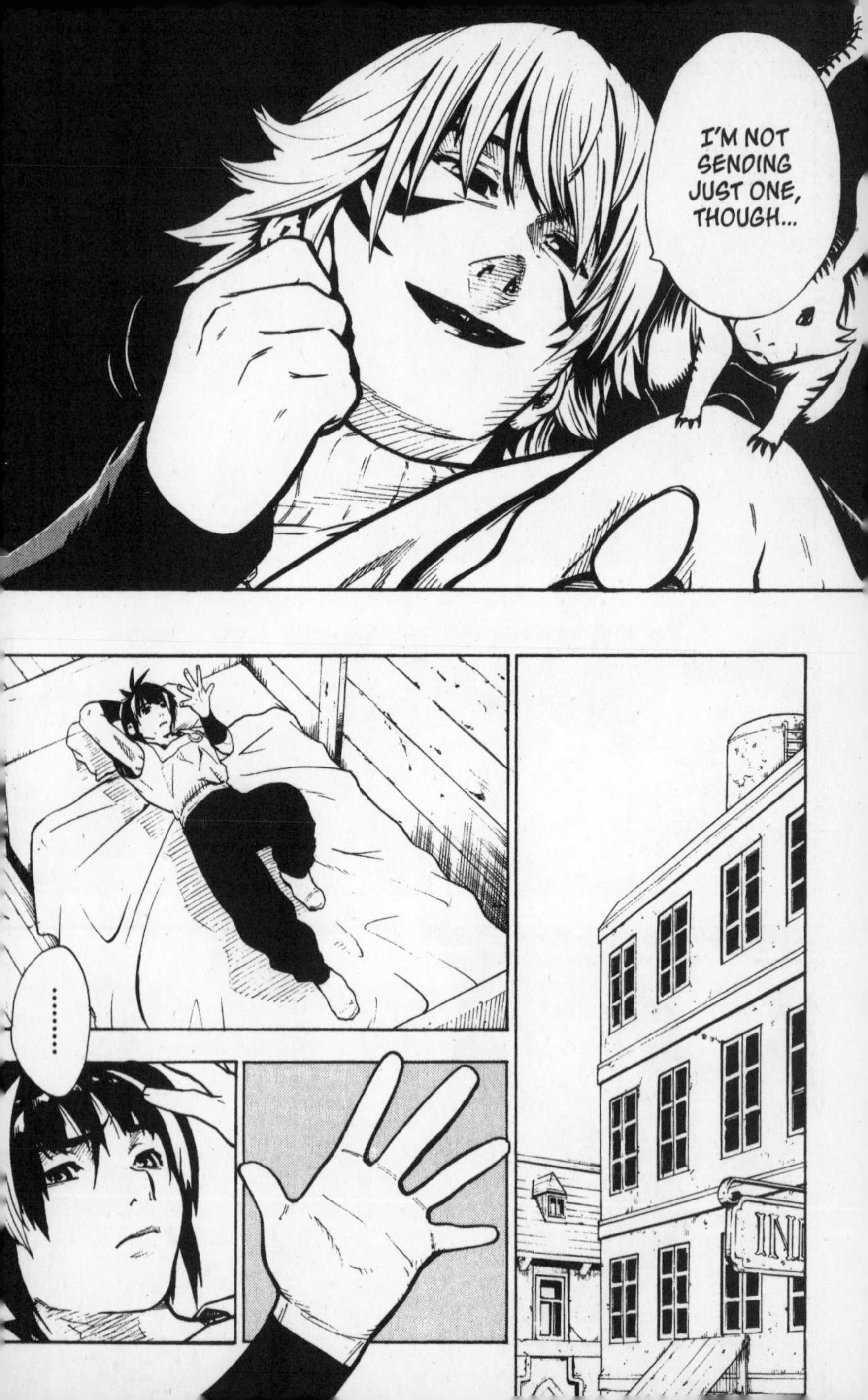
I'M NOT SENDING JUST ONE, THOUGH...
......
INN

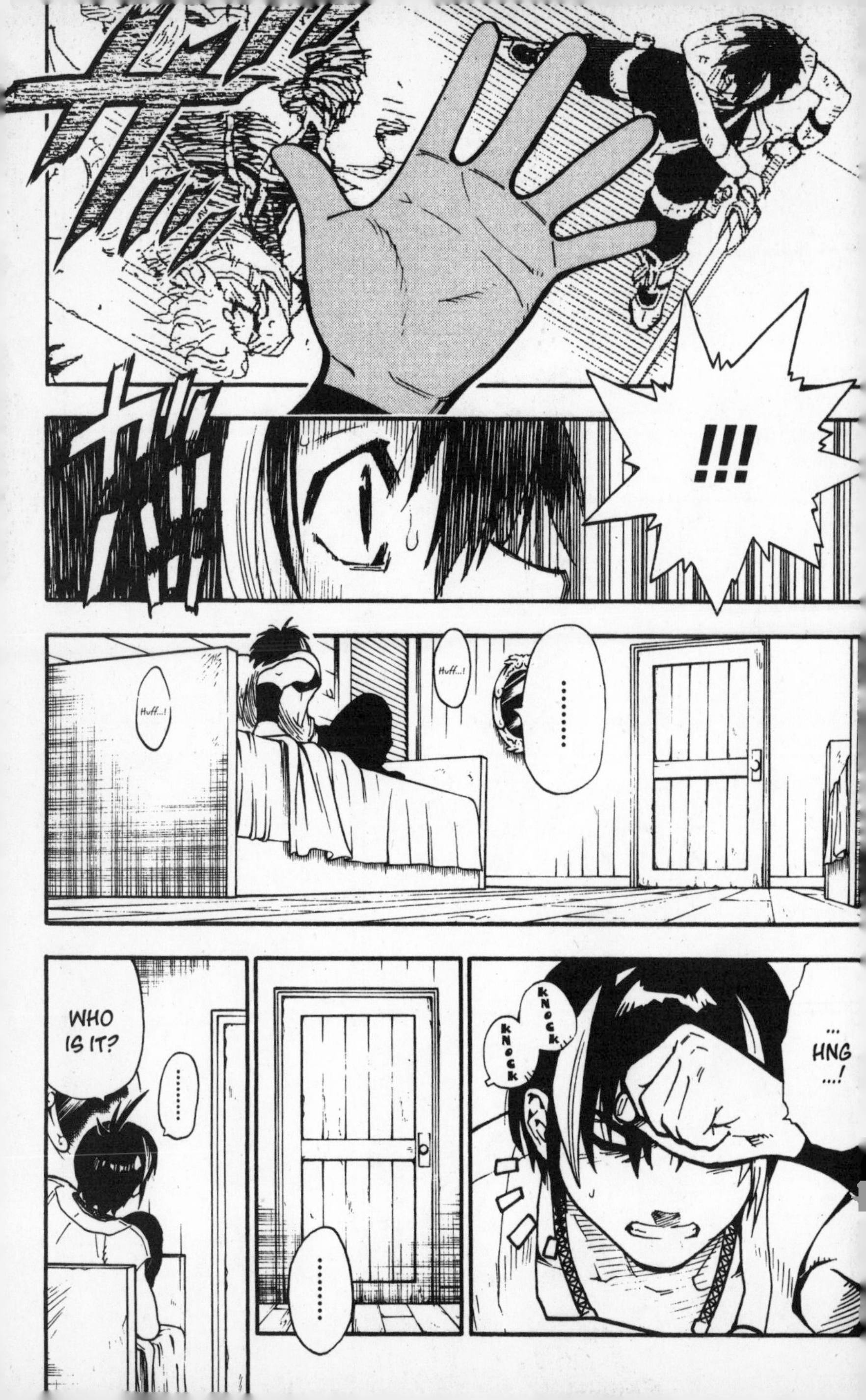
!!!
....
Huff...!
Huff...!
... HNG ...!
KNOCK KNOCK
....
WHO IS IT?
....

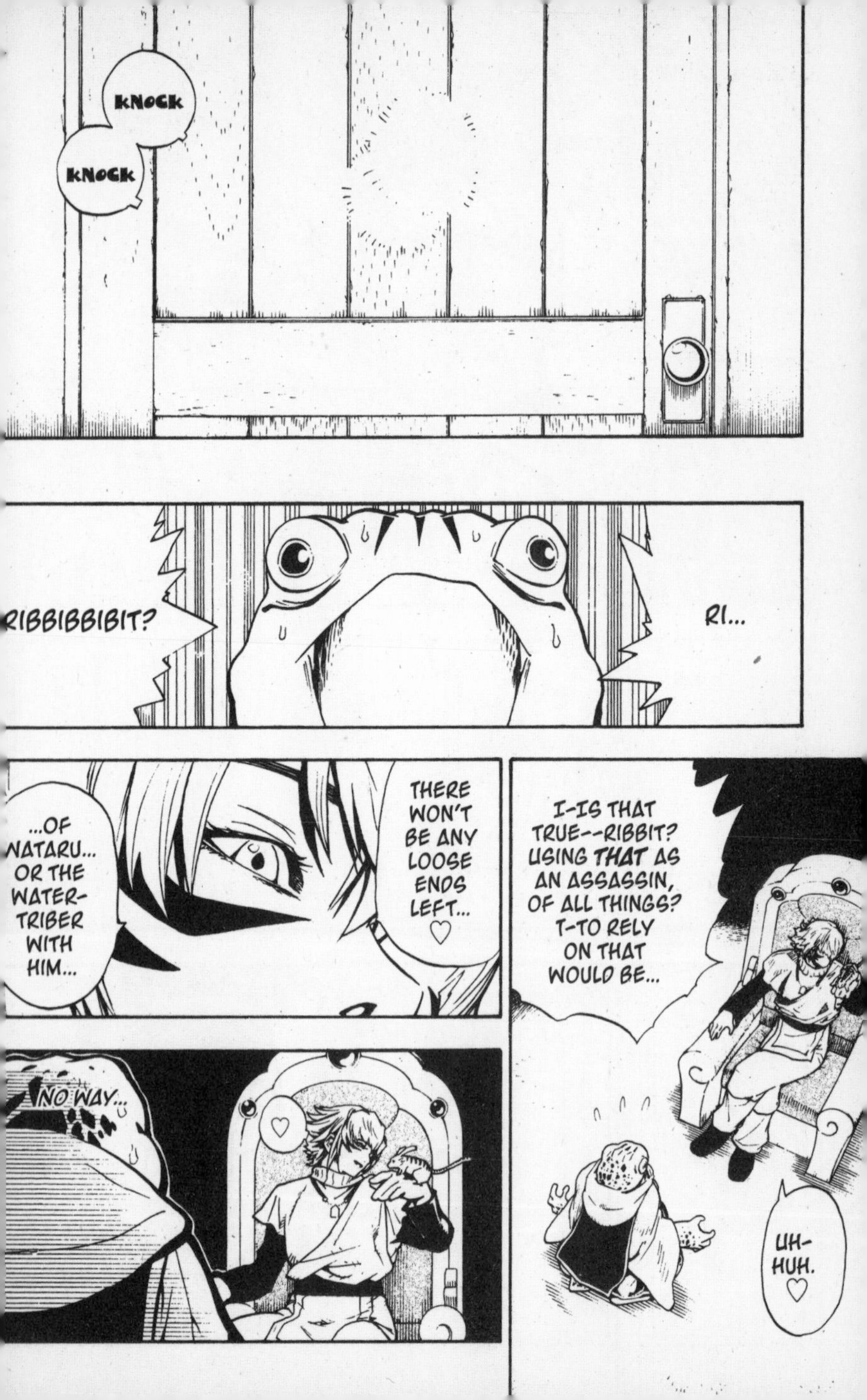
KNOCK
KNOCK
RI...
RIBBIBBIBIT?
I-IS THAT TRUE--RIBBIT? USING *THAT* AS AN ASSASSIN, OF ALL THINGS? T-TO RELY ON THAT WOULD BE...
UH-HUH. ♥
THERE WON'T BE ANY LOOSE ENDS LEFT... ♥
...OF WATARU... OR THE WATER-TRIBER WITH HIM...
NO WAY...

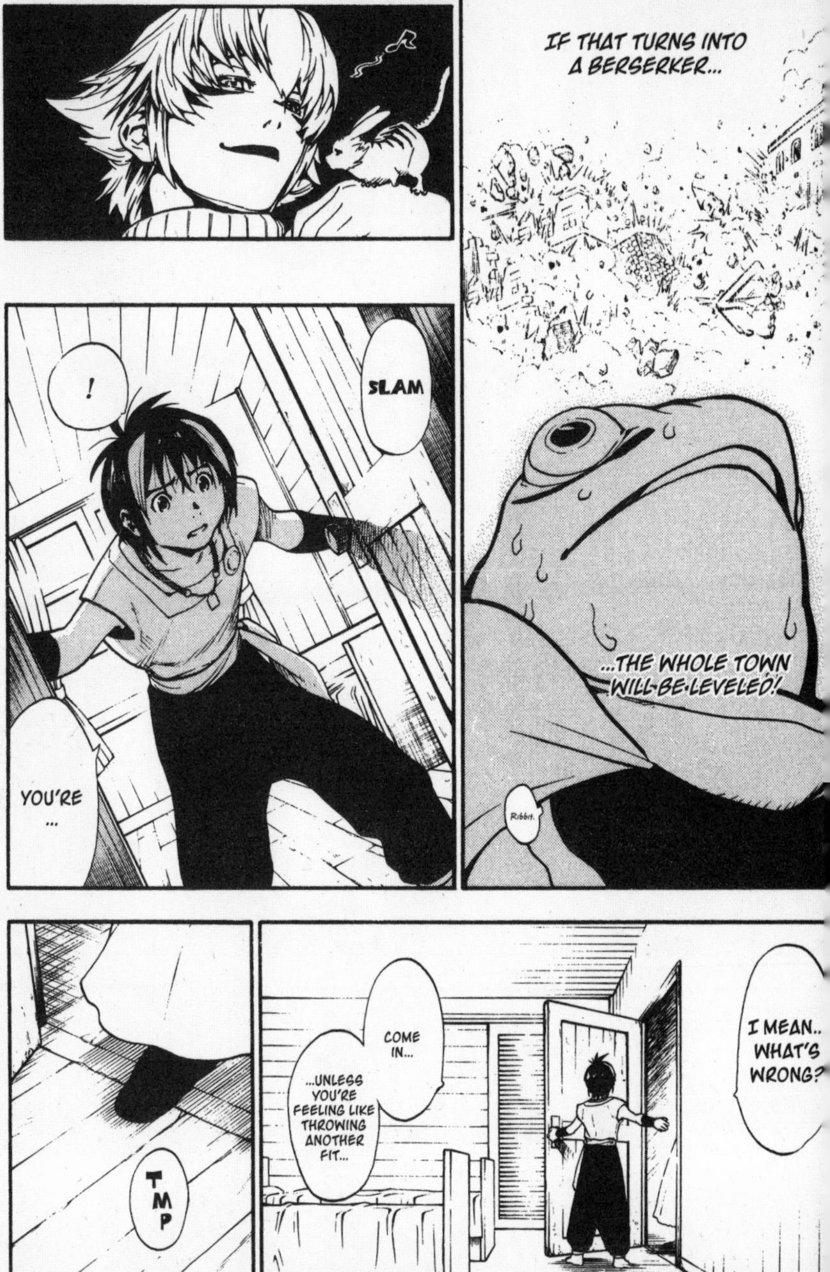
IF THAT TURNS INTO A BERSERKER...
...THE WHOLE TOWN WILL BE LEVELED!
Ribbit.
SLAM
!
YOU'RE ...
I MEAN.. WHAT'S WRONG?
COME IN...
...UNLESS YOU'RE FEELING LIKE THROWING ANOTHER FIT...
TMP

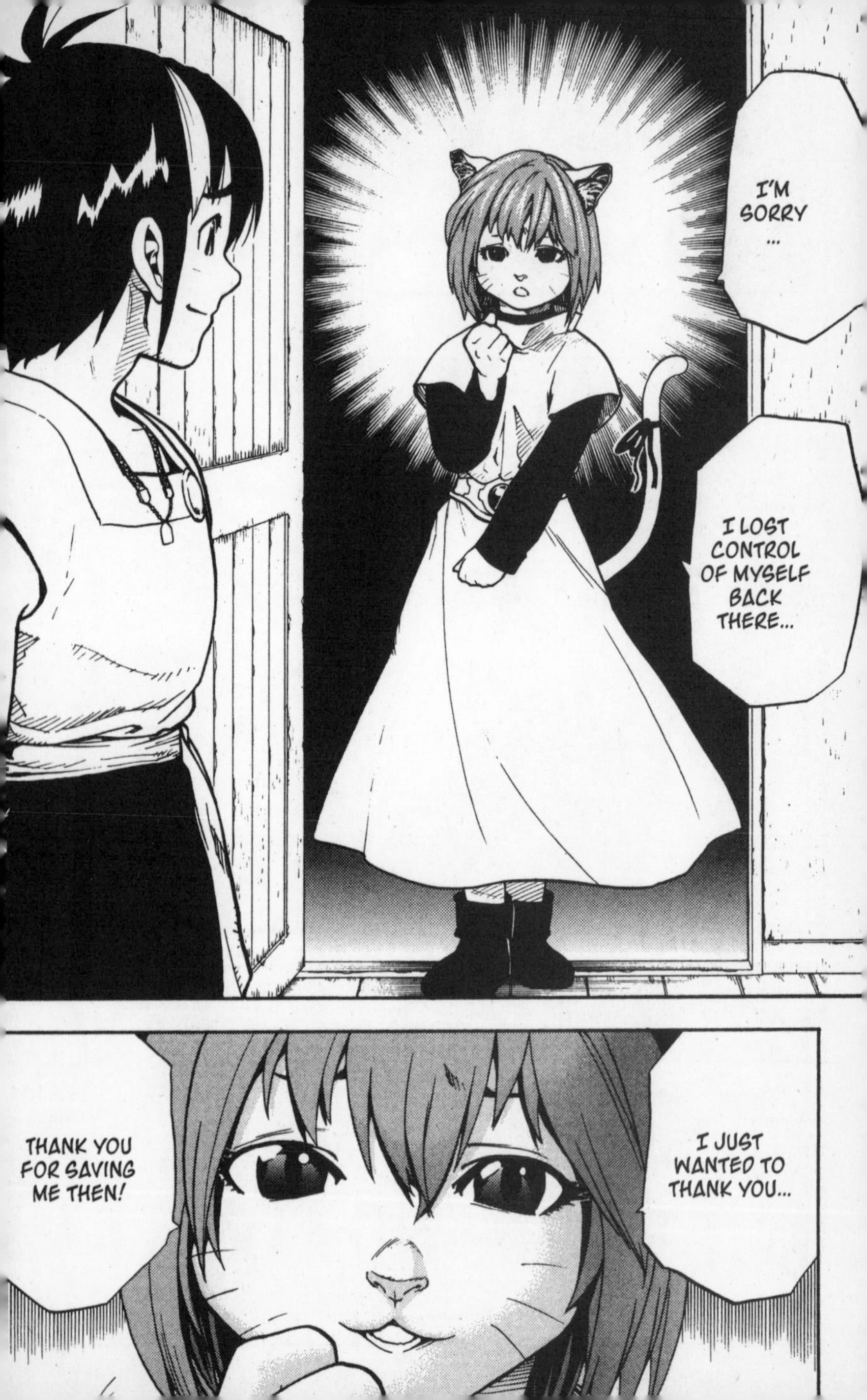
I'M SORRY ...
I LOST CONTROL OF MYSELF BACK THERE...
I JUST WANTED TO THANK YOU...
THANK YOU FOR SAVING ME THEN!

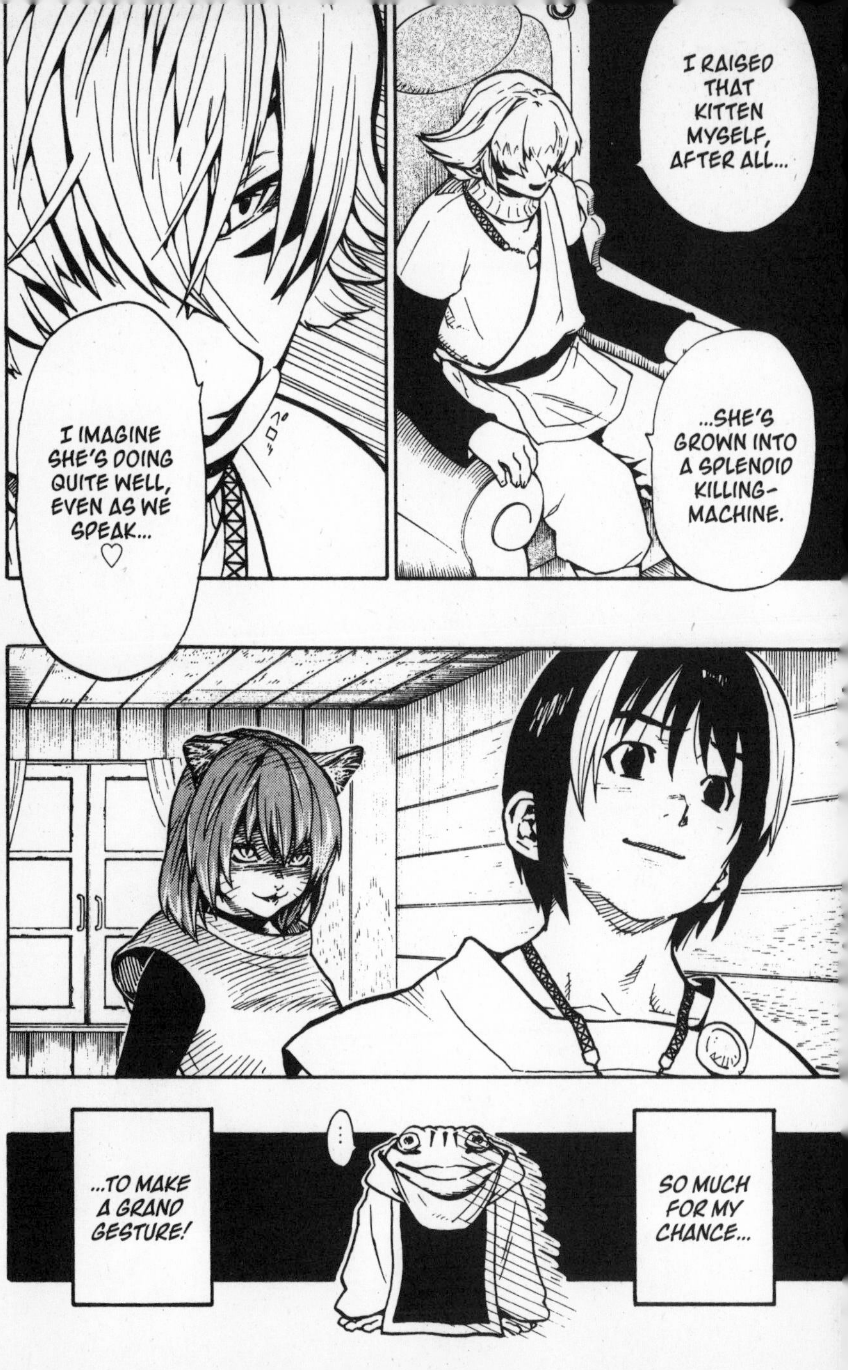
I RAISED THAT KITTEN MYSELF, AFTER ALL...
...SHE'S GROWN INTO A SPLENDID KILLING-MACHINE.
I IMAGINE SHE'S DOING QUITE WELL, EVEN AS WE SPEAK... ♡
SO MUCH FOR MY CHANCE...
...
...TO MAKE A GRAND GESTURE!

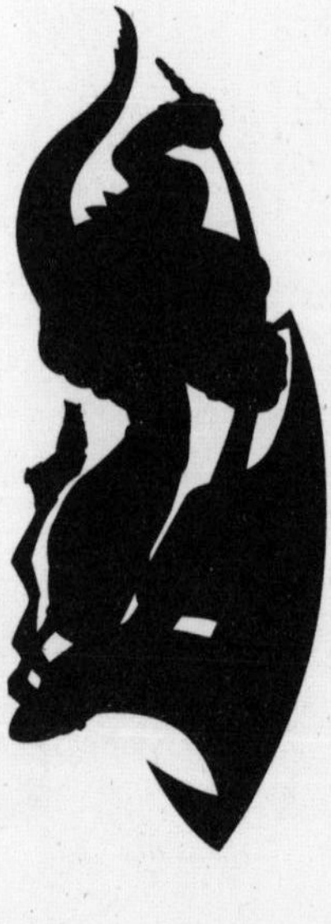

A Retelling of a Classic

BRAVE STORY

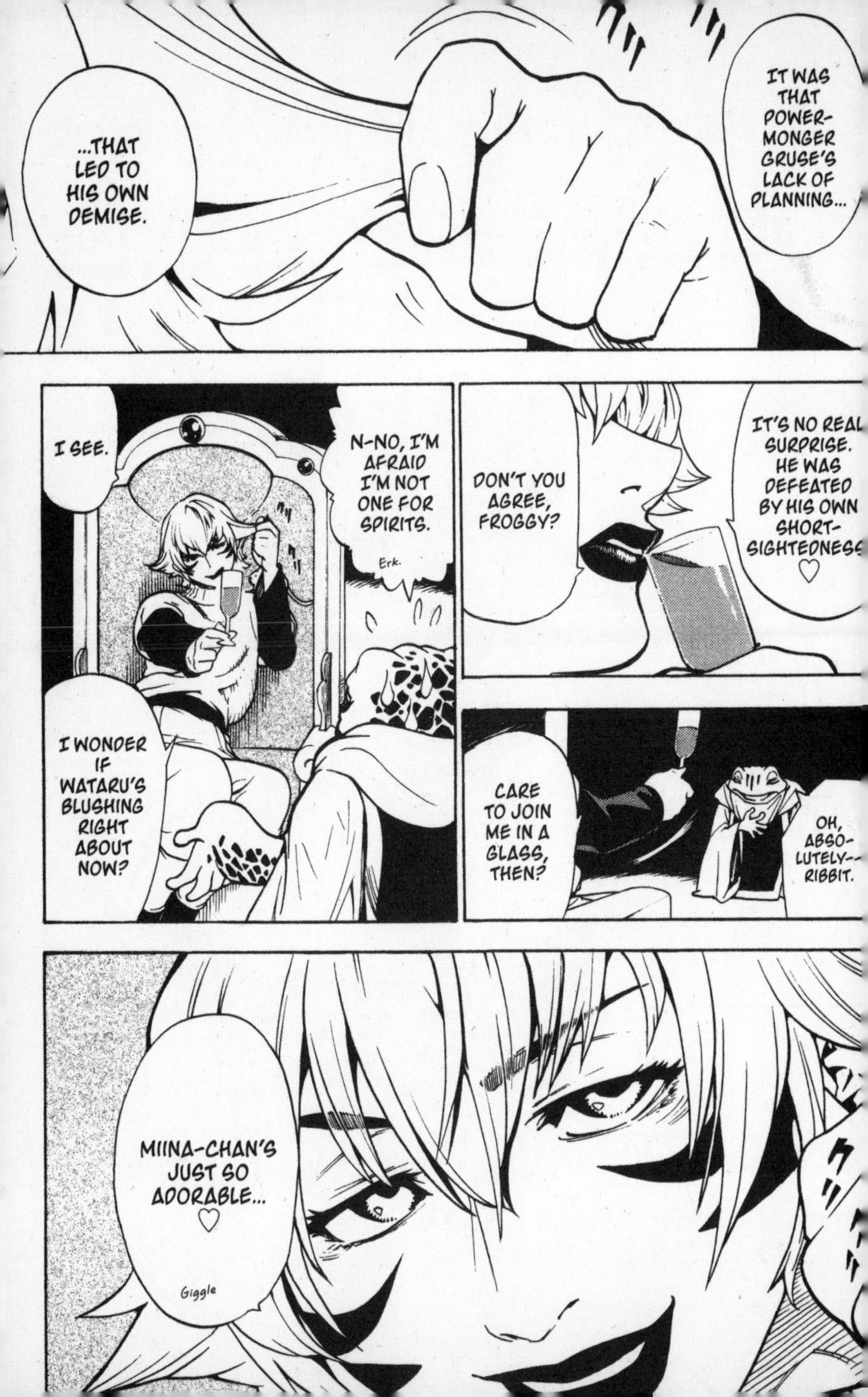
IT WAS THAT POWER-MONGER GRUSE'S LACK OF PLANNING...
...THAT LED TO HIS OWN DEMISE.
IT'S NO REAL SURPRISE. HE WAS DEFEATED BY HIS OWN SHORT-SIGHTEDNESS ♡
DON'T YOU AGREE, FROGGY?
OH, ABSOLUTELY--RIBBIT.
CARE TO JOIN ME IN A GLASS, THEN?
N-NO, I'M AFRAID I'M NOT ONE FOR SPIRITS.
Erk.
I SEE.
I WONDER IF WATARU'S BLUSHING RIGHT ABOUT NOW?
MIINA-CHAN'S JUST SO ADORABLE... ♡
Giggle

Chapter 33 The Unluckiest Assassin

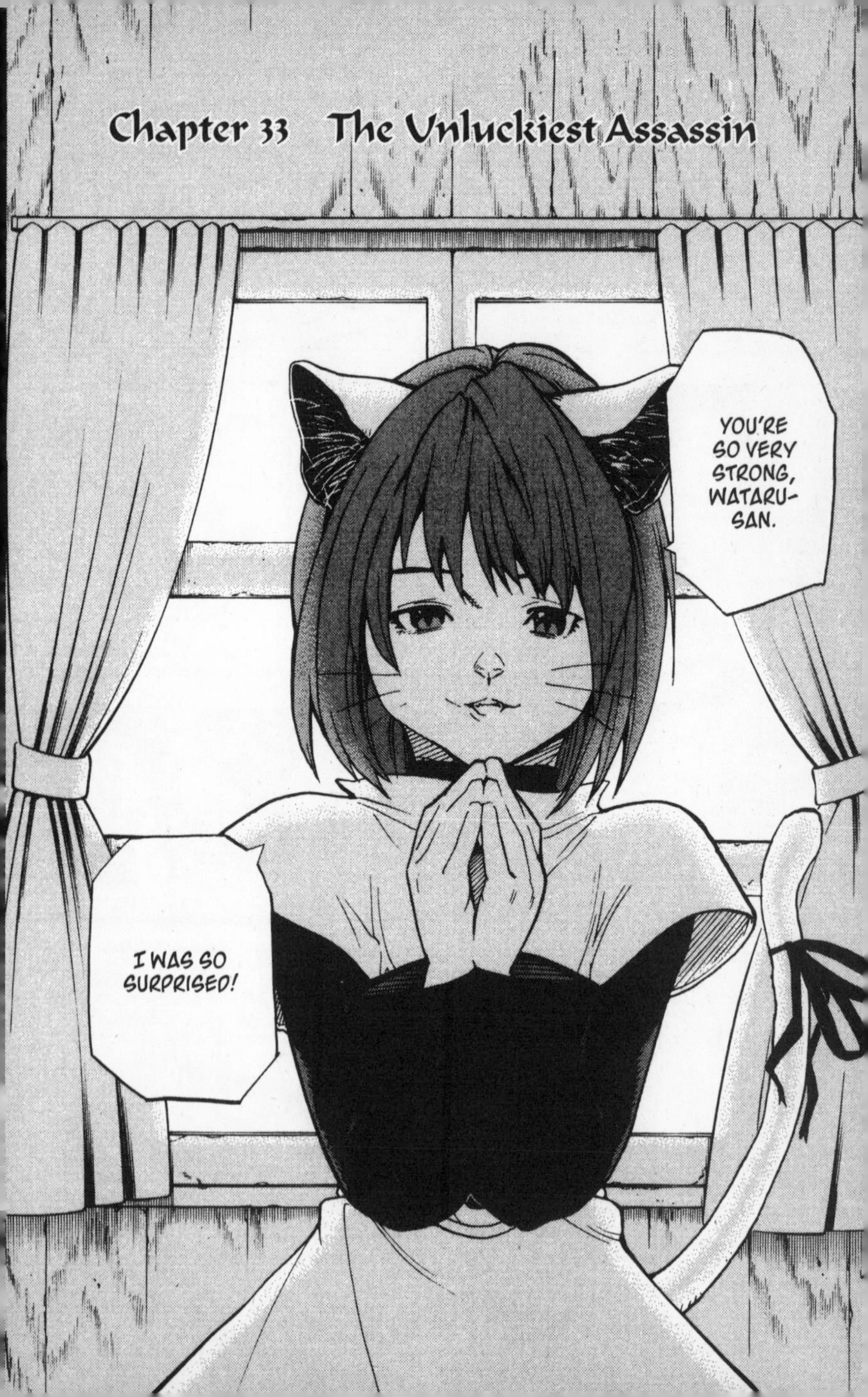

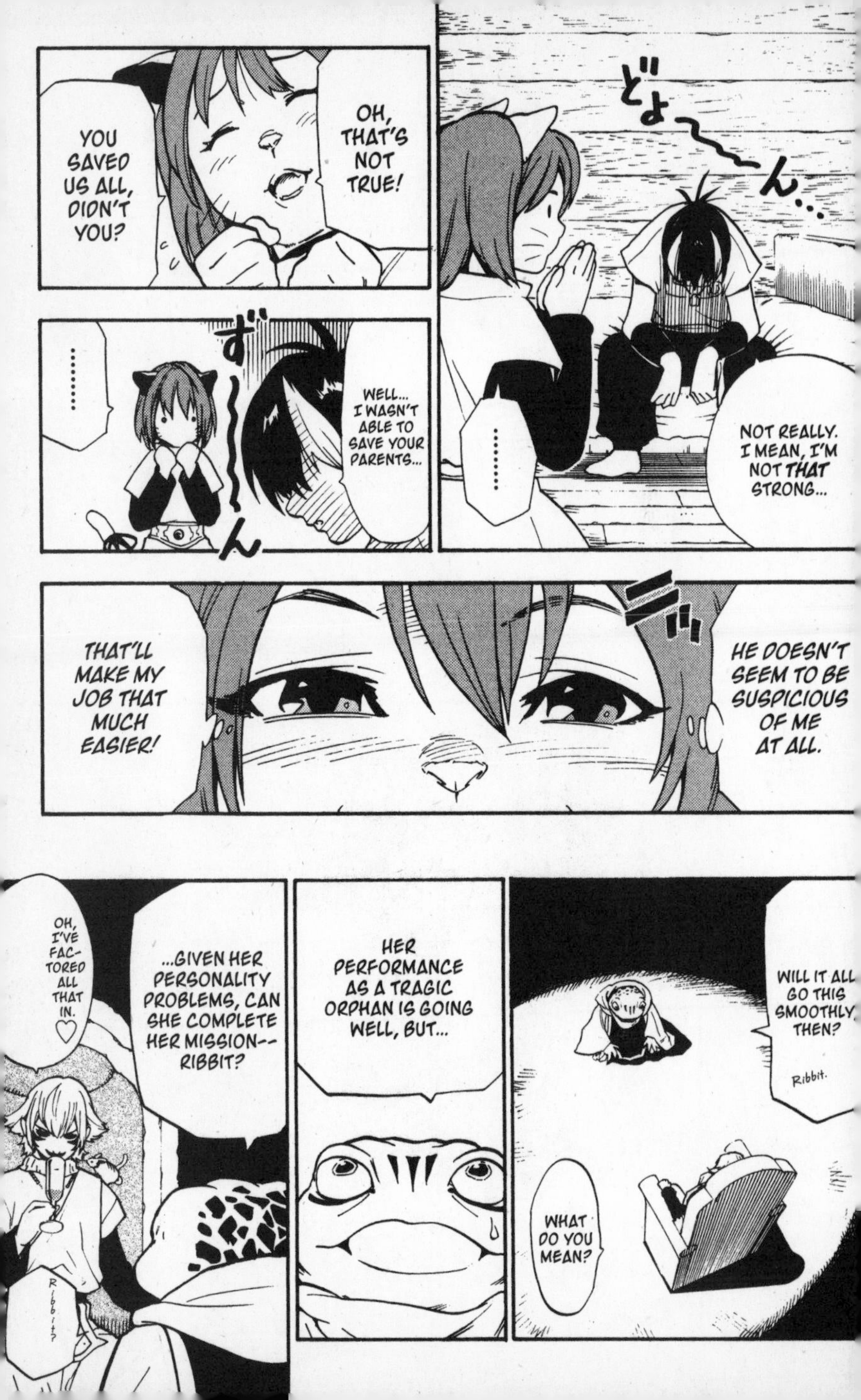
どよ〜〜〜ん…
NOT REALLY. I MEAN, I'M NOT THAT STRONG...
....
OH, THAT'S NOT TRUE!
YOU SAVED US ALL, DIDN'T YOU?
WELL... I WASN'T ABLE TO SAVE YOUR PARENTS...
ずーん
....
HE DOESN'T SEEM TO BE SUSPICIOUS OF ME AT ALL.
THAT'LL MAKE MY JOB THAT MUCH EASIER!
WILL IT ALL GO THIS SMOOTHLY, THEN?
Ribbit.
WHAT DO YOU MEAN?
HER PERFORMANCE AS A TRAGIC ORPHAN IS GOING WELL, BUT...
...GIVEN HER PERSONALITY PROBLEMS, CAN SHE COMPLETE HER MISSION--RIBBIT?
OH, I'VE FACTORED ALL THAT IN. ♡
Ribbit?

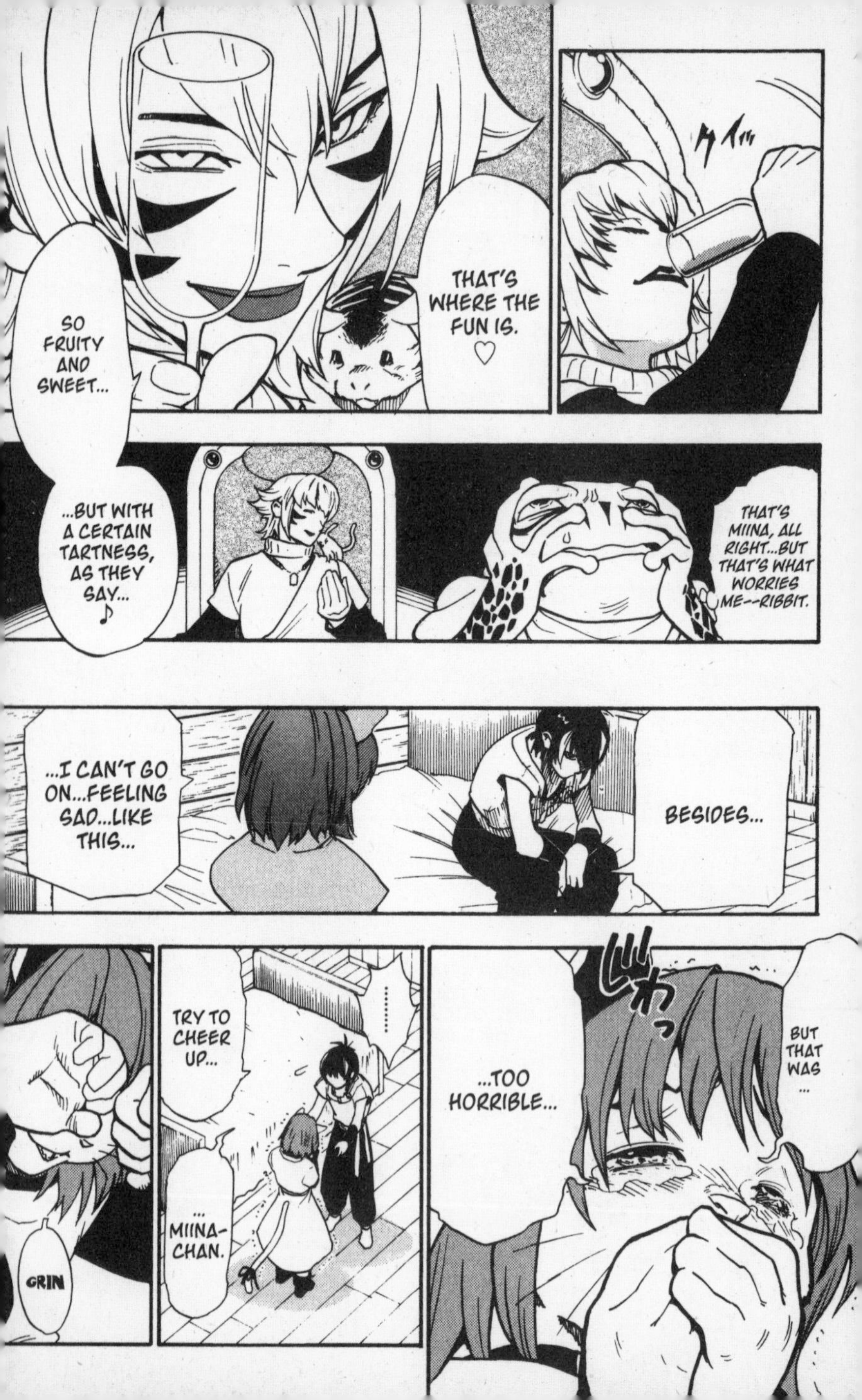
THAT'S WHERE THE FUN IS. ♡
SO FRUITY AND SWEET...
THAT'S MIINA, ALL RIGHT...BUT THAT'S WHAT WORRIES ME--RIBBIT.
...BUT WITH A CERTAIN TARTNESS, AS THEY SAY... ♪
BESIDES...
...I CAN'T GO ON...FEELING SAD...LIKE THIS...
BUT THAT WAS ...
...TOO HORRIBLE...
......
TRY TO CHEER UP...
... MIINA-CHAN.
GRIN

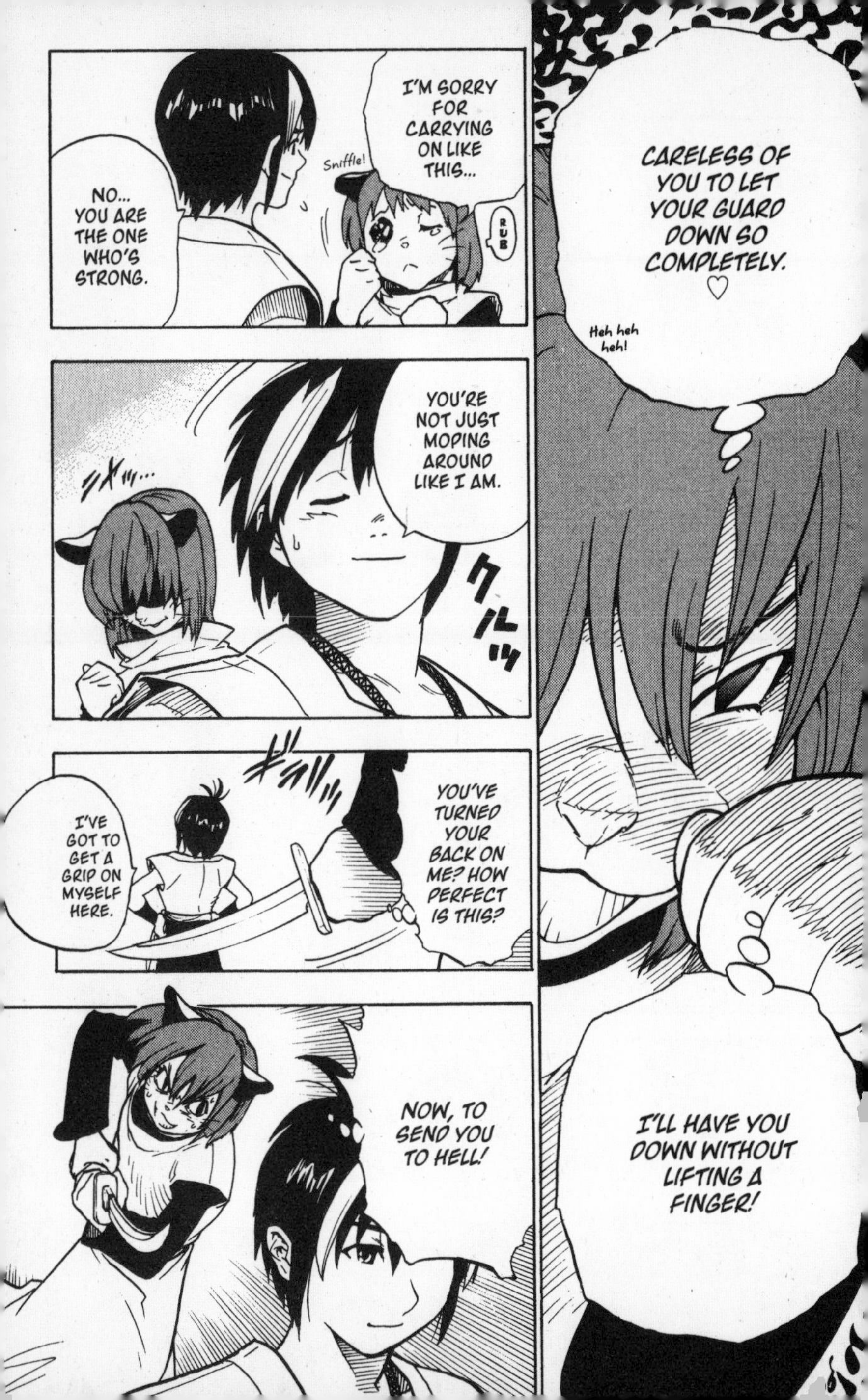
CARELESS OF YOU TO LET YOUR GUARD DOWN SO COMPLETELY. ♡
Heh heh heh!
I'LL HAVE YOU DOWN WITHOUT LIFTING A FINGER!
I'M SORRY FOR CARRYING ON LIKE THIS...
Sniffle!
RUB
NO... YOU ARE THE ONE WHO'S STRONG.
YOU'RE NOT JUST MOPING AROUND LIKE I AM.
YOU'VE TURNED YOUR BACK ON ME? HOW PERFECT IS THIS?
I'VE GOT TO GET A GRIP ON MYSELF HERE.
NOW, TO SEND YOU TO HELL!

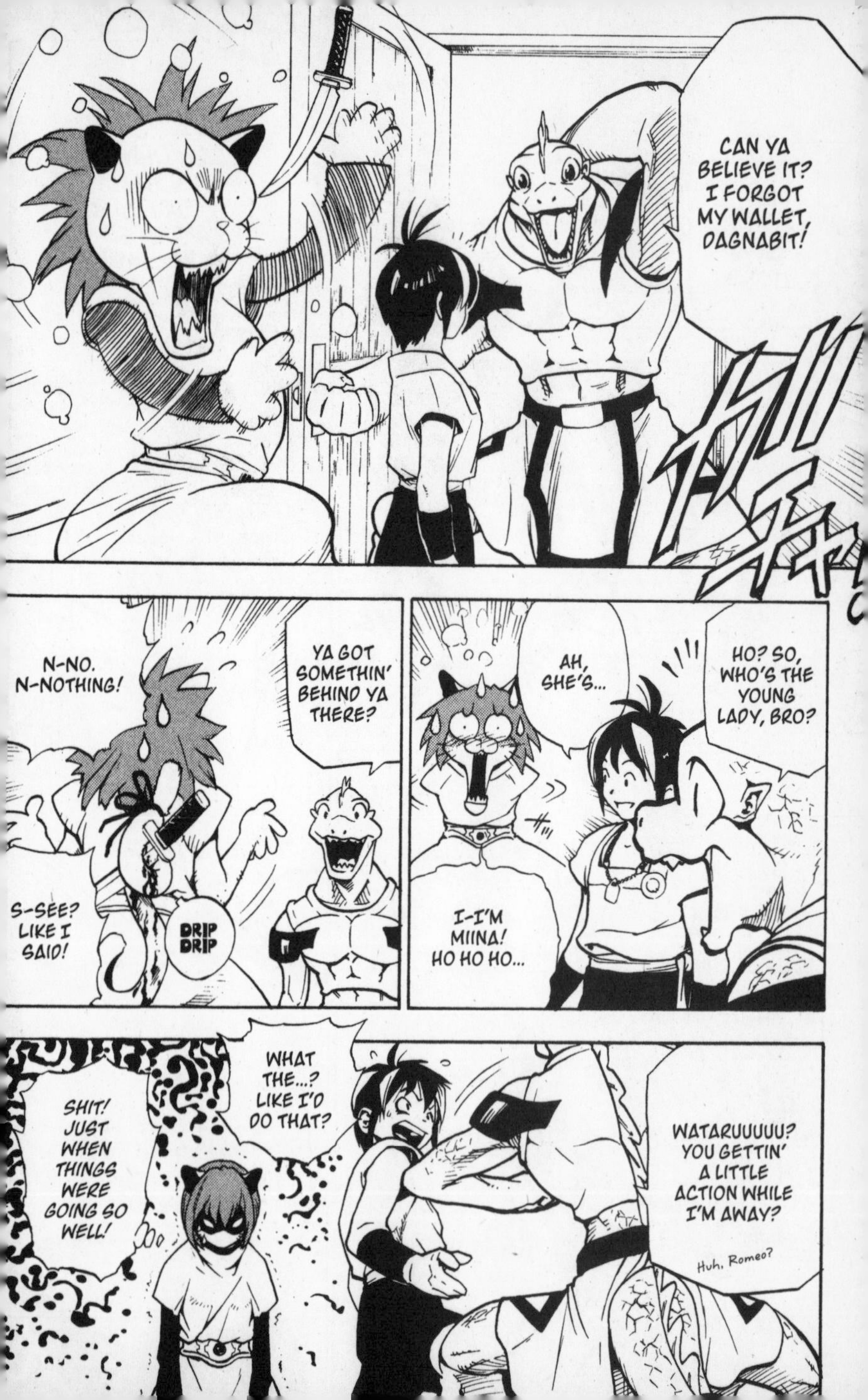
CAN YA BELIEVE IT? I FORGOT MY WALLET, DAGNABIT!
HO? SO, WHO'S THE YOUNG LADY, BRO?
AH, SHE'S...
I-I'M MIINA! HO HO HO...
YA GOT SOMETHIN' BEHIND YA THERE?
N-NO. N-NOTHING!
DRIP DRIP
S-SEE? LIKE I SAID!
WATARUUUUU? YOU GETTIN' A LITTLE ACTION WHILE I'M AWAY?
Huh, Romeo?
WHAT THE...? LIKE I'D DO THAT?
SHIT! JUST WHEN THINGS WERE GOING SO WELL!

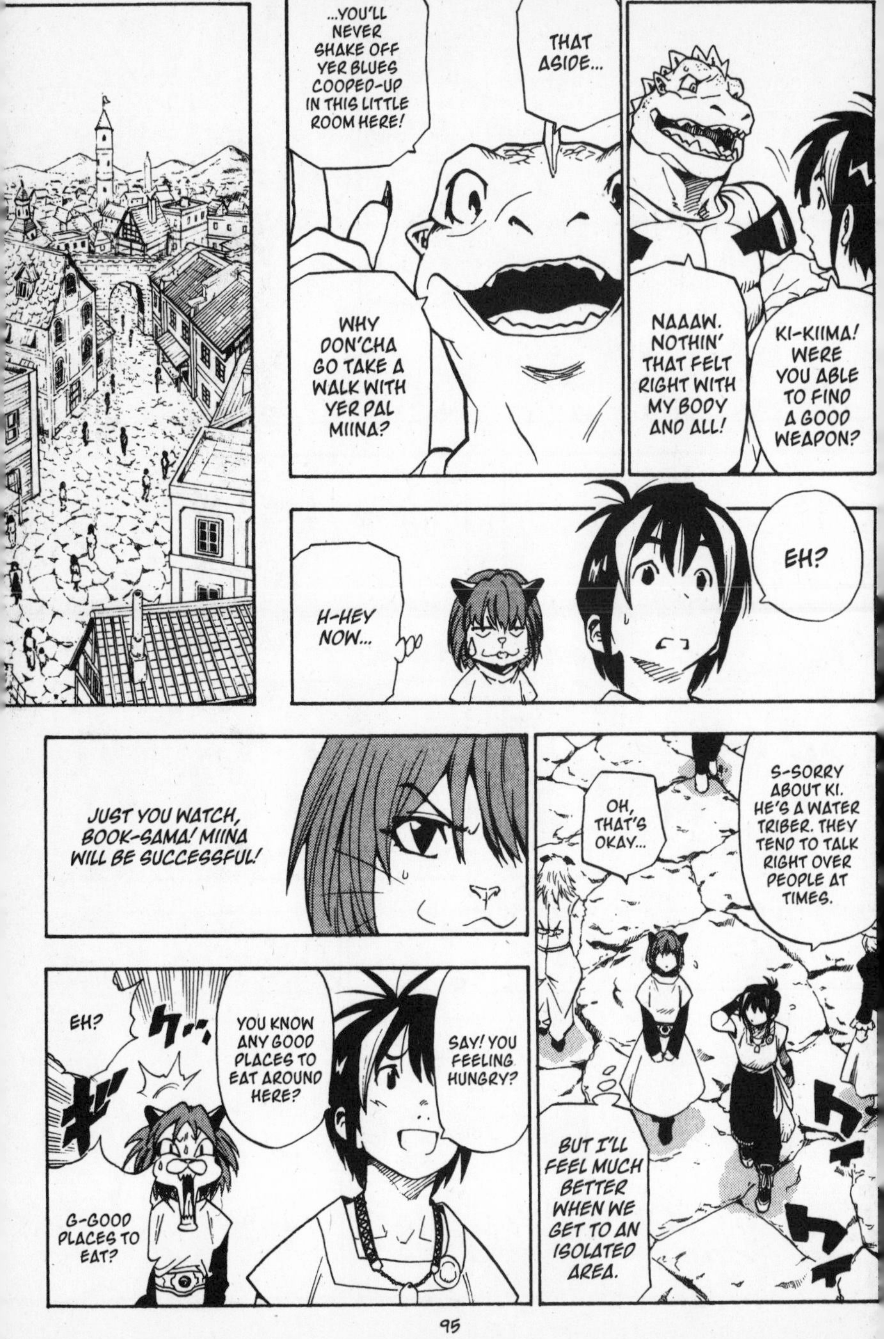
KI-KIIMA! WERE YOU ABLE TO FIND A GOOD WEAPON?
NAAAW. NOTHIN' THAT FELT RIGHT WITH MY BODY AND ALL!
THAT ASIDE...
...YOU'LL NEVER SHAKE OFF YER BLUES COOPED-UP IN THIS LITTLE ROOM HERE!
WHY DON'CHA GO TAKE A WALK WITH YER PAL MIINA?
EH?
H-HEY NOW...
S-SORRY ABOUT KI. HE'S A WATER TRIBER. THEY TEND TO TALK RIGHT OVER PEOPLE AT TIMES.
OH, THAT'S OKAY...
BUT I'LL FEEL MUCH BETTER WHEN WE GET TO AN ISOLATED AREA.
JUST YOU WATCH, BOOK-SAMA! MIINA WILL BE SUCCESSFUL!
SAY! YOU FEELING HUNGRY?
YOU KNOW ANY GOOD PLACES TO EAT AROUND HERE?
EH?
G-GOOD PLACES TO EAT?

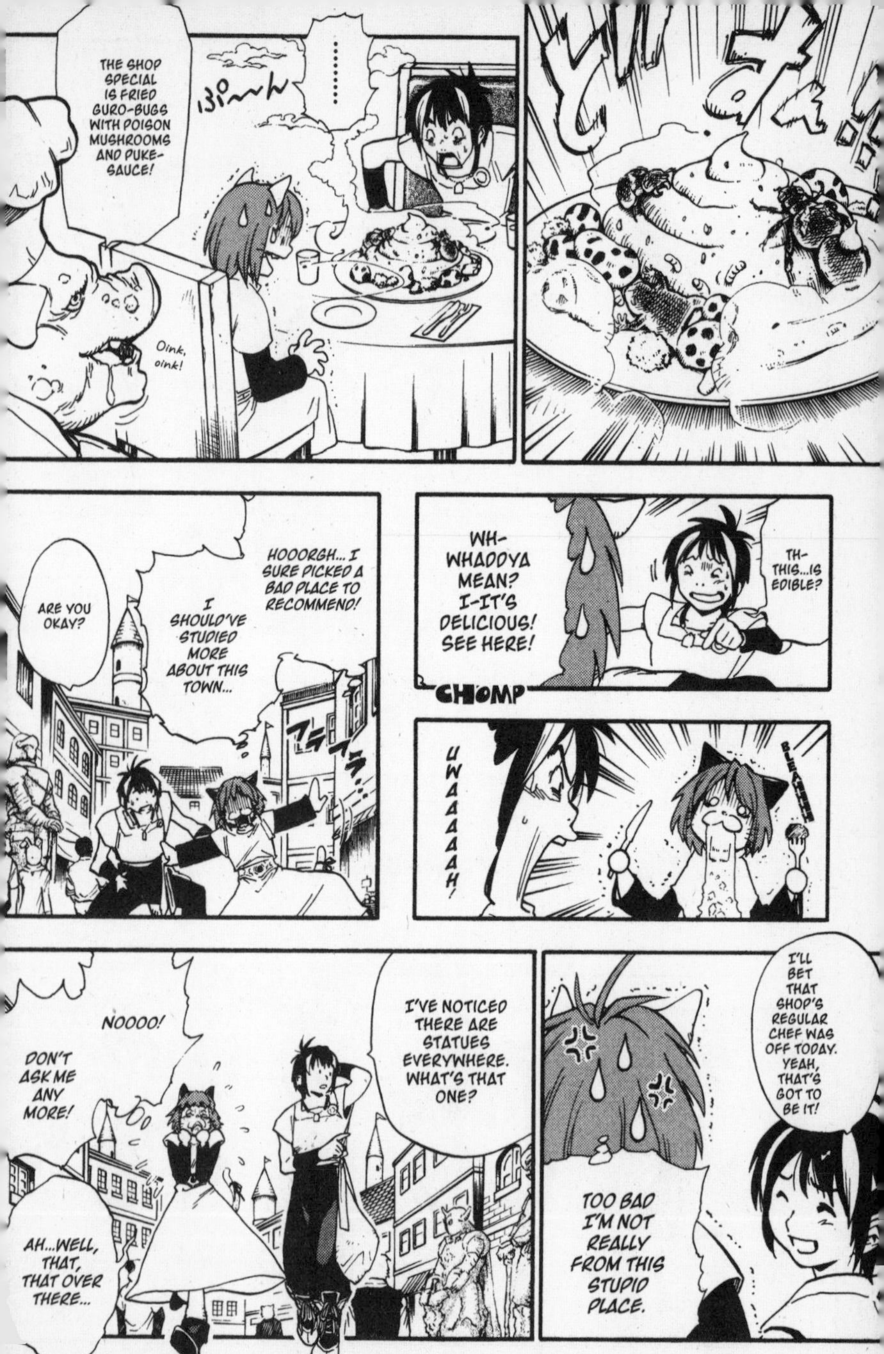
......
ぷ〜ん
THE SHOP SPECIAL IS FRIED GURO-BUGS WITH POISON MUSHROOMS AND PUKE-SAUCE!
Oink, oink!
TH-THIS...IS EDIBLE?
WH-WHADDYA MEAN? I-IT'S DELICIOUS! SEE HERE!
CHOMP
BLEAHHHH
UWAAAAAAAH!
HOOORGH... I SURE PICKED A BAD PLACE TO RECOMMEND!
I SHOULD'VE STUDIED MORE ABOUT THIS TOWN...
ARE YOU OKAY?
I'LL BET THAT SHOP'S REGULAR CHEF WAS OFF TODAY. YEAH, THAT'S GOT TO BE IT!
TOO BAD I'M NOT REALLY FROM THIS STUPID PLACE.
I'VE NOTICED THERE ARE STATUES EVERYWHERE. WHAT'S THAT ONE?
NOOOO!
DON'T ASK ME ANY MORE!
AH...WELL, THAT, THAT OVER THERE...

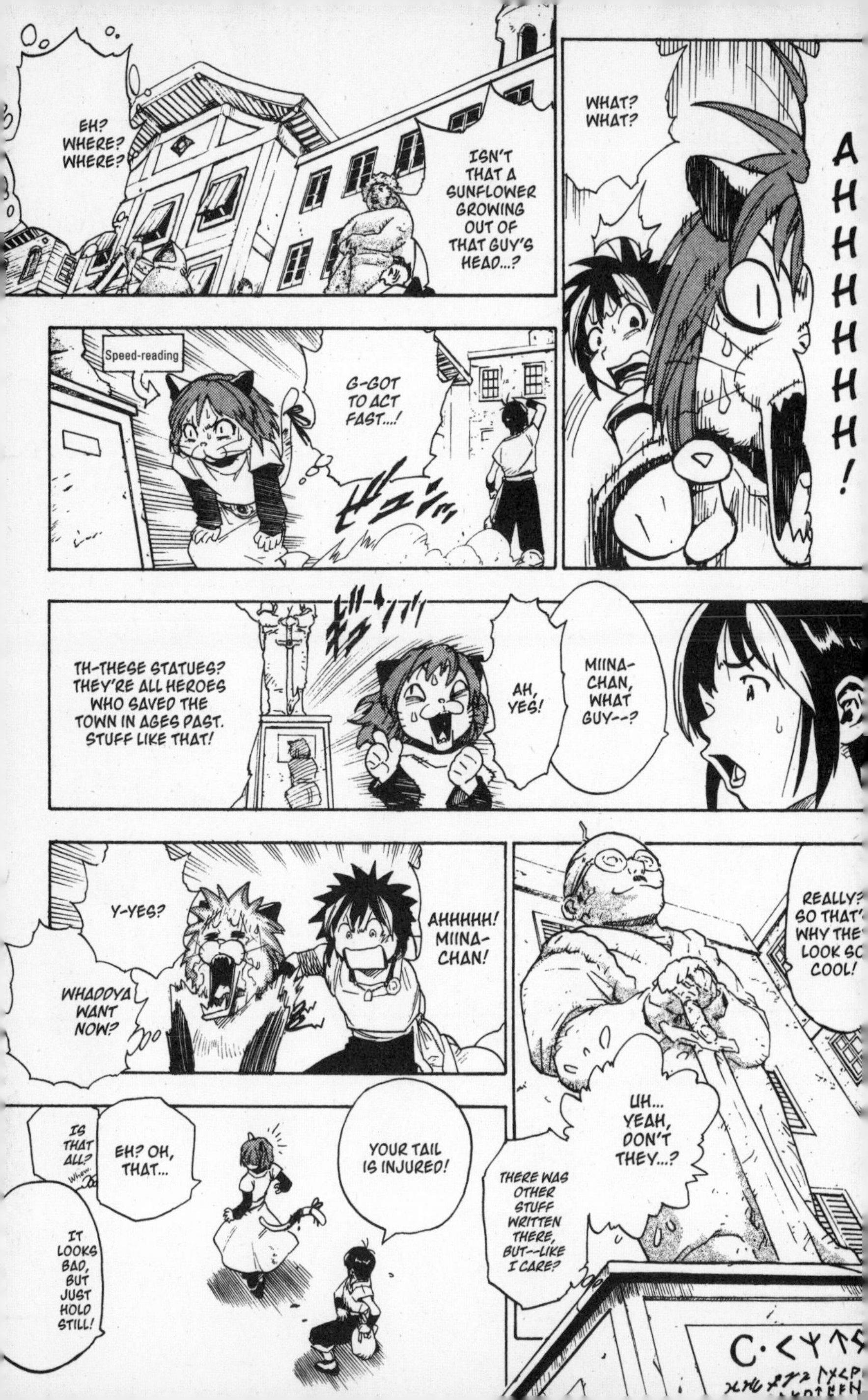
WHAT? WHAT?
AHHHHHHH!
ISN'T THAT A SUNFLOWER GROWING OUT OF THAT GUY'S HEAD...?
EH? WHERE? WHERE?
Speed-reading
G-GOT TO ACT FAST...!
MIINA-CHAN, WHAT GUY--?
AH, YES!
TH-THESE STATUES? THEY'RE ALL HEROES WHO SAVED THE TOWN IN AGES PAST. STUFF LIKE THAT!
REALLY? SO THAT' WHY THE LOOK SO COOL!
UH... YEAH, DON'T THEY...?
THERE WAS OTHER STUFF WRITTEN THERE, BUT--LIKE I CARE?
AHHHHH! MIINA-CHAN!
Y-YES?
WHADDYA WANT NOW?
YOUR TAIL IS INJURED!
EH? OH, THAT...
IS THAT ALL?
Whew.
IT LOOKS BAD, BUT JUST HOLD STILL!

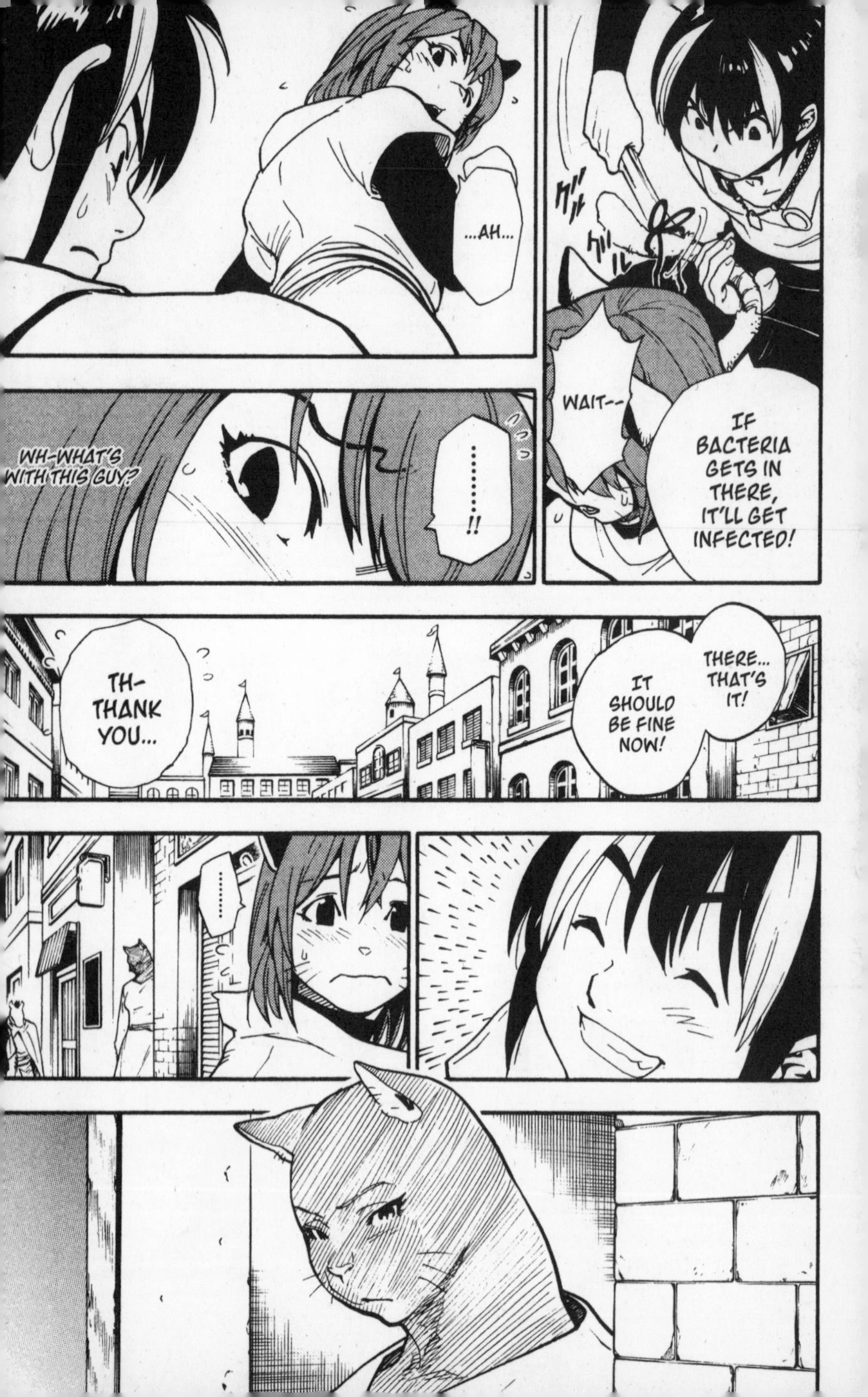
WAIT--
IF BACTERIA GETS IN THERE, IT'LL GET INFECTED!
...AH...
........!!
WH-WHAT'S WITH THIS GUY?
THERE... THAT'S IT!
IT SHOULD BE FINE NOW!
TH-THANK YOU...
....

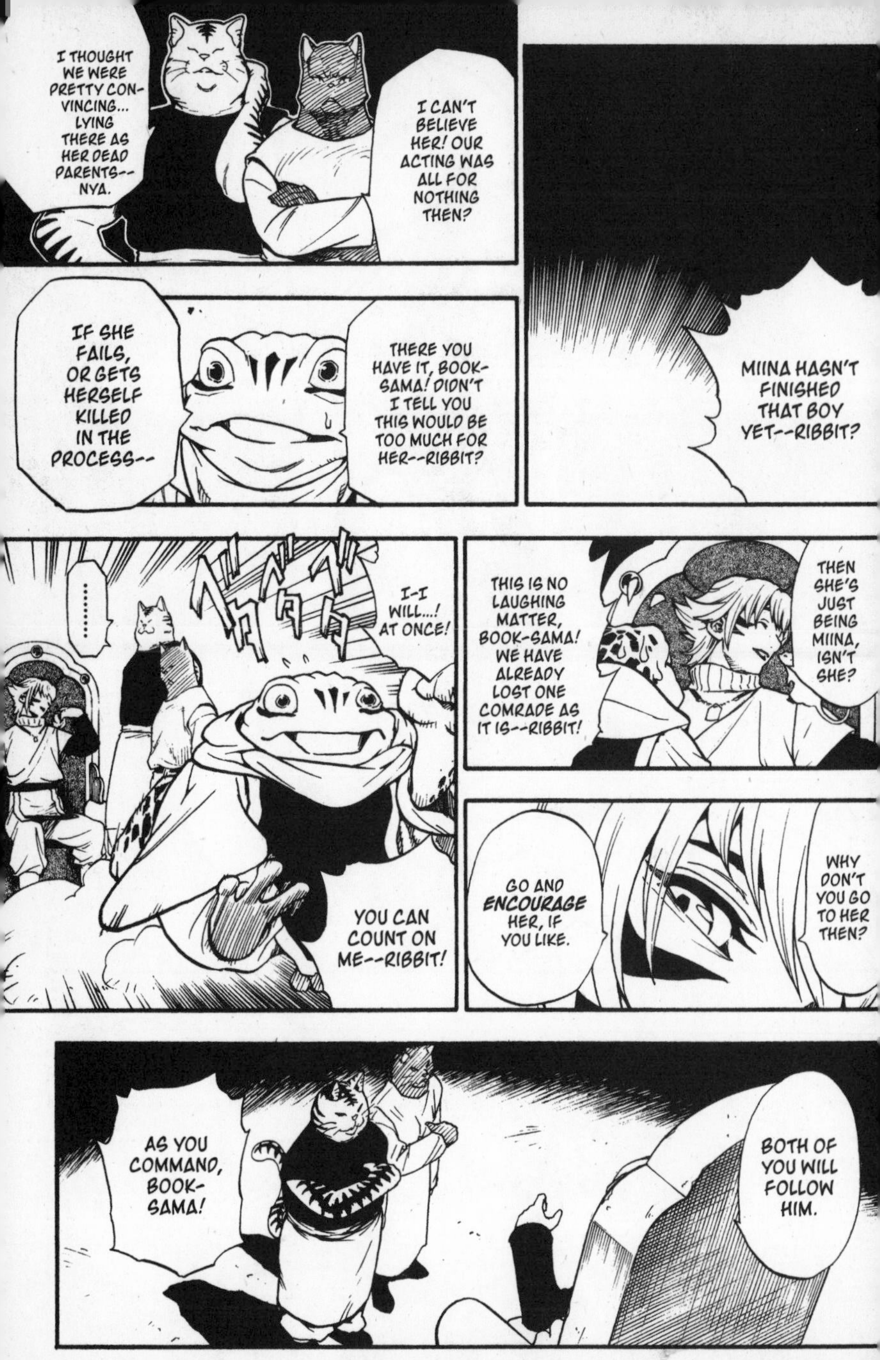
MIINA HASN'T FINISHED THAT BOY YET--RIBBIT?
I CAN'T BELIEVE HER! OUR ACTING WAS ALL FOR NOTHING THEN?
I THOUGHT WE WERE PRETTY CON-VINCING... LYING THERE AS HER DEAD PARENTS--NYA.
THERE YOU HAVE IT, BOOK-SAMA! DIDN'T I TELL YOU THIS WOULD BE TOO MUCH FOR HER--RIBBIT?
IF SHE FAILS, OR GETS HERSELF KILLED IN THE PROCESS--
THEN SHE'S JUST BEING MIINA, ISN'T SHE?
THIS IS NO LAUGHING MATTER, BOOK-SAMA! WE HAVE ALREADY LOST ONE COMRADE AS IT IS--RIBBIT!
WHY DON'T YOU GO TO HER THEN?
GO AND ENCOURAGE HER, IF YOU LIKE.
I-I WILL...! AT ONCE!
....
YOU CAN COUNT ON ME--RIBBIT!
BOTH OF YOU WILL FOLLOW HIM.
AS YOU COMMAND, BOOK-SAMA!

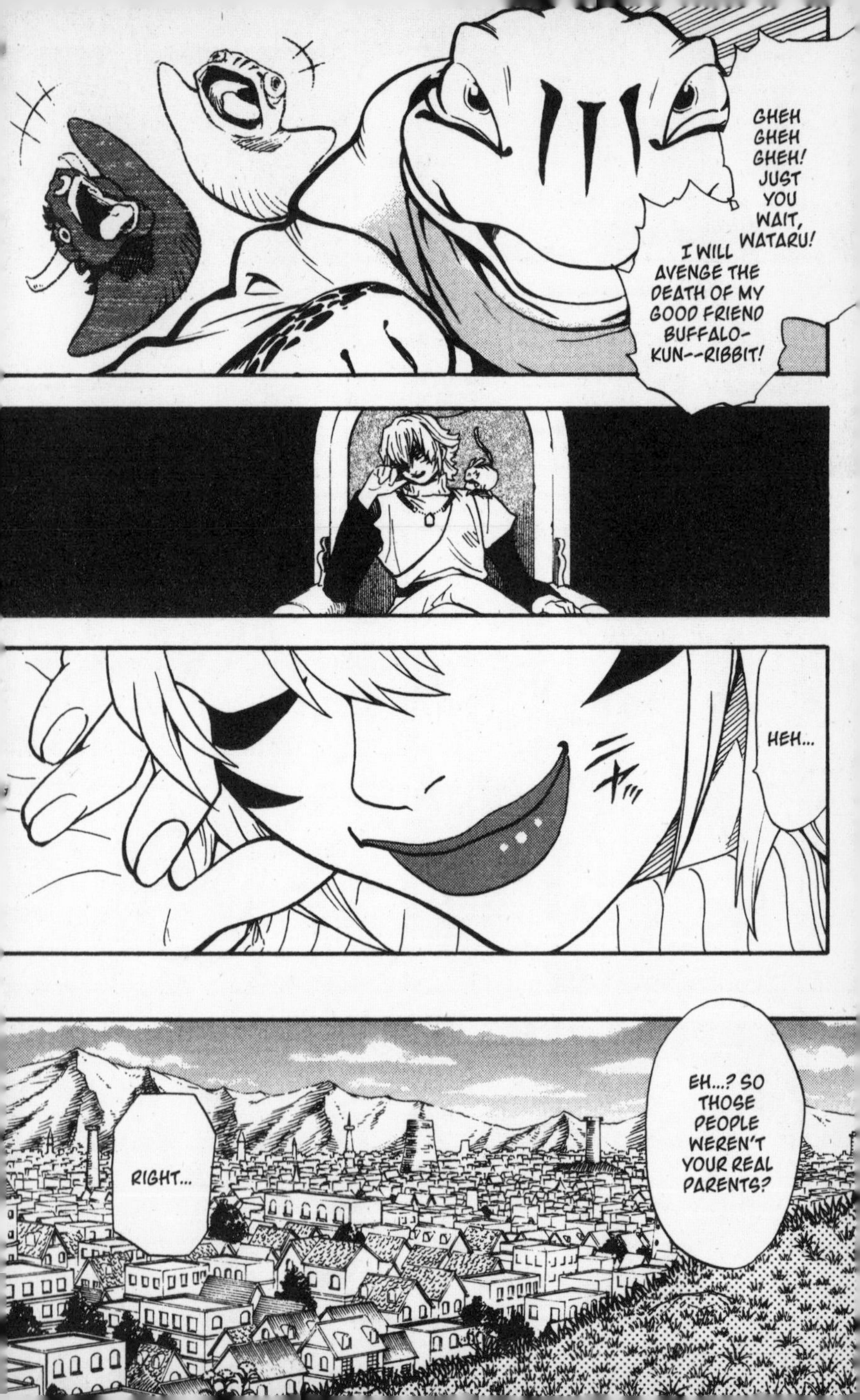
GHEH GHEH GHEH! JUST YOU WAIT, WATARU!
I WILL AVENGE THE DEATH OF MY GOOD FRIEND BUFFALO-KUN--RIBBIT!
HEH...
EH...? SO THOSE PEOPLE WEREN'T YOUR REAL PARENTS?
RIGHT...

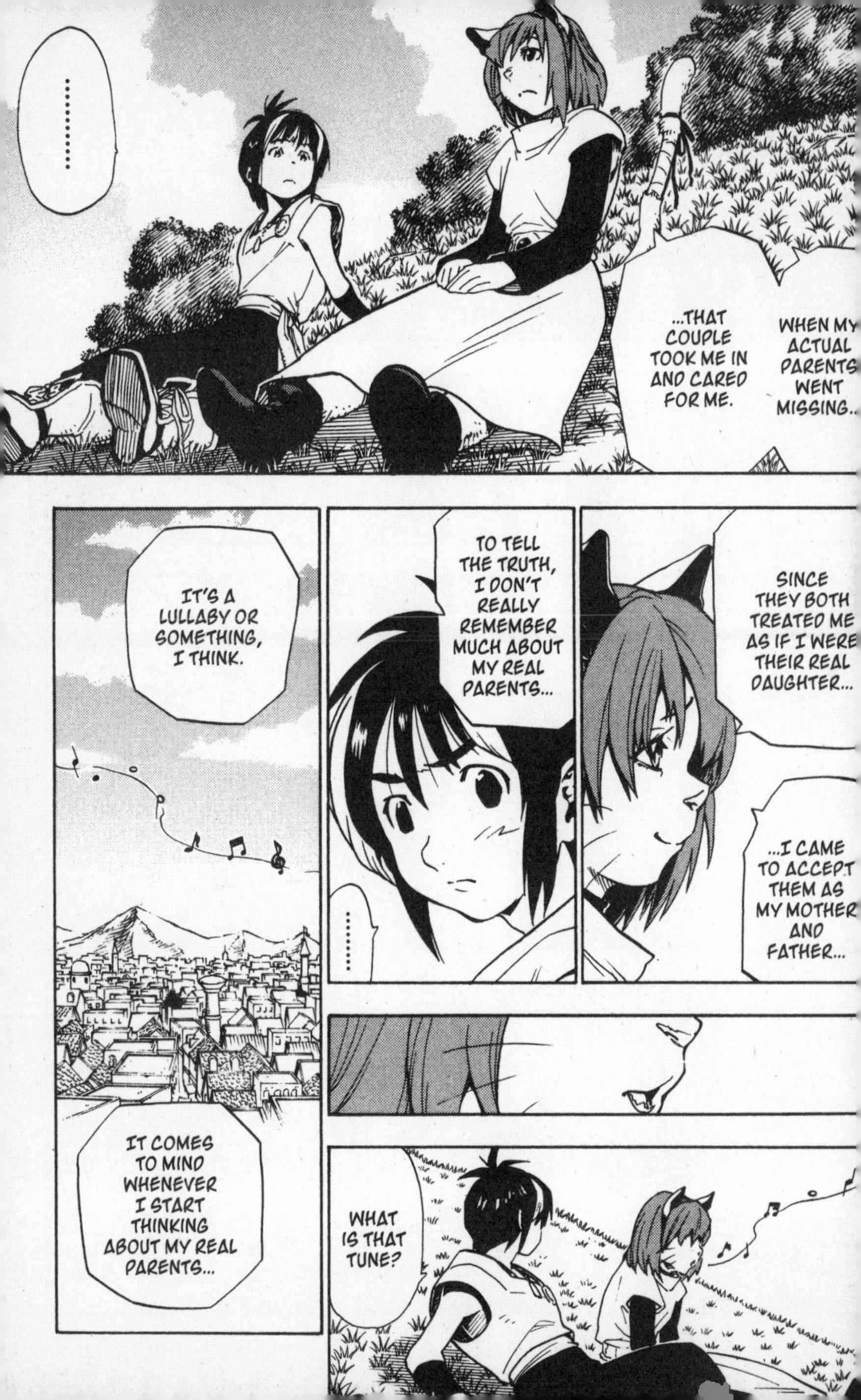
WHEN MY ACTUAL PARENTS WENT MISSING...
...THAT COUPLE TOOK ME IN AND CARED FOR ME.
......
SINCE THEY BOTH TREATED ME AS IF I WERE THEIR REAL DAUGHTER...
...I CAME TO ACCEPT THEM AS MY MOTHER AND FATHER...
TO TELL THE TRUTH, I DON'T REALLY REMEMBER MUCH ABOUT MY REAL PARENTS...
......
WHAT IS THAT TUNE?
IT'S A LULLABY OR SOMETHING, I THINK.
IT COMES TO MIND WHENEVER I START THINKING ABOUT MY REAL PARENTS...

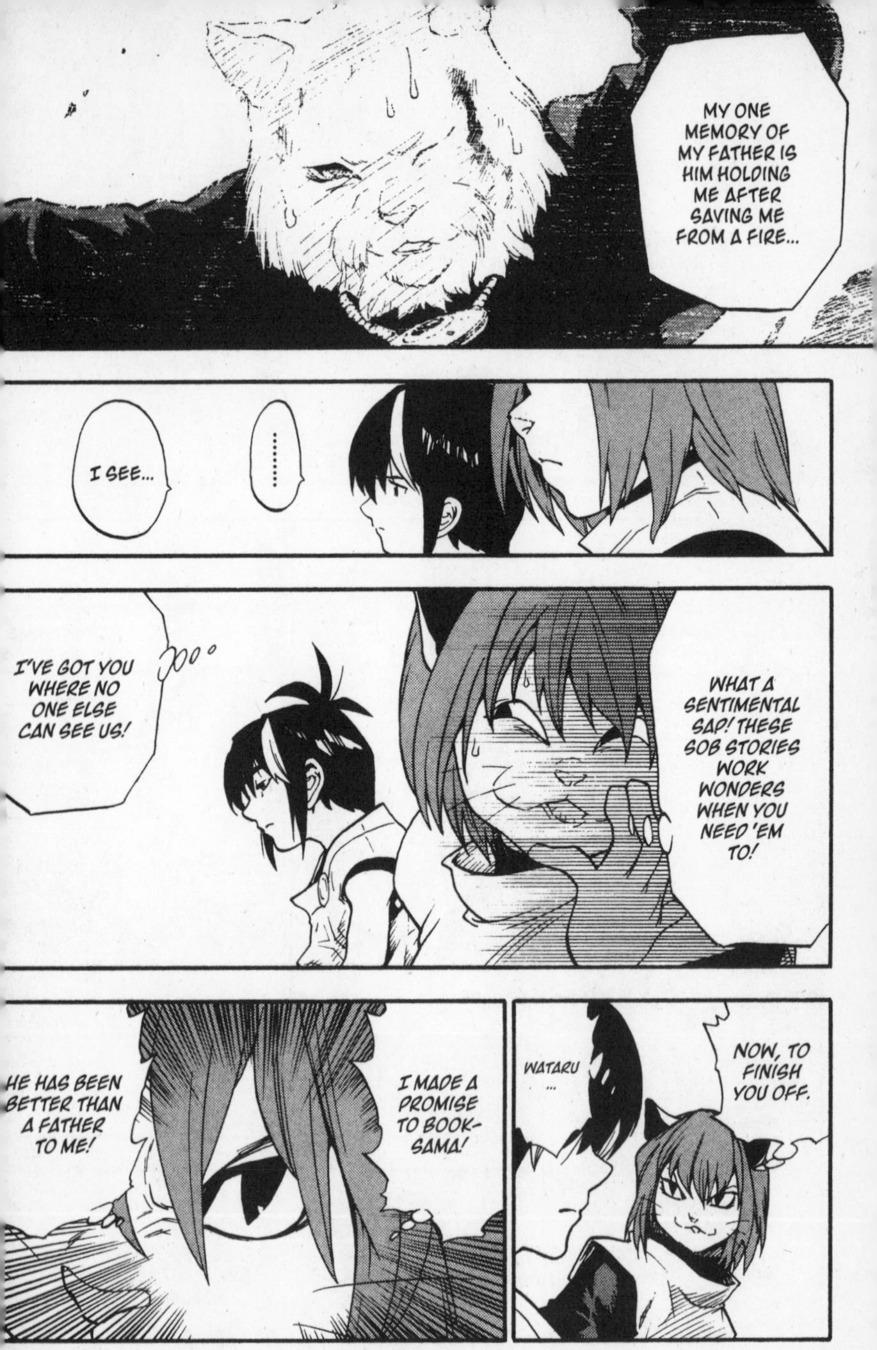
MY ONE MEMORY OF MY FATHER IS HIM HOLDING ME AFTER SAVING ME FROM A FIRE...
......
I SEE...
WHAT A SENTIMENTAL SAP! THESE SOB STORIES WORK WONDERS WHEN YOU NEED 'EM TO!
I'VE GOT YOU WHERE NO ONE ELSE CAN SEE US!
NOW, TO FINISH YOU OFF.
WATARU ...
I MADE A PROMISE TO BOOK-SAMA!
HE HAS BEEN BETTER THAN A FATHER TO ME!

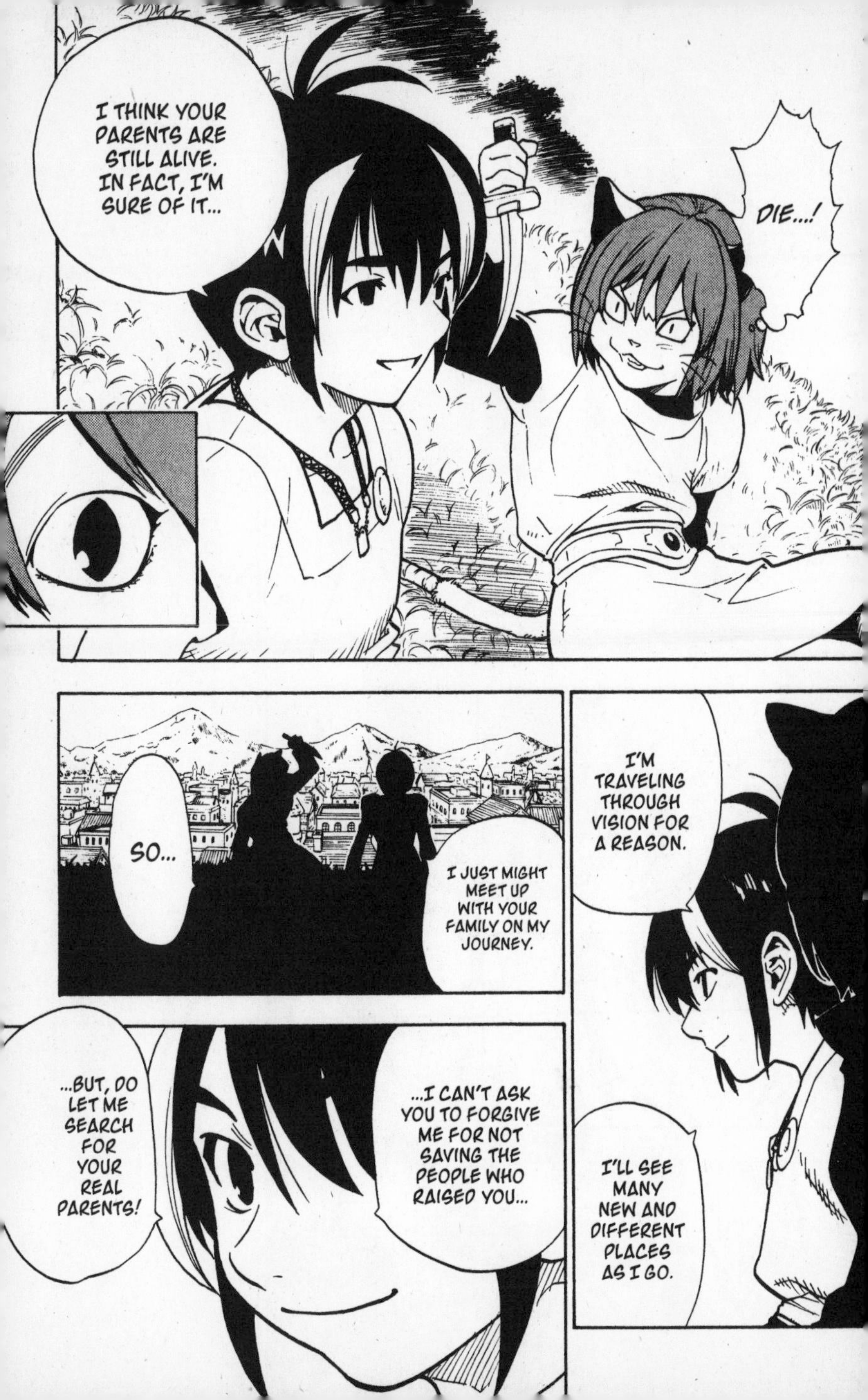
DIE...!
I THINK YOUR PARENTS ARE STILL ALIVE. IN FACT, I'M SURE OF IT...
I'M TRAVELING THROUGH VISION FOR A REASON.
I'LL SEE MANY NEW AND DIFFERENT PLACES AS I GO.
SO...
I JUST MIGHT MEET UP WITH YOUR FAMILY ON MY JOURNEY.
...I CAN'T ASK YOU TO FORGIVE ME FOR NOT SAVING THE PEOPLE WHO RAISED YOU...
...BUT, DO LET ME SEARCH FOR YOUR REAL PARENTS!

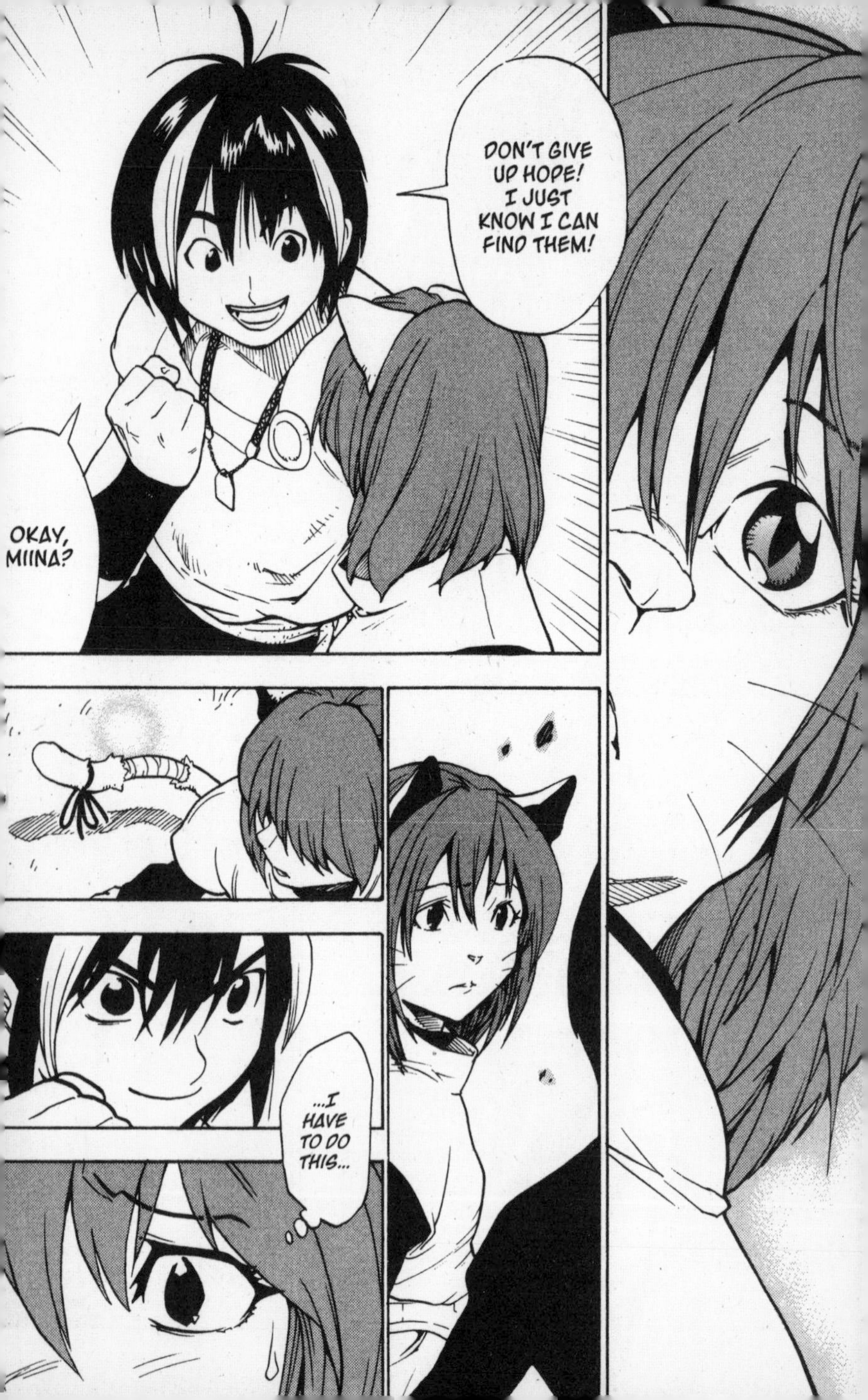
DON'T GIVE UP HOPE! I JUST KNOW I CAN FIND THEM!
OKAY, MIINA?
...I HAVE TO DO THIS...

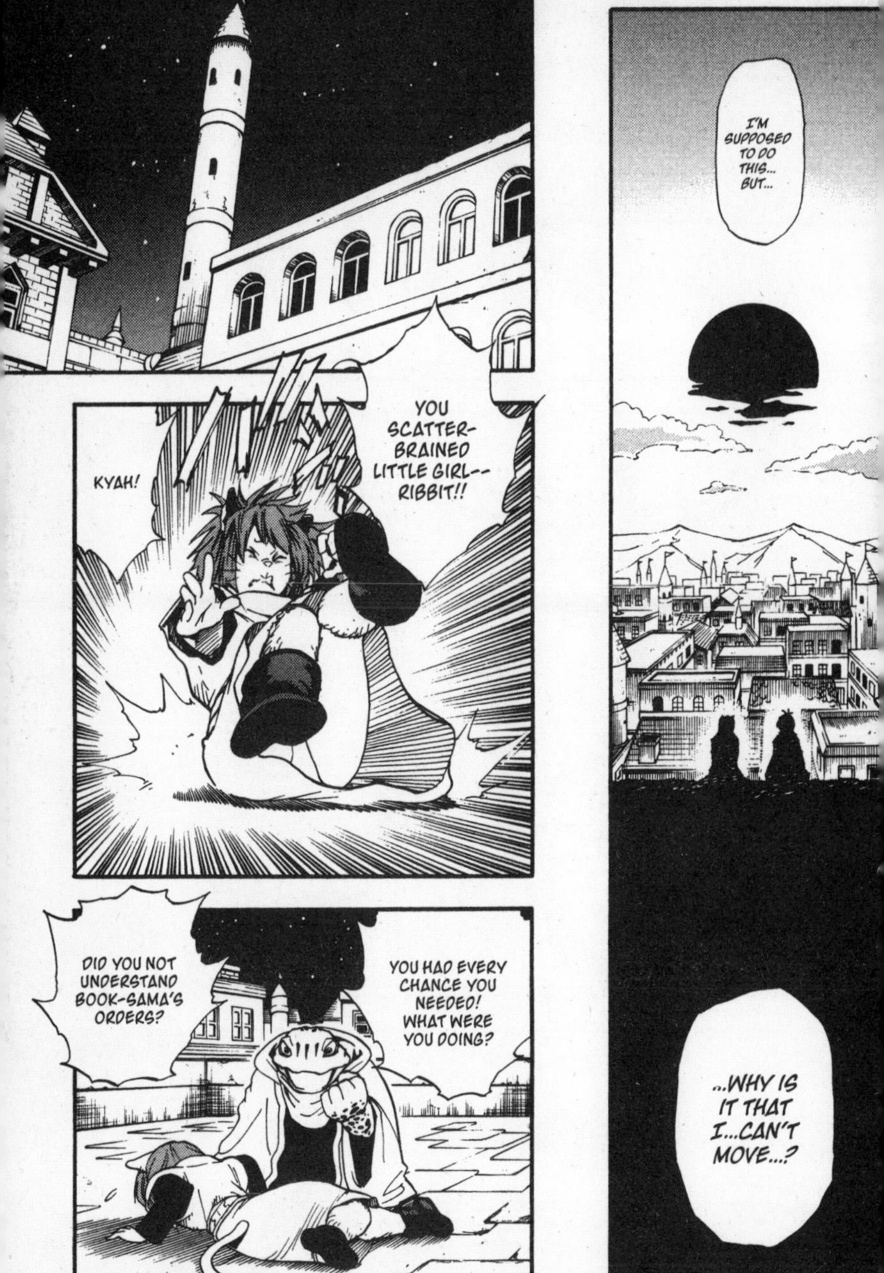
I'M SUPPOSED TO DO THIS... BUT...
...WHY IS IT THAT I...CAN'T MOVE...?
YOU SCATTER-BRAINED LITTLE GIRL--RIBBIT!!
KYAH!
YOU HAD EVERY CHANCE YOU NEEDED! WHAT WERE YOU DOING?
DID YOU NOT UNDERSTAND BOOK-SAMA'S ORDERS?

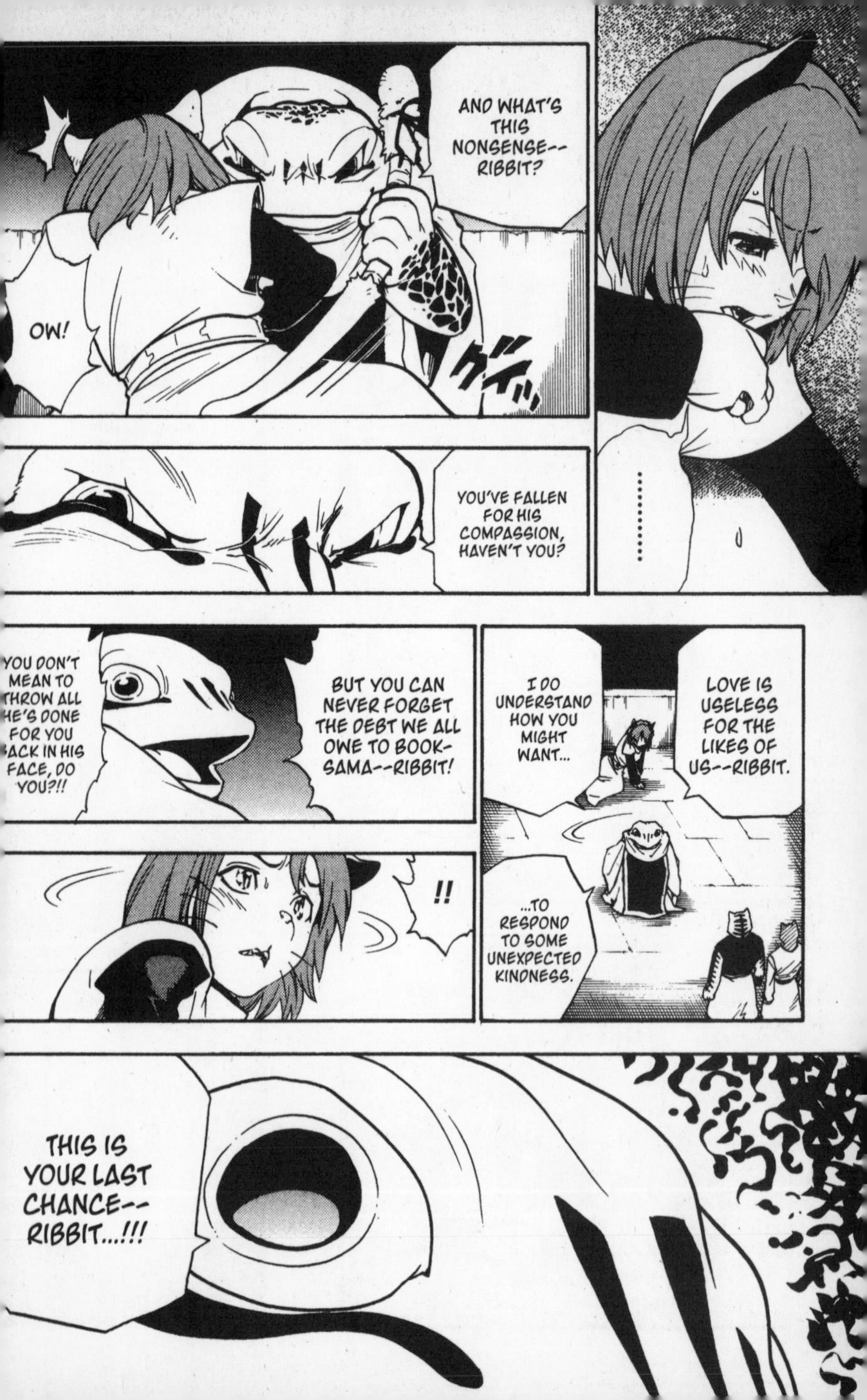
......
AND WHAT'S THIS NONSENSE--RIBBIT?
OW!
YOU'VE FALLEN FOR HIS COMPASSION, HAVEN'T YOU?
LOVE IS USELESS FOR THE LIKES OF US--RIBBIT.
I DO UNDERSTAND HOW YOU MIGHT WANT...
...TO RESPOND TO SOME UNEXPECTED KINDNESS.
BUT YOU CAN NEVER FORGET THE DEBT WE ALL OWE TO BOOK-SAMA--RIBBIT!
YOU DON'T MEAN TO THROW ALL HE'S DONE FOR YOU BACK IN HIS FACE, DO YOU?!!
!!
THIS IS YOUR LAST CHANCE--RIBBIT...!!!

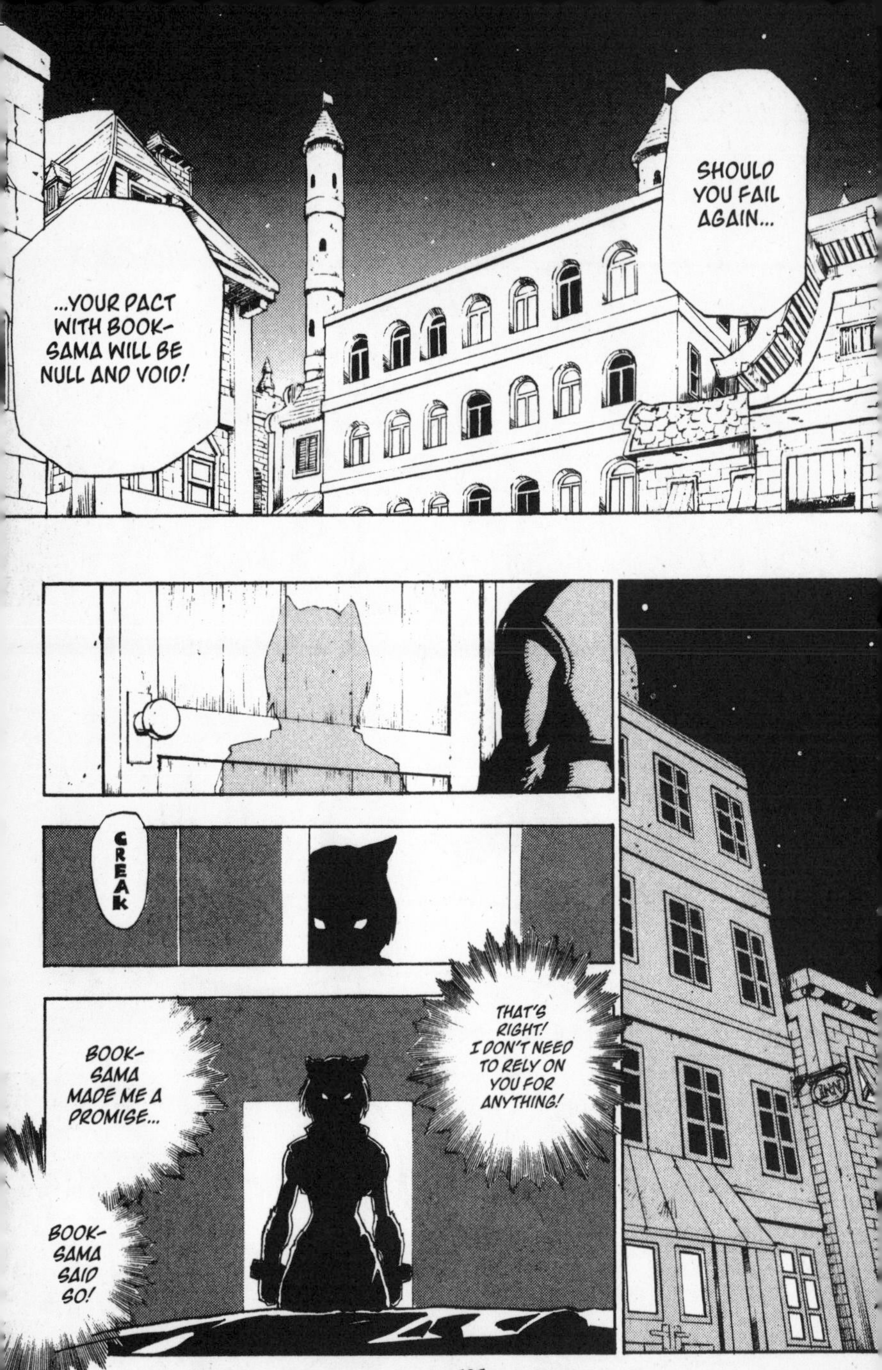
SHOULD YOU FAIL AGAIN...
...YOUR PACT WITH BOOK-SAMA WILL BE NULL AND VOID!
CREAK
THAT'S RIGHT! I DON'T NEED TO RELY ON YOU FOR ANYTHING!
BOOK-SAMA MADE ME A PROMISE...
BOOK-SAMA SAID SO!

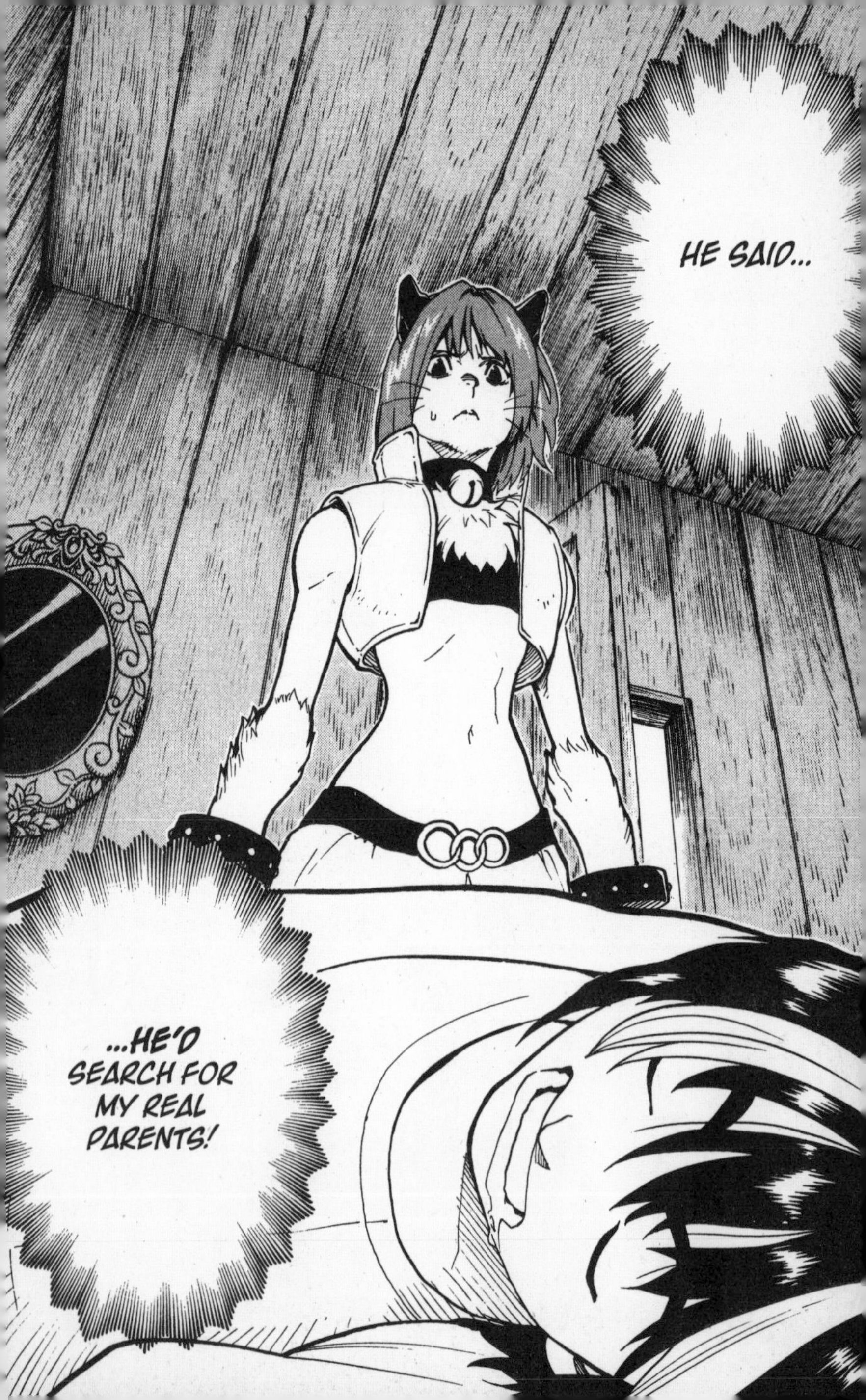
HE SAID...
...HE'D SEARCH FOR MY REAL PARENTS!

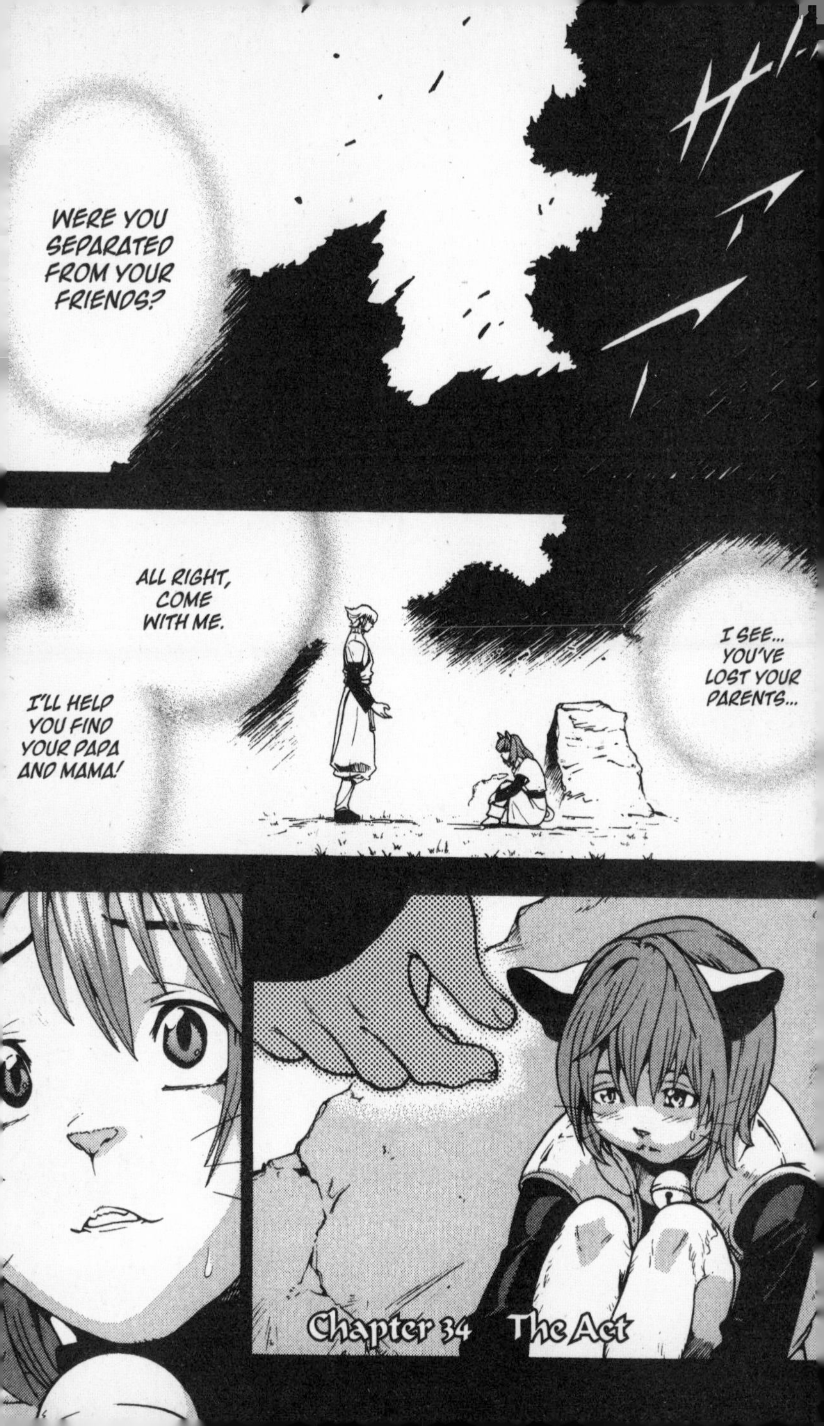
WERE YOU SEPARATED FROM YOUR FRIENDS?
I SEE... YOU'VE LOST YOUR PARENTS...
ALL RIGHT, COME WITH ME.
I'LL HELP YOU FIND YOUR PAPA AND MAMA!
Chapter 34 The Act

Chapter 34 The Act

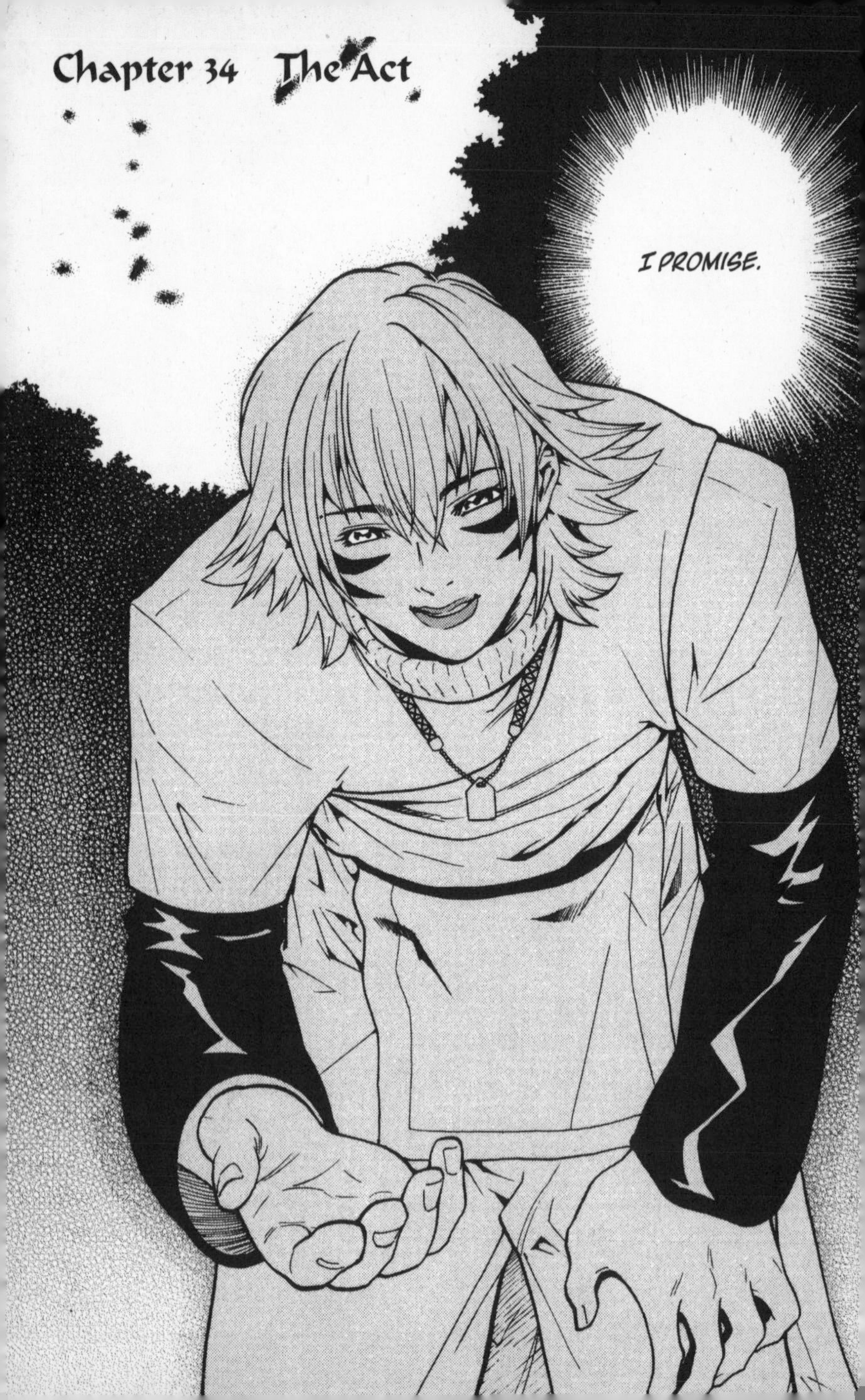
I PROMISE.

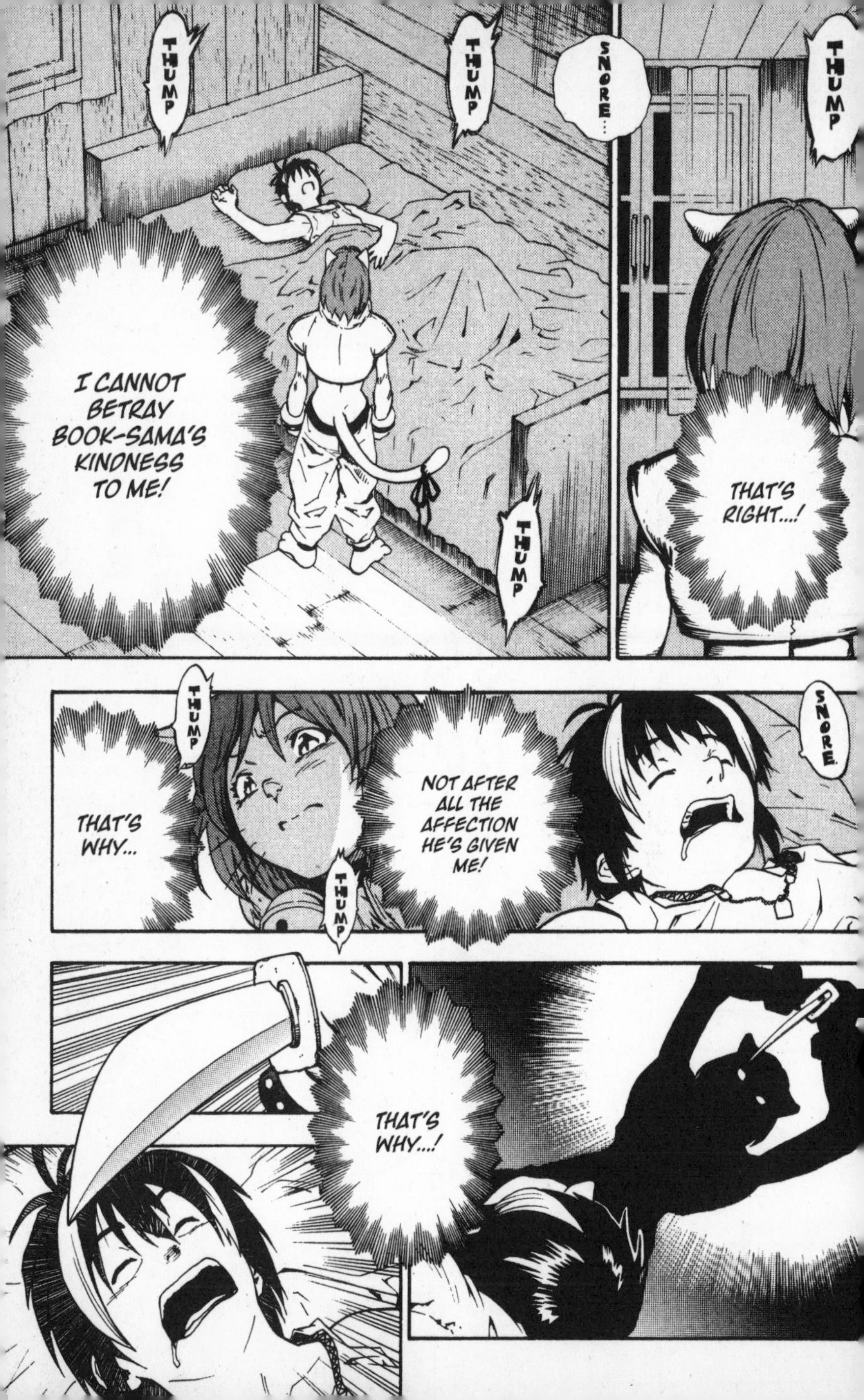
THUMP
THAT'S RIGHT...!
SNORE...
THUMP
THUMP
THUMP
I CANNOT BETRAY BOOK-SAMA'S KINDNESS TO ME!
SNORE.
NOT AFTER ALL THE AFFECTION HE'S GIVEN ME!
THUMP
THUMP
THAT'S WHY...
THAT'S WHY...!

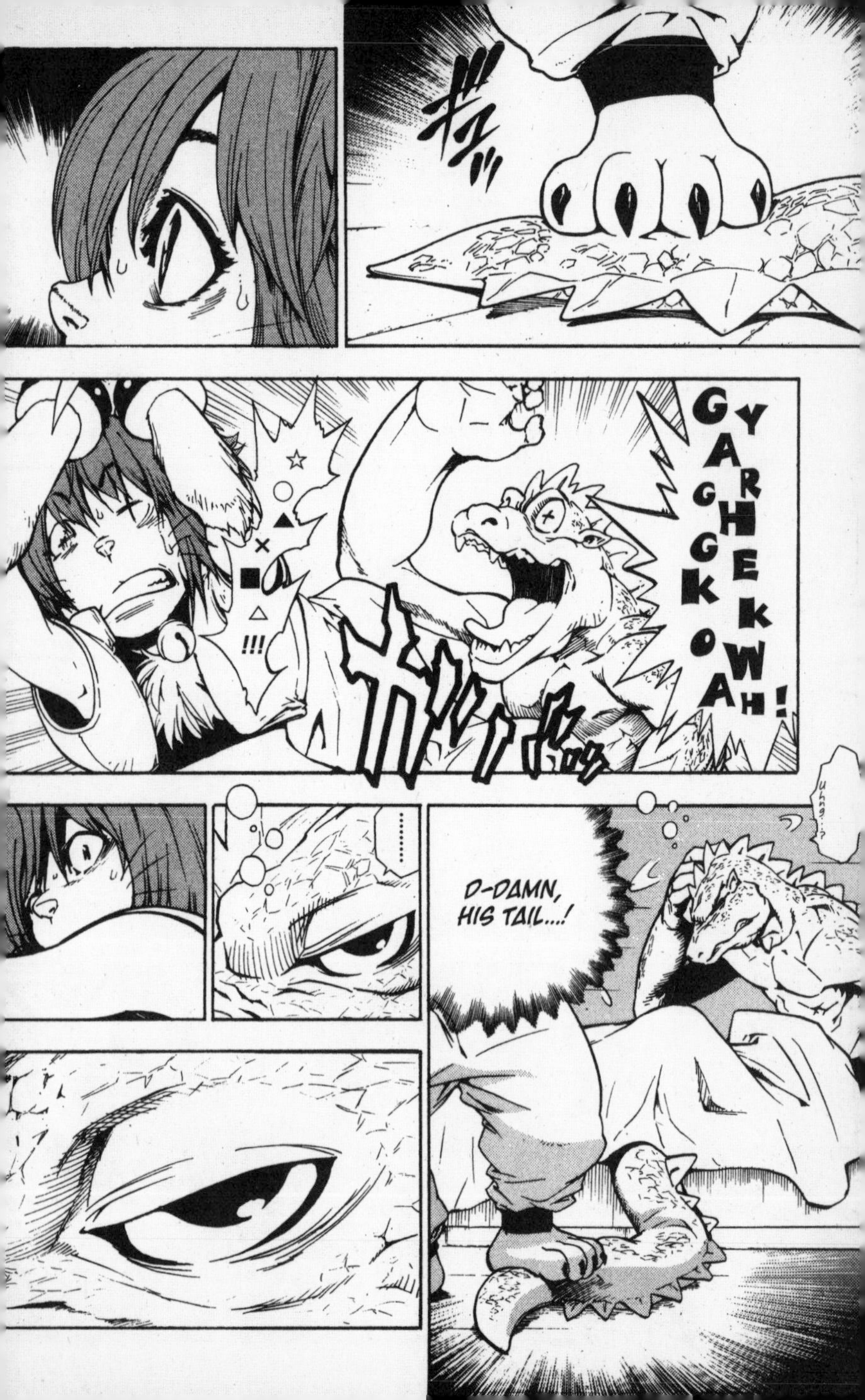

!!!
GYARGHGEKKOWAH!
Uhng...?
D-DAMN, HIS TAIL...!
....

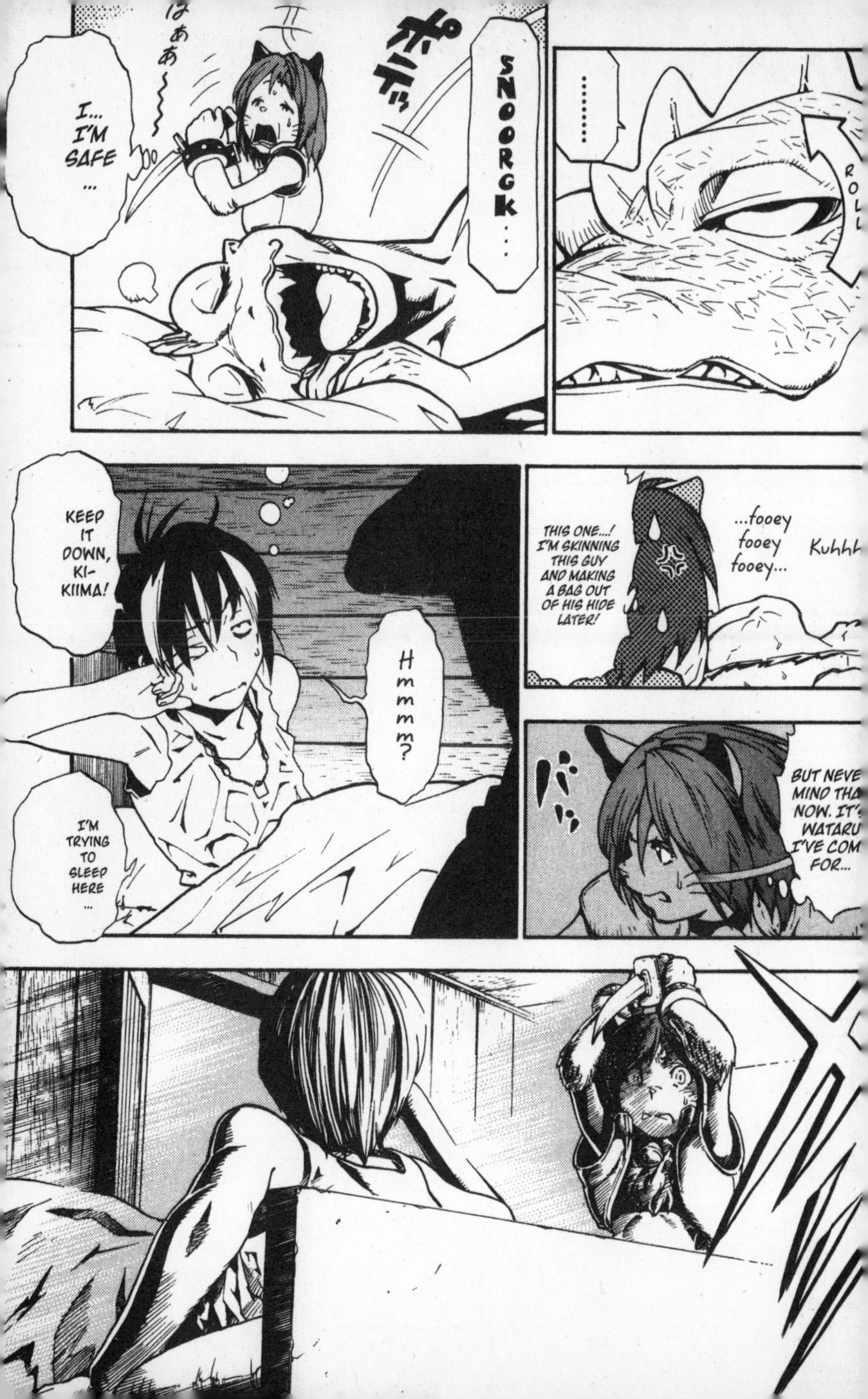
......
ROLL
SNOORGK...
ポテッ
はぁあ~~~
I... I'M SAFE...
...fooey fooey fooey...
Kuhhh
THIS ONE...! I'M SKINNING THIS GUY AND MAKING A BAG OUT OF HIS HIDE LATER!
バッ
BUT NEVE MIND THA NOW. IT'S WATARU I'VE COM FOR...
Hmmmm?
KEEP IT DOWN, KI-KIIMA!
I'M TRYING TO SLEEP HERE...

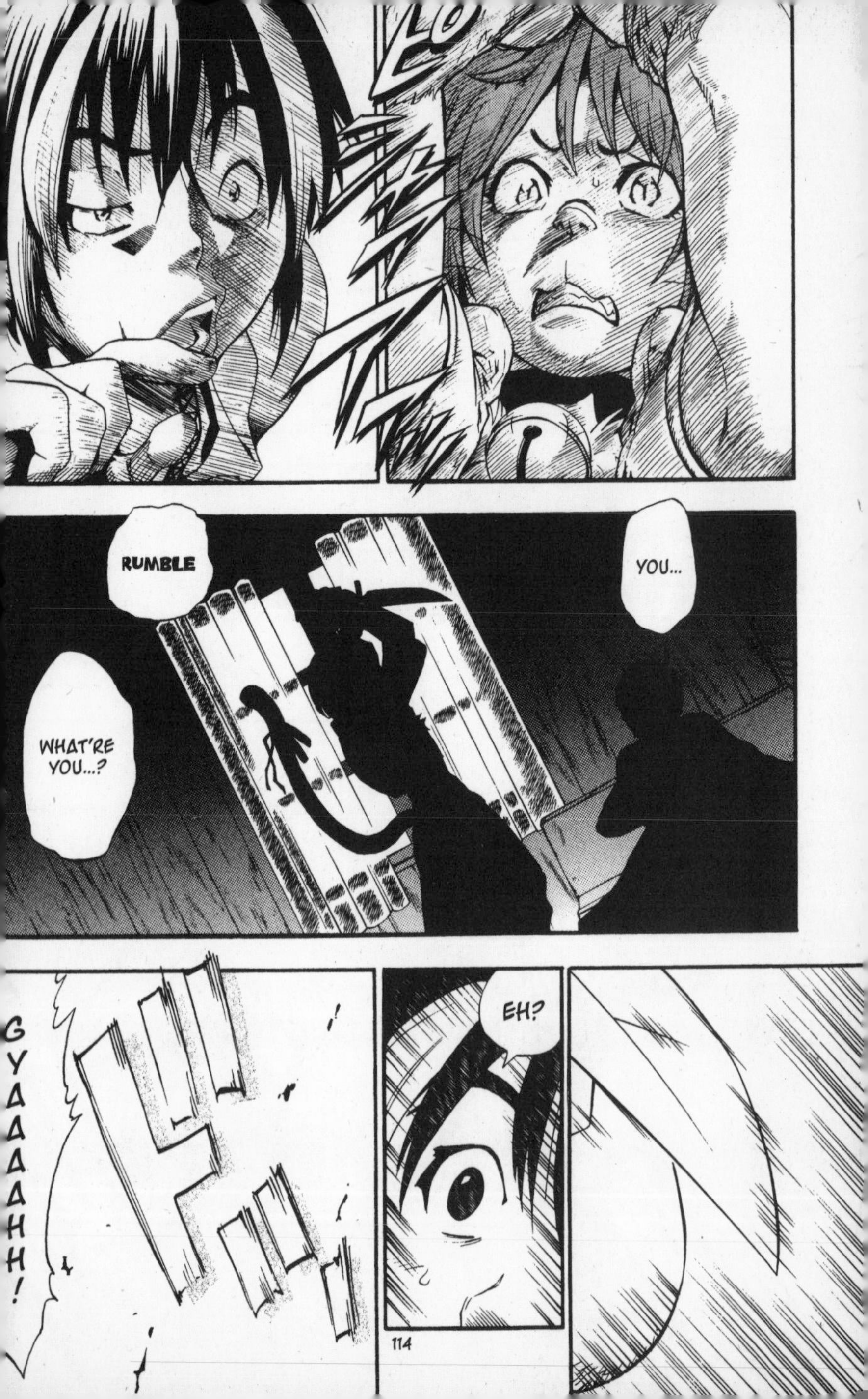
YOU...
RUMBLE
WHAT'RE YOU...?
EH?
GYAAAAAHH!

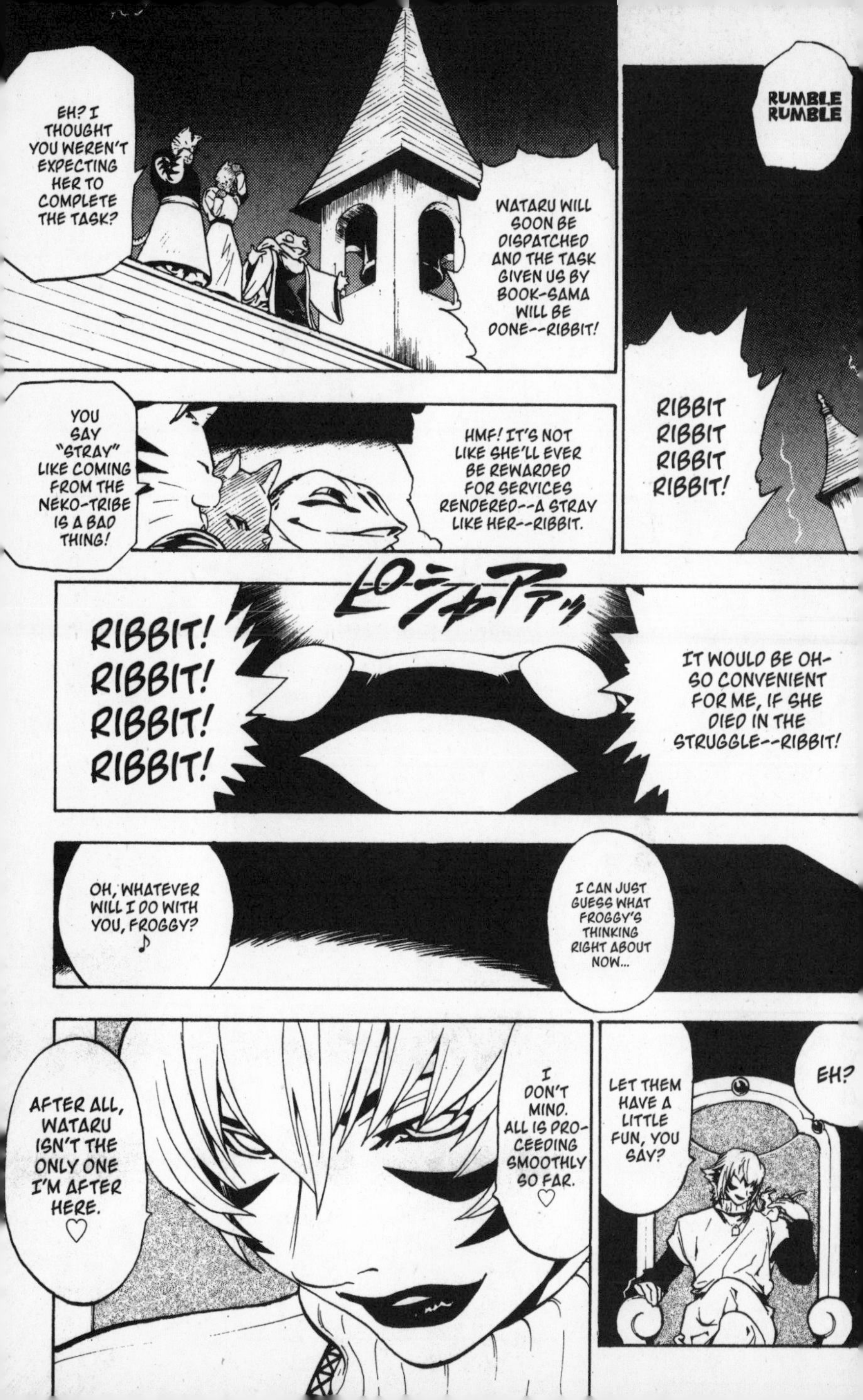
RUMBLE RUMBLE
RIBBIT RIBBIT RIBBIT RIBBIT!
WATARU WILL SOON BE DISPATCHED AND THE TASK GIVEN US BY BOOK-SAMA WILL BE DONE--RIBBIT!
EH? I THOUGHT YOU WEREN'T EXPECTING HER TO COMPLETE THE TASK?
HMF! IT'S NOT LIKE SHE'LL EVER BE REWARDED FOR SERVICES RENDERED--A STRAY LIKE HER--RIBBIT.
YOU SAY "STRAY" LIKE COMING FROM THE NEKO-TRIBE IS A BAD THING!
IT WOULD BE OH-SO CONVENIENT FOR ME, IF SHE DIED IN THE STRUGGLE--RIBBIT!
RIBBIT! RIBBIT! RIBBIT! RIBBIT!
I CAN JUST GUESS WHAT FROGGY'S THINKING RIGHT ABOUT NOW...
OH, WHATEVER WILL I DO WITH YOU, FROGGY? ♪
EH?
LET THEM HAVE A LITTLE FUN, YOU SAY?
I DON'T MIND. ALL IS PROCEEDING SMOOTHLY SO FAR. ♡
AFTER ALL, WATARU ISN'T THE ONLY ONE I'M AFTER HERE. ♡

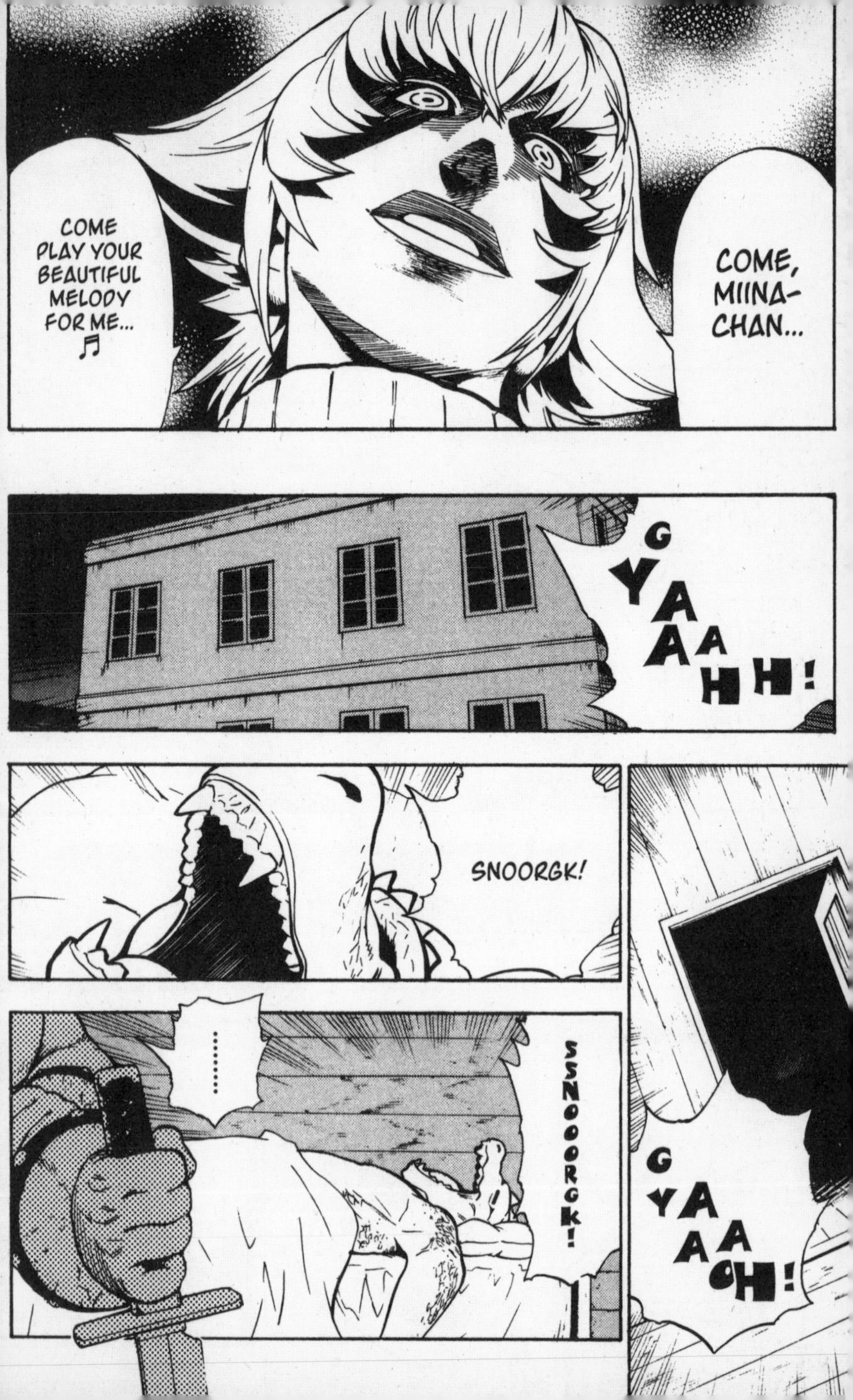
COME, MIINA-CHAN...
COME PLAY YOUR BEAUTIFUL MELODY FOR ME... ♬
GYAAAHH!
SNOORGK!
....
SSNOOOORGK!
GYAAACH!

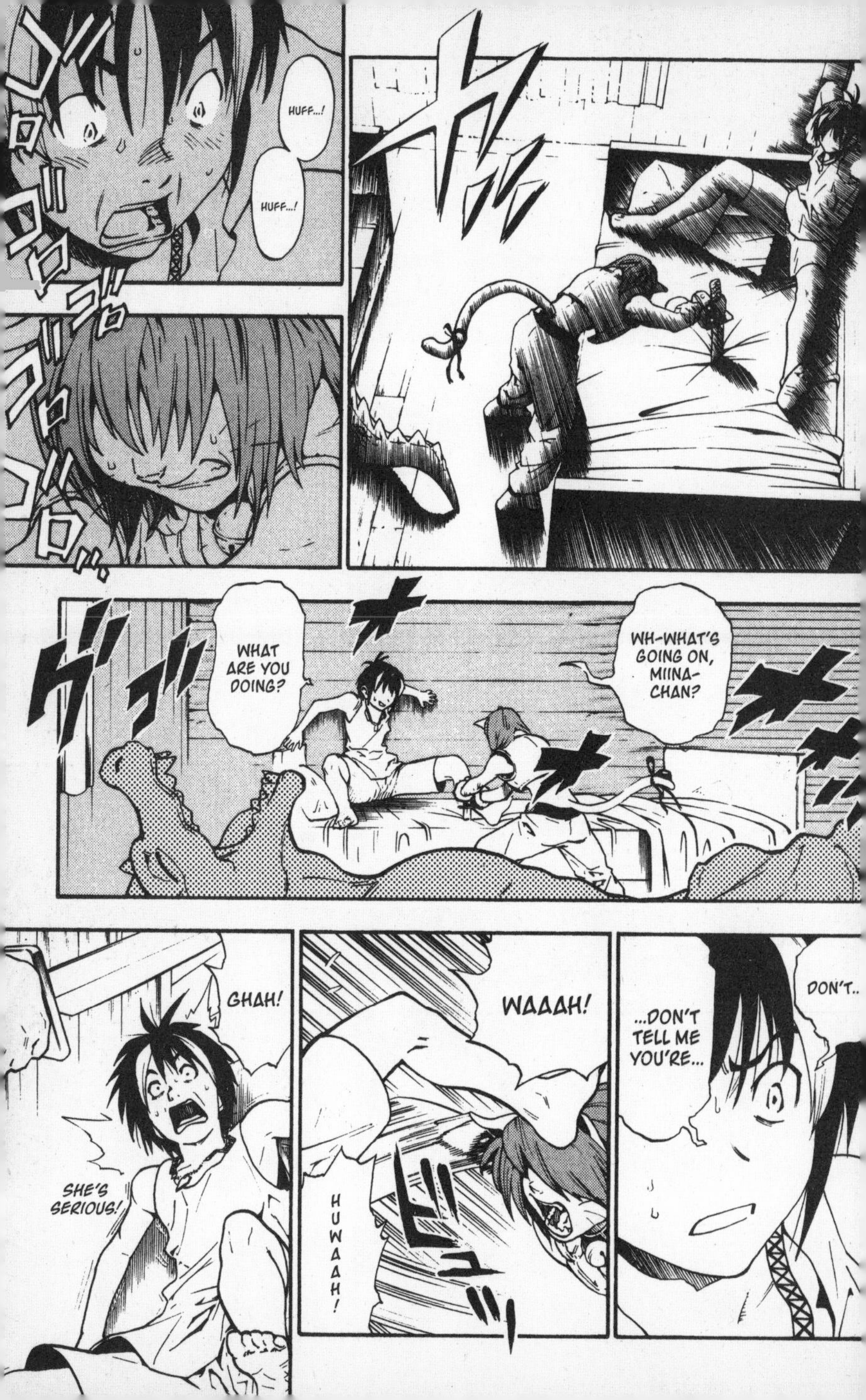
HUFF...!
HUFF...!
WH-WHAT'S GOING ON, MIINA-CHAN?
WHAT ARE YOU DOING?
DON'T...
...DON'T TELL ME YOU'RE...
WAAAH!
HUWAAAH!
GHAH!
SHE'S SERIOUS!

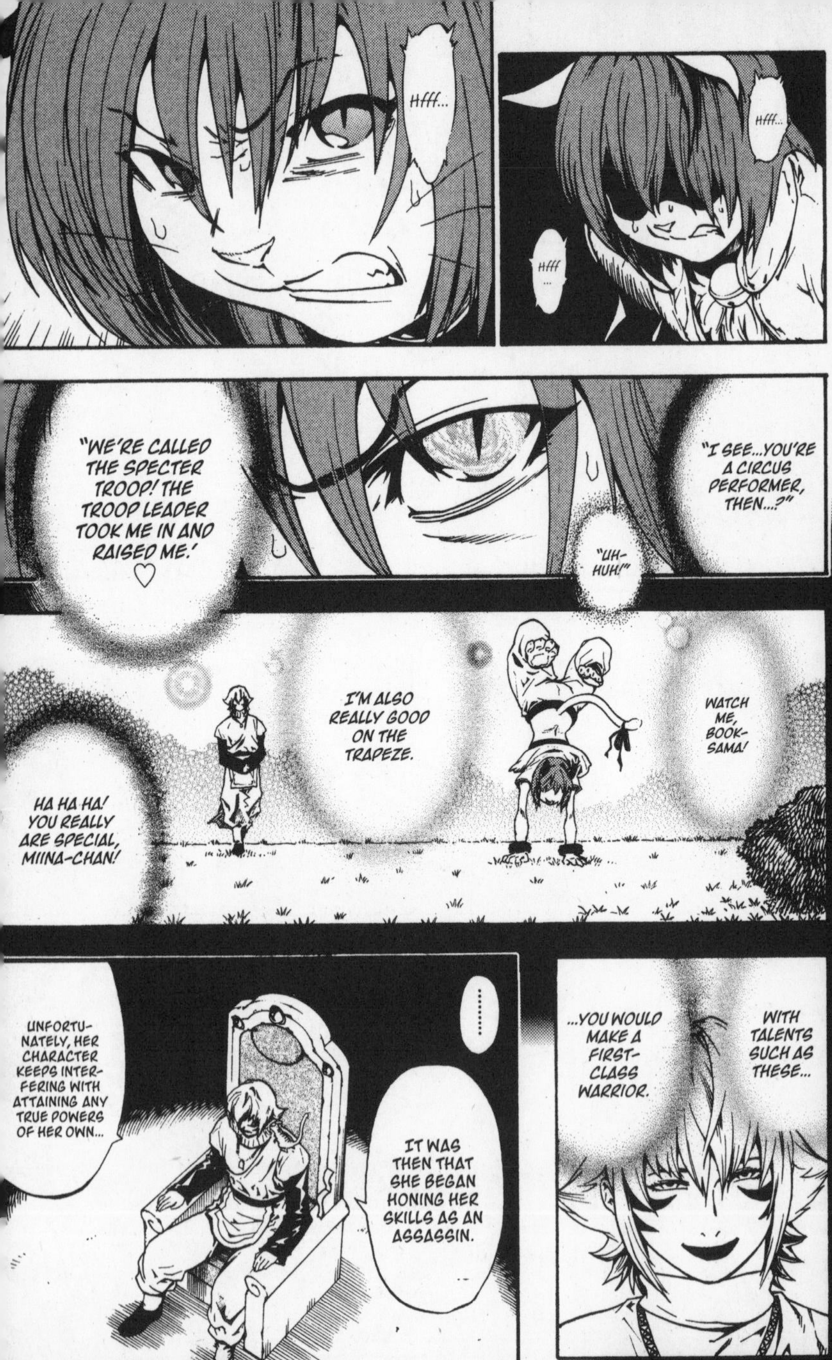
Hfff...
Hfff...
Hfff...
"I SEE...YOU'RE A CIRCUS PERFORMER, THEN...?"
"UH-HUH!"
"WE'RE CALLED THE SPECTER TROOP! THE TROOP LEADER TOOK ME IN AND RAISED ME.' ♡
WATCH ME, BOOK-SAMA!
I'M ALSO REALLY GOOD ON THE TRAPEZE.
HA HA HA! YOU REALLY ARE SPECIAL, MIINA-CHAN!
WITH TALENTS SUCH AS THESE...
...YOU WOULD MAKE A FIRST-CLASS WARRIOR.
....
UNFORTUNATELY, HER CHARACTER KEEPS INTERFERING WITH ATTAINING ANY TRUE POWERS OF HER OWN...
IT WAS THEN THAT SHE BEGAN HONING HER SKILLS AS AN ASSASSIN.

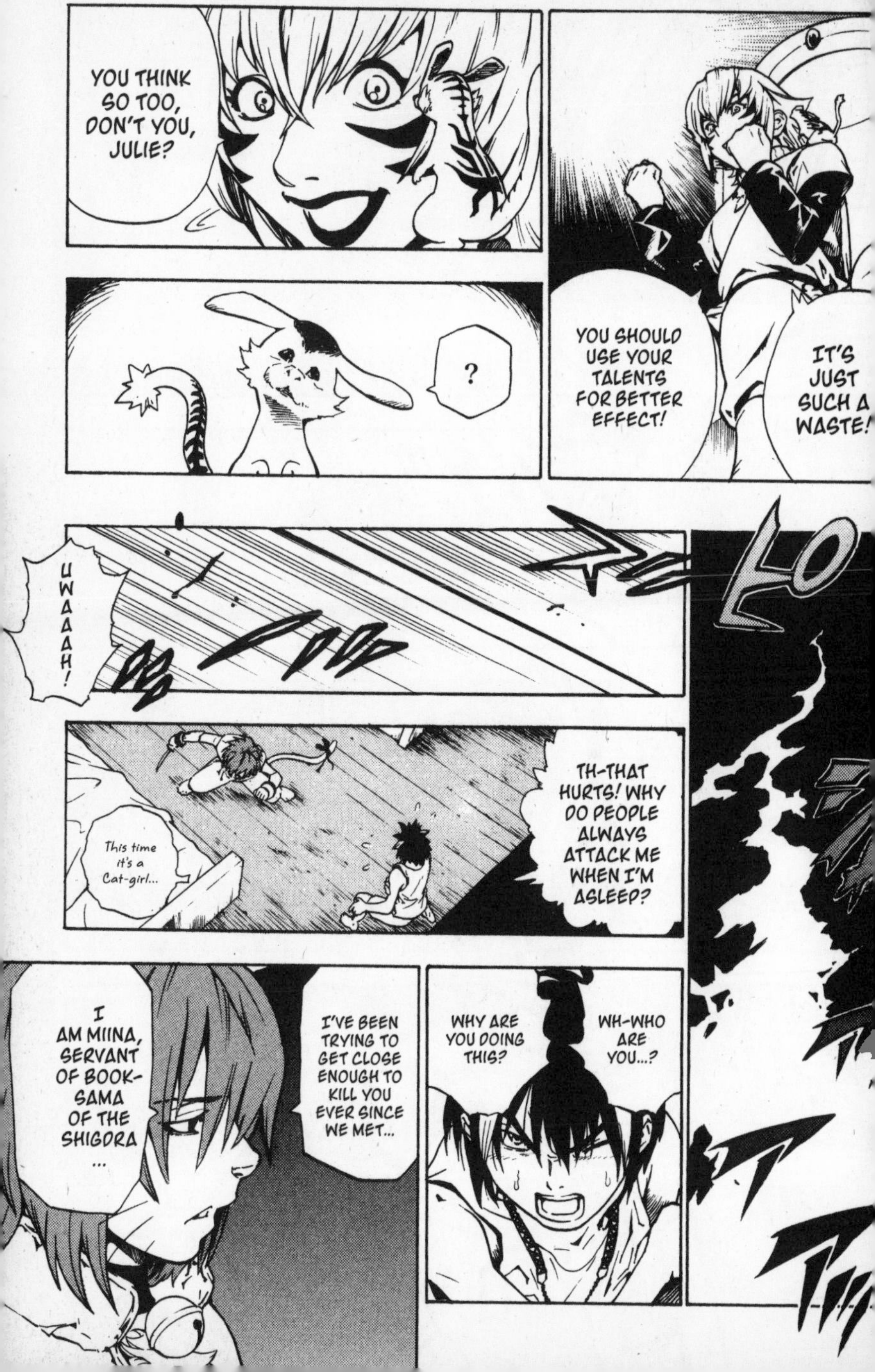
IT'S JUST SUCH A WASTE!
YOU SHOULD USE YOUR TALENTS FOR BETTER EFFECT!
YOU THINK SO TOO, DON'T YOU, JULIE?
?
UWAAAAH!
TH-THAT HURTS! WHY DO PEOPLE ALWAYS ATTACK ME WHEN I'M ASLEEP?
This time it's a Cat-girl...
WH-WHO ARE YOU...?
WHY ARE YOU DOING THIS?
I'VE BEEN TRYING TO GET CLOSE ENOUGH TO KILL YOU EVER SINCE WE MET...
I AM MIINA, SERVANT OF BOOK-SAMA OF THE SHIGORA ...

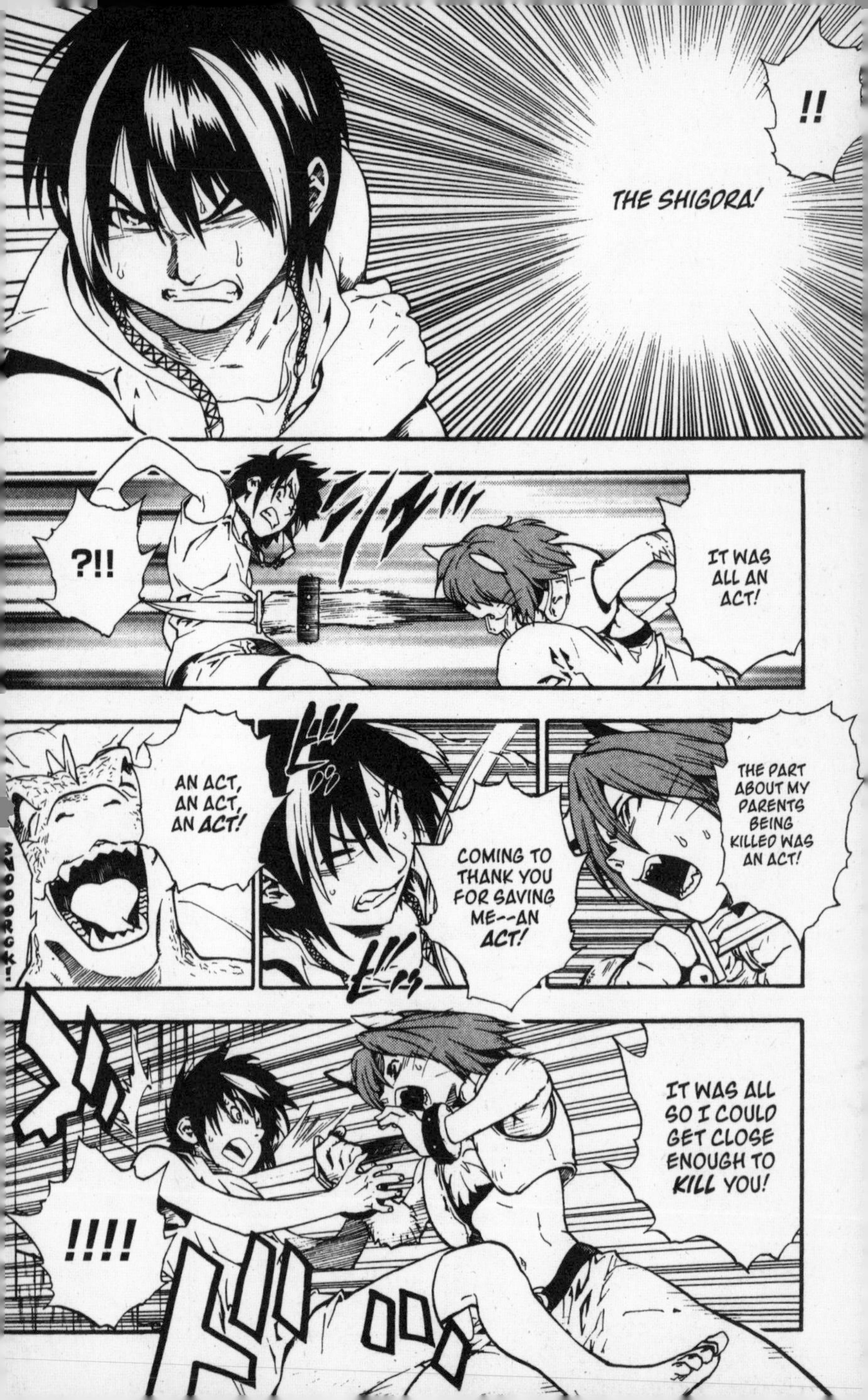
!!
THE SHIGORA!
IT WAS ALL AN ACT!
?!!
THE PART ABOUT MY PARENTS BEING KILLED WAS AN ACT!
COMING TO THANK YOU FOR SAVING ME--AN ACT!
AN ACT, AN ACT, AN ACT!
SWOOOORGK!!
IT WAS ALL SO I COULD GET CLOSE ENOUGH TO KILL YOU!
!!!!

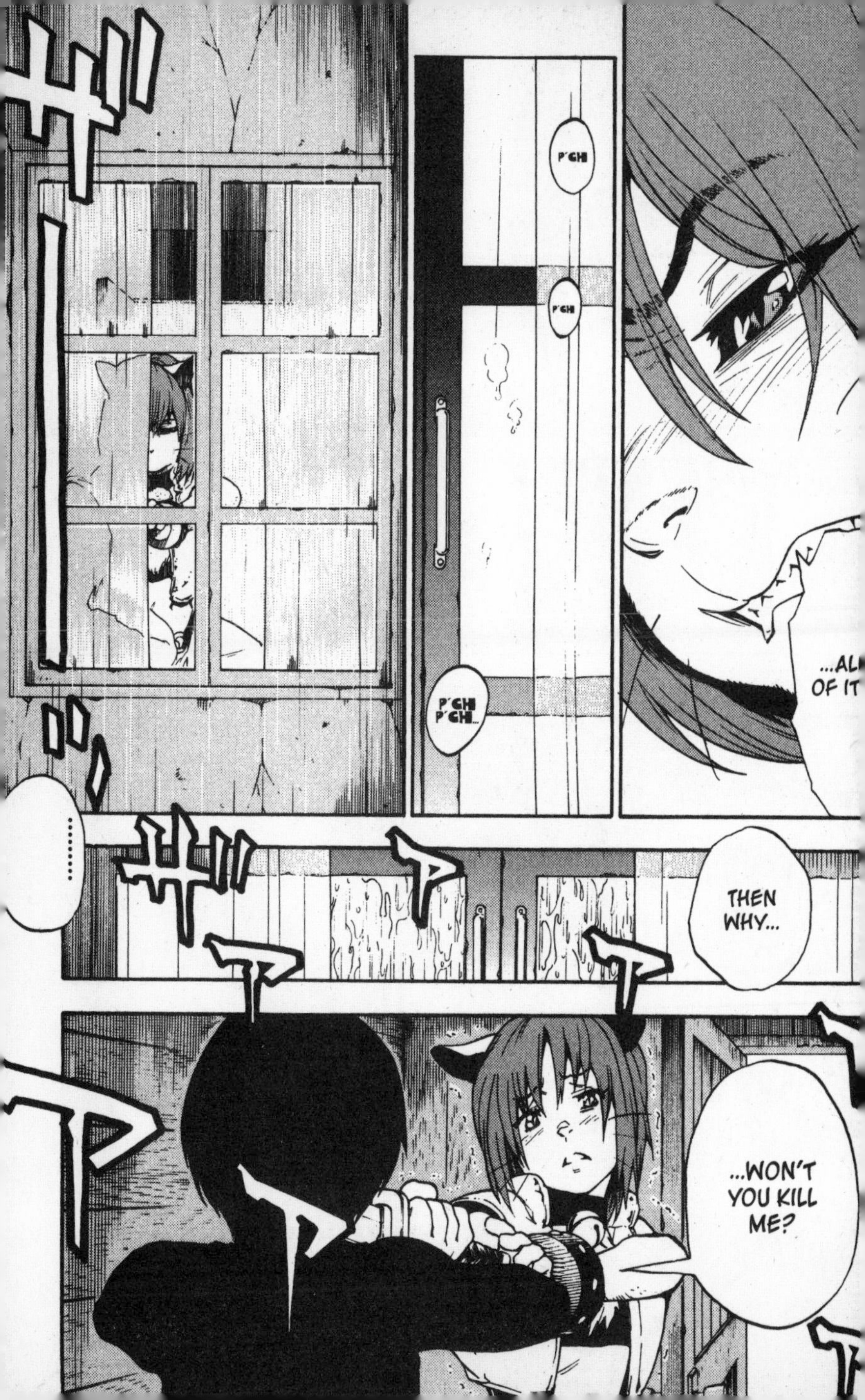
...AL OF IT
P'CHI
P'CHI
P'CHI P'CHI...
THEN WHY...
......
...WON'T YOU KILL ME?

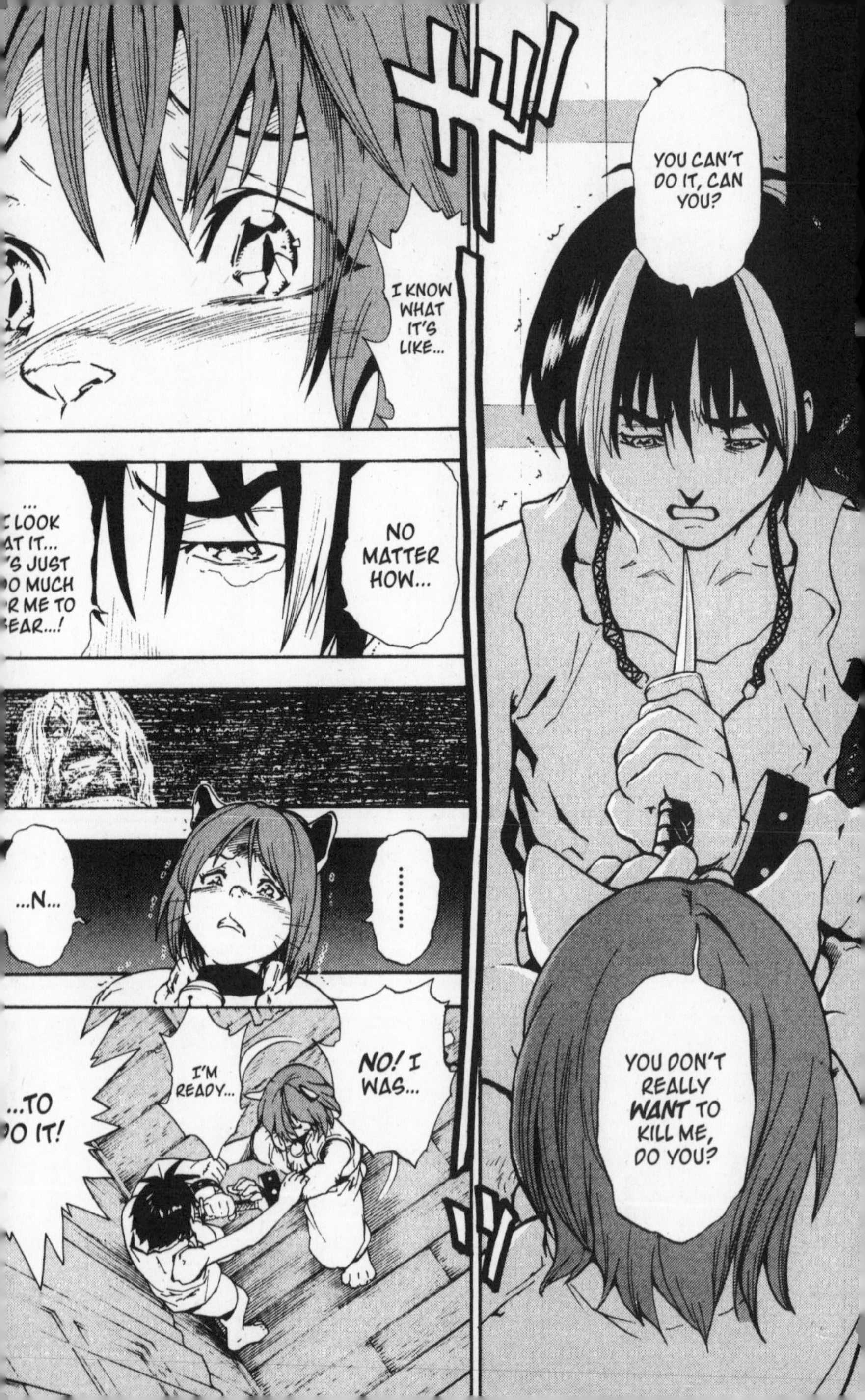
YOU CAN'T DO IT, CAN YOU?
YOU DON'T REALLY WANT TO KILL ME, DO YOU?
I KNOW WHAT IT'S LIKE...
NO MATTER HOW...
... LOOK AT IT... 'S JUST O MUCH R ME TO EAR...!
....
...N...
NO! I WAS...
I'M READY...
...TO O IT!

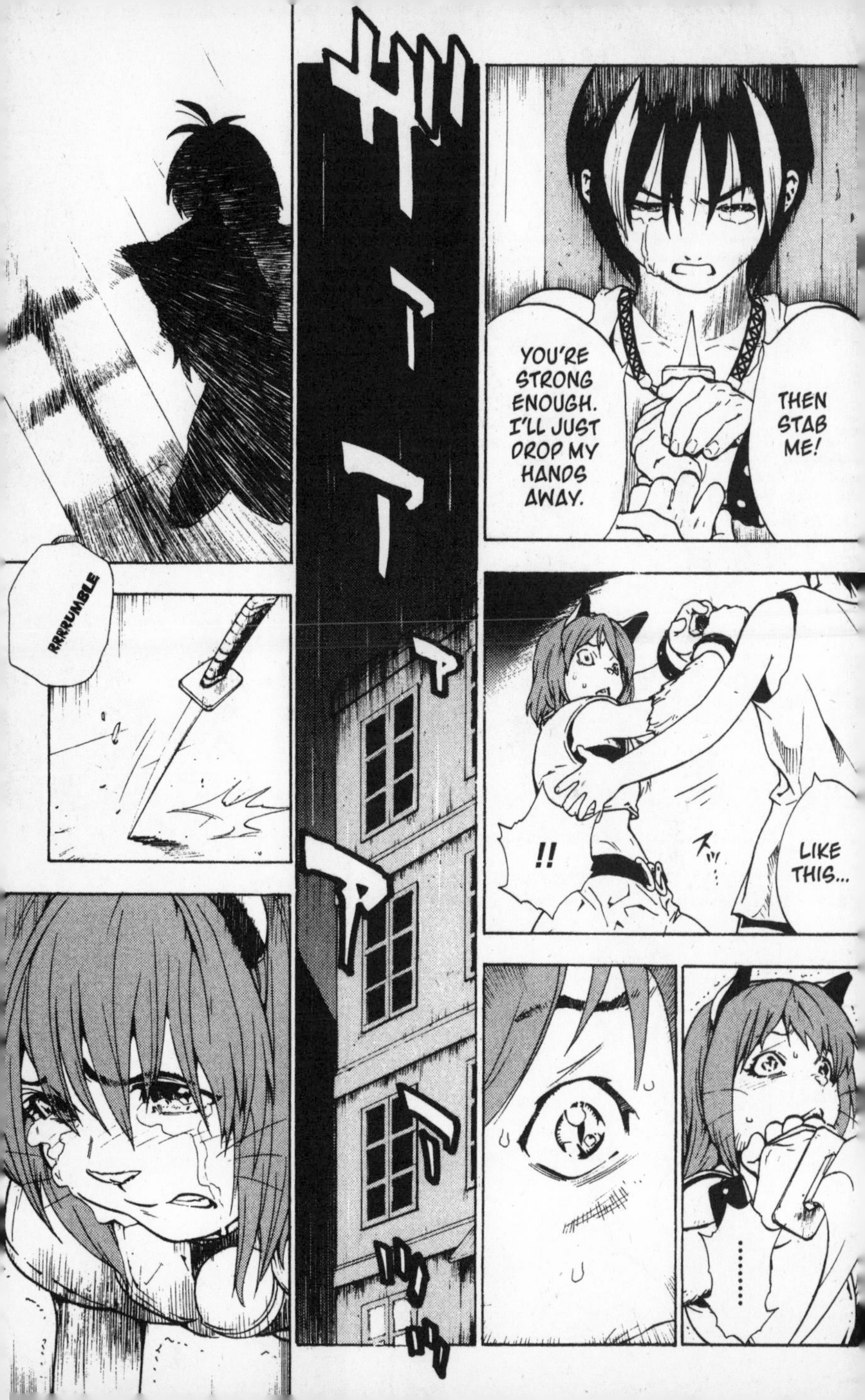
YOU'RE STRONG ENOUGH. I'LL JUST DROP MY HANDS AWAY.
THEN STAB ME!
LIKE THIS...
!!
......
RRRRUMBLE

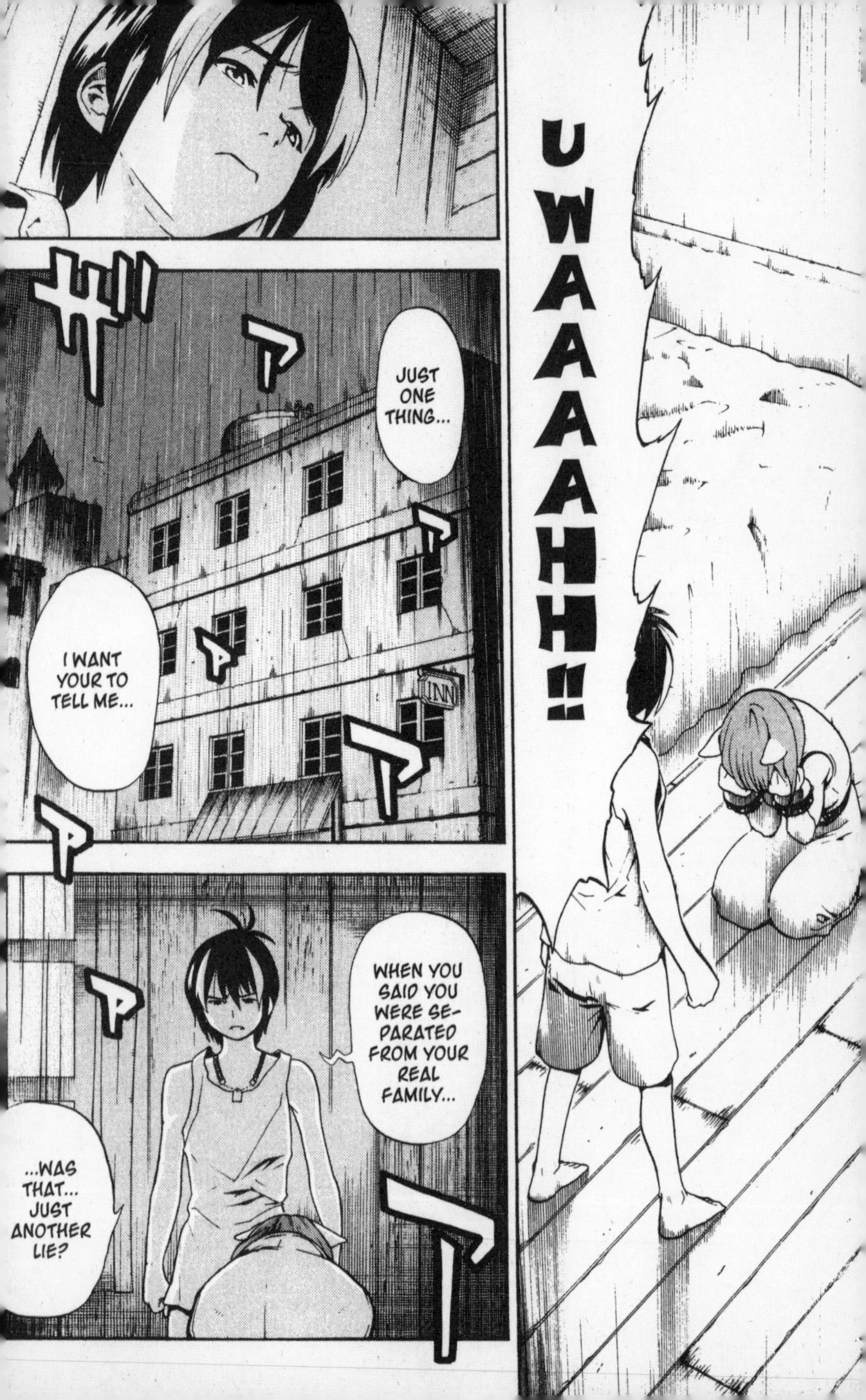
UWAAAAAHH!!
JUST ONE THING...
I WANT YOUR TO TELL ME...
INN
WHEN YOU SAID YOU WERE SE-PARATED FROM YOUR REAL FAMILY...
...WAS THAT... JUST ANOTHER LIE?

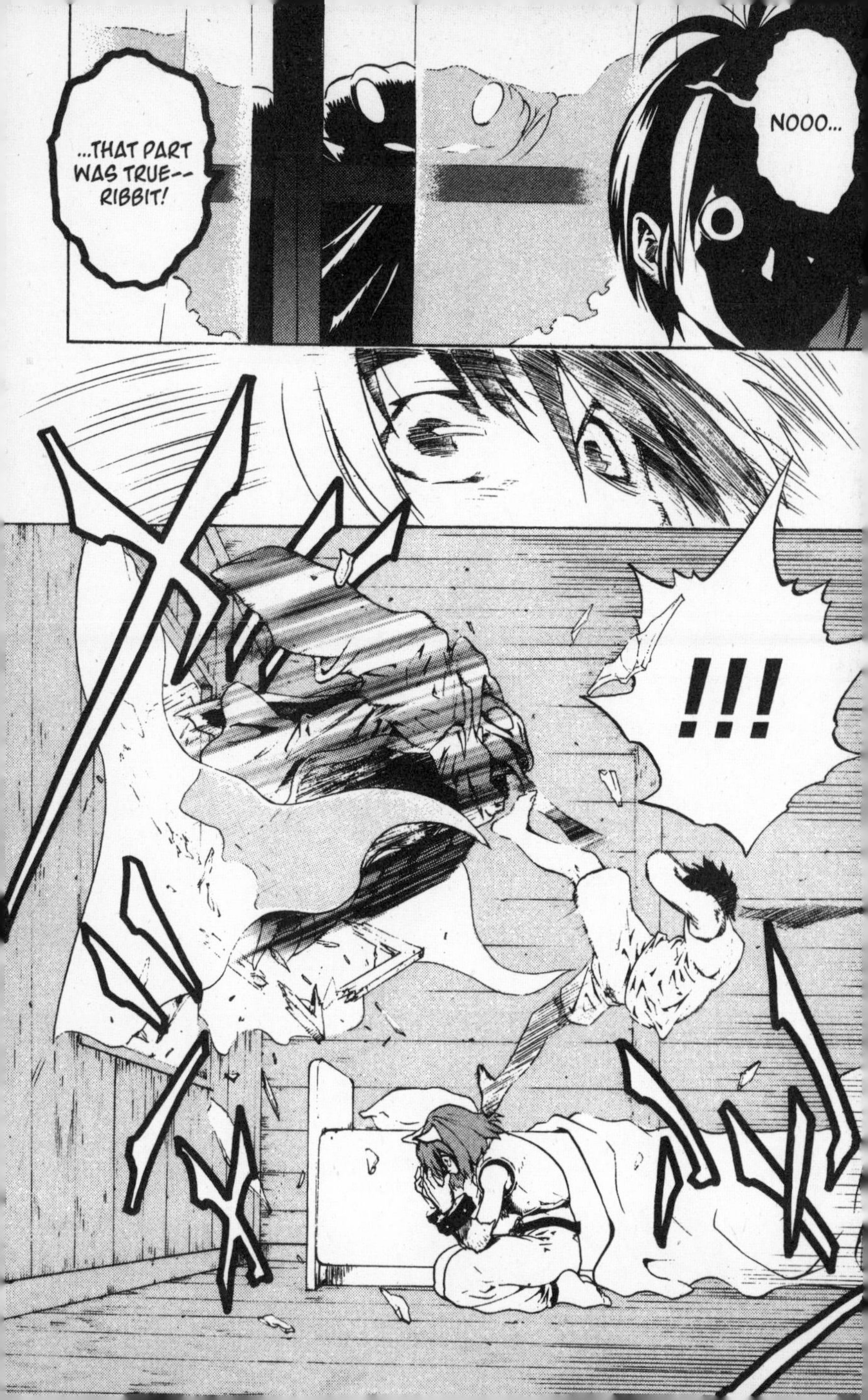
NOOO...
...THAT PART WAS TRUE--RIBBIT!
!!!

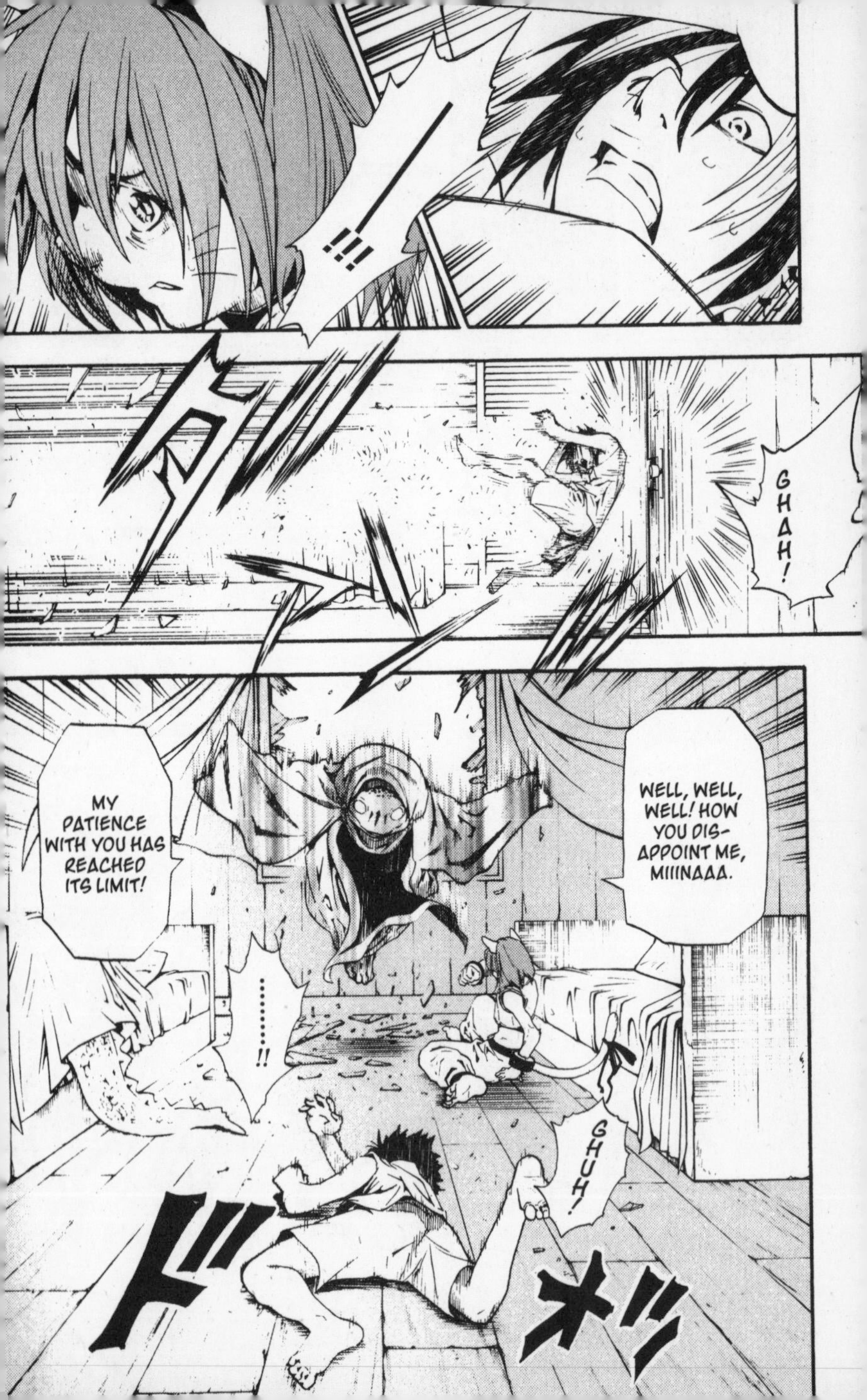
!!!
GHAH!
WELL, WELL, WELL! HOW YOU DIS-APPOINT ME, MIIINAAA.
MY PATIENCE WITH YOU HAS REACHED ITS LIMIT!
......!!
GHUH!

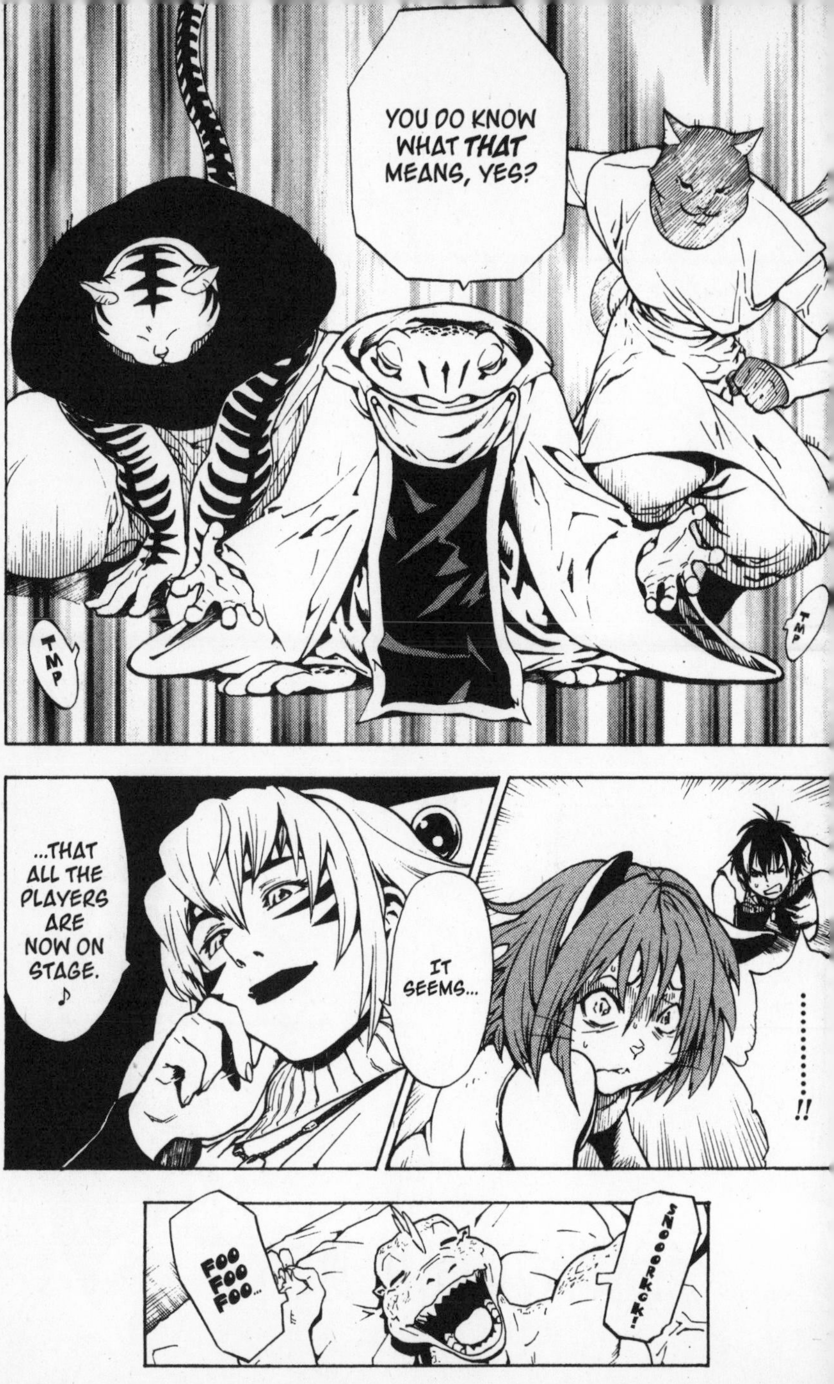
YOU DO KNOW WHAT THAT MEANS, YES?
TMP
TMP
..........!!
IT SEEMS...
...THAT ALL THE PLAYERS ARE NOW ON STAGE. ♪
SNOOORKCK!
FOO FOO FOO...

A Retelling of a Classic

BRAVE STORY

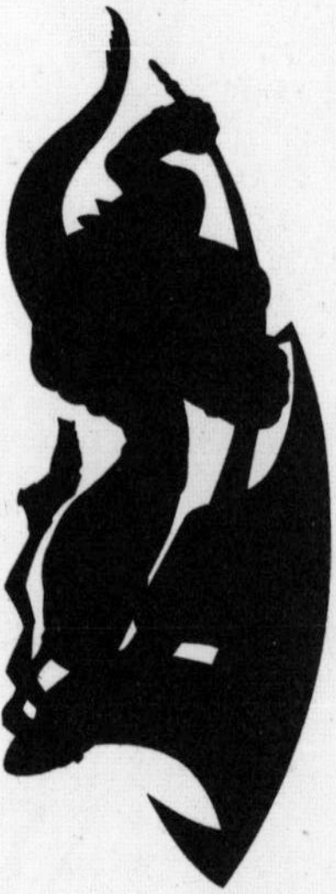

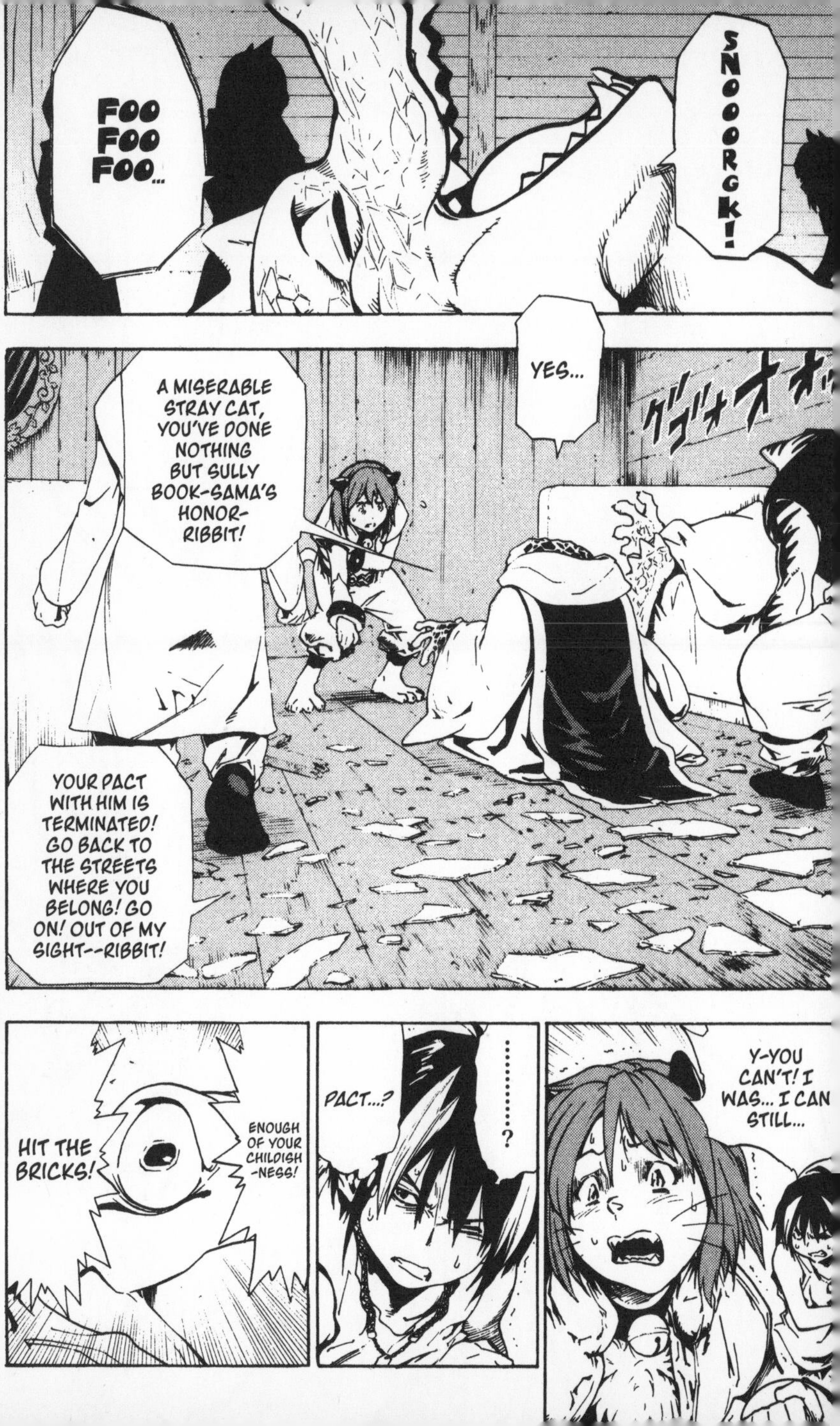
SNOOOORGK!
FOO FOO FOO...
YES...
グゴォオオッ
A MISERABLE STRAY CAT, YOU'VE DONE NOTHING BUT SULLY BOOK-SAMA'S HONOR-RIBBIT!
YOUR PACT WITH HIM IS TERMINATED! GO BACK TO THE STREETS WHERE YOU BELONG! GO ON! OUT OF MY SIGHT--RIBBIT!
Y-YOU CAN'T! I WAS... I CAN STILL...
.........?
PACT...?
ENOUGH OF YOUR CHILDISH-NESS!
HIT THE BRICKS!

Chapter 35 The Girl Who Hungered for Love

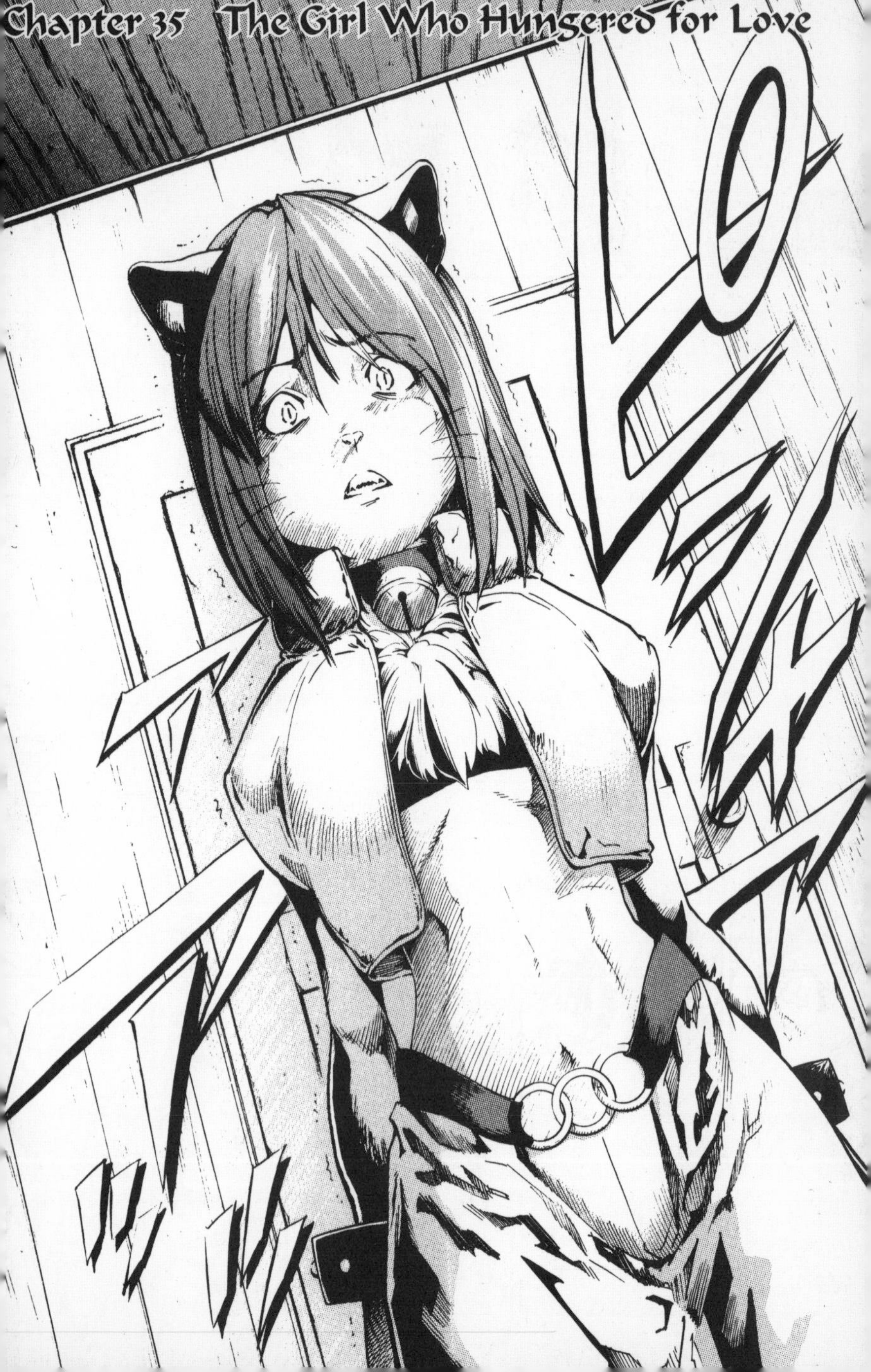

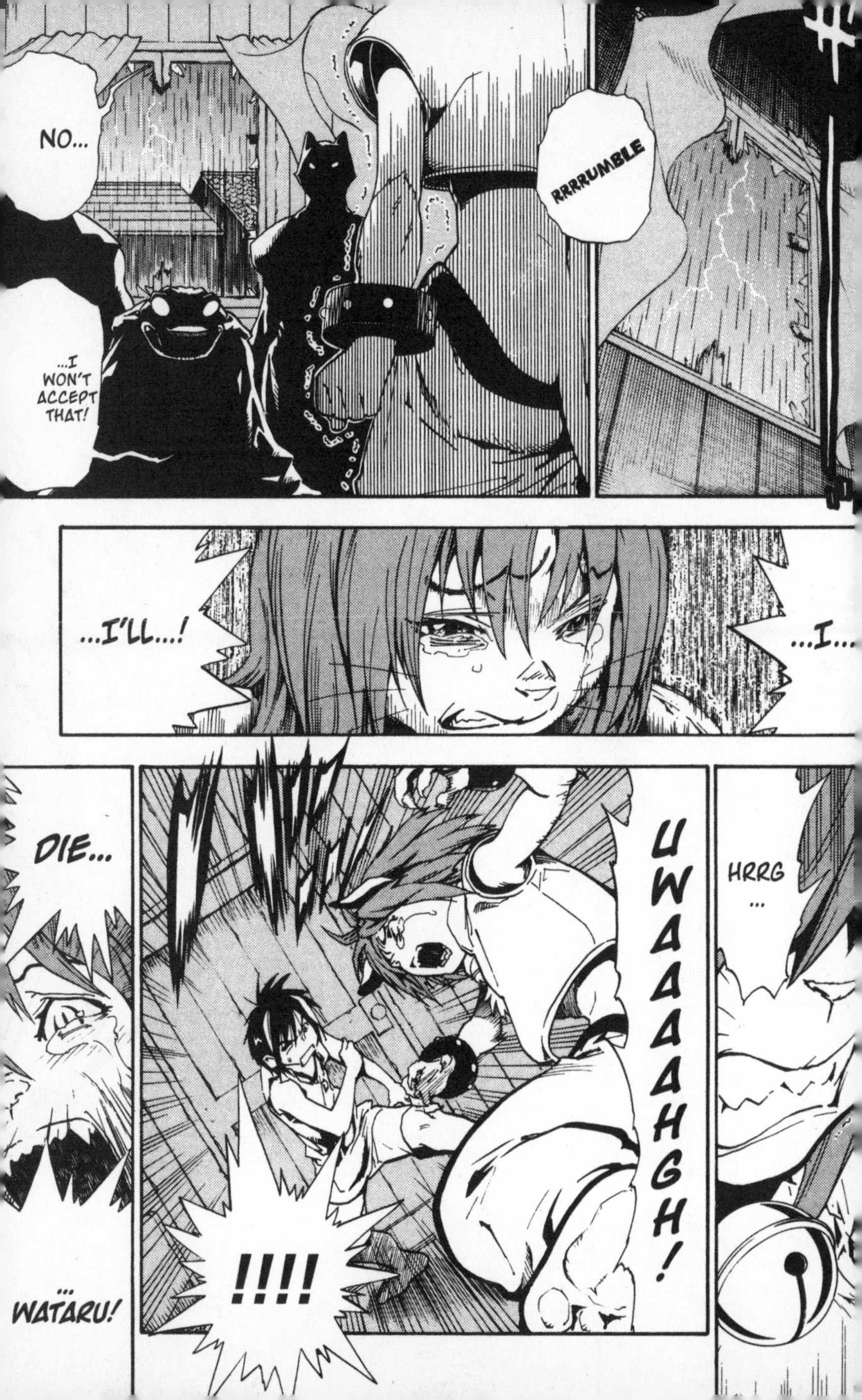
RRRRUMBLE
NO...
...I WON'T ACCEPT THAT!
...I...
...I'LL...!
HRRG ...
UWAAAAAHGH!
!!!!
DIE...
... WATARU!

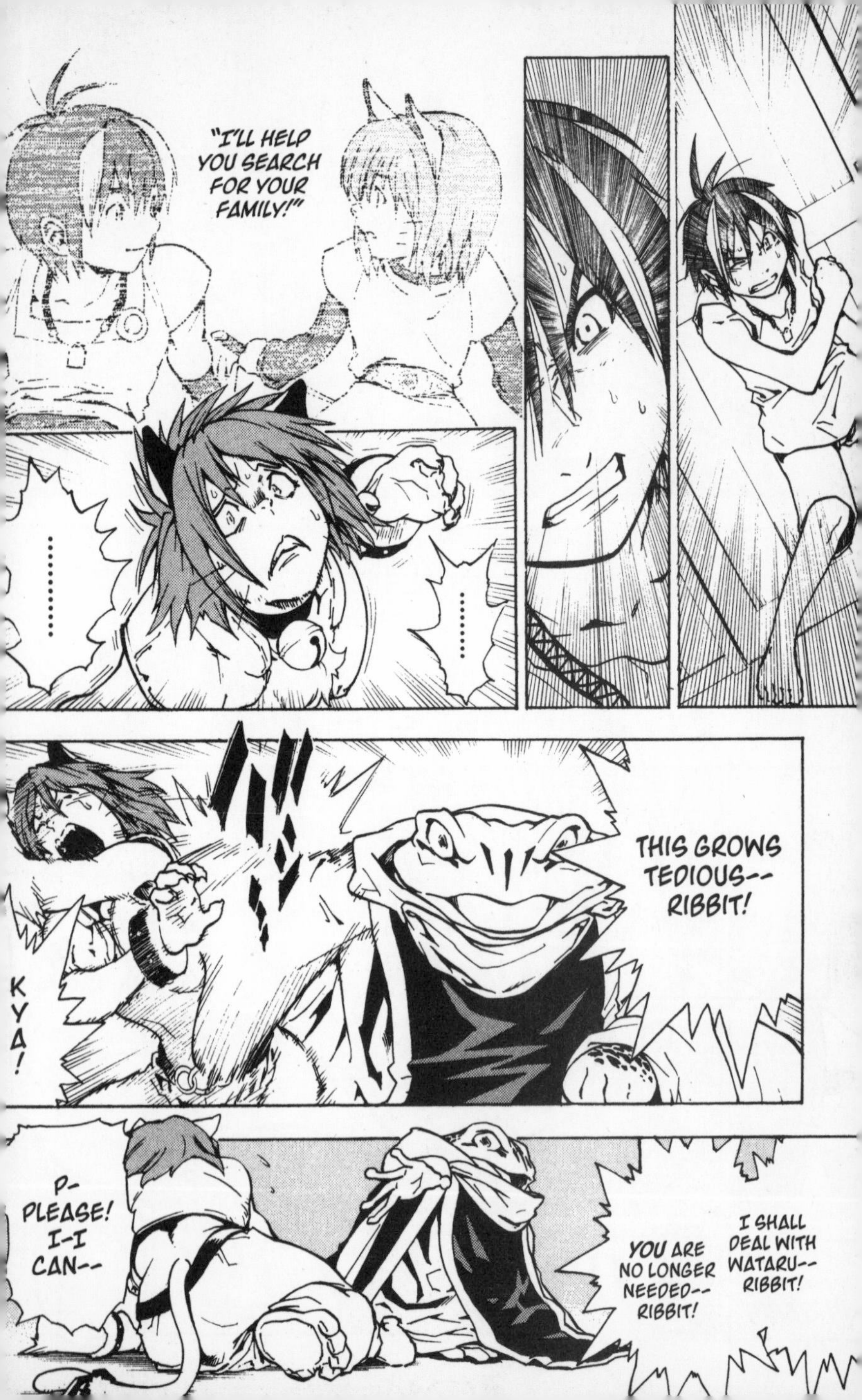
"I'LL HELP YOU SEARCH FOR YOUR FAMILY!"
......
......
THIS GROWS TEDIOUS--RIBBIT!
KYA!
I SHALL DEAL WITH WATARU--RIBBIT!
YOU ARE NO LONGER NEEDED--RIBBIT!
P-PLEASE! I-I CAN--

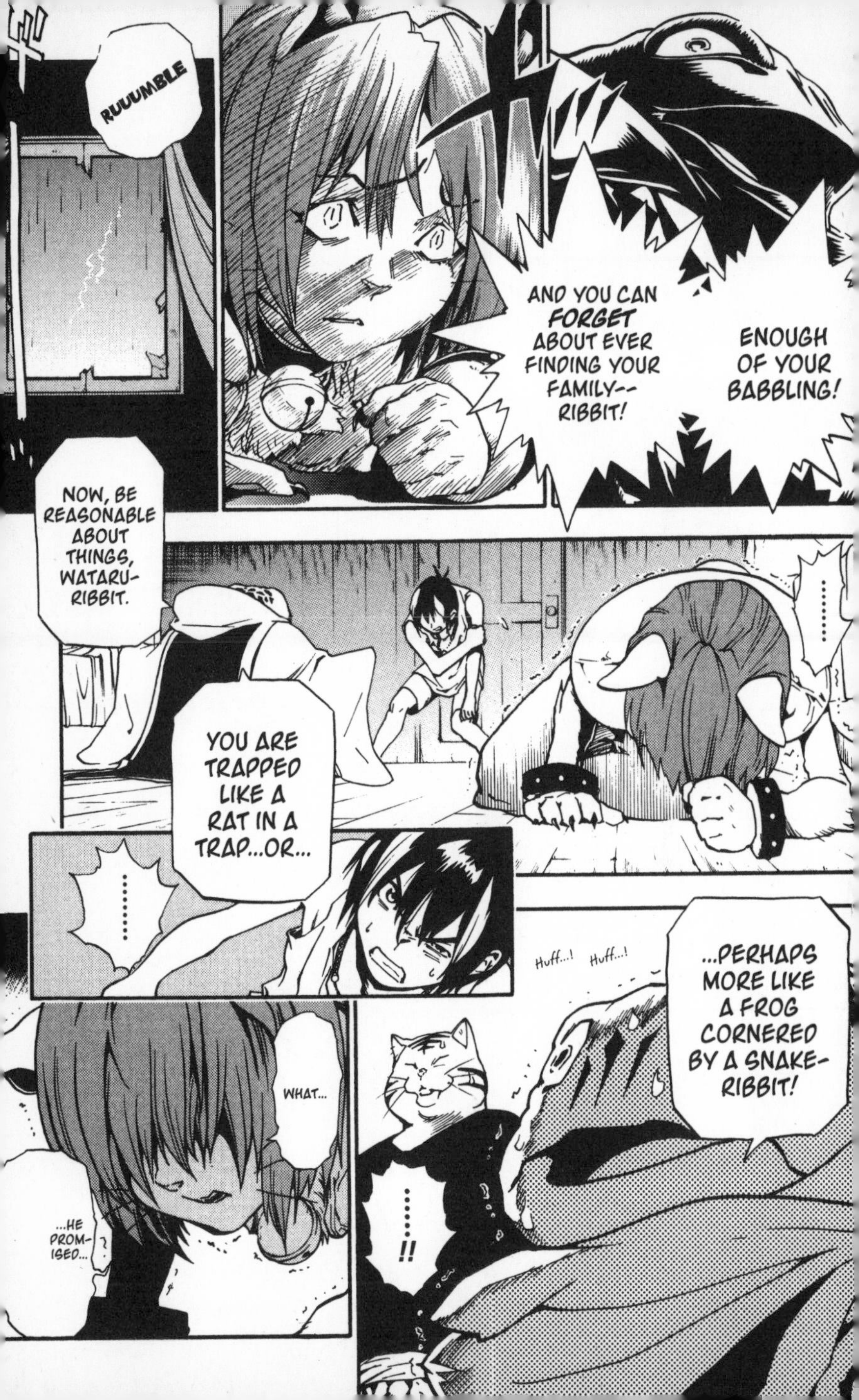
ENOUGH OF YOUR BABBLING!
AND YOU CAN FORGET ABOUT EVER FINDING YOUR FAMILY--RIBBIT!
RUUUMBLE
NOW, BE REASONABLE ABOUT THINGS, WATARU-RIBBIT.
......
YOU ARE TRAPPED LIKE A RAT IN A TRAP...OR...
Huff...! Huff...!
...PERHAPS MORE LIKE A FROG CORNERED BY A SNAKE-RIBBIT!
......
......!!
WHAT...
...HE PROMISED...

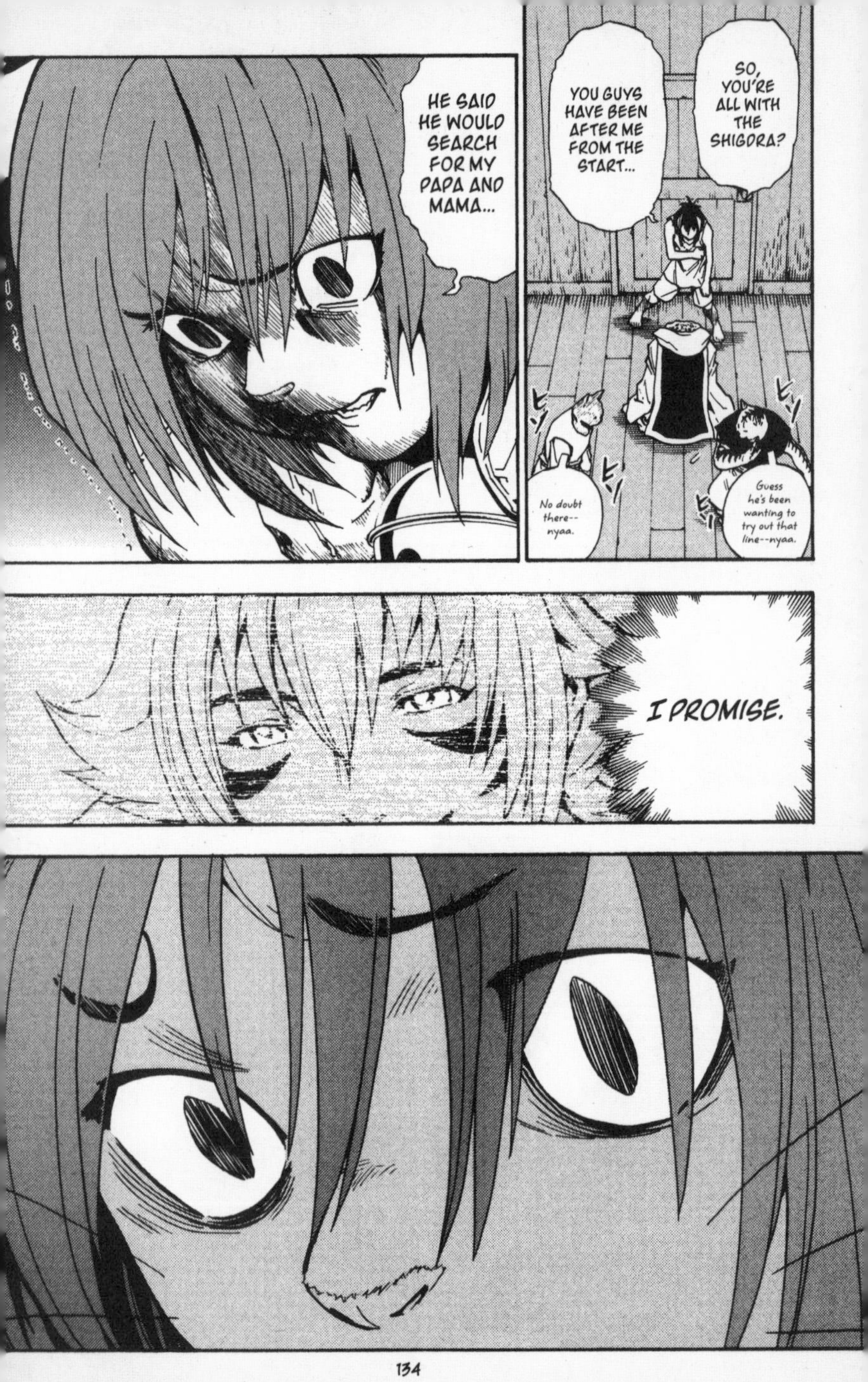
SO, YOU'RE ALL WITH THE SHIGORA?
YOU GUYS HAVE BEEN AFTER ME FROM THE START...
Guess he's been wanting to try out that line--nyaa.
No doubt there--nyaa.
HE SAID HE WOULD SEARCH FOR MY PAPA AND MAMA...
I PROMISE.

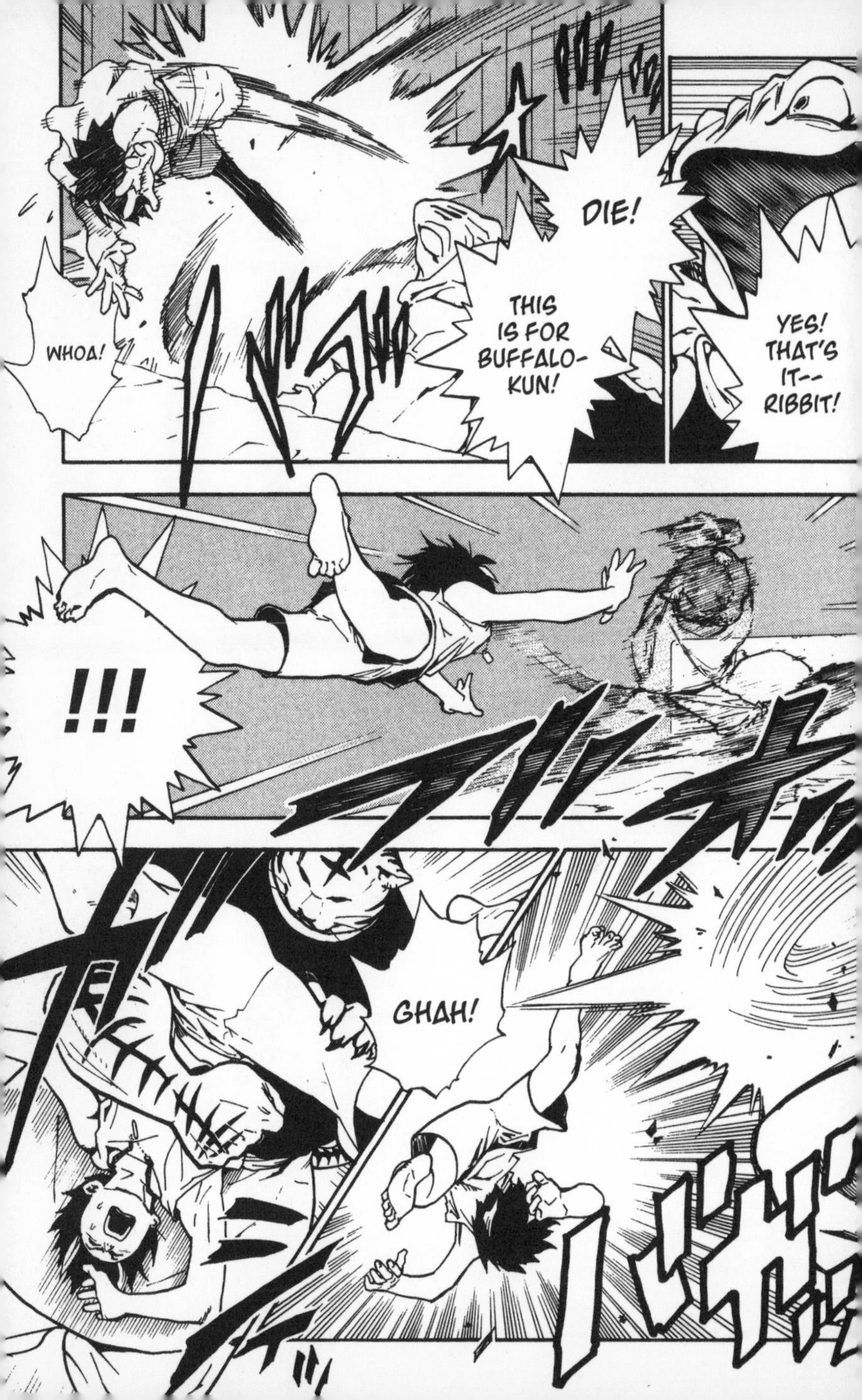
YES! THAT'S IT-- RIBBIT!
DIE!
THIS IS FOR BUFFALO-KUN!
WHOA!
!!!
GHAH!

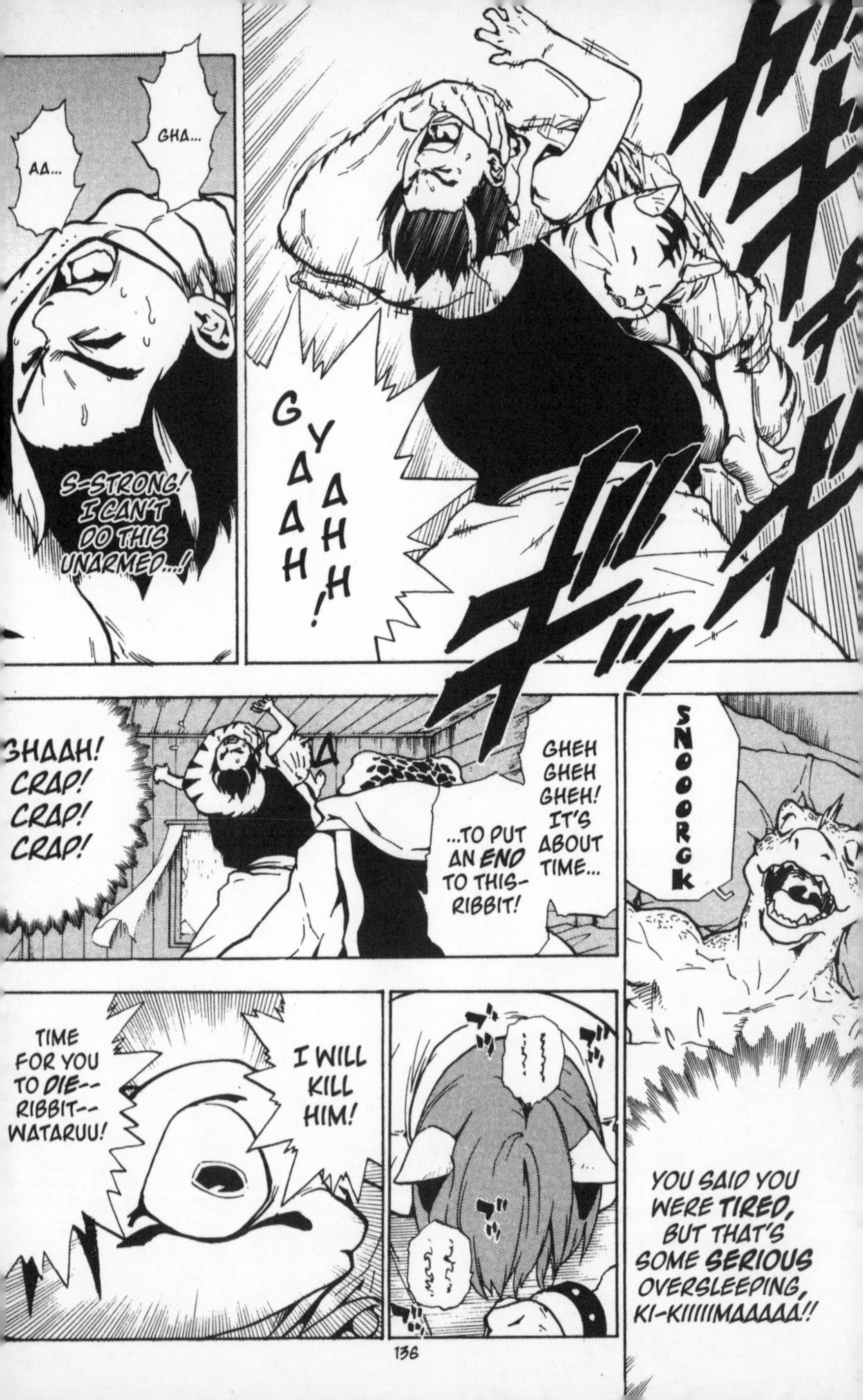
GYAAAHHH!
GHA...
AA...
S-STRONG! I CAN'T DO THIS UNARMED...!
SNOOOORGK
YOU SAID YOU WERE TIRED, BUT THAT'S SOME SERIOUS OVERSLEEPING, KI-KIIIIIMAAAAA!!
GHEH GHEH GHEH! IT'S ABOUT TIME...
...TO PUT AN END TO THIS-RIBBIT!
GHAAH! CRAP! CRAP! CRAP!
I WILL KILL HIM!
TIME FOR YOU TO DIE--RIBBIT--WATARUU!

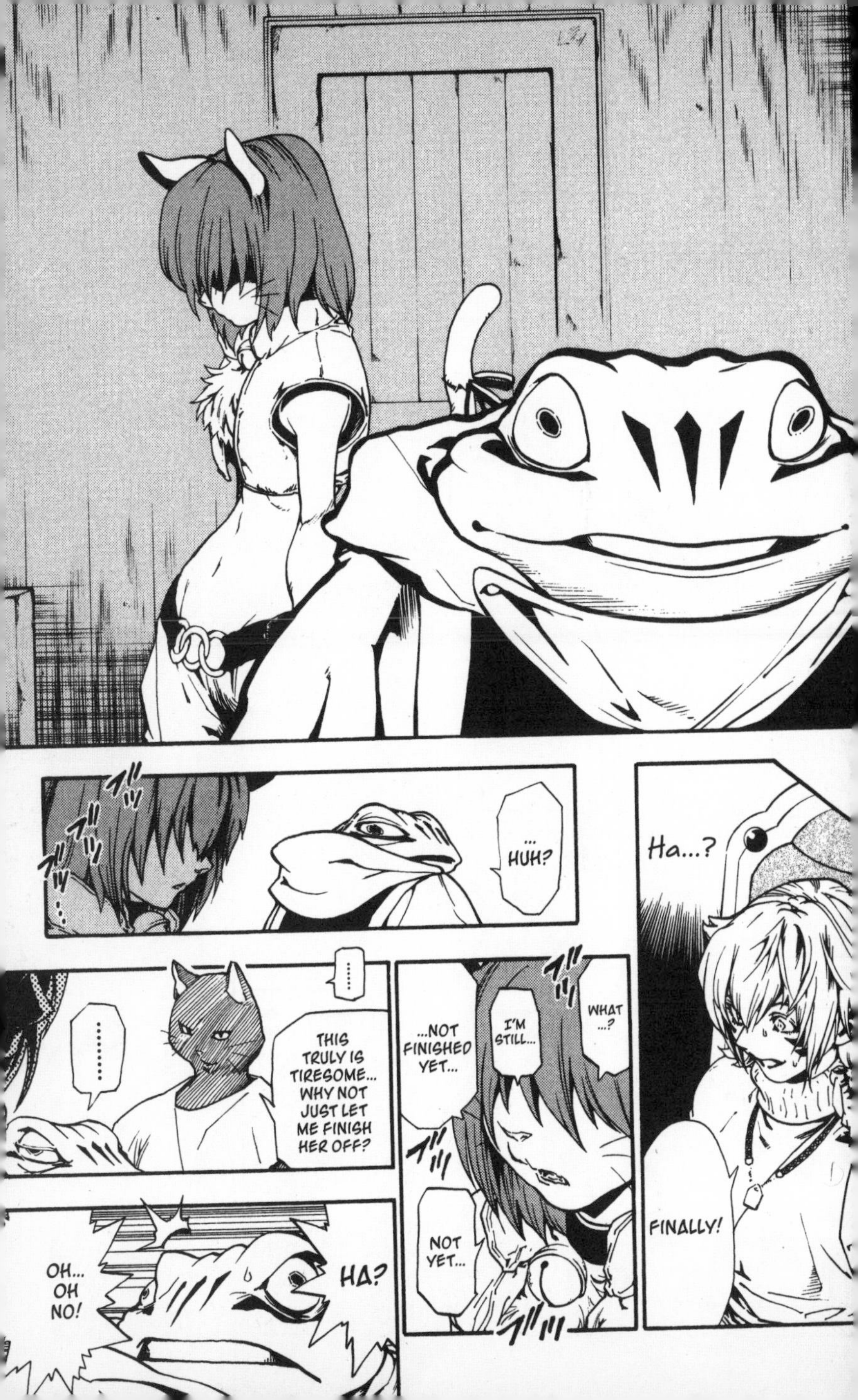
Ha...?
FINALLY!
... HUH?
...
WHAT ...?
I'M STILL...
...NOT FINISHED YET...
NOT YET...
......
THIS TRULY IS TIRESOME... WHY NOT JUST LET ME FINISH HER OFF?
....
HA?
OH... OH NO!

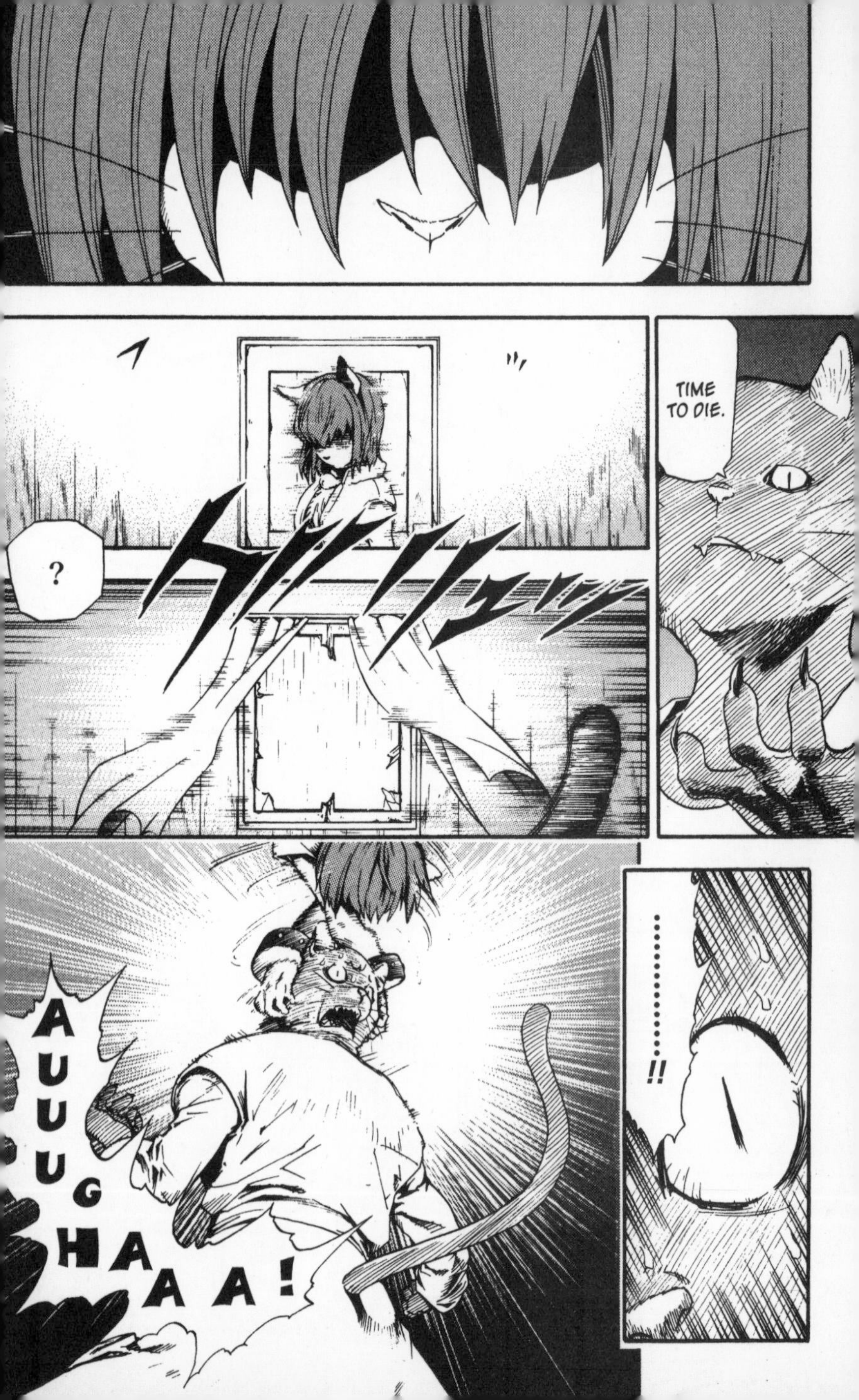

TIME TO DIE.
?
......!!
AUUUGHAAAA!

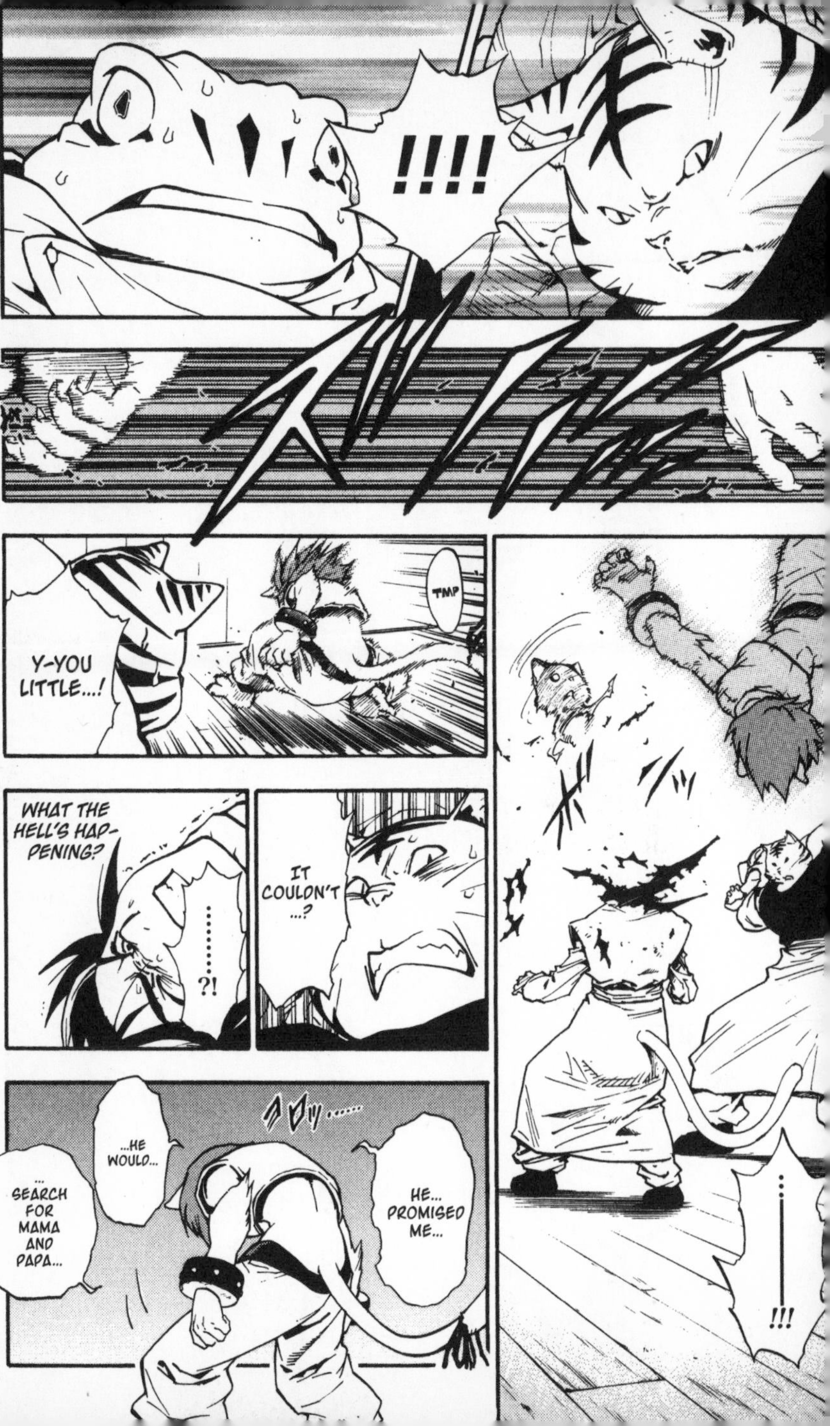
!!!!
......!!!
TMP
Y-YOU LITTLE...!
IT COULDN'T ...?
WHAT THE HELL'S HAP-PENING?
......?!
HE... PROMISED ME...
...HE WOULD...
... SEARCH FOR MAMA AND PAPA...

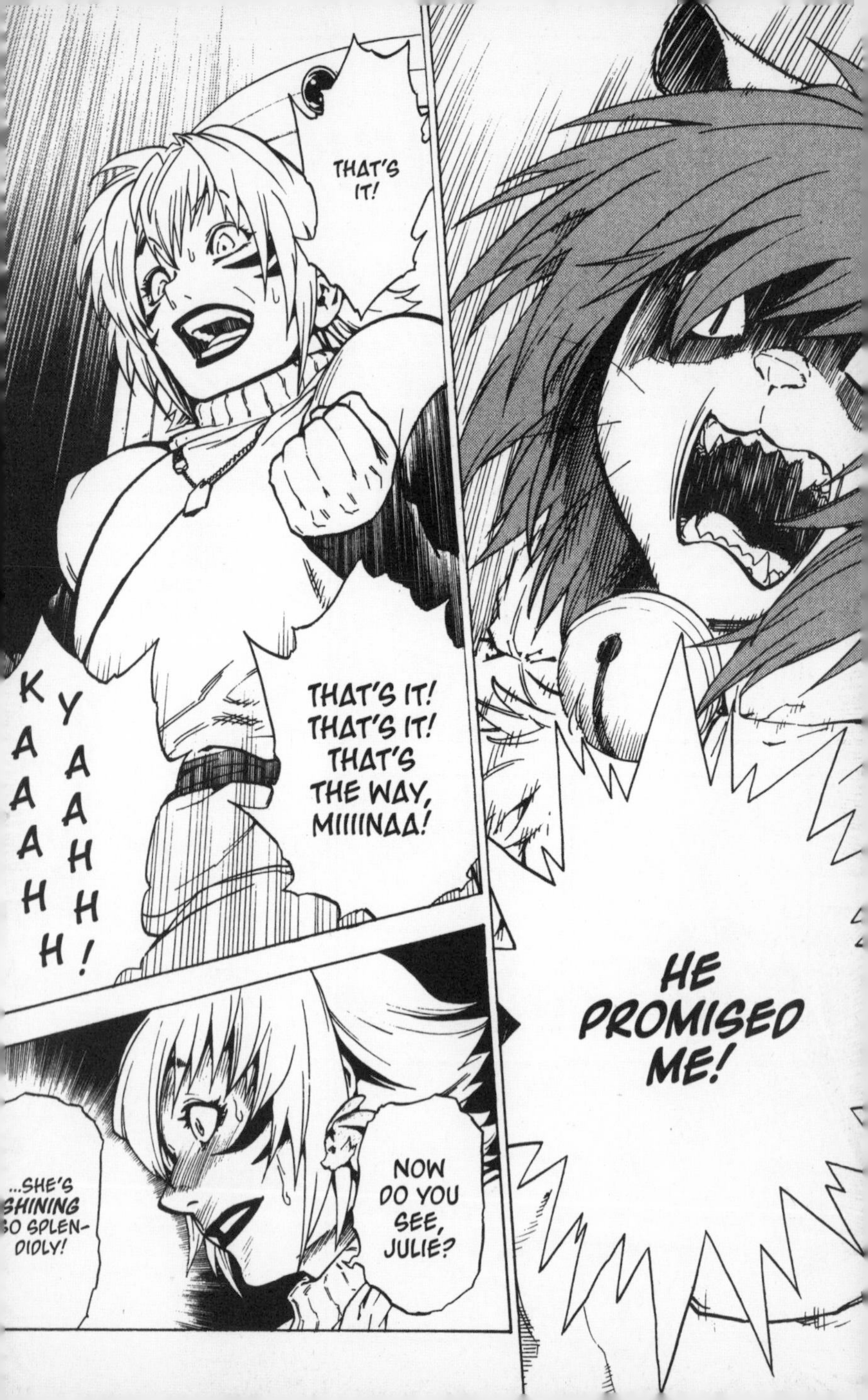
HE PROMISED ME!
THAT'S IT!
THAT'S IT! THAT'S IT! THAT'S THE WAY, MIIIINAA!
KAAAAHH
YAAHHH!
NOW DO YOU SEE, JULIE?
...SHE'S SHINING SO SPLEN-DIDLY!

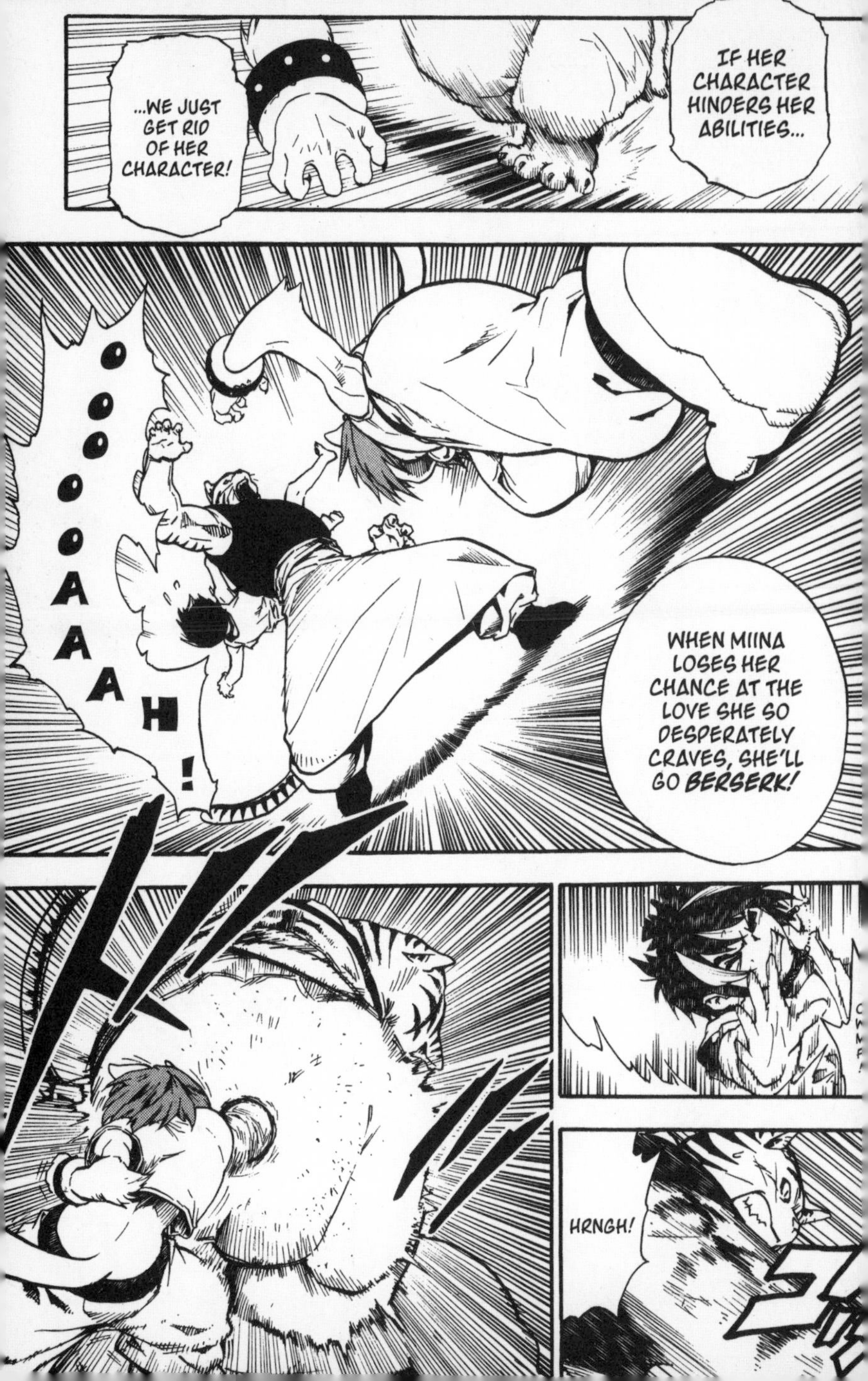
IF HER CHARACTER HINDERS HER ABILITIES...
...WE JUST GET RID OF HER CHARACTER!
WHEN MIINA LOSES HER CHANCE AT THE LOVE SHE SO DESPERATELY CRAVES, SHE'LL GO BERSERK!
OOOOOAAAAH!
HRNGH!

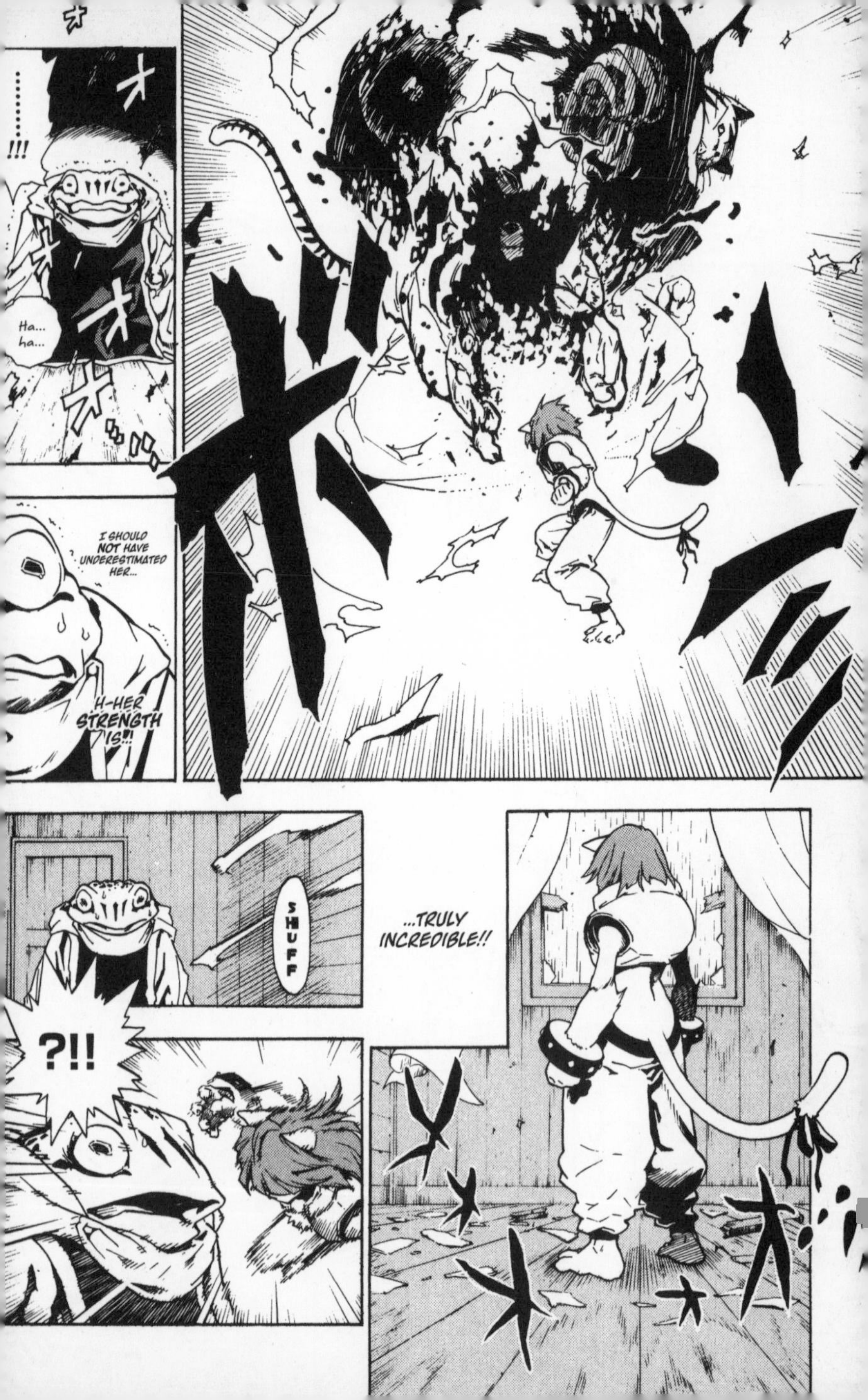
......!!!
Ha... ha...
I SHOULD NOT HAVE UNDERESTIMATED HER...
H-HER STRENGTH IS!!
...TRULY INCREDIBLE!!
SHUFF
?!!

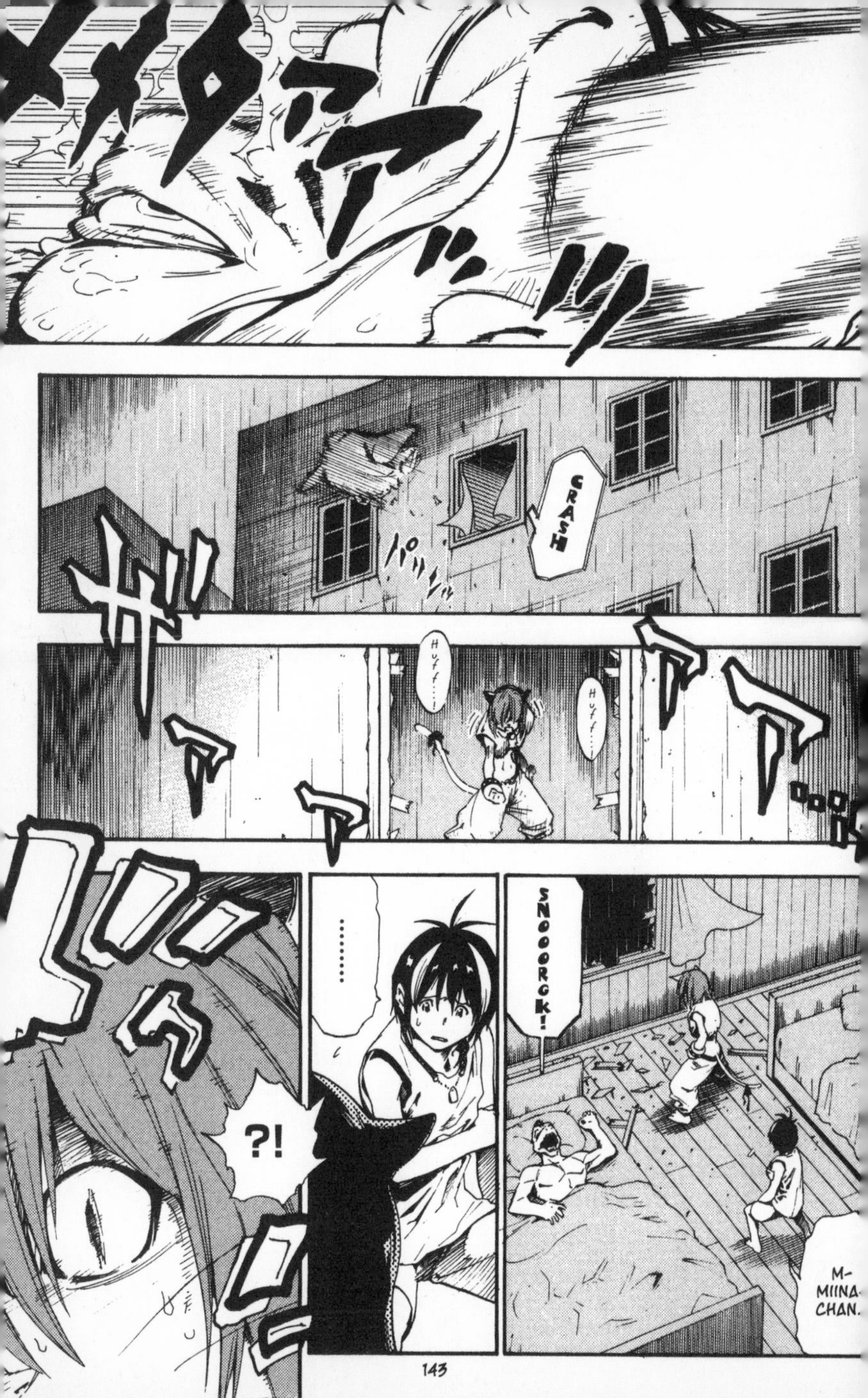
CRASH
Huff...!
Huff...!
SNOOORGK!
M-MIINA-CHAN.
....
?!

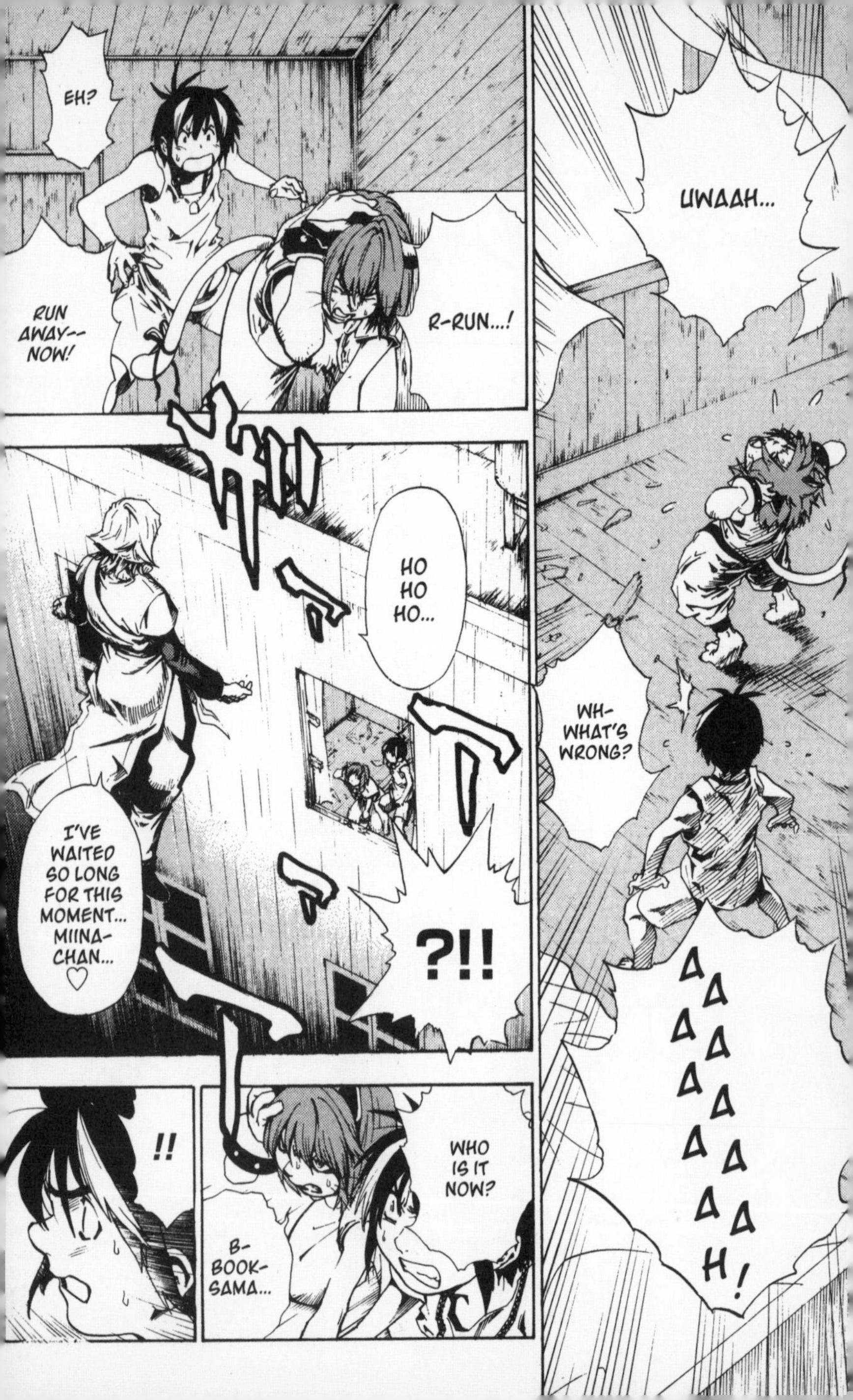

UWAAH...
WH-WHAT'S WRONG?
AAAAAAAAAAAH!
R-RUN...!
RUN AWAY--NOW!
EH?
HO HO HO...
I'VE WAITED SO LONG FOR THIS MOMENT... MIINA-CHAN... ♡
?!!
WHO IS IT NOW?
B-BOOK-SAMA...
!!

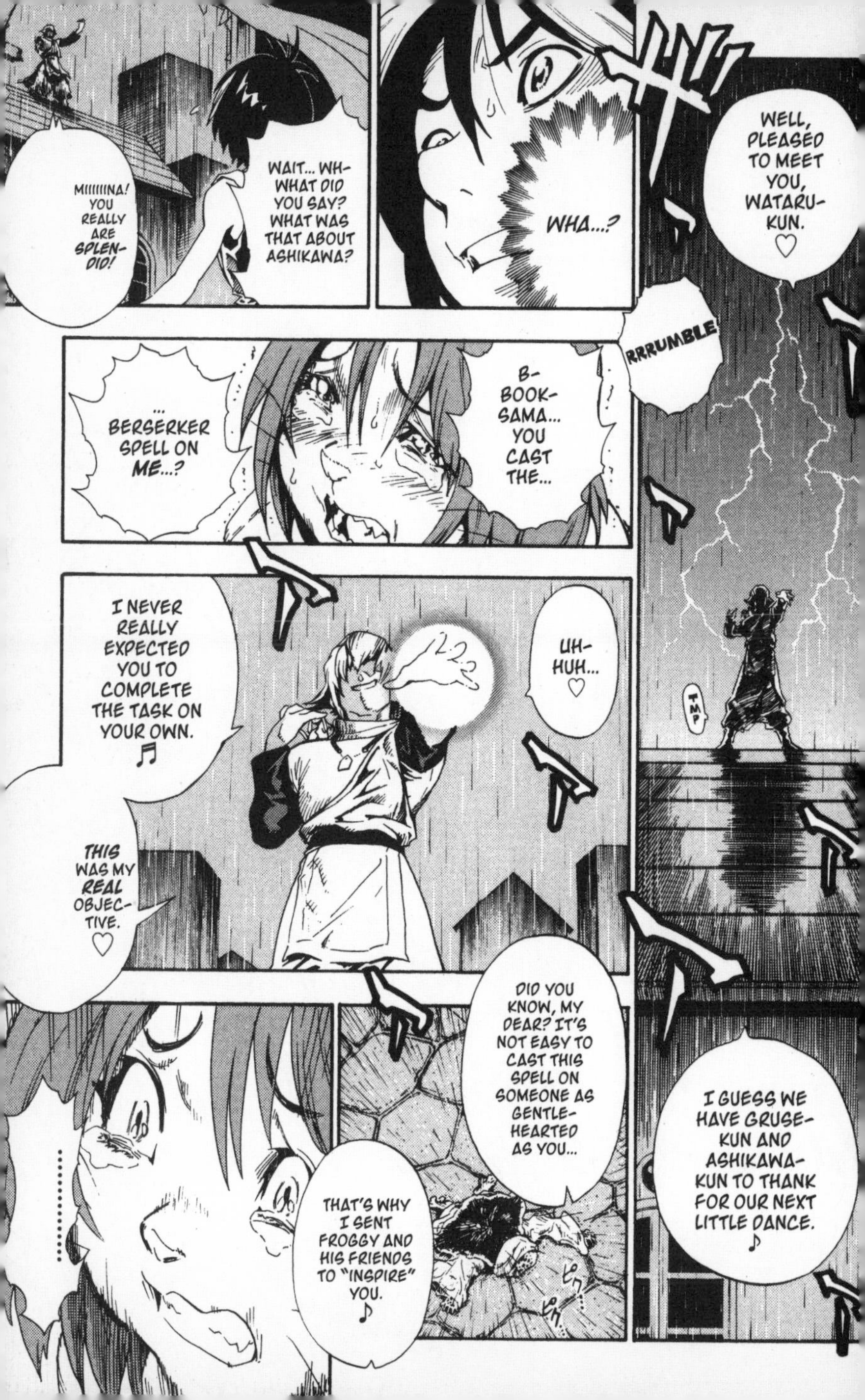
WELL, PLEASED TO MEET YOU, WATARU-KUN. ♡
RRRUMBLE
TMP
I GUESS WE HAVE GRUSE-KUN AND ASHIKAWA-KUN TO THANK FOR OUR NEXT LITTLE DANCE. ♪
WHA...?
WAIT... WH-WHAT DID YOU SAY? WHAT WAS THAT ABOUT ASHIKAWA?
MIIIIINA! YOU REALLY ARE SPLEN-DID!
B-BOOK-SAMA... YOU CAST THE...
... BERSERKER SPELL ON ME...?
UH-HUH... ♡
I NEVER REALLY EXPECTED YOU TO COMPLETE THE TASK ON YOUR OWN. ♫
THIS WAS MY REAL OBJEC-TIVE. ♡
DID YOU KNOW, MY DEAR? IT'S NOT EASY TO CAST THIS SPELL ON SOMEONE AS GENTLE-HEARTED AS YOU...
THAT'S WHY I SENT FROGGY AND HIS FRIENDS TO "INSPIRE" YOU. ♪

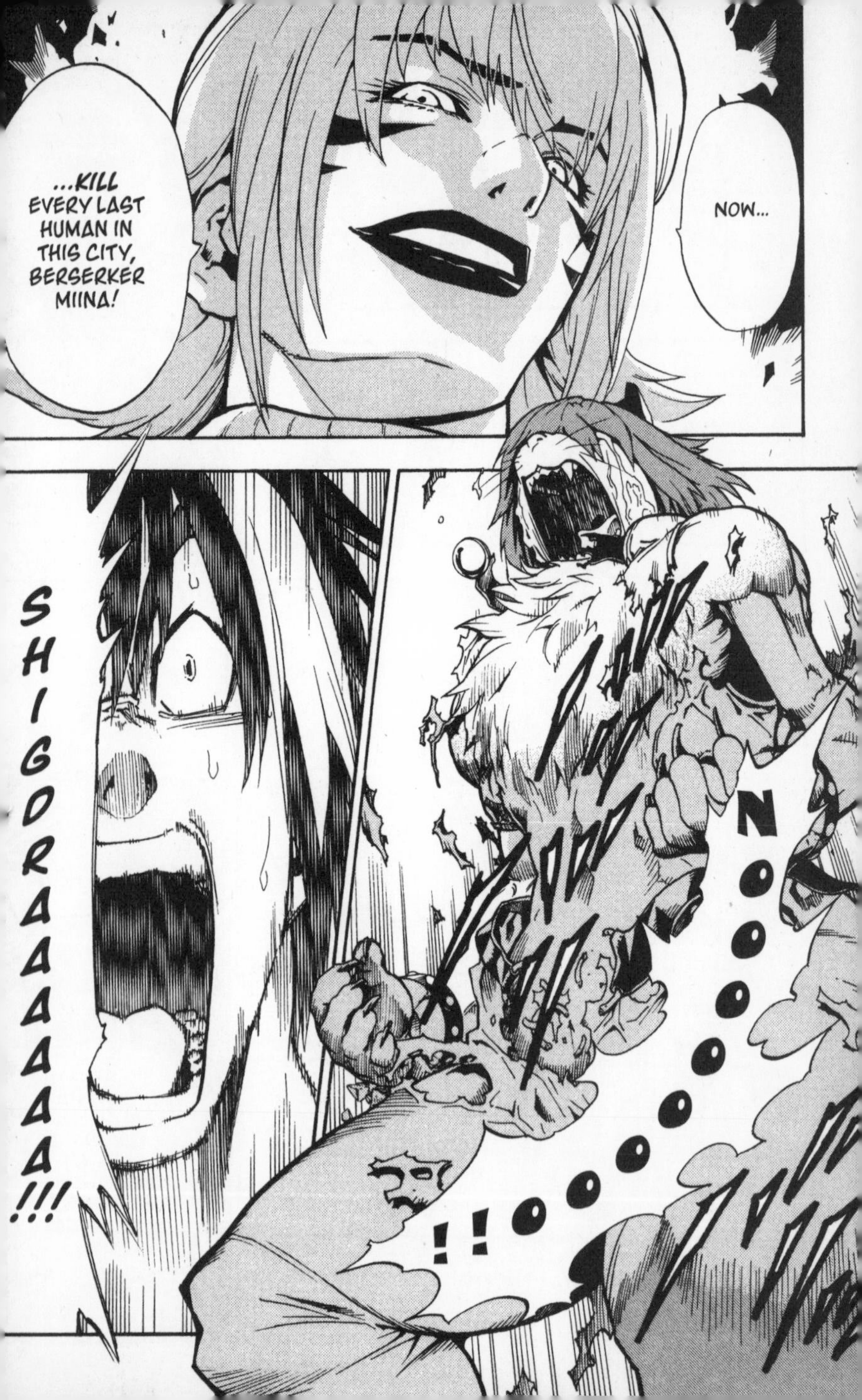
NOW...
...KILL EVERY LAST HUMAN IN THIS CITY, BERSERKER MIINA!
NOOOOOOOOO!!
SHIGORAAAAAAAA!!!

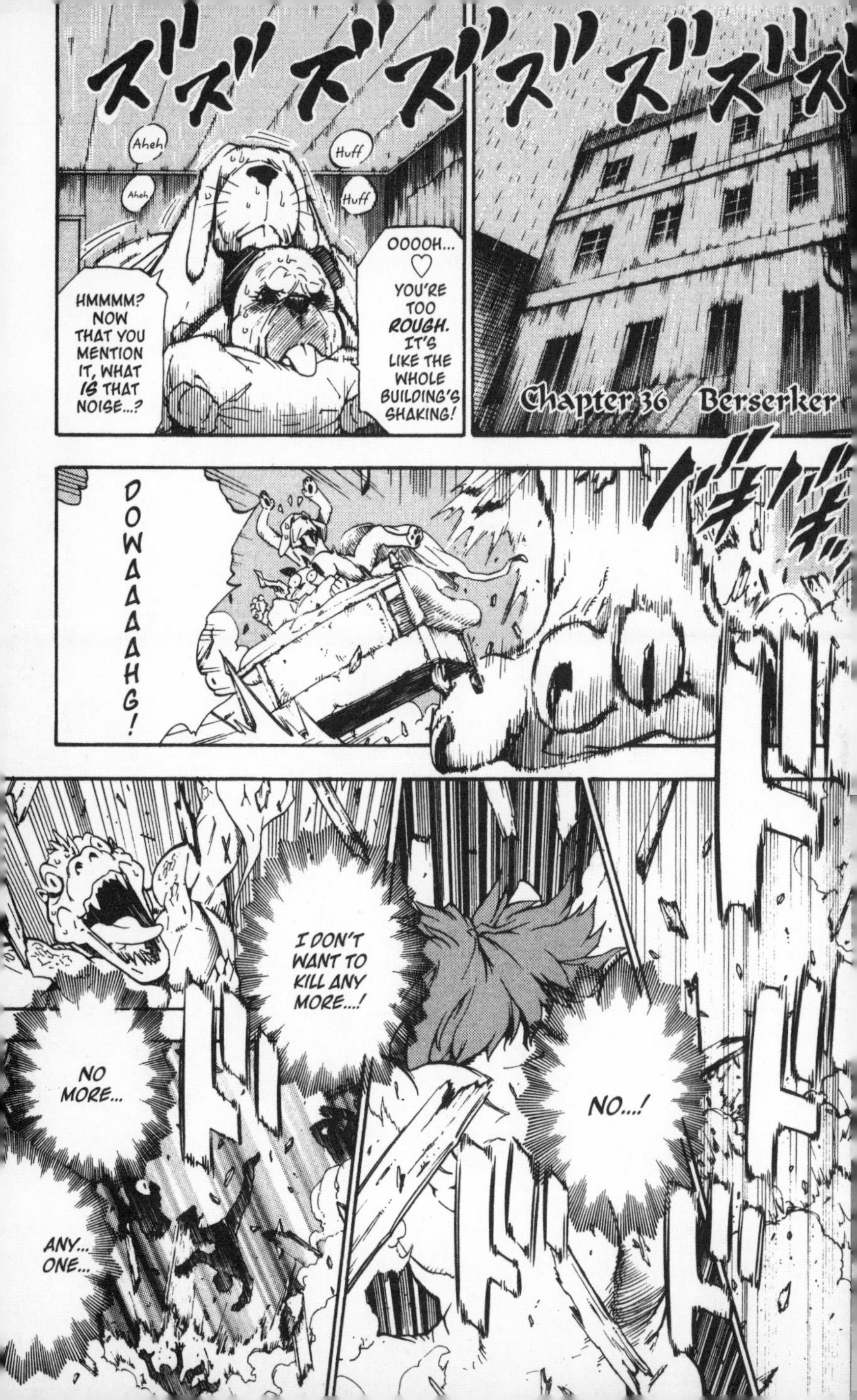
Chapter 36 Berserker
Huff
Aheh
Huff
Aheh
OOOOH...♡ YOU'RE TOO ROUGH. IT'S LIKE THE WHOLE BUILDING'S SHAKING!
HMMMM? NOW THAT YOU MENTION IT, WHAT IS THAT NOISE...?
DOWAAAAHG!
I DON'T WANT TO KILL ANY MORE...!
NO...!
NO MORE...
ANY... ONE...

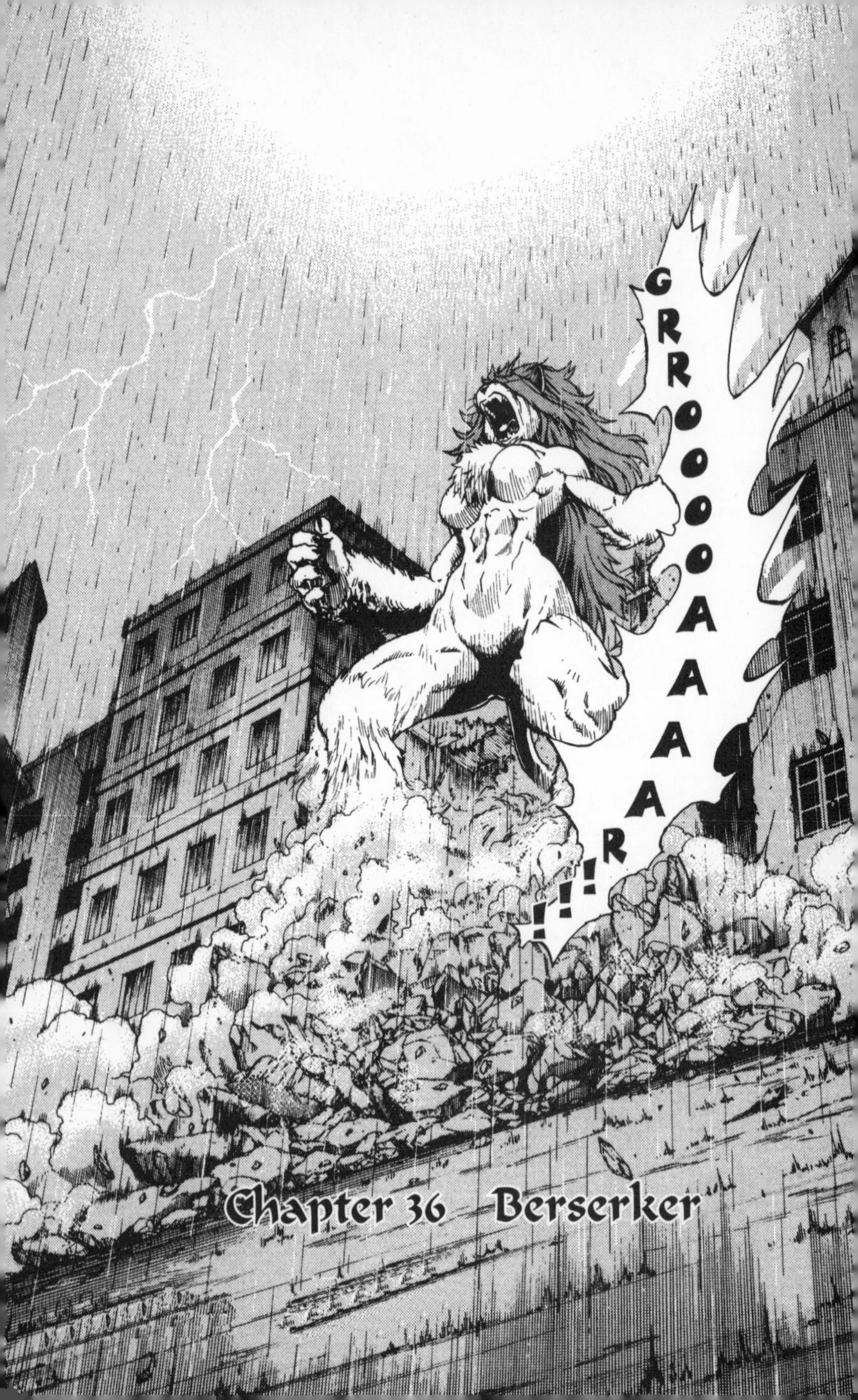
GRROOOOAAAAR!!!

Chapter 36 Berserker

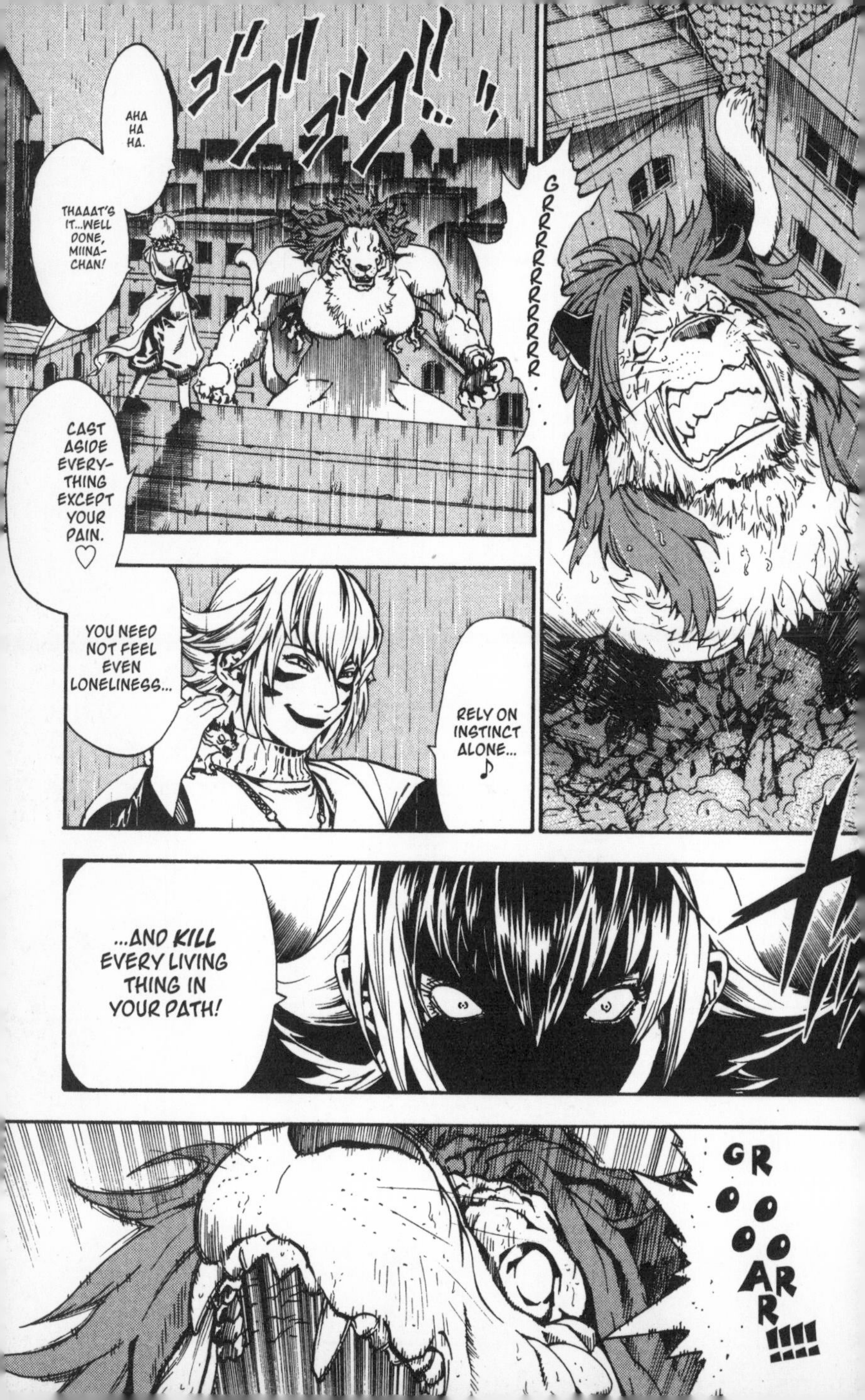
GRRRRRRRRRR
AHA HA HA.
THAAAT'S IT...WELL DONE, MIINA-CHAN!
CAST ASIDE EVERY-THING EXCEPT YOUR PAIN. ♡
YOU NEED NOT FEEL EVEN LONELINESS...
RELY ON INSTINCT ALONE... ♪
...AND **KILL** EVERY LIVING THING IN YOUR PATH!
GROOOOAR!!!!

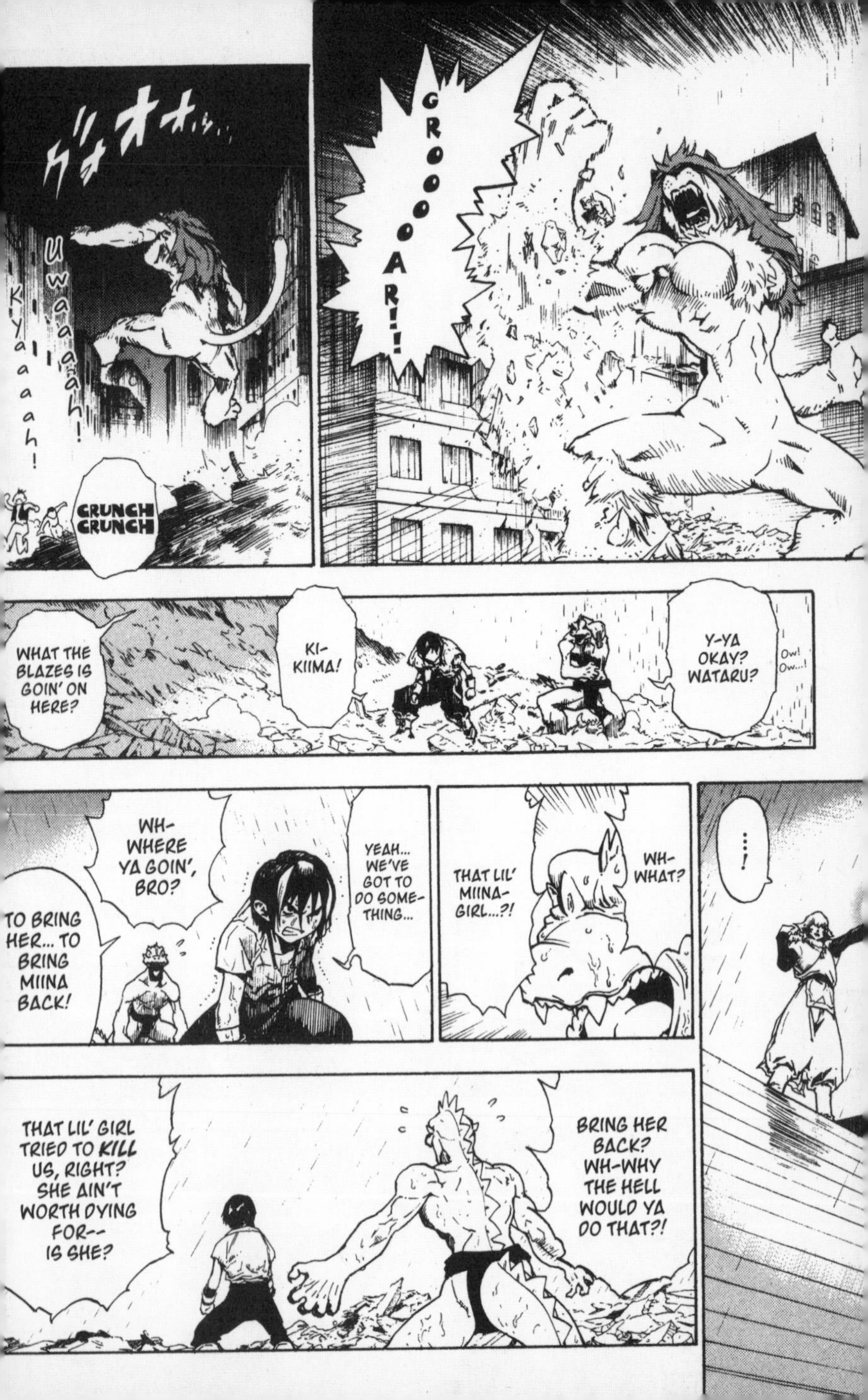

GROOOOAR!!!
グォオオォッ...
Uwaaaaah!
Kyaaaah!
CRUNCH CRUNCH
Ow! Ow...!
Y-YA OKAY? WATARU?
KI-KIIMA!
WHAT THE BLAZES IS GOIN' ON HERE?
...!
WH-WHAT?
THAT LIL' MIINA-GIRL...?!
YEAH... WE'VE GOT TO DO SOME-THING...
WH-WHERE YA GOIN', BRO?
TO BRING HER... TO BRING MIINA BACK!
BRING HER BACK? WH-WHY THE HELL WOULD YA DO THAT?!
THAT LIL' GIRL TRIED TO KILL US, RIGHT? SHE AIN'T WORTH DYING FOR-- IS SHE?

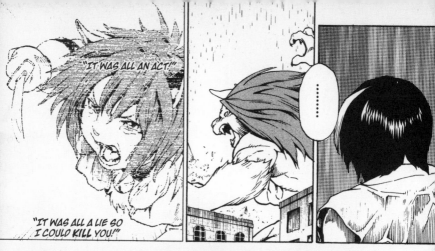

"......"
"IT WAS ALL AN ACT!"
"IT WAS ALL A LIE SO I COULD KILL YOU!"
"WHEN YOU SAID YOU WERE SEPARATED FROM YOUR FAMILY..."
"...WAS THAT A LIE, TOO?"
"NOOO..."
"THAT PART WAS TRUE--RIBBIT!"
"HE PROMISED..."
"...TO SEARCH FOR MY MAMA AND PAPA!"
"YOU CAN FORGET ABOUT ..."
"...EVER FINDING YOUR FAMILY--RIBBIT!"

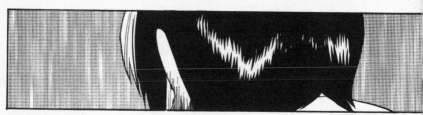

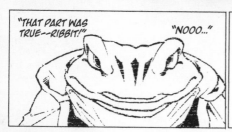

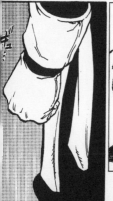

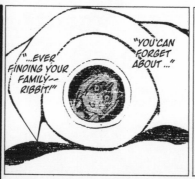

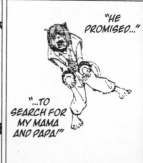

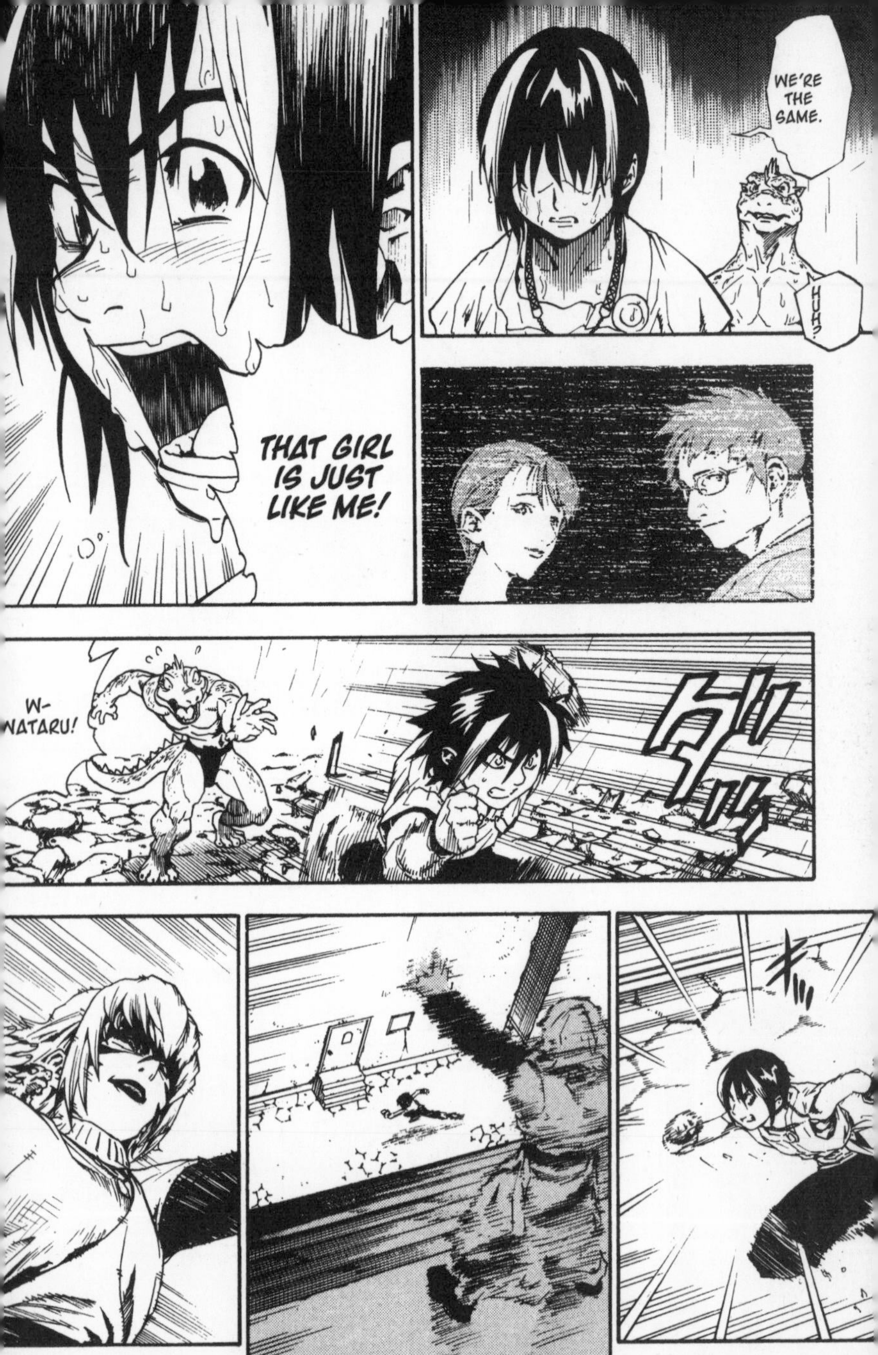
WE'RE THE SAME.
HUH?
THAT GIRL IS JUST LIKE ME!
W-WATARU!

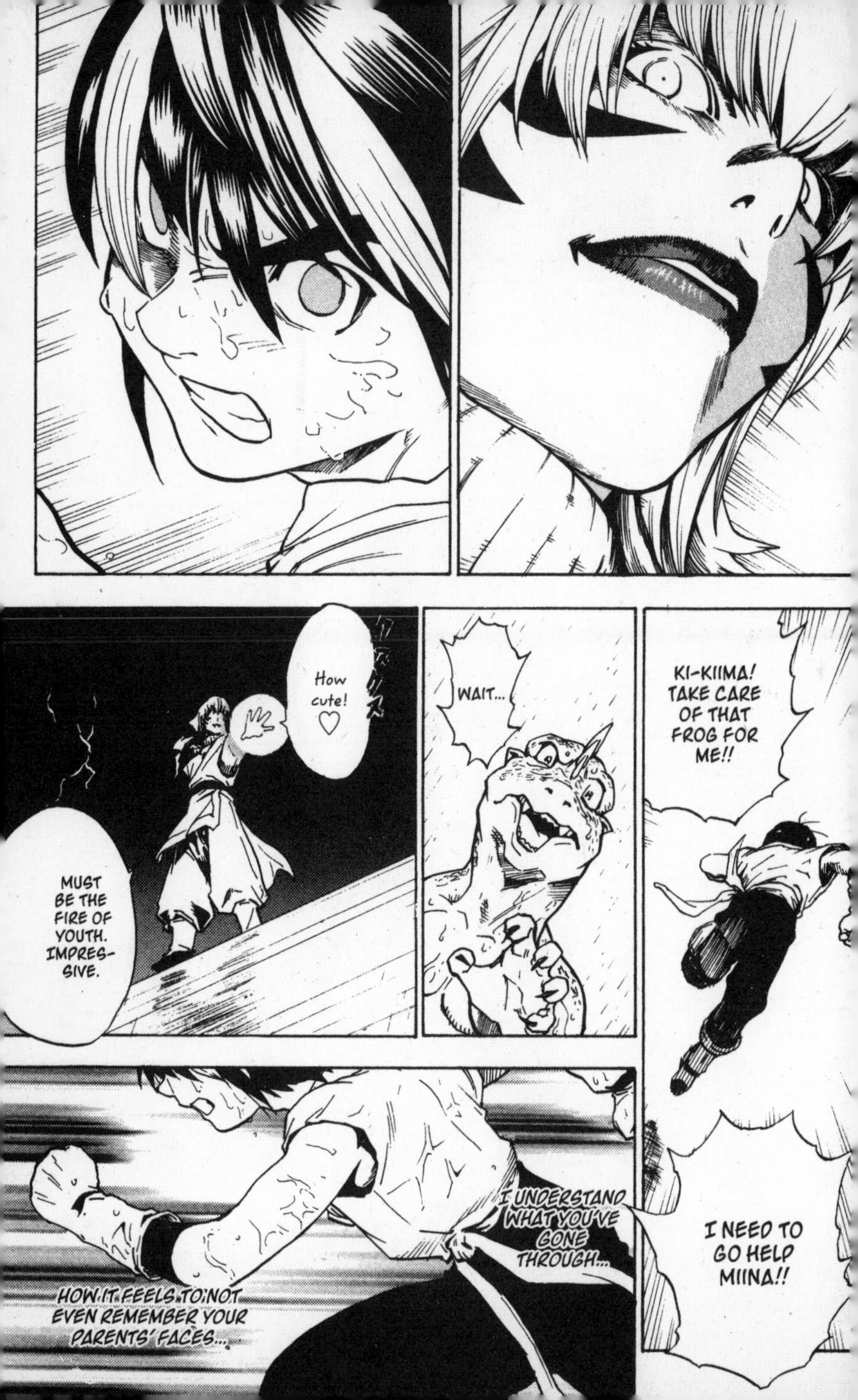
KI-KIIMA! TAKE CARE OF THAT FROG FOR ME!!
I NEED TO GO HELP MIINA!!
WAIT...
How cute! ♥
MUST BE THE FIRE OF YOUTH. IMPRESSIVE.
I UNDERSTAND WHAT YOU'VE GONE THROUGH...
HOW IT FEELS TO NOT EVEN REMEMBER YOUR PARENTS' FACES...

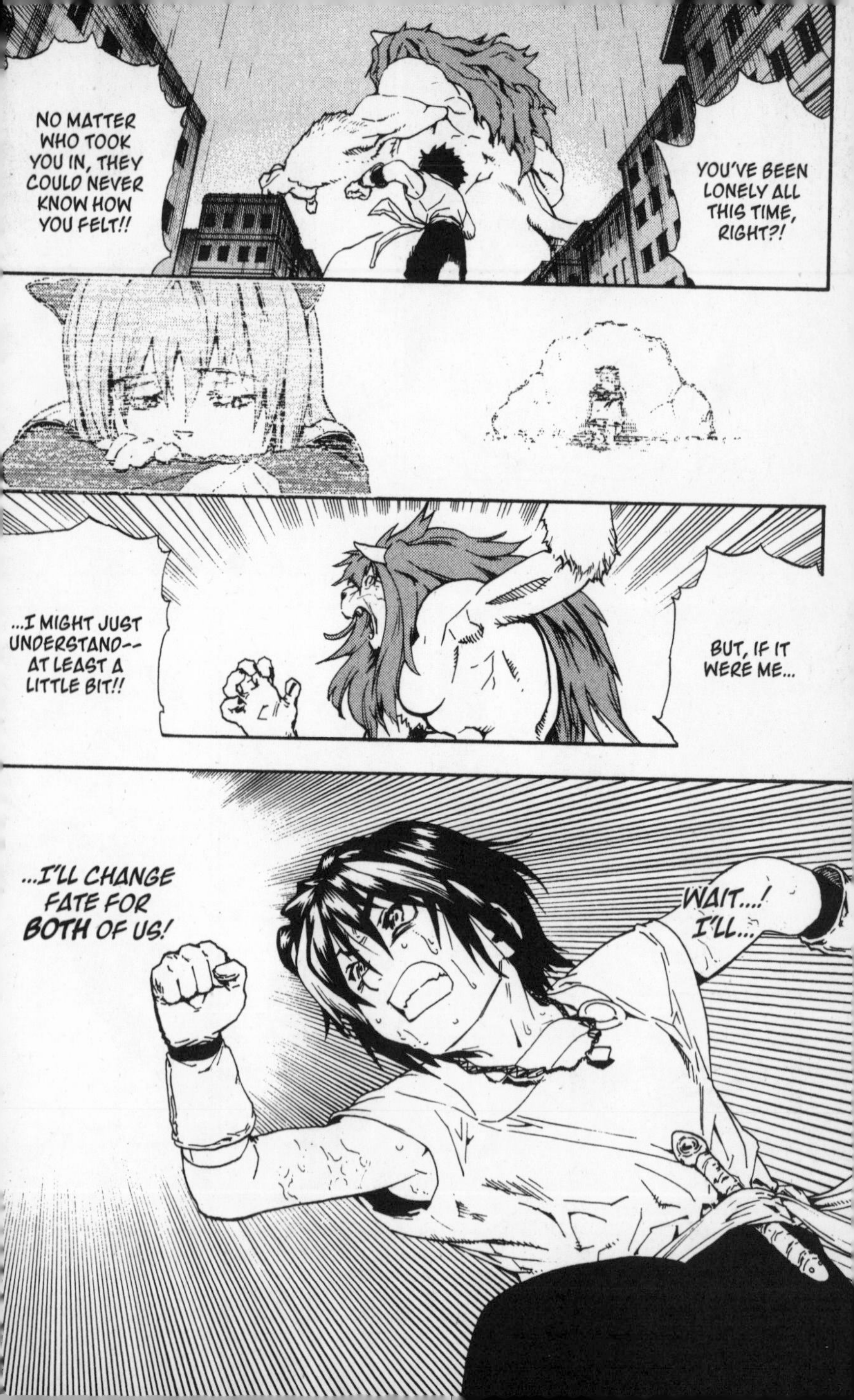
YOU'VE BEEN LONELY ALL THIS TIME, RIGHT?!
NO MATTER WHO TOOK YOU IN, THEY COULD NEVER KNOW HOW YOU FELT!!
BUT, IF IT WERE ME...
...I MIGHT JUST UNDERSTAND-- AT LEAST A LITTLE BIT!!
WAIT...! I'LL...
...I'LL CHANGE FATE FOR BOTH OF US!

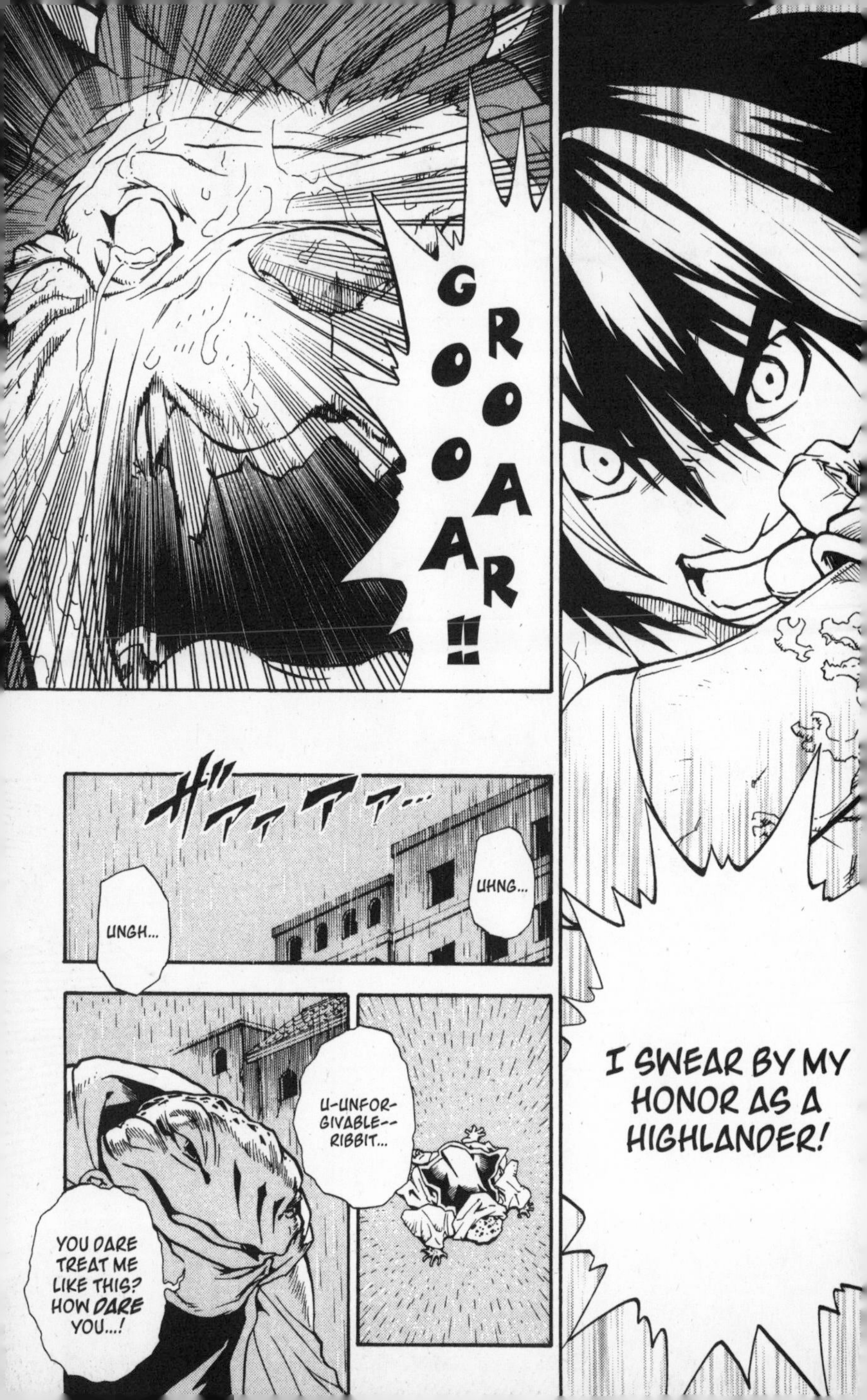
I SWEAR BY MY HONOR AS A HIGHLANDER!
GROOOAR!!
ザァァァァ…
UHNG...
UNGH...
U-UNFORGIVABLE--RIBBIT...
YOU DARE TREAT ME LIKE THIS? HOW DARE YOU...!

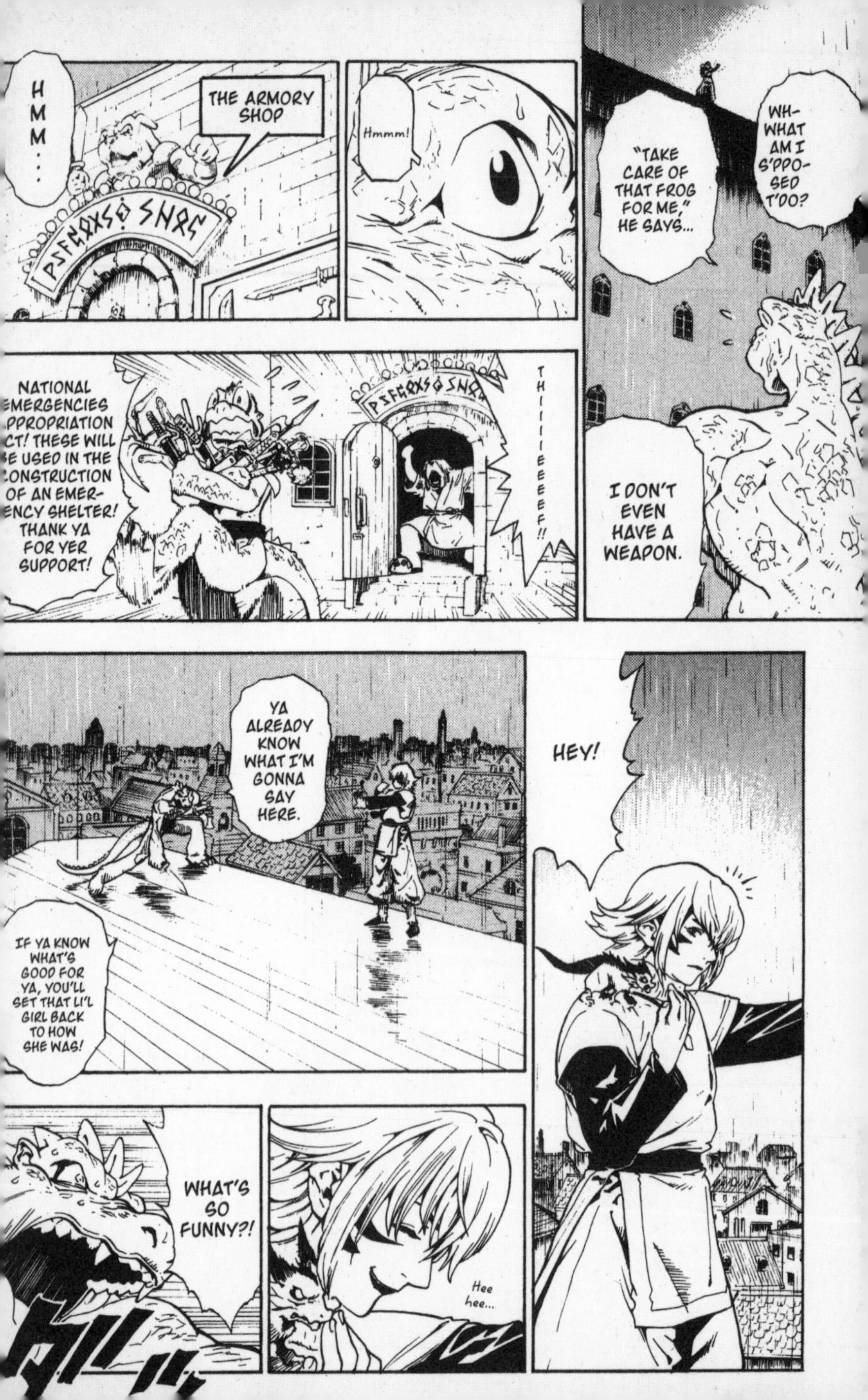
WH-WHAT AM I S'PPOSED T'DO?
"TAKE CARE OF THAT FROG FOR ME," HE SAYS...
I DON'T EVEN HAVE A WEAPON.
Hmmm!
THE ARMORY SHOP
HMM...
THIIIEEEEF!!
NATIONAL EMERGENCIES APPROPRIATION ACT! THESE WILL BE USED IN THE CONSTRUCTION OF AN EMERGENCY SHELTER! THANK YA FOR YER SUPPORT!
HEY!
YA ALREADY KNOW WHAT I'M GONNA SAY HERE.
IF YA KNOW WHAT'S GOOD FOR YA, YOU'LL SET THAT LI'L GIRL BACK TO HOW SHE WAS!
Hee hee...
WHAT'S SO FUNNY?!

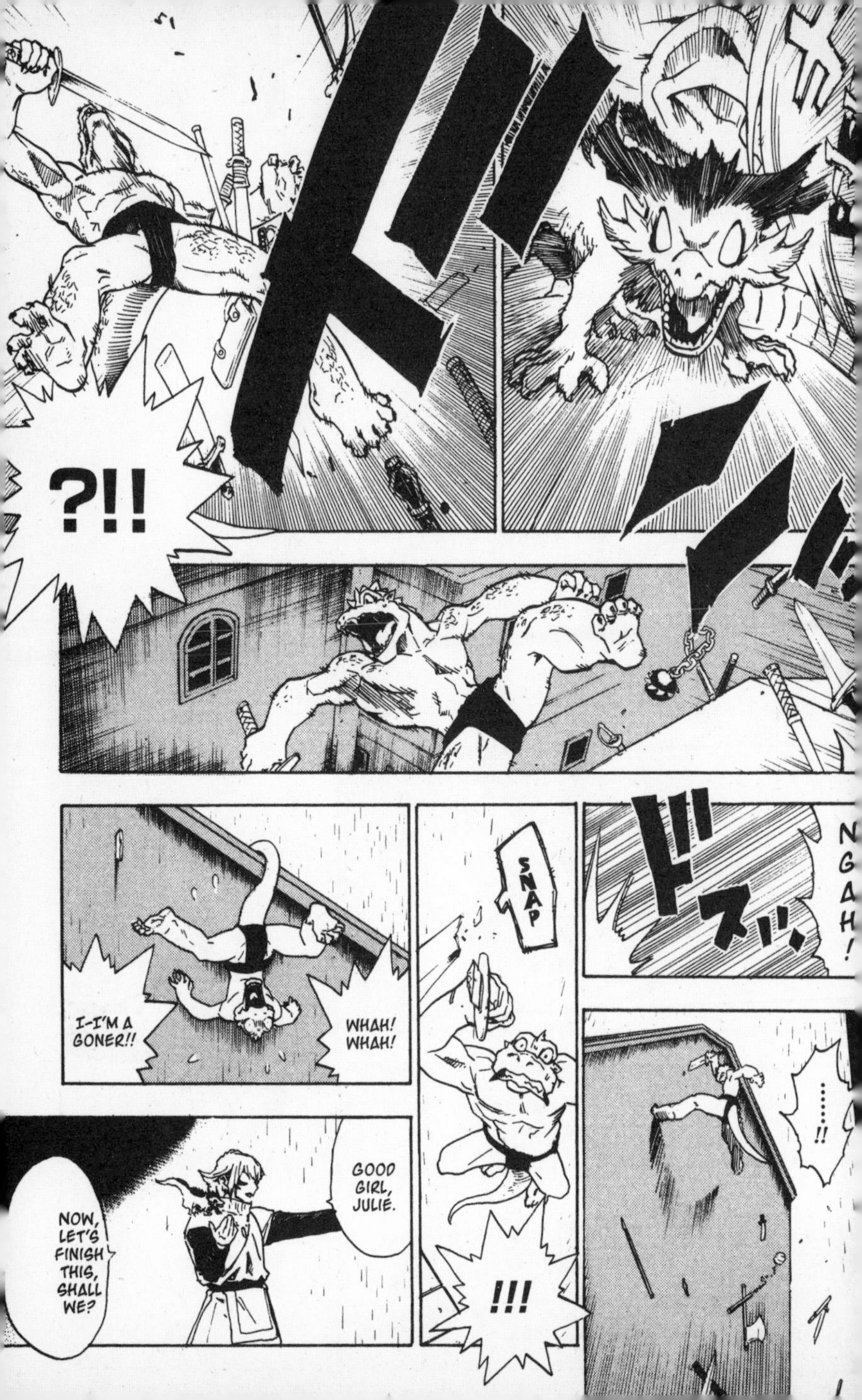
?!!
NGAAH!
......!!
SNAP
!!!
WHAH! WHAH!
I-I'M A GONER!!
GOOD GIRL, JULIE.
NOW, LET'S FINISH THIS, SHALL WE?

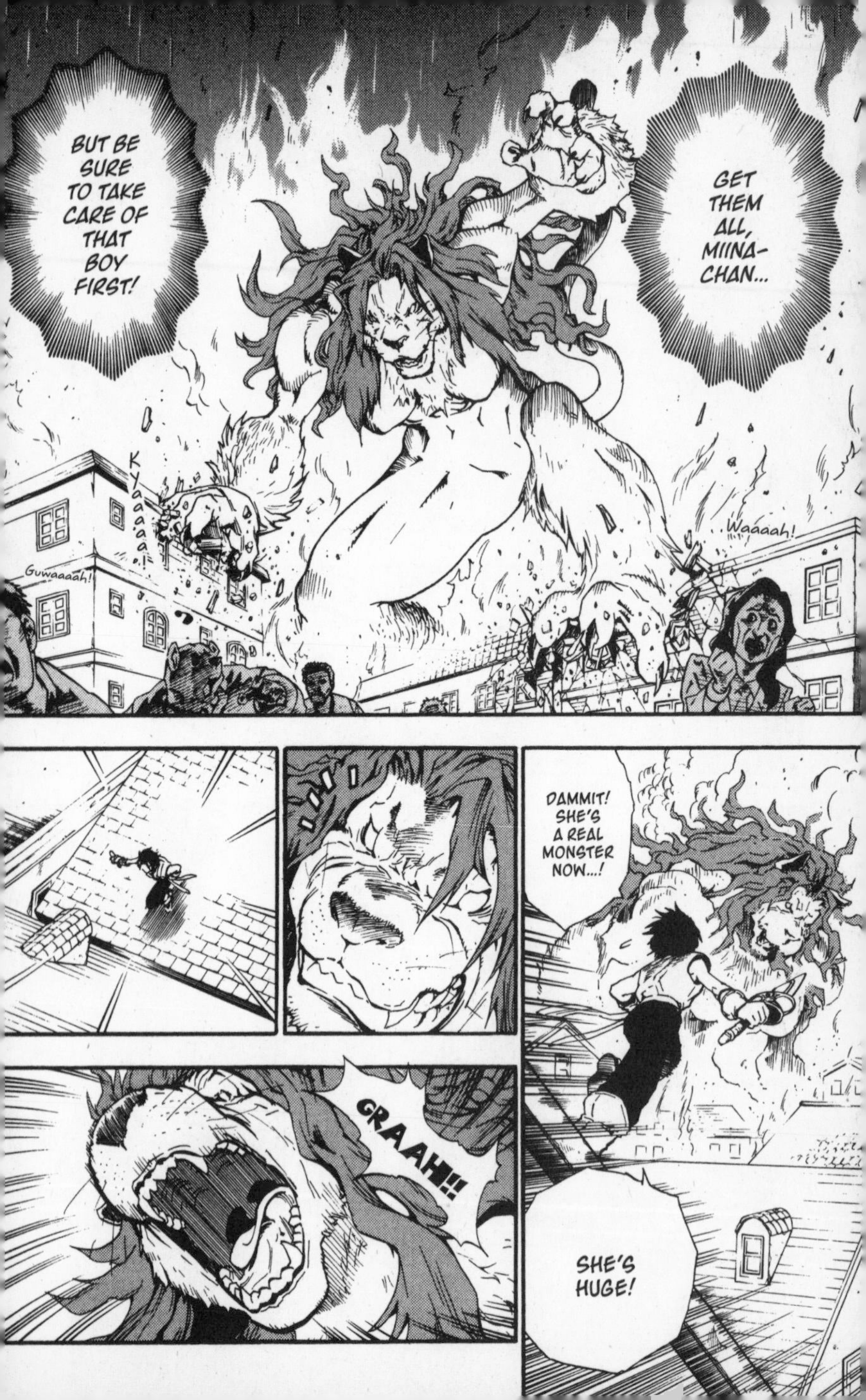
GET THEM ALL, MIINA-CHAN...
BUT BE SURE TO TAKE CARE OF THAT BOY FIRST!
Waaaah!
Kyaaaaa!
Guwaaaah!
DAMMIT! SHE'S A REAL MONSTER NOW...!
SHE'S HUGE!
GRAAH!!

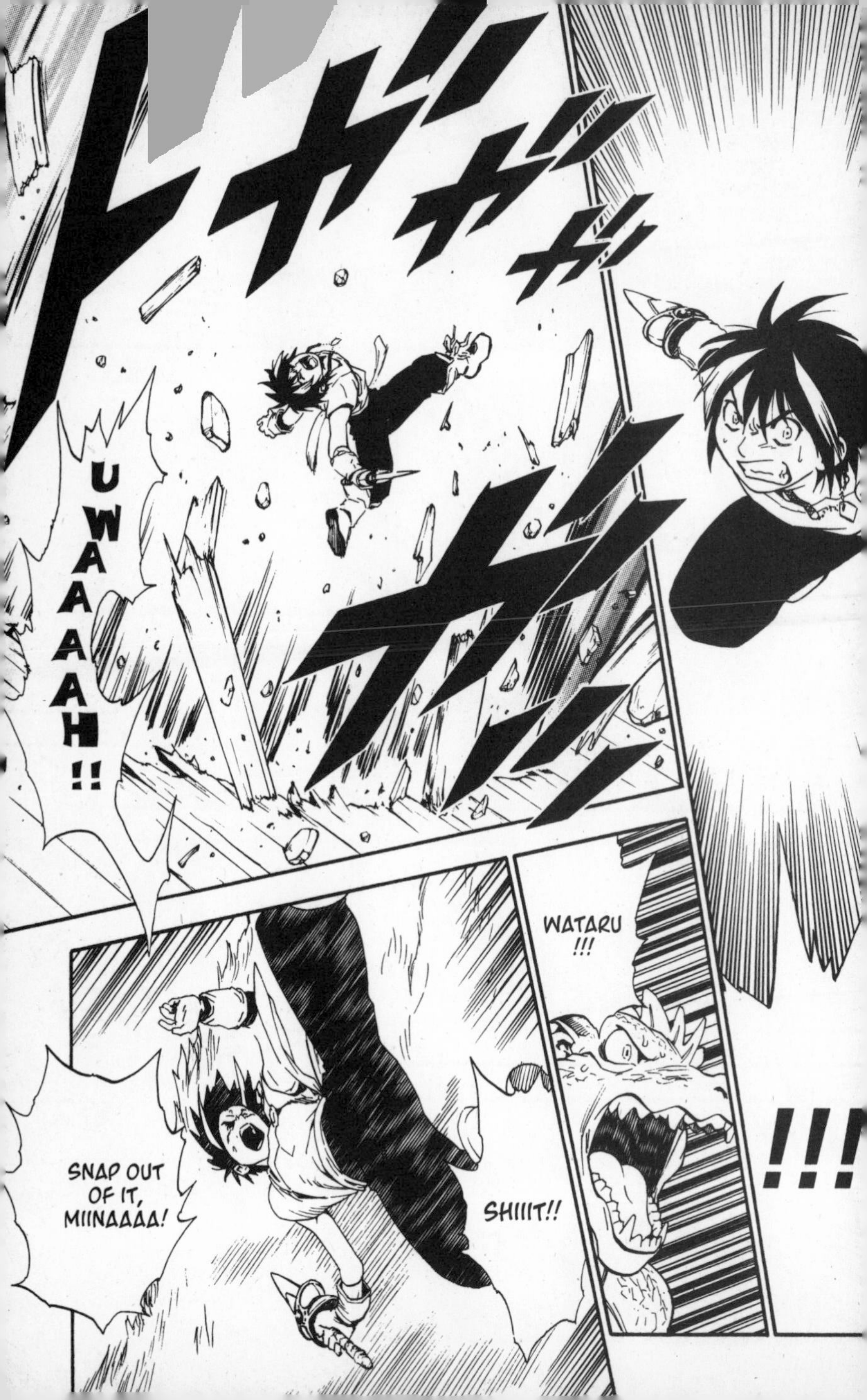
UWAAAAAH!!
!!!
WATARU !!!
SHIIIT!!
SNAP OUT OF IT, MIINAAAA!

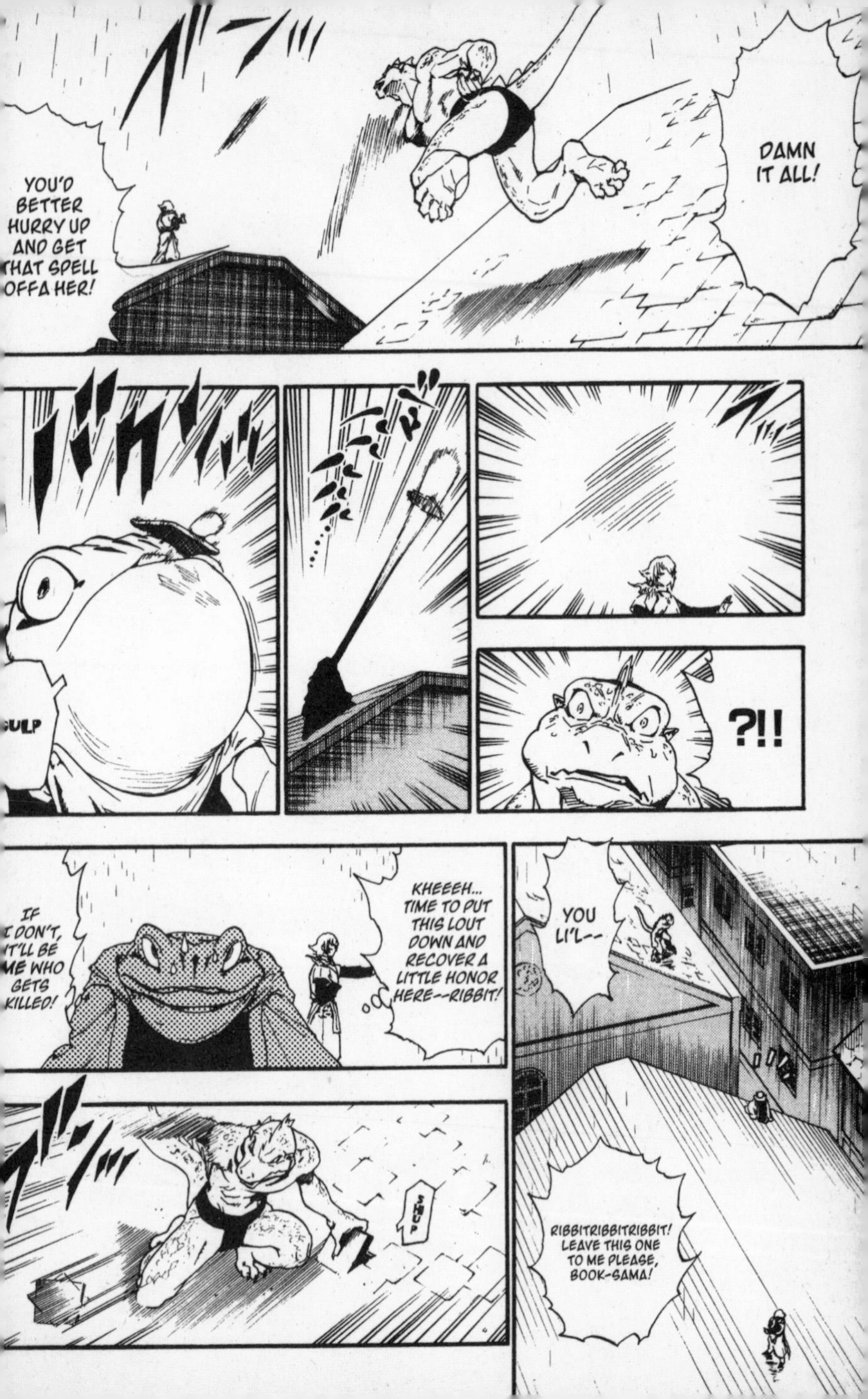
DAMN IT ALL!
YOU'D BETTER HURRY UP AND GET THAT SPELL OFFA HER!
?!!
GULP
YOU LI'L--
RIBBITRIBBITRIBBIT! LEAVE THIS ONE TO ME PLEASE, BOOK-SAMA!
KHEEEH... TIME TO PUT THIS LOUT DOWN AND RECOVER A LITTLE HONOR HERE--RIBBIT!
IF I DON'T, IT'LL BE ME WHO GETS KILLED!
SHUP

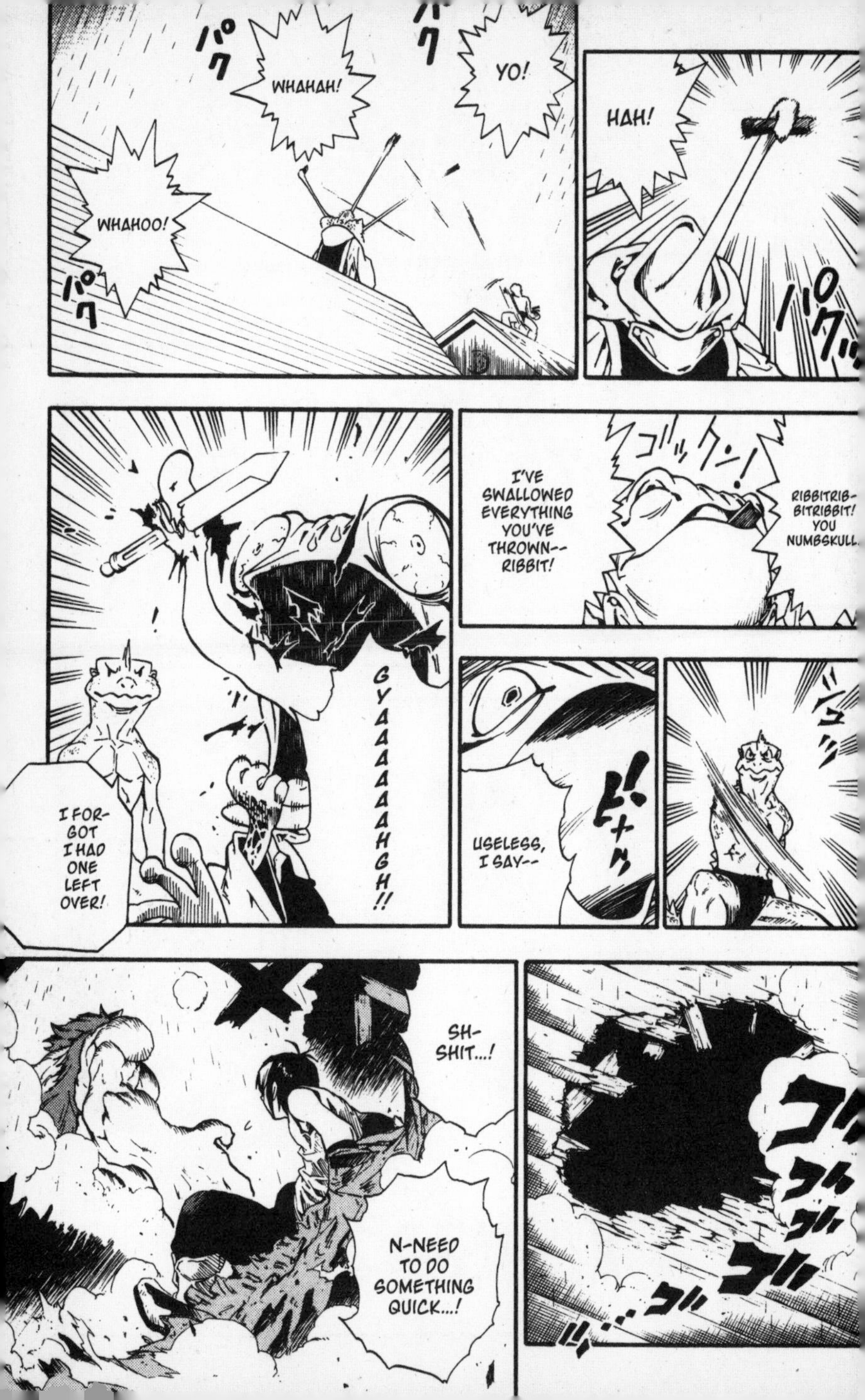
HAH!
YO!
WHAHAH!
WHAHOO!
RIBBITRIBBITRIBBIT! YOU NUMBSKULL.
I'VE SWALLOWED EVERYTHING YOU'VE THROWN--RIBBIT!
USELESS, I SAY--
GYAAAAAAAAAHGH!!
I FORGOT I HAD ONE LEFT OVER!
SH-SHIT...!
N-NEED TO DO SOMETHING QUICK...!

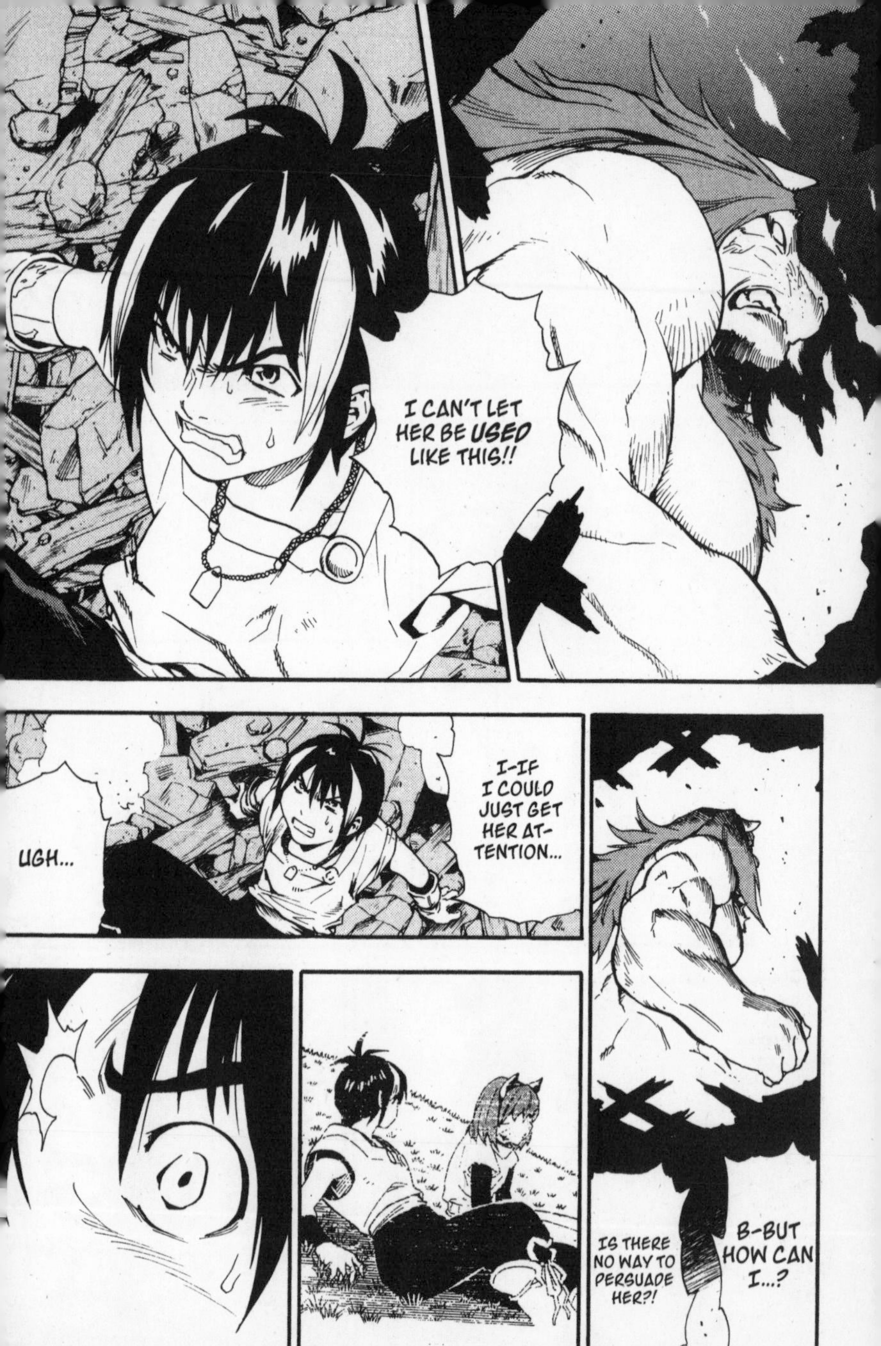
I CAN'T LET HER BE USED LIKE THIS!!
B-BUT HOW CAN I...?
IS THERE NO WAY TO PERSUADE HER?!
I-IF I COULD JUST GET HER AT-TENTION...
UGH...

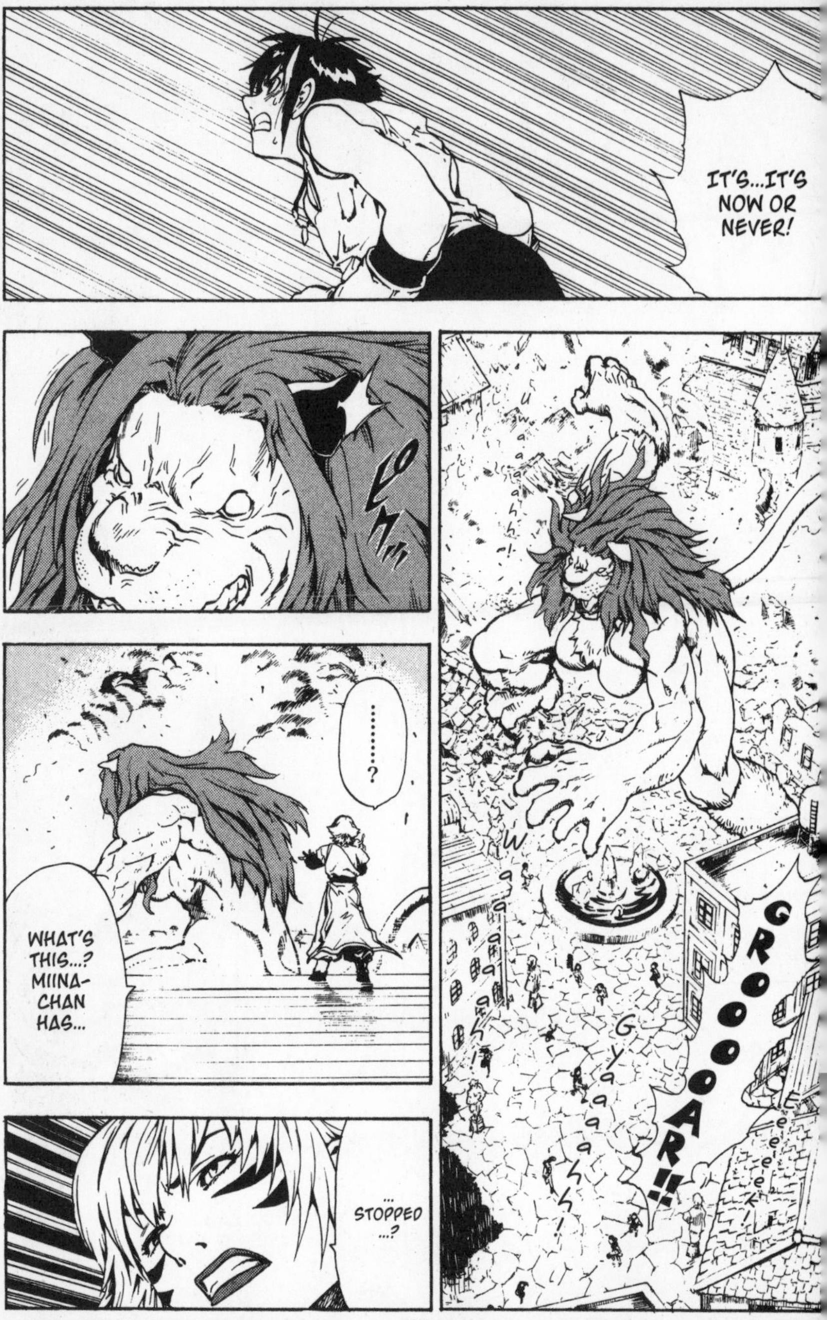
IT'S...IT'S NOW OR NEVER!
Uwaaaahh!
Waaaaaaah!
Gyaaaahhh!
GROOOOAR!!
Eeeeek!
......?
WHAT'S THIS...? MIINA-CHAN HAS...
...STOPPED...?

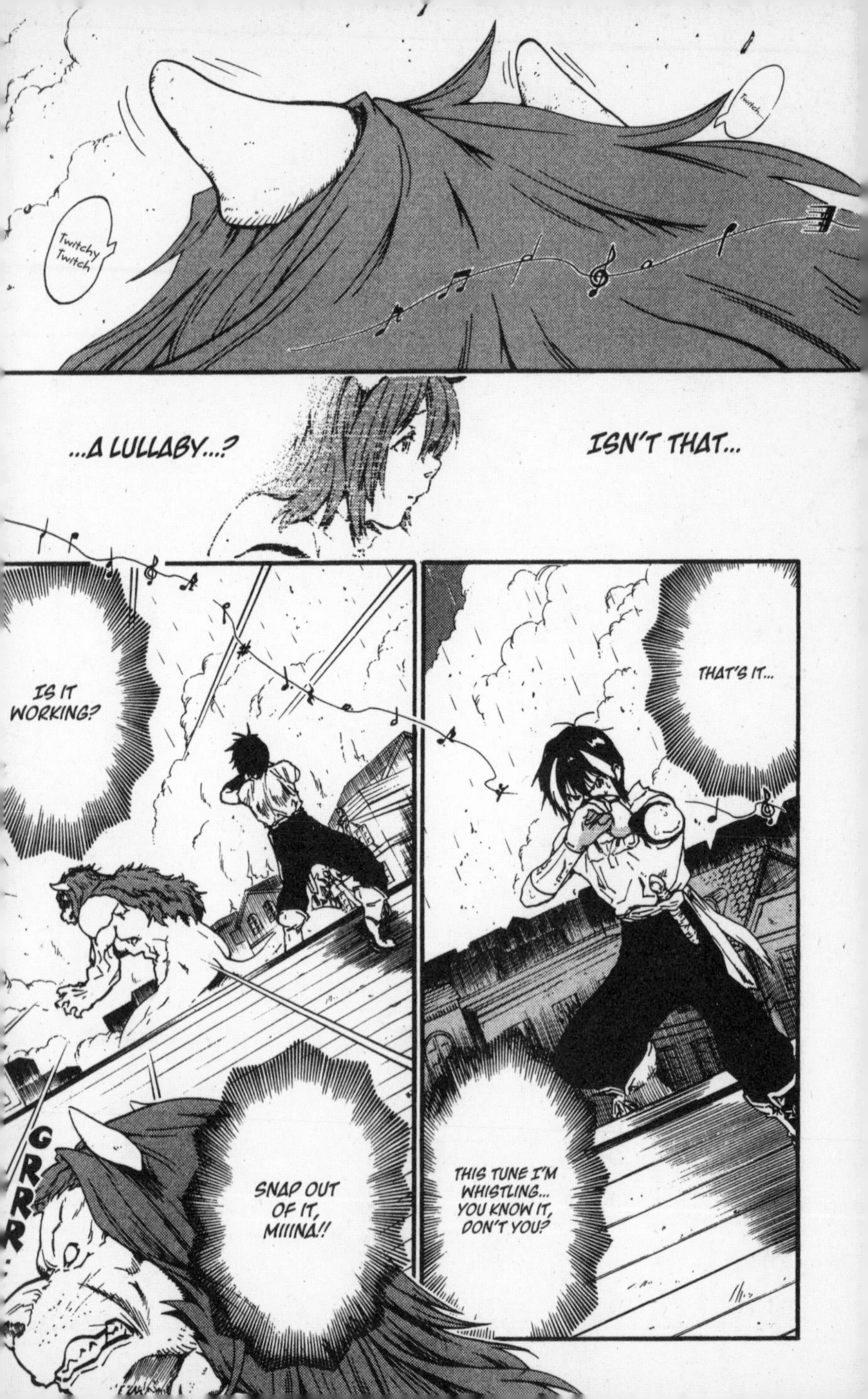
Twitch...
Twitchy Twitch
ISN'T THAT...
...A LULLABY...?
THAT'S IT...
THIS TUNE I'M WHISTLING... YOU KNOW IT, DON'T YOU?
IS IT WORKING?
SNAP OUT OF IT, MIIINA!!
GRRR...

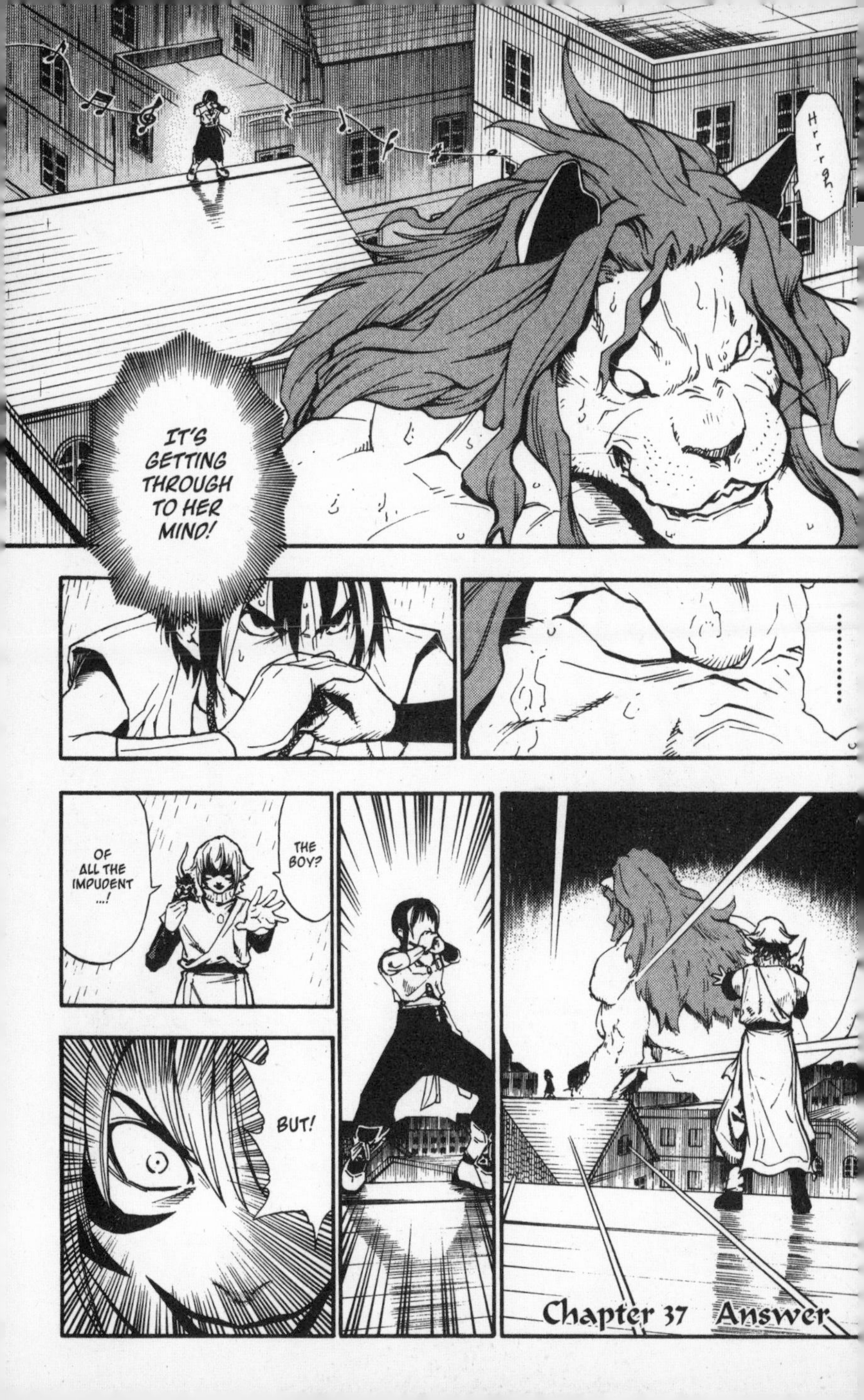
Hrrrgh...
IT'S GETTING THROUGH TO HER MIND!
......
Chapter 37 Answer
THE BOY?
OF ALL THE IMPUDENT ...!
BUT!

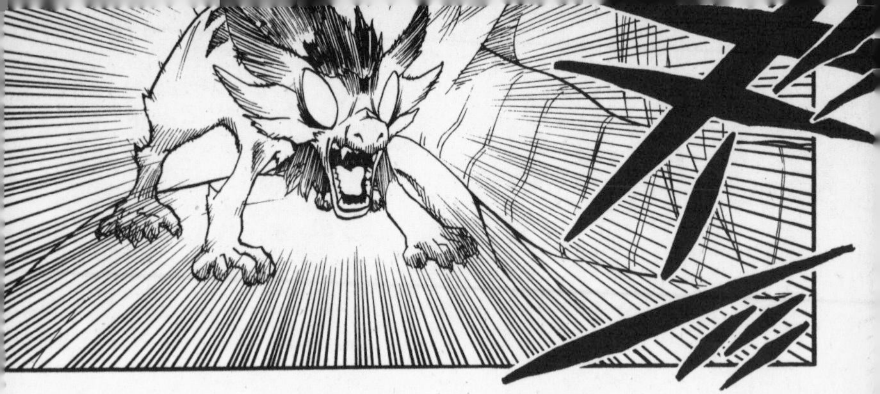

Chapter 37 Answer

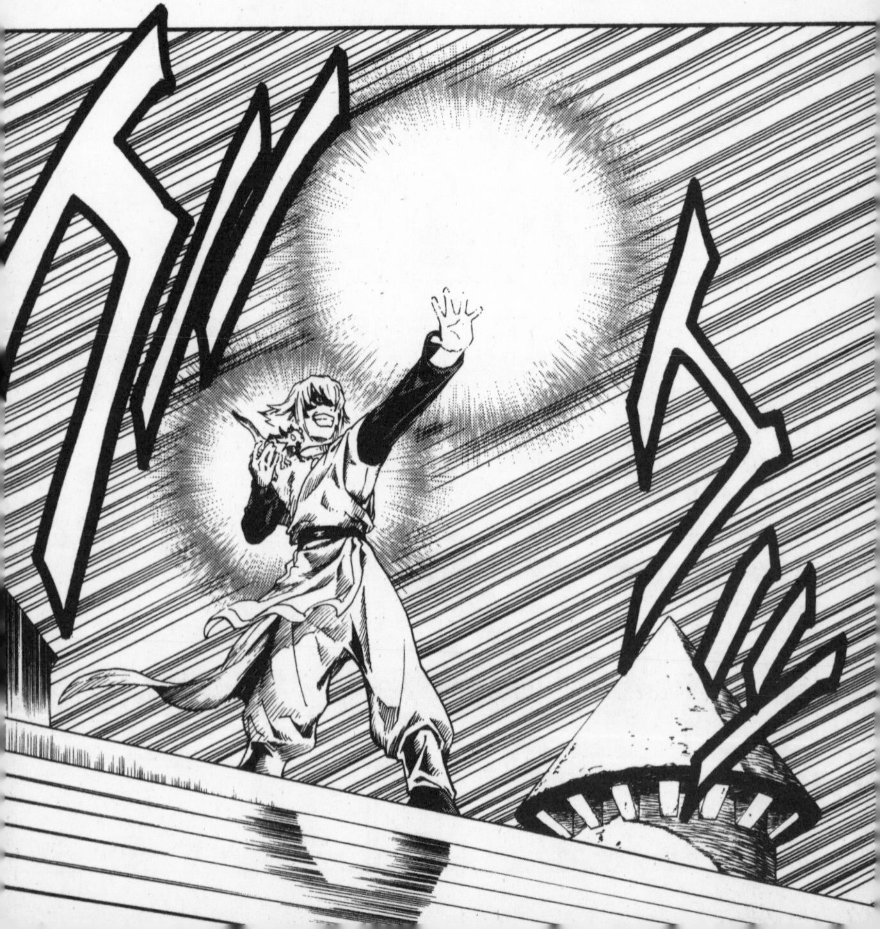

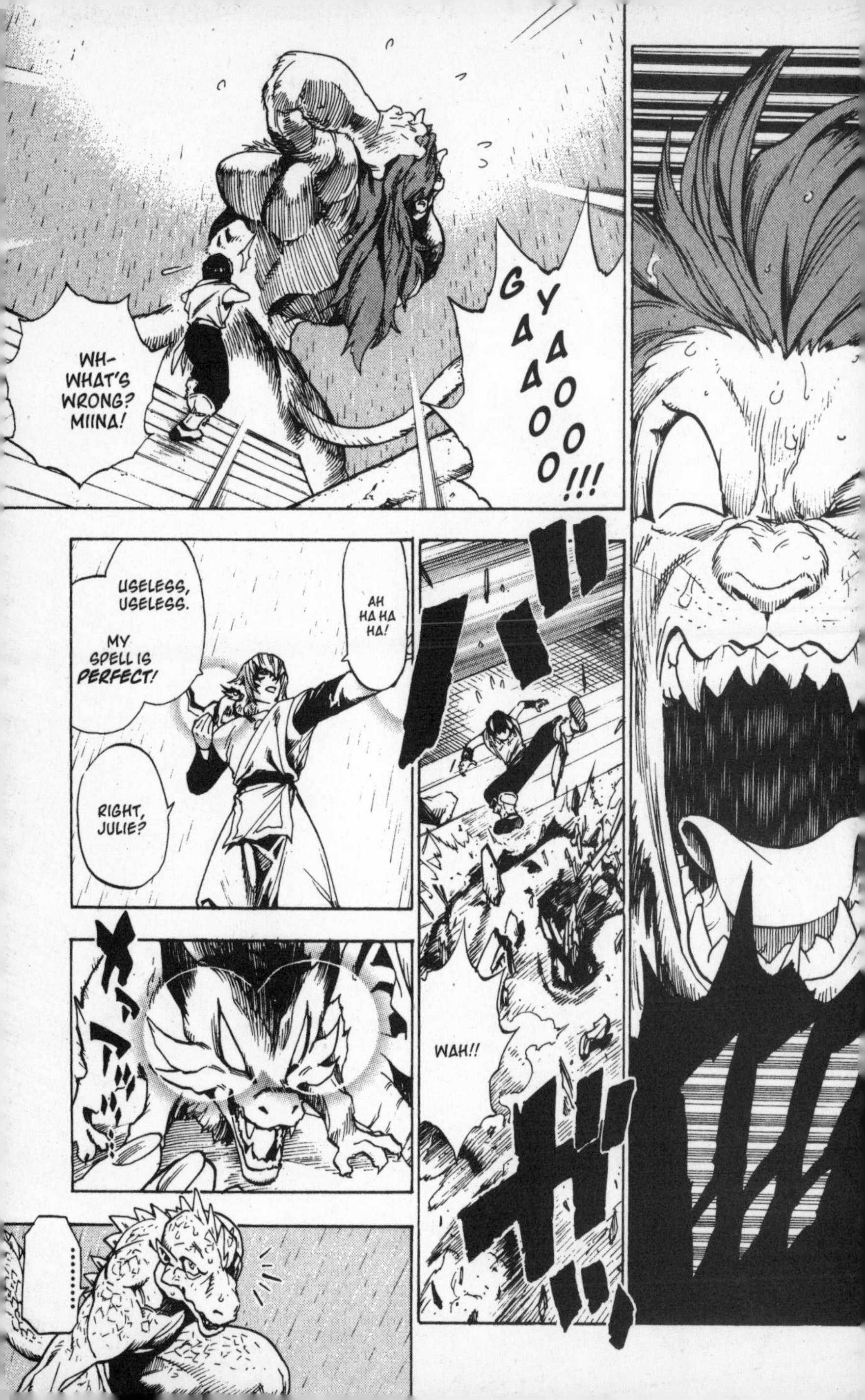
GYAAAOOOOO!!!
WH- WHAT'S WRONG? MIINA!
WAH!!
AH HA HA HA!
USELESS, USELESS.
MY SPELL IS PERFECT!
RIGHT, JULIE?
......

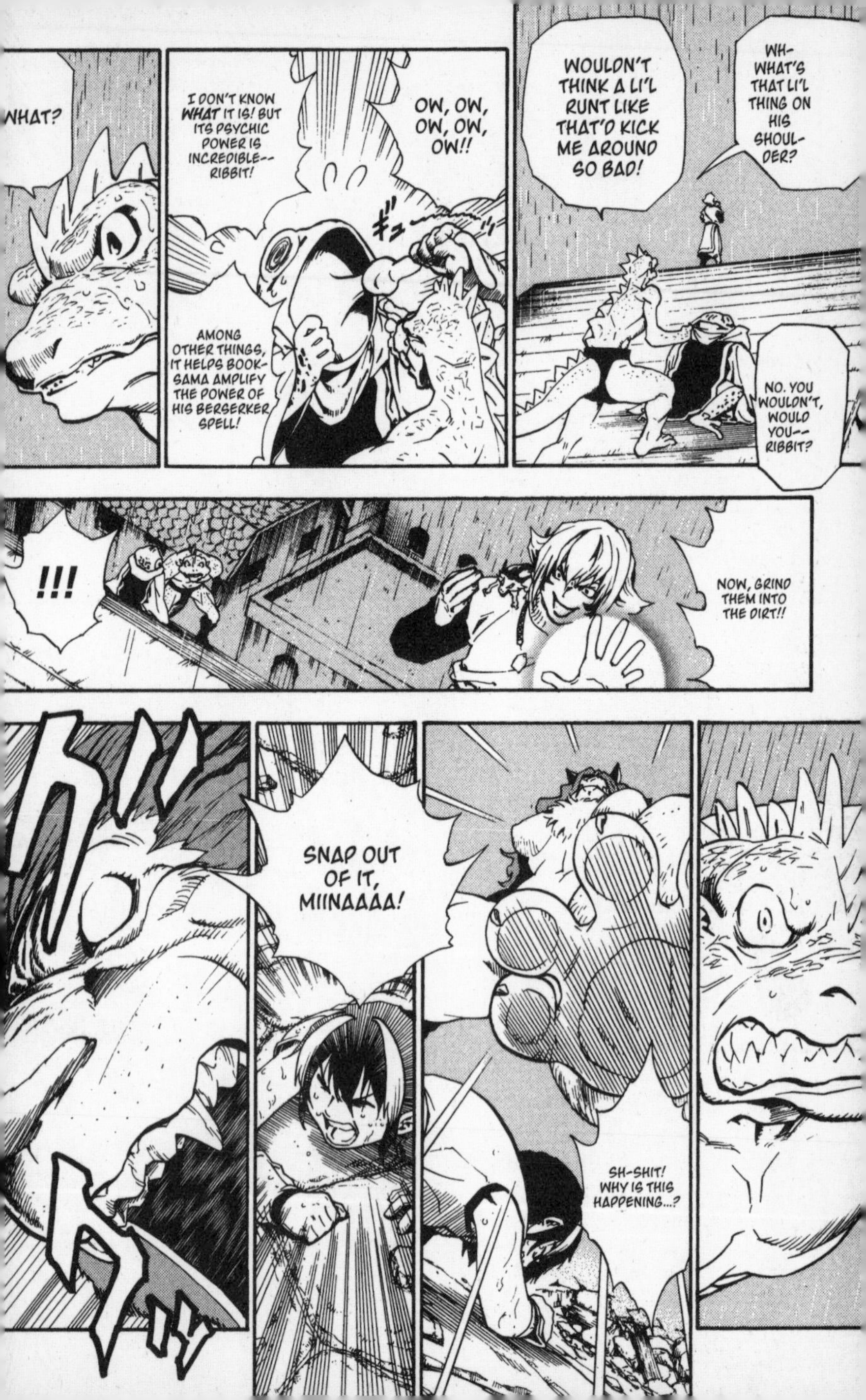
WH-WHAT'S THAT LI'L THING ON HIS SHOULDER?
WOULDN'T THINK A LI'L RUNT LIKE THAT'D KICK ME AROUND SO BAD!
NO. YOU WOULDN'T, WOULD YOU--RIBBIT?
OW, OW, OW, OW, OW!!
I DON'T KNOW **WHAT** IT IS! BUT ITS PSYCHIC POWER IS INCREDIBLE--RIBBIT!
AMONG OTHER THINGS, IT HELPS BOOK-SAMA AMPLIFY THE POWER OF HIS BERSERKER SPELL!
WHAT?
NOW, GRIND THEM INTO THE DIRT!!
!!!
SH-SHIT! WHY IS THIS HAPPENING...?
SNAP OUT OF IT, MIINAAAA!

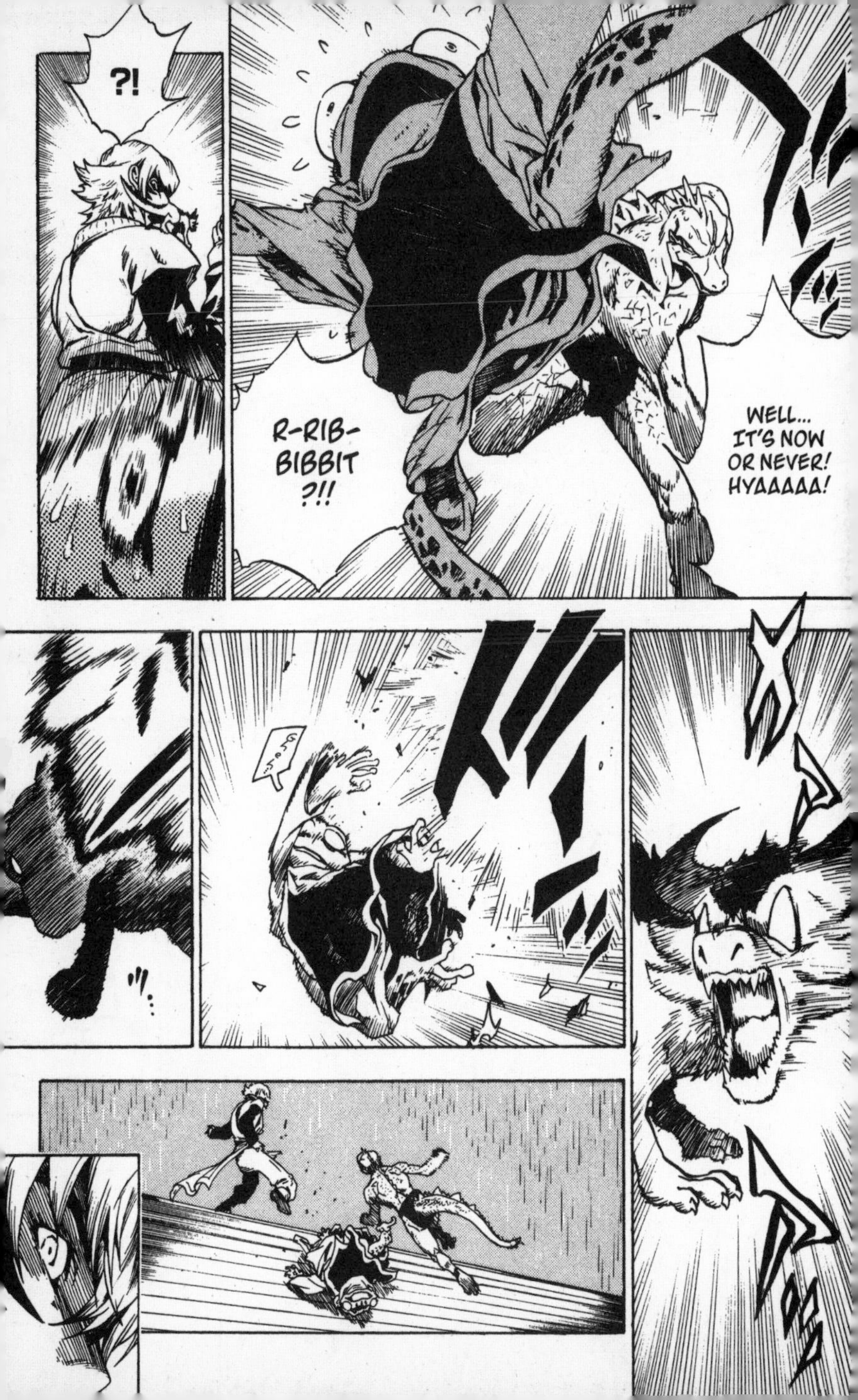
WELL... IT'S NOW OR NEVER! HYAAAAA!
R-RIB-BIBBIT ?!!
?!

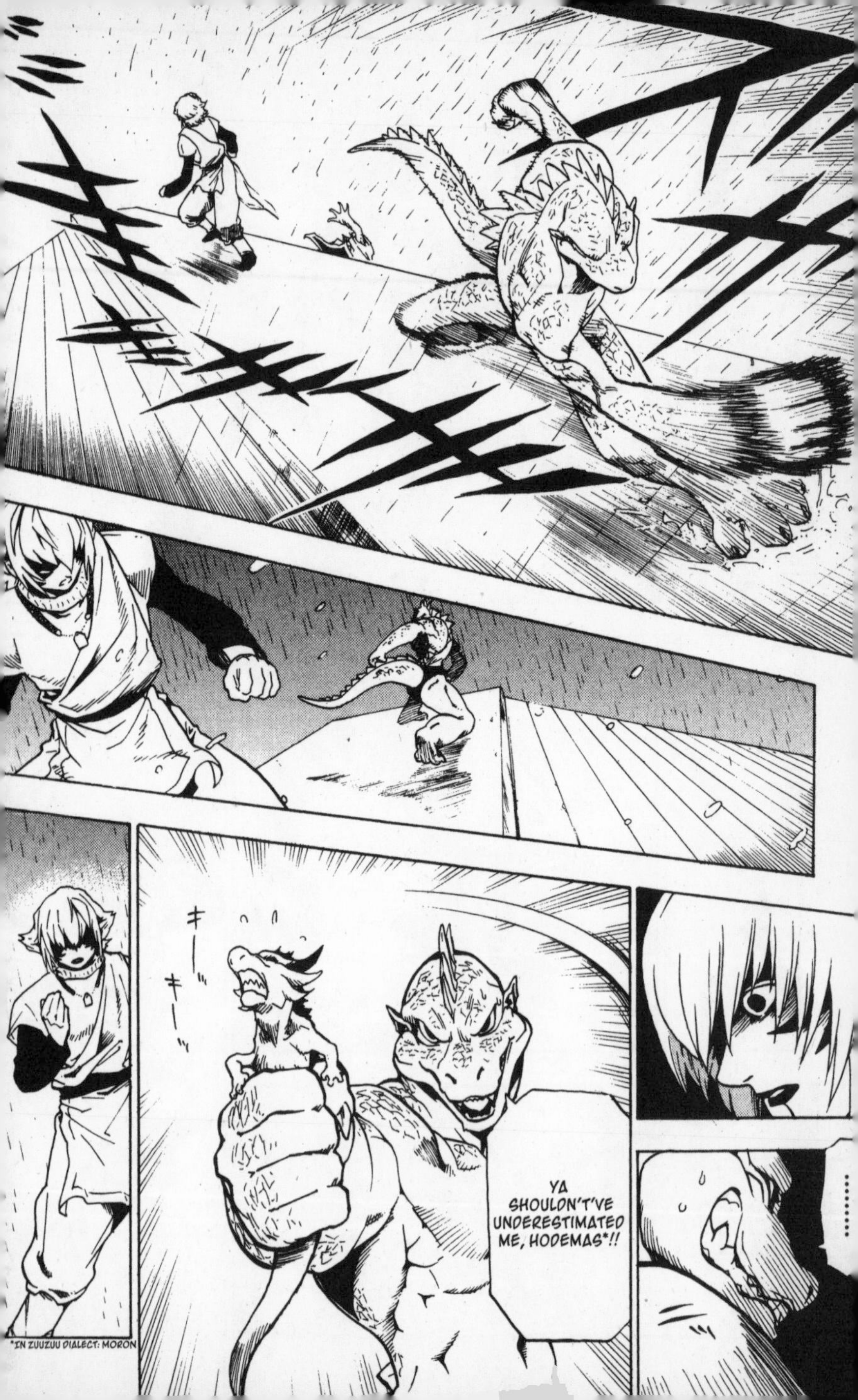
YA SHOULDN'T'VE UNDERESTIMATED ME, HODEMAS*!!
キー
キーッ
*IN ZUUZUU DIALECT: MORON

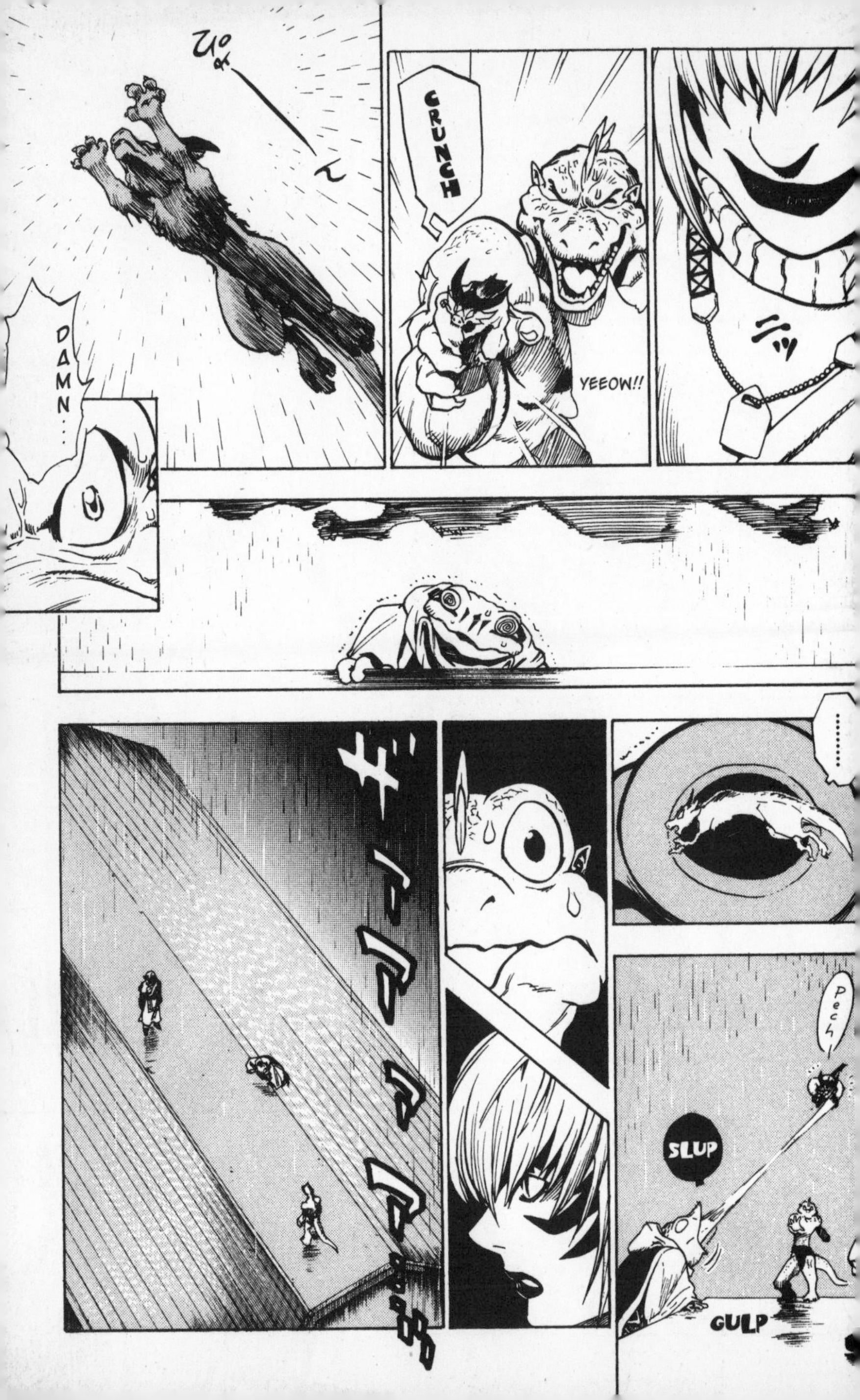
ニッ
CRUNCH
YEEOW!!
ぴょん
DAMN...
......
Pech
SLUP
GULP
ギャアアア

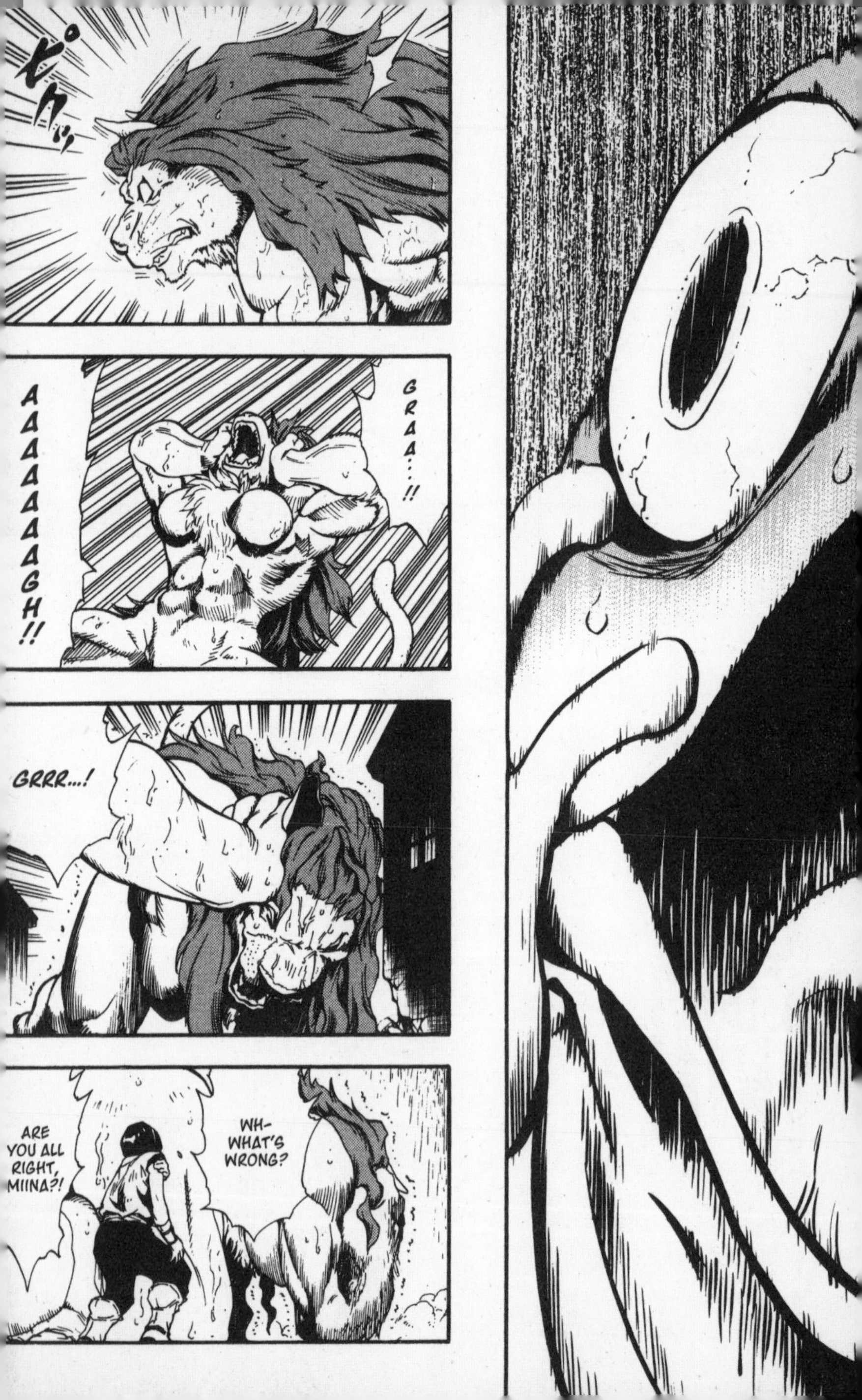
GRAA...!!
AAAAAAAAAAGH!!
GRRR...!
WH-WHAT'S WRONG?
ARE YOU ALL RIGHT, MIINA?!

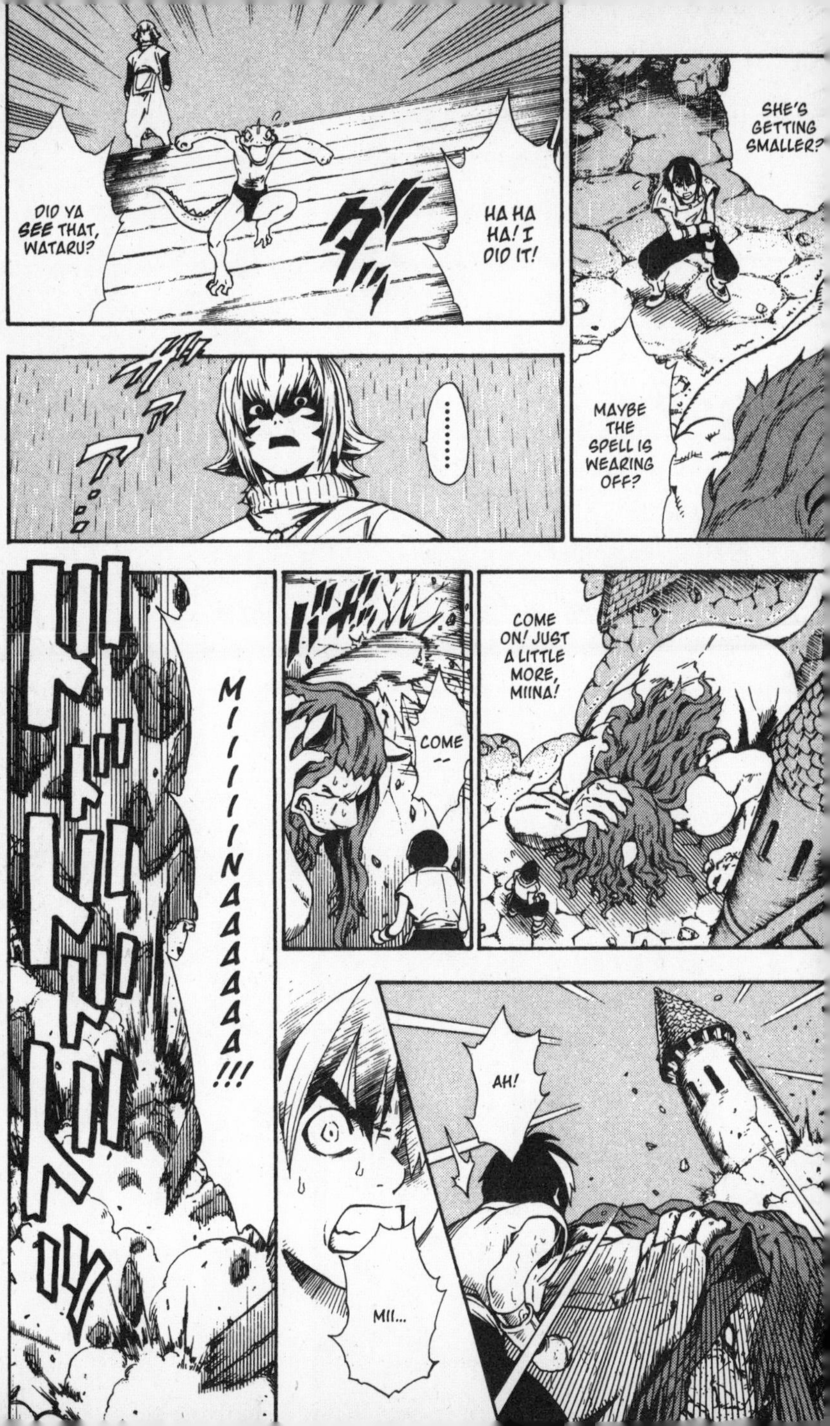
SHE'S GETTING SMALLER?
MAYBE THE SPELL IS WEARING OFF?
HA HA HA! I DID IT!
DID YA SEE THAT, WATARU?
......
COME ON! JUST A LITTLE MORE, MIINA!
COME--
AH!
MII...
MIIIIINAAAAAA!!!

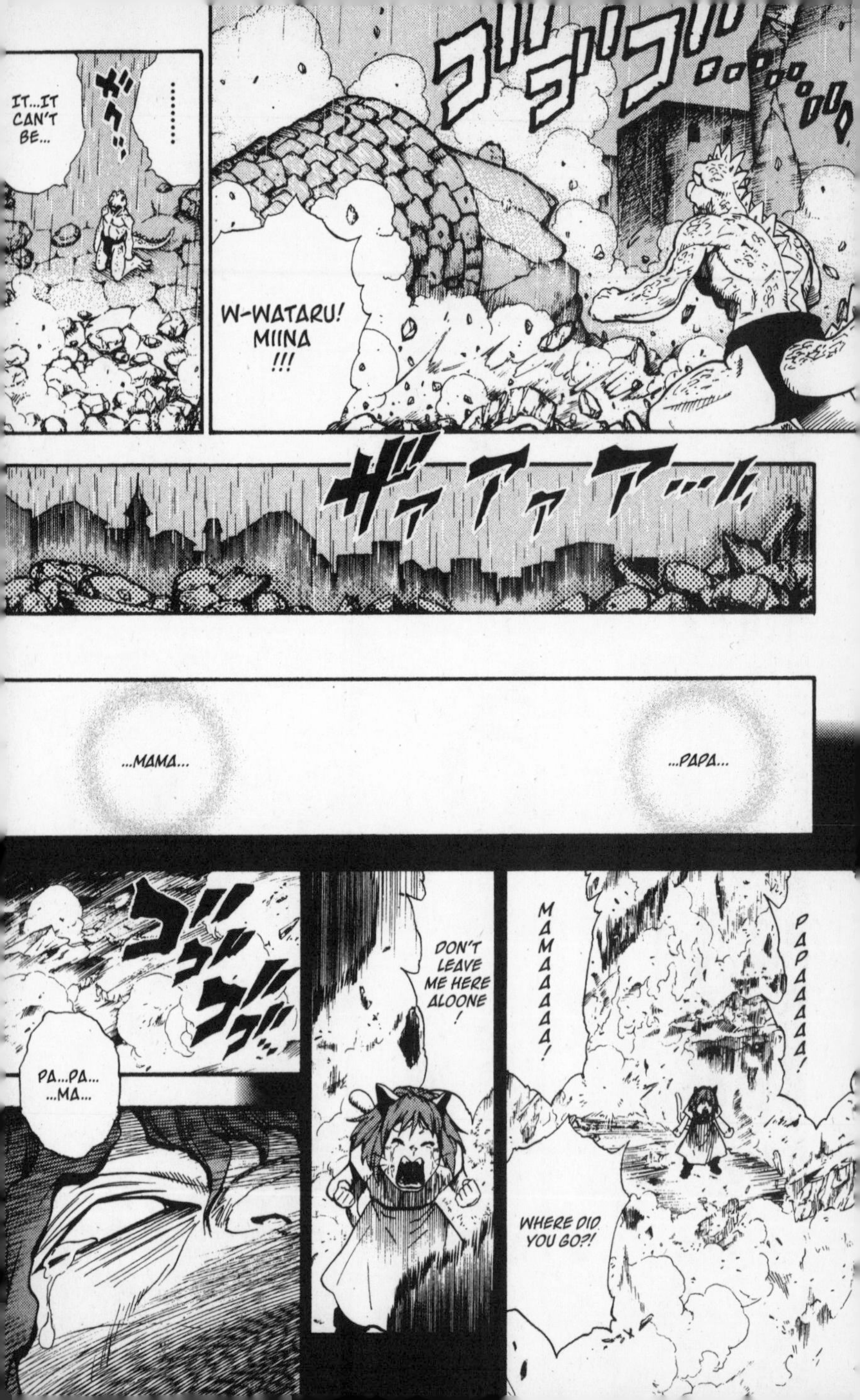
W-WATARU! MIINA !!!
IT...IT CAN'T BE...
......
...PAPA...
...MAMA...
PAPAAAAAAA!
MAMAAAAAA!
WHERE DID YOU GO?!
DON'T LEAVE ME HERE ALOONE!
PA...PA... ...MA...

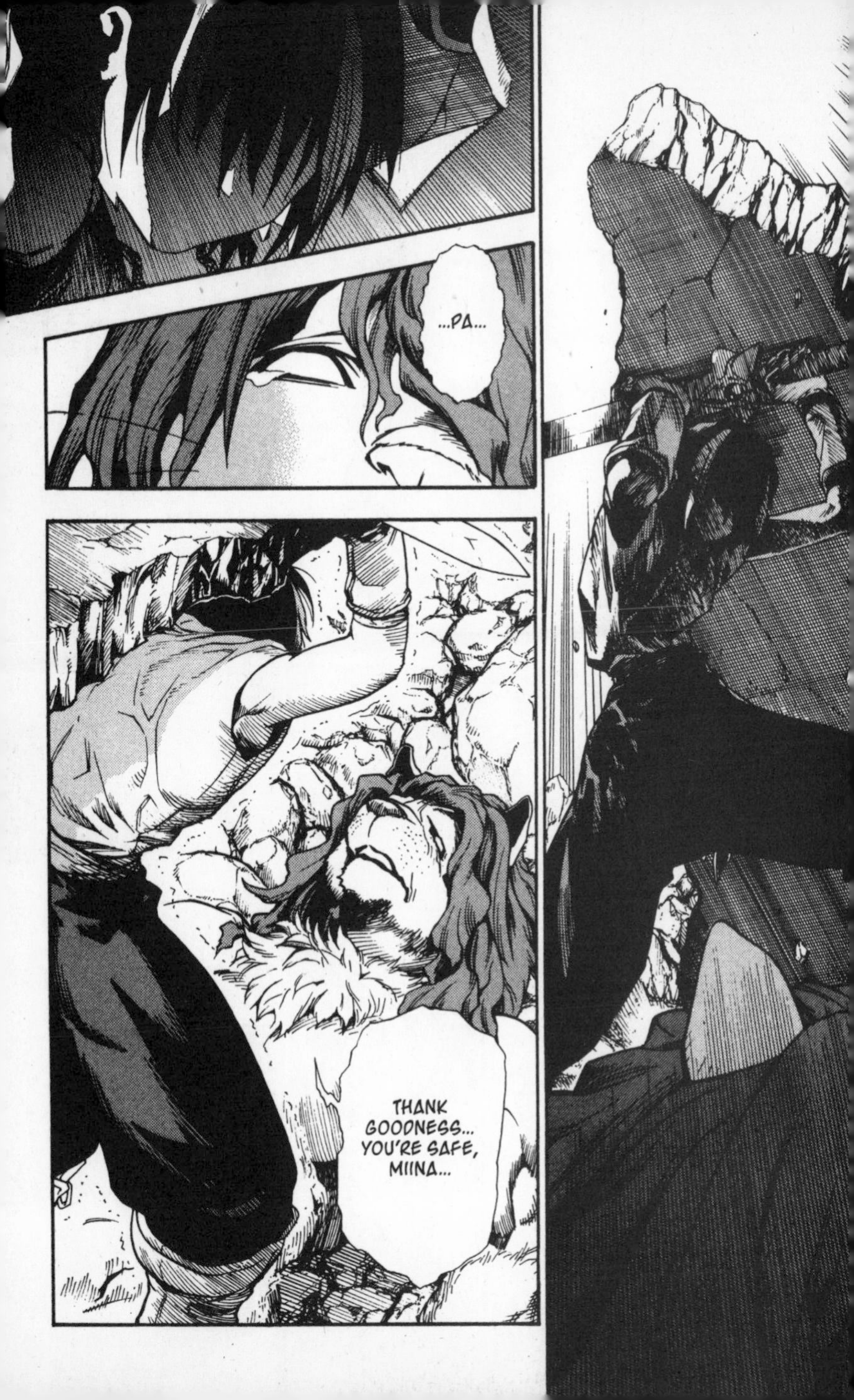
...PA...
THANK GOODNESS... YOU'RE SAFE, MIINA...

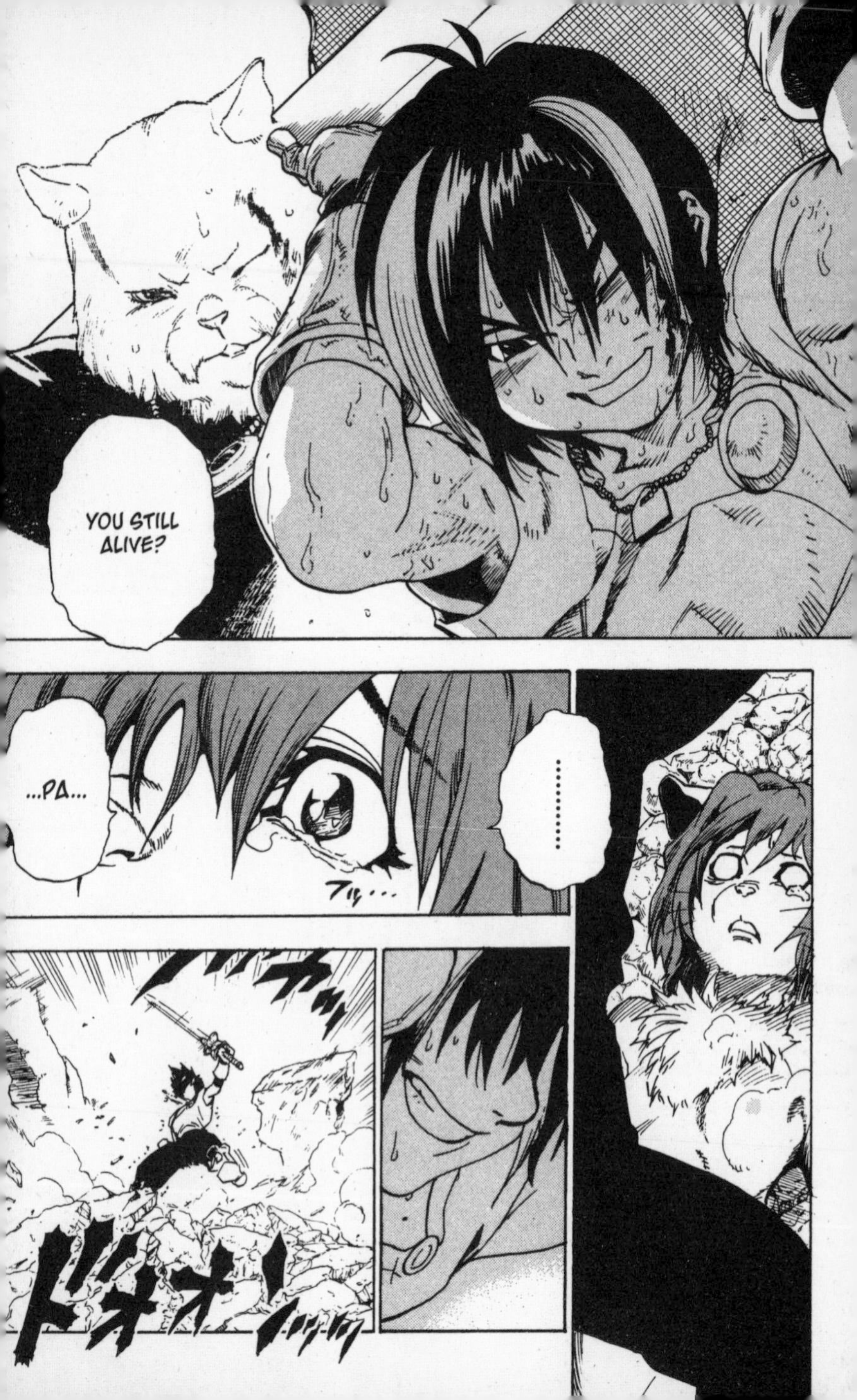
YOU STILL ALIVE?
....
...PA...

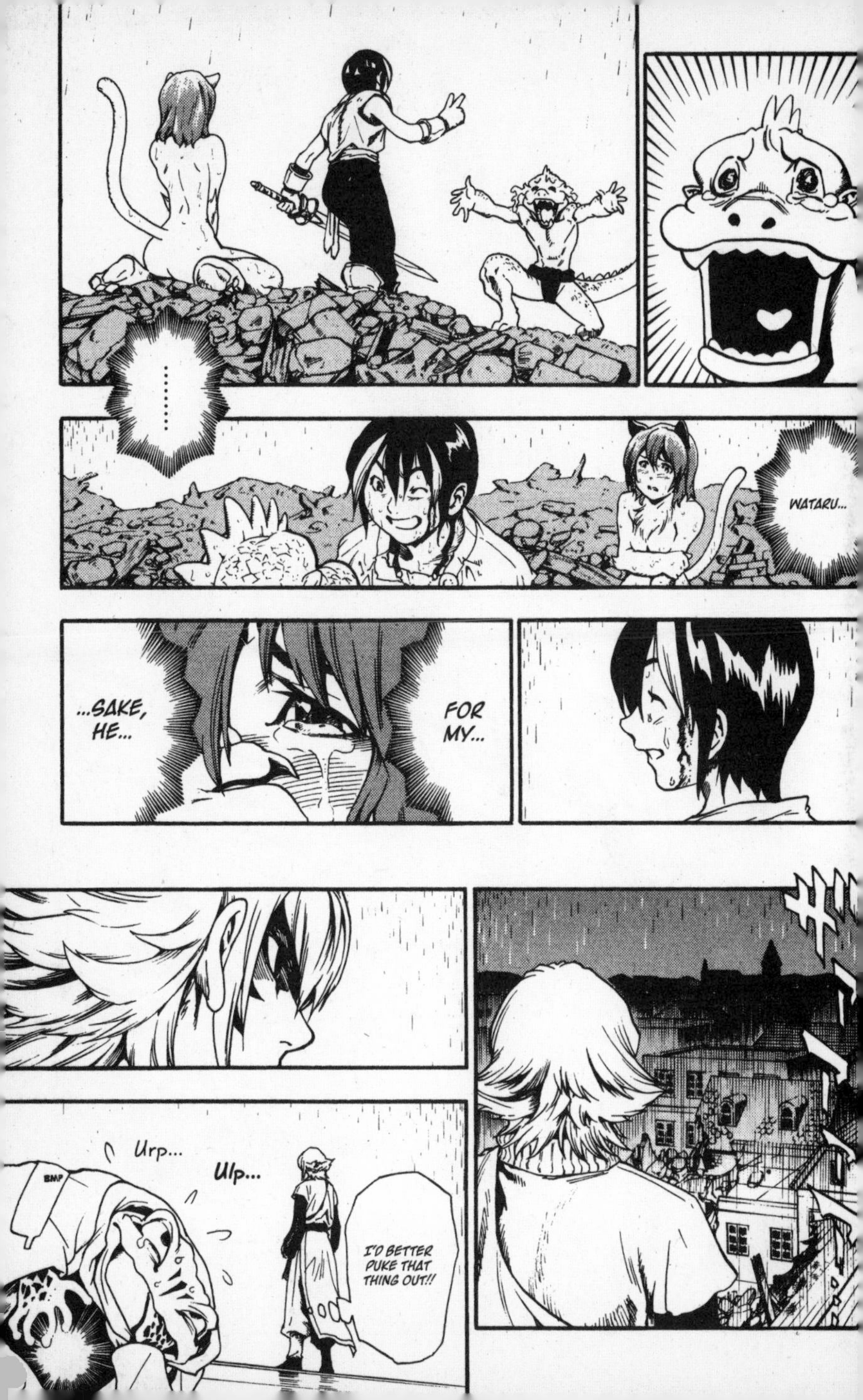
......
WATARU...
FOR MY...
...SAKE, HE...
I'D BETTER PUKE THAT THING OUT!!
Ulp...
Urp...
BMP

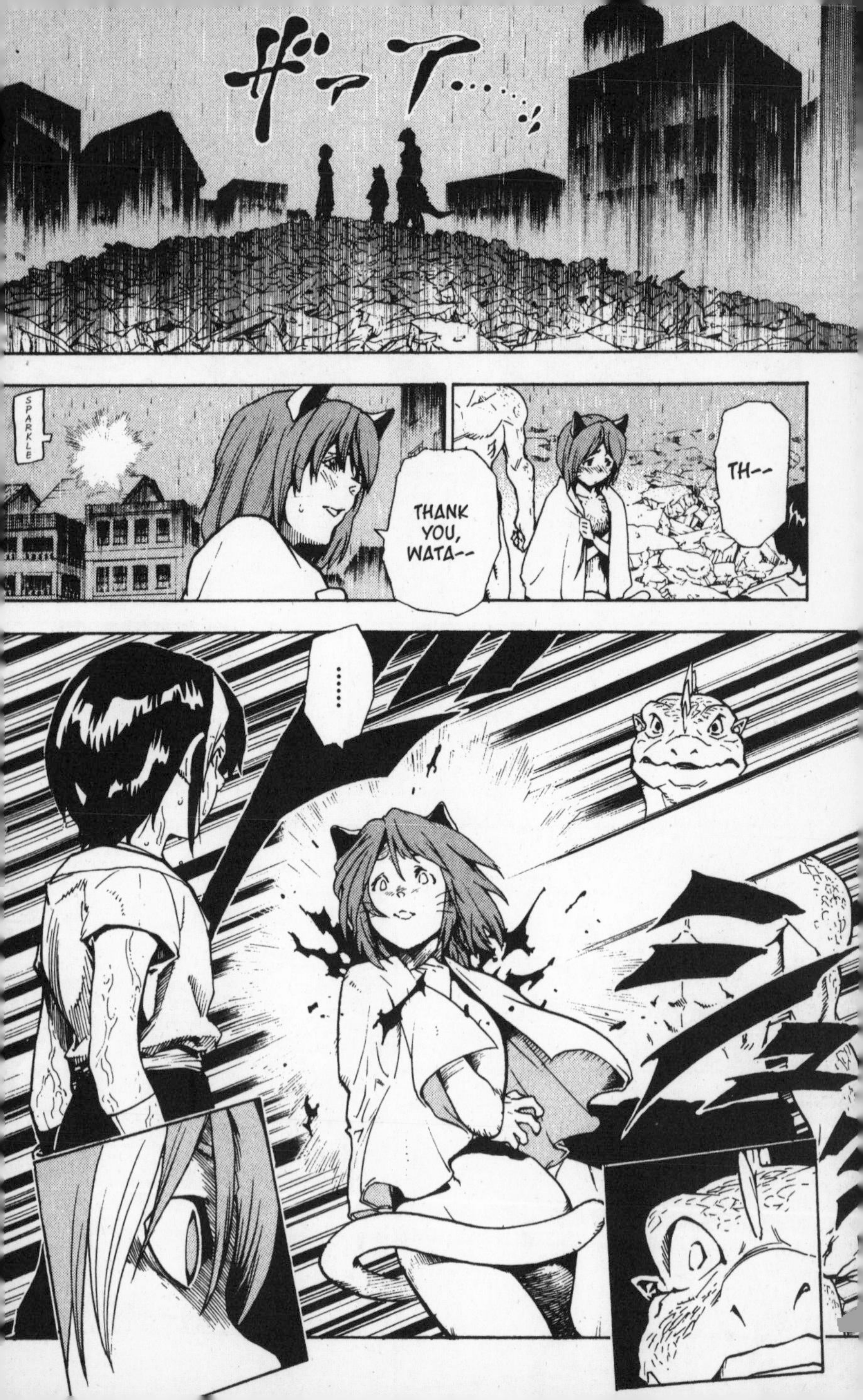
ザァア……
TH--
SPARKLE
THANK YOU, WATA--
......

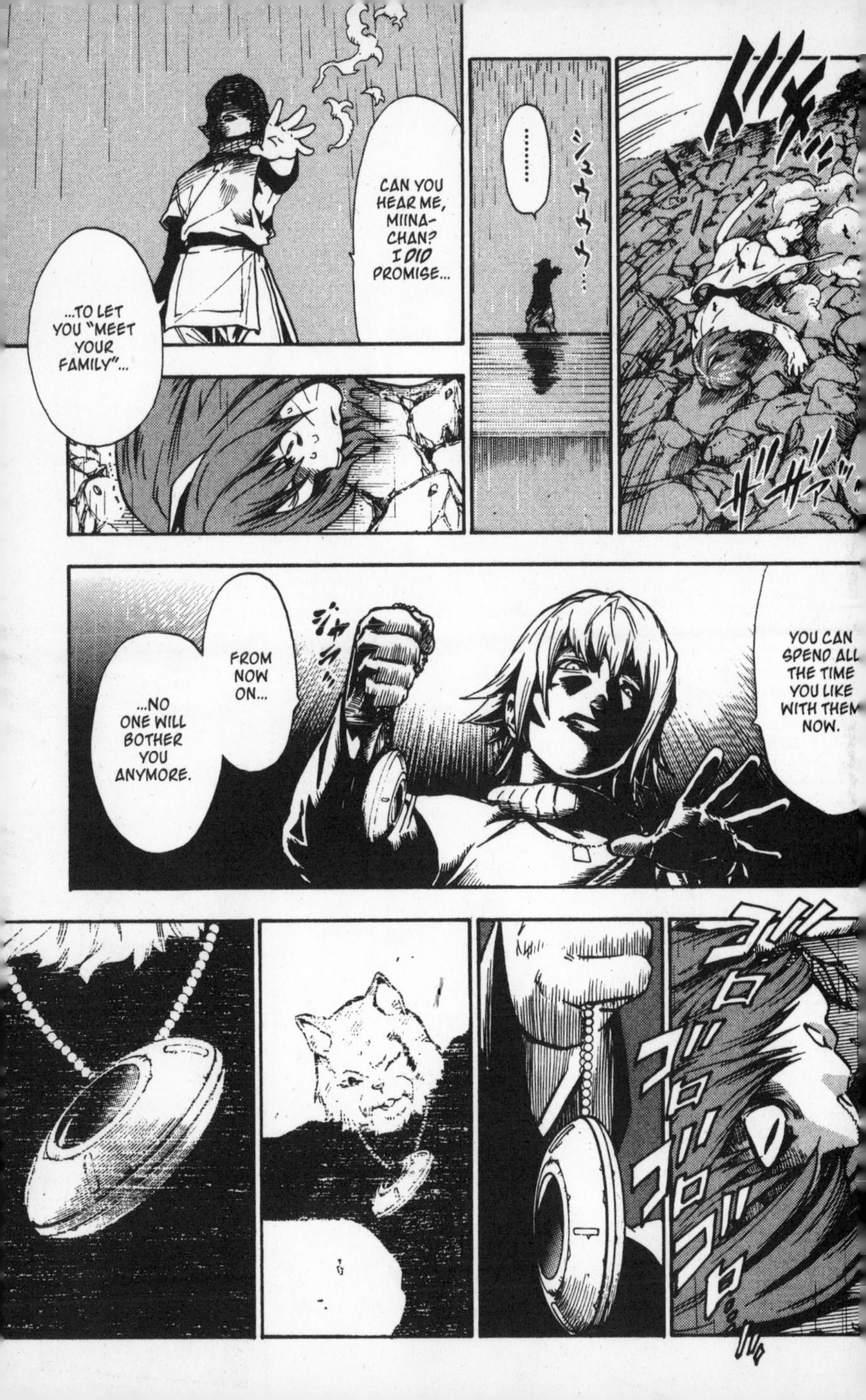
......
CAN YOU HEAR ME, MIINA-CHAN? I DID PROMISE...
...TO LET YOU "MEET YOUR FAMILY"...
YOU CAN SPEND ALL THE TIME YOU LIKE WITH THEM NOW.
FROM NOW ON...
...NO ONE WILL BOTHER YOU ANYMORE.

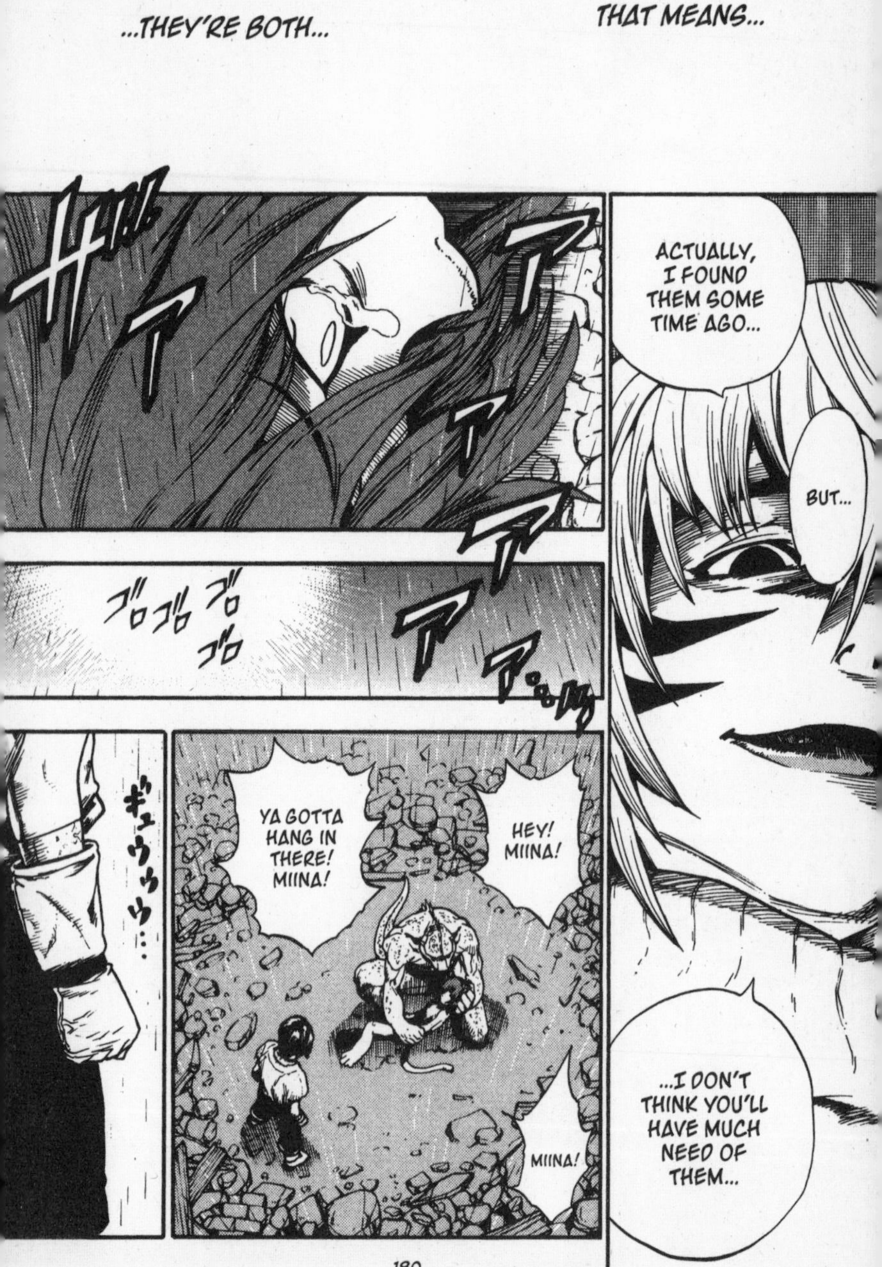
THAT MEANS...
...THEY'RE BOTH...
ACTUALLY, I FOUND THEM SOME TIME AGO...
BUT...
...I DON'T THINK YOU'LL HAVE MUCH NEED OF THEM...
HEY! MIINA!
YA GOTTA HANG IN THERE! MIINA!
MIINA!

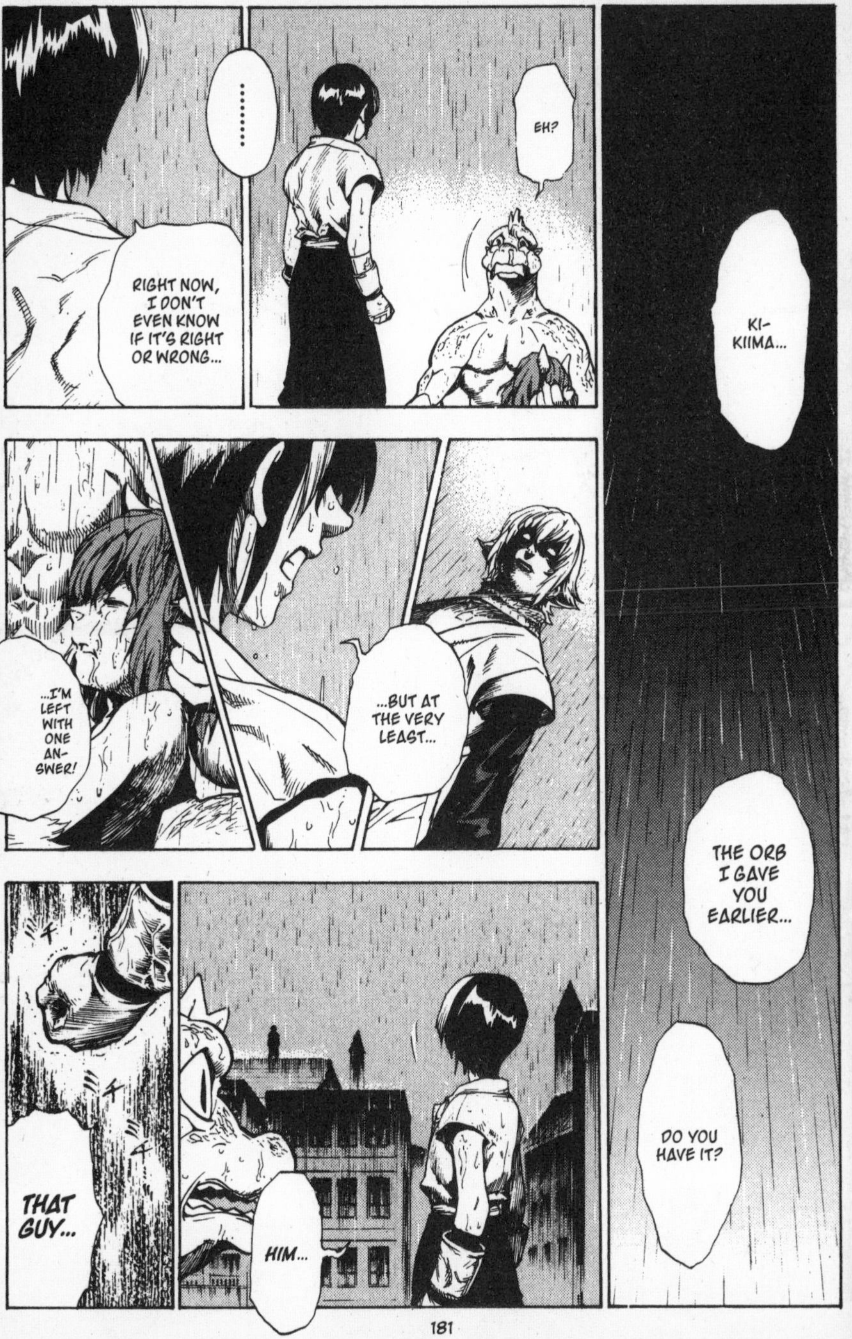
KI-KIIMA...
THE ORB I GAVE YOU EARLIER...
DO YOU HAVE IT?
EH?
......
RIGHT NOW, I DON'T EVEN KNOW IF IT'S RIGHT OR WRONG...
...BUT AT THE VERY LEAST...
...I'M LEFT WITH ONE AN-SWER!
HIM...
THAT GUY...

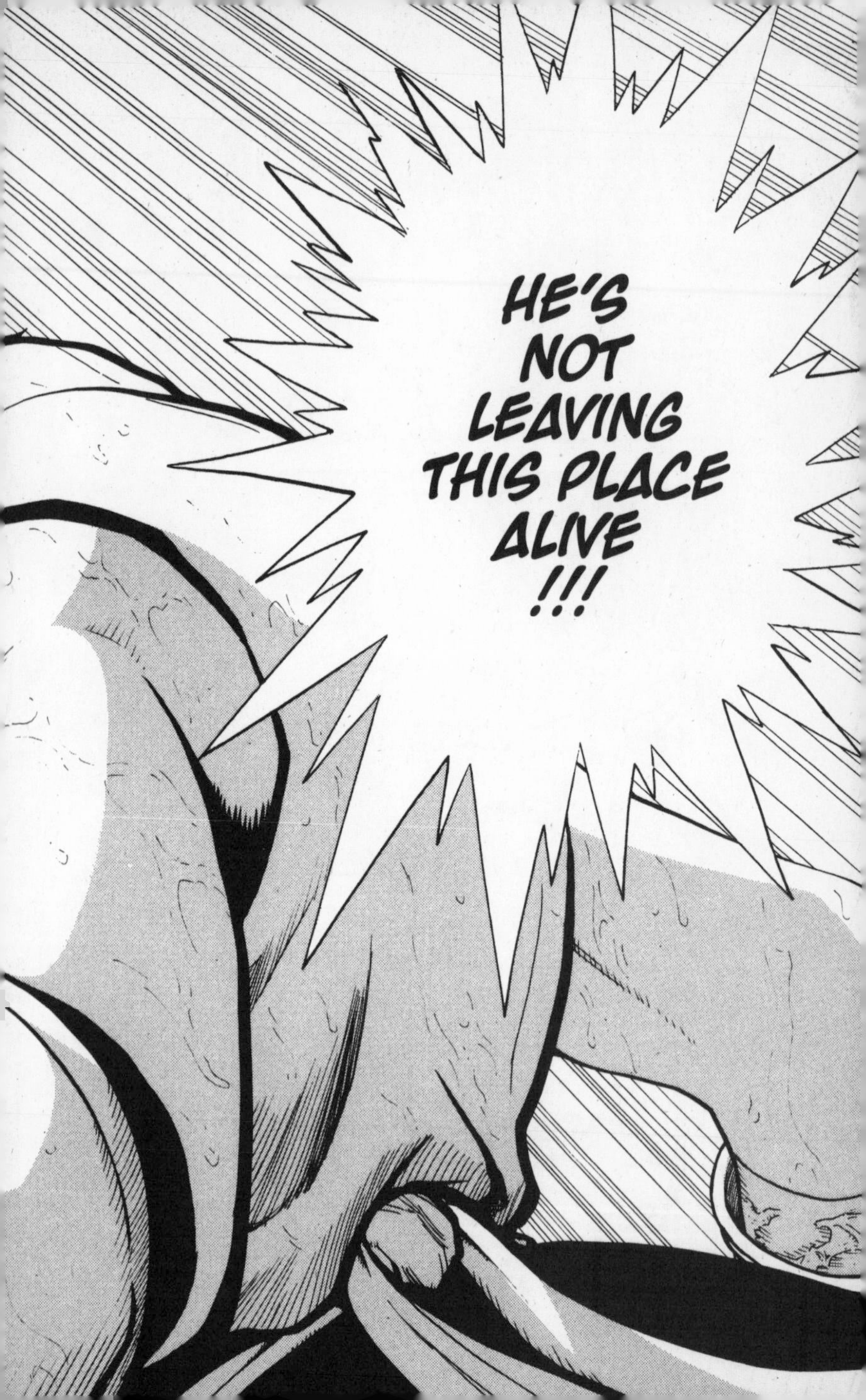
HE'S NOT LEAVING THIS PLACE ALIVE !!!

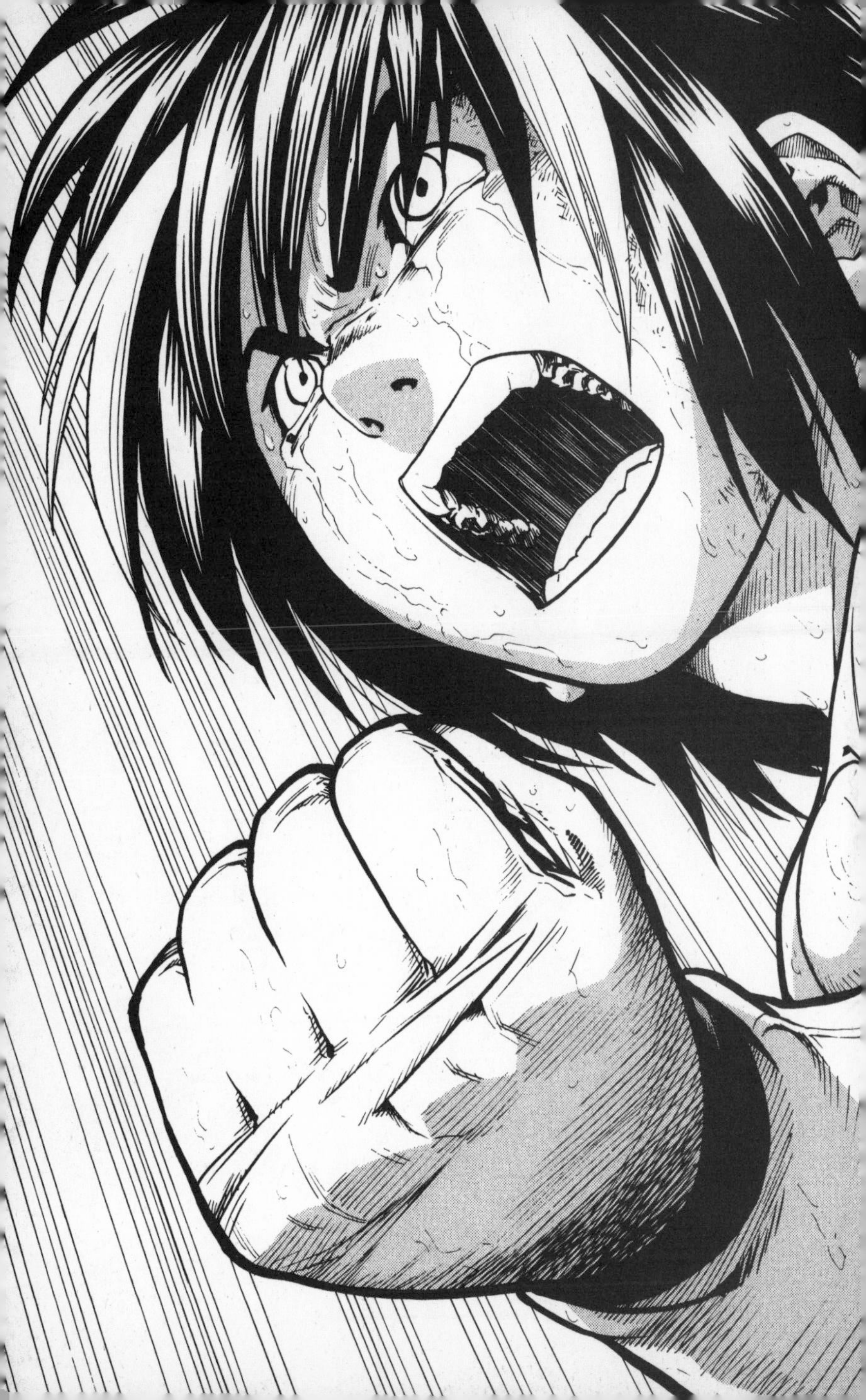

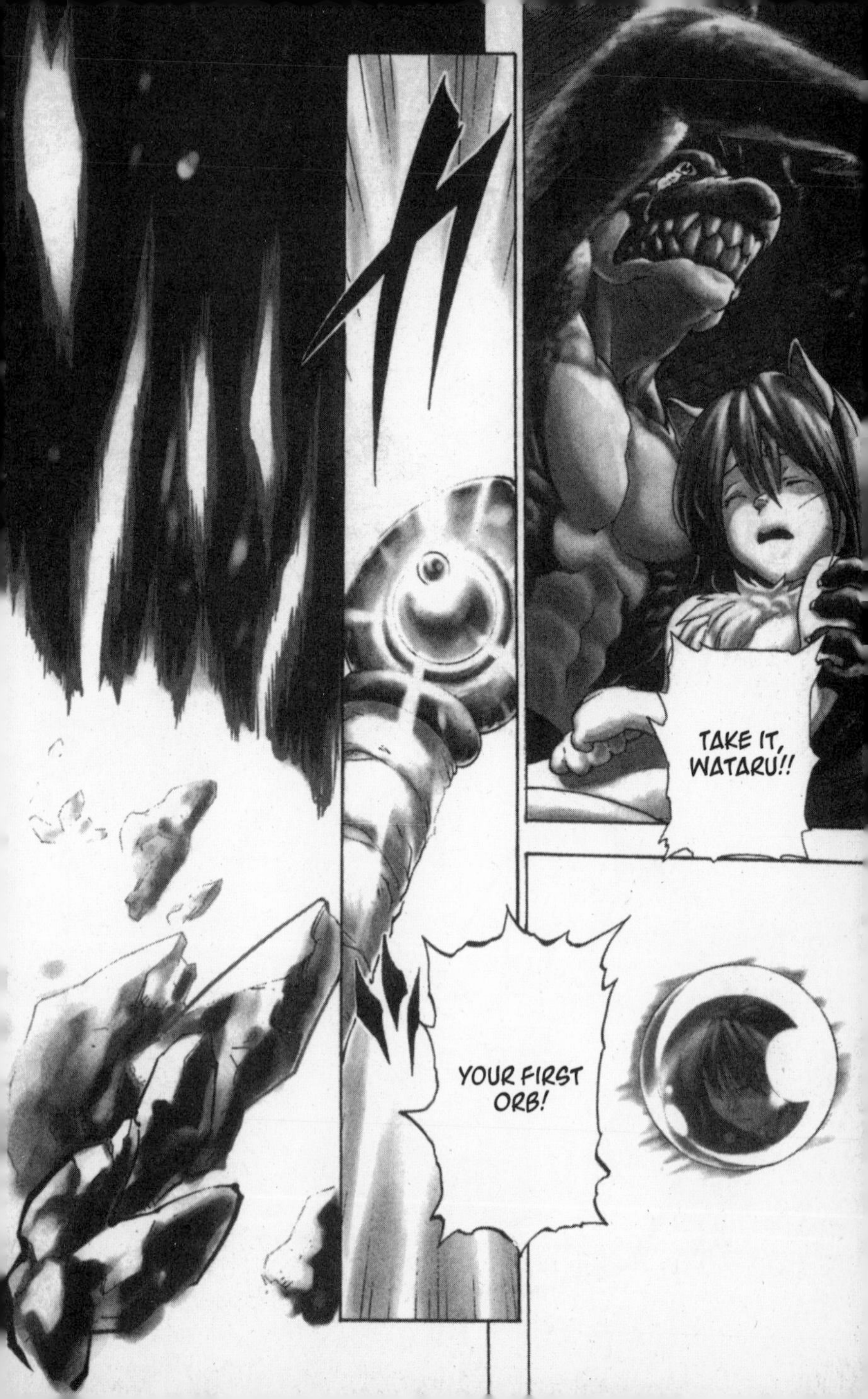
TAKE IT, WATARU!!
YOUR FIRST ORB!

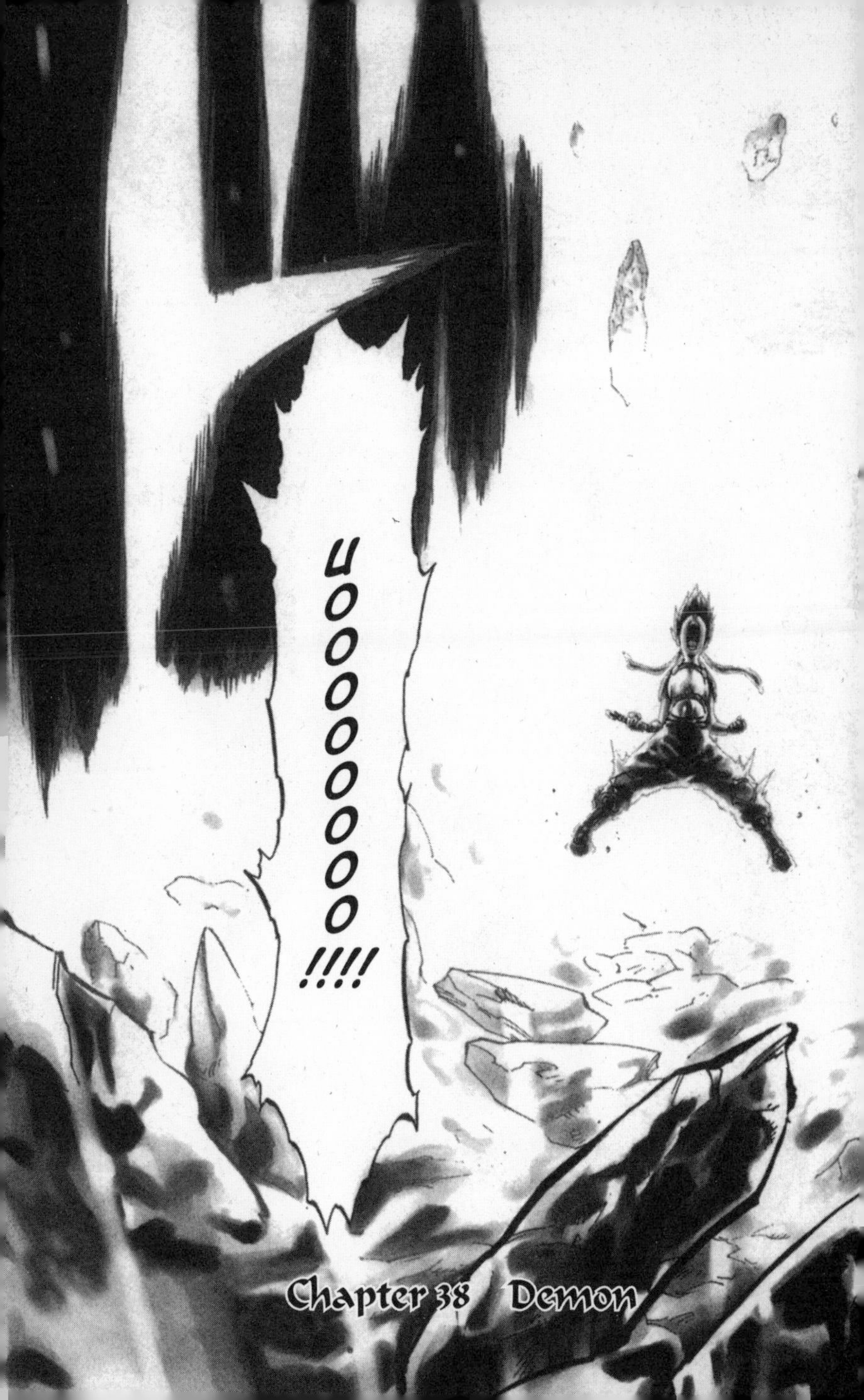
UOOOOOOOOOO!!!!

Chapter 38 Demon

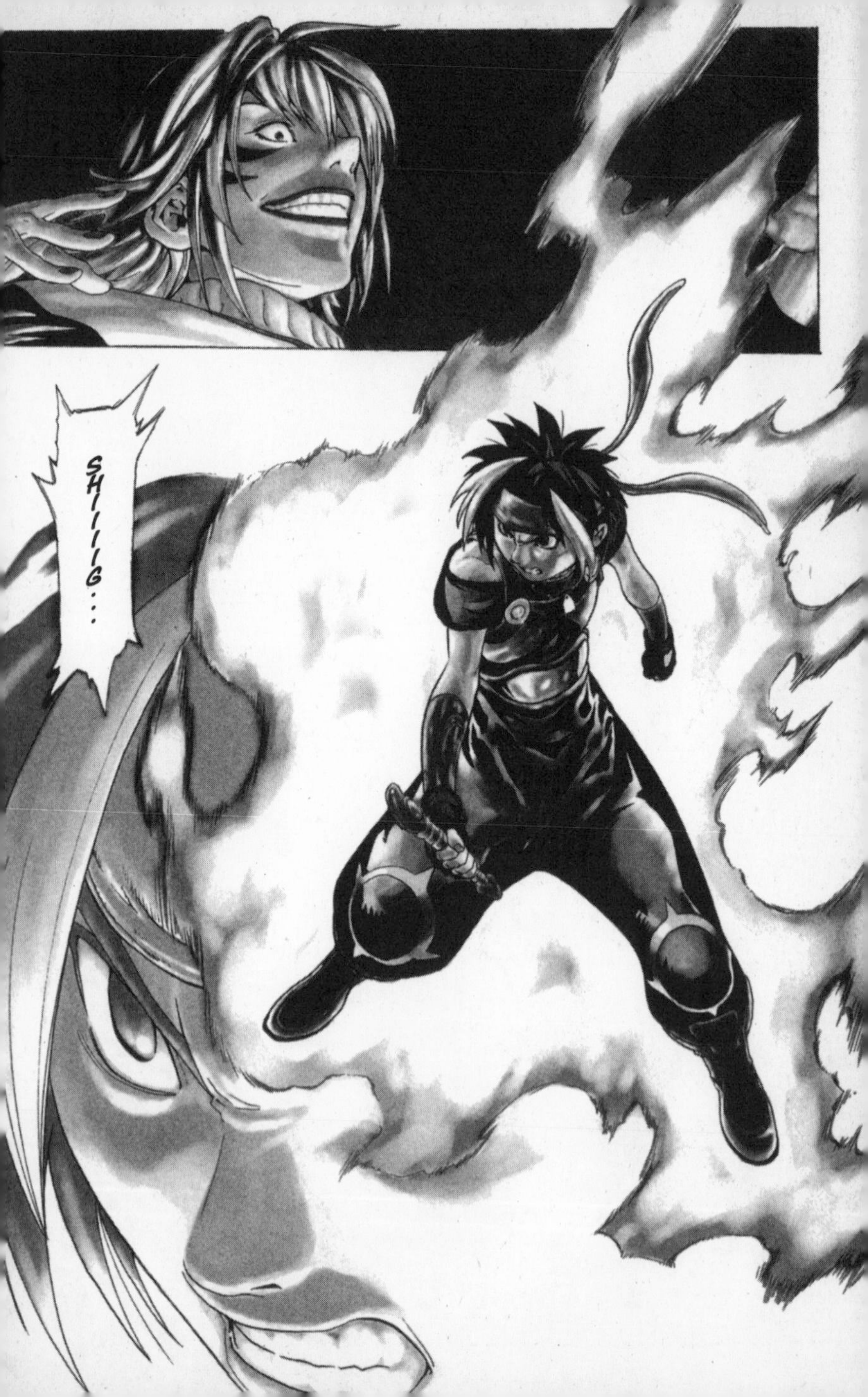
SHIIIIG...

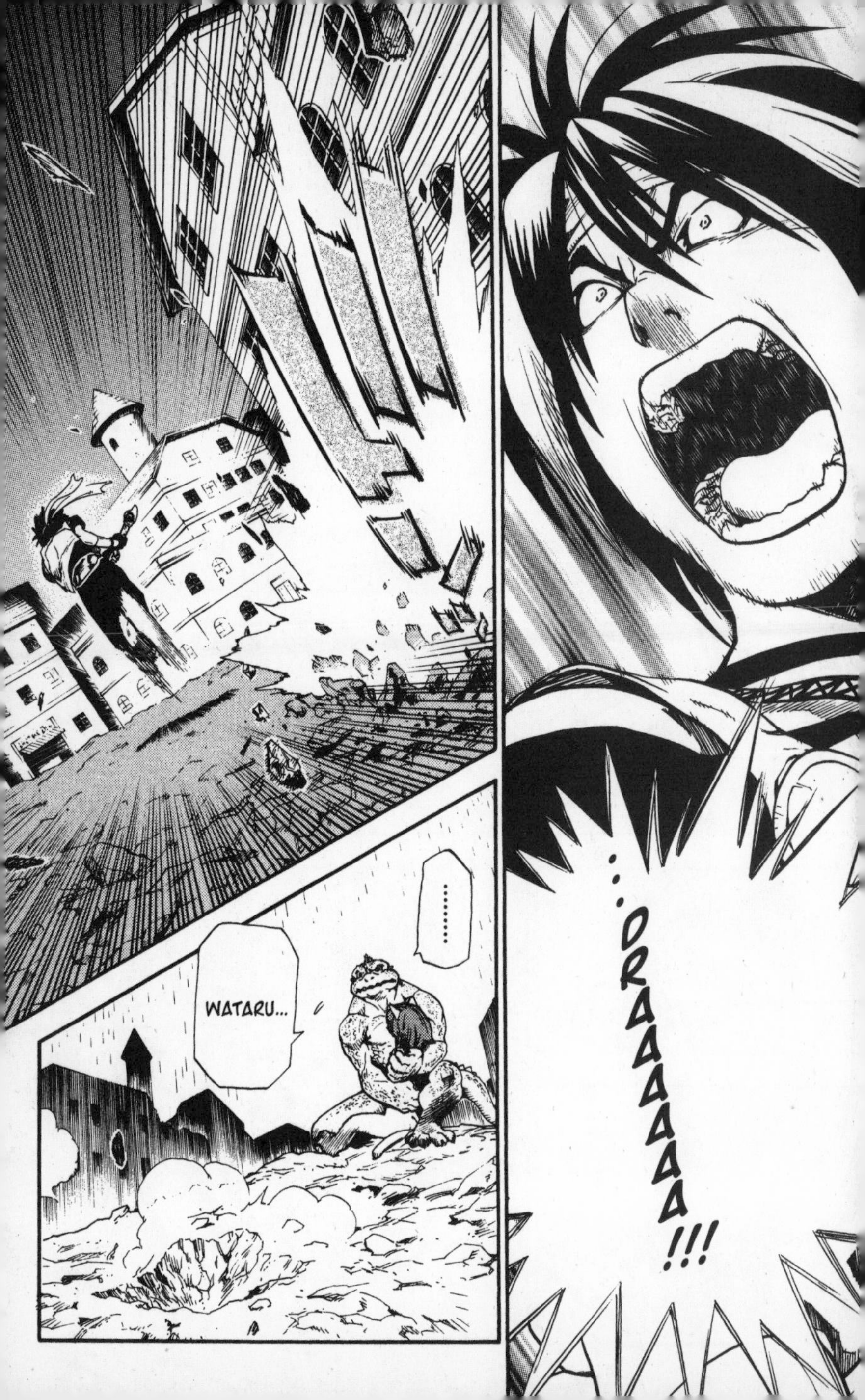
...ORAAAAAA!!!
......
WATARU...

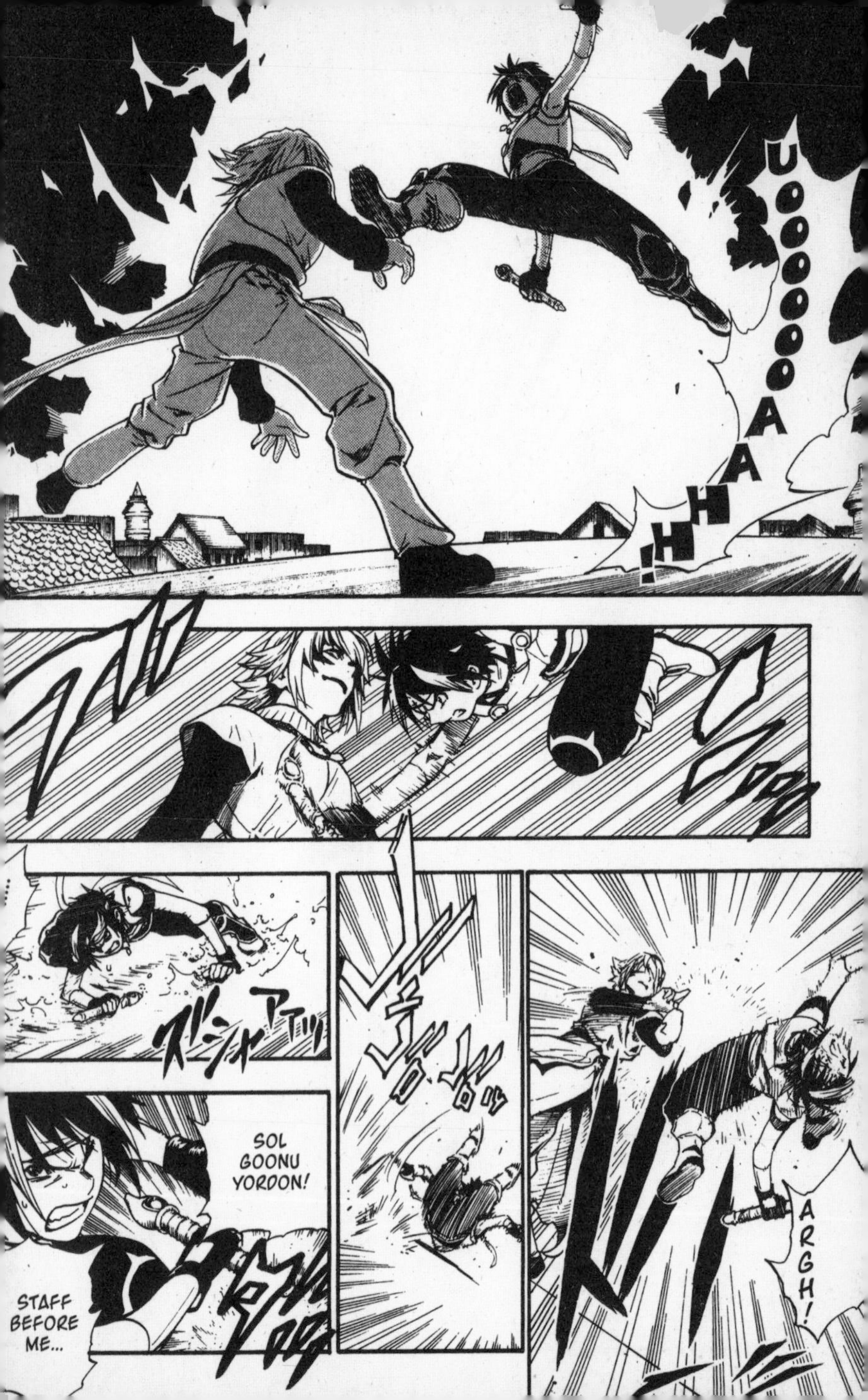
UOOOOOOAAHHH!
ARGH!
SOL GOONU YORDON!
STAFF BEFORE ME...

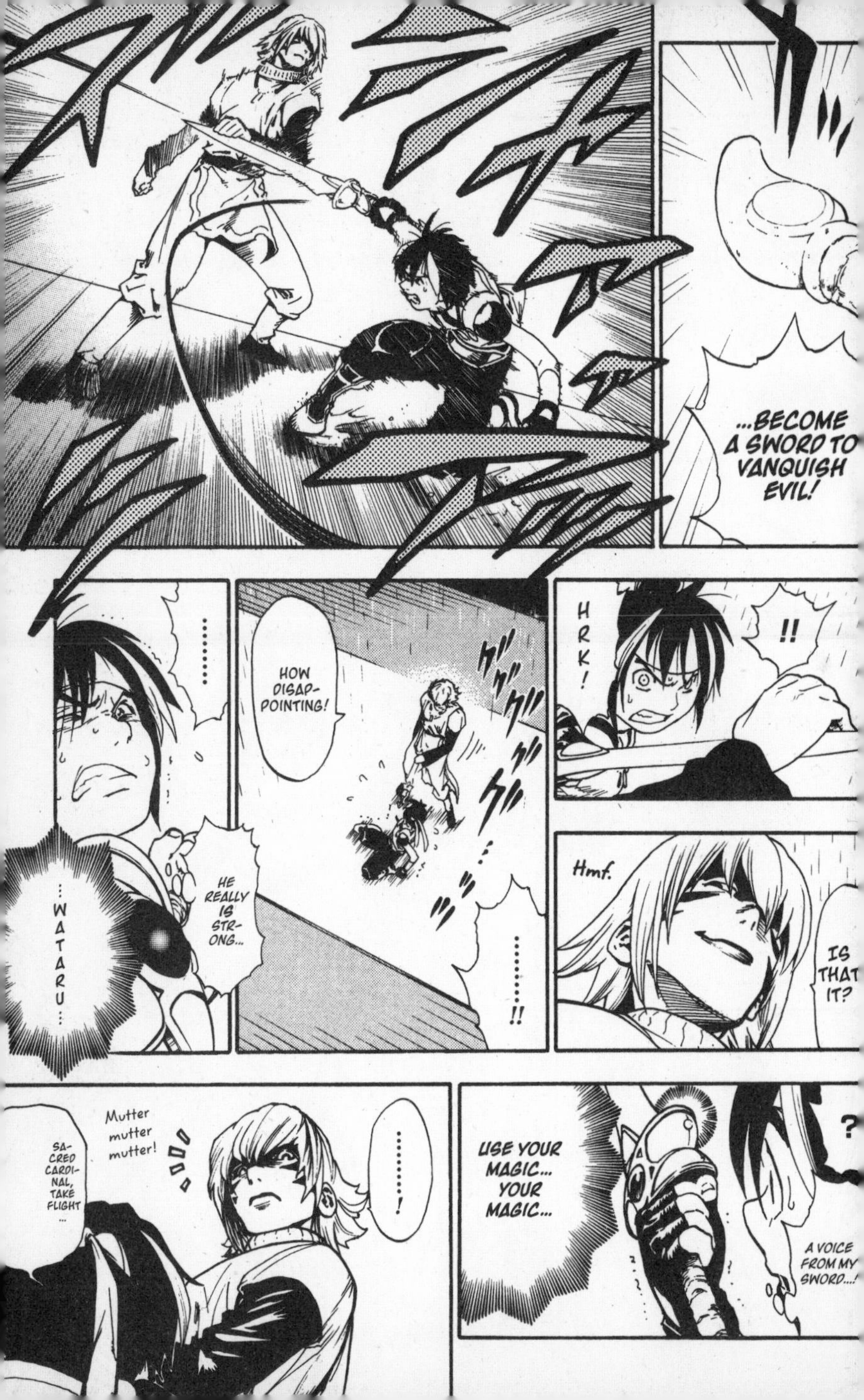
...BECOME A SWORD TO VANQUISH EVIL!
!!
HRK!
HOW DISAP-POINTING!
......
IS THAT IT?
Hmf.
......!!
HE REALLY IS STR-ONG...
...WATARU...
?
A VOICE FROM MY SWORD...!
USE YOUR MAGIC... YOUR MAGIC...
......!
Mutter mutter mutter!
SA-CRED CARDI-NAL, TAKE FLIGHT ...

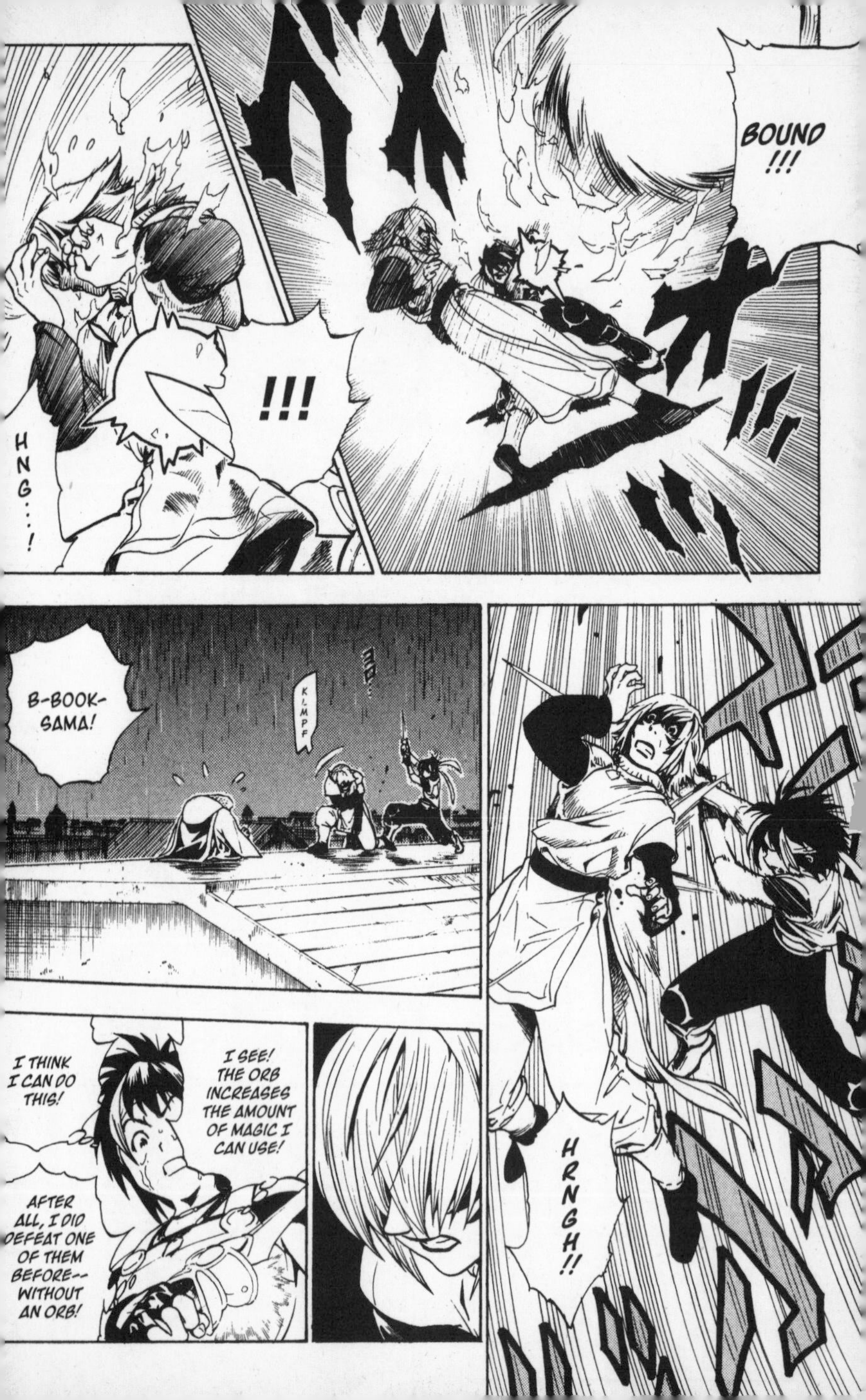
BOUND !!!
!!!
HNG...!
HRNGH!!
B-BOOK-SAMA!
KLMPF
I SEE! THE ORB INCREASES THE AMOUNT OF MAGIC I CAN USE!
I THINK I CAN DO THIS!
AFTER ALL, I DID DEFEAT ONE OF THEM BEFORE--WITHOUT AN ORB!

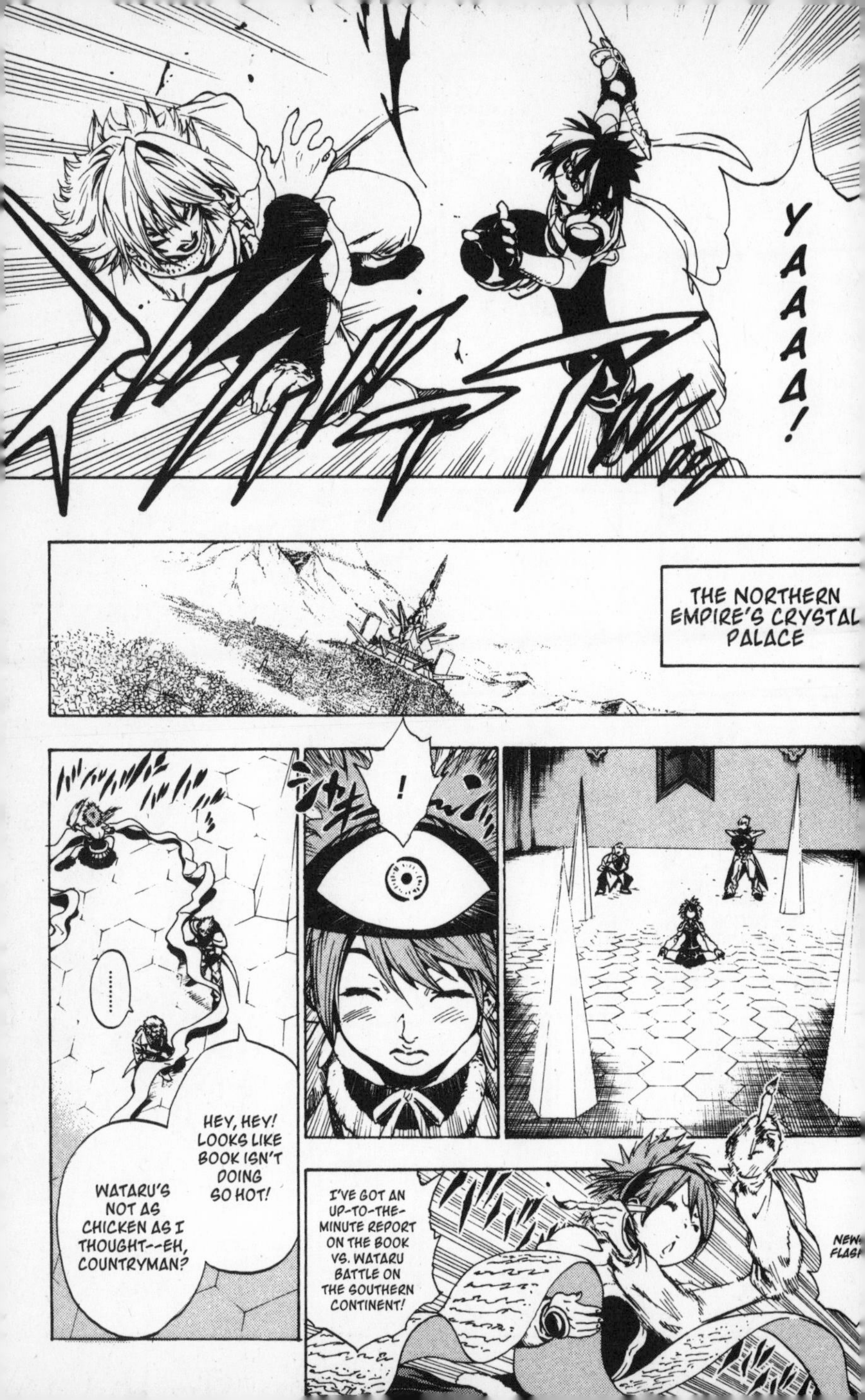
YAAAAA!
THE NORTHERN EMPIRE'S CRYSTAL PALACE
!
NEW FLAS
I'VE GOT AN UP-TO-THE-MINUTE REPORT ON THE BOOK VS. WATARU BATTLE ON THE SOUTHERN CONTINENT!
......
HEY, HEY! LOOKS LIKE BOOK ISN'T DOING SO HOT!
WATARU'S NOT AS CHICKEN AS I THOUGHT--EH, COUNTRYMAN?

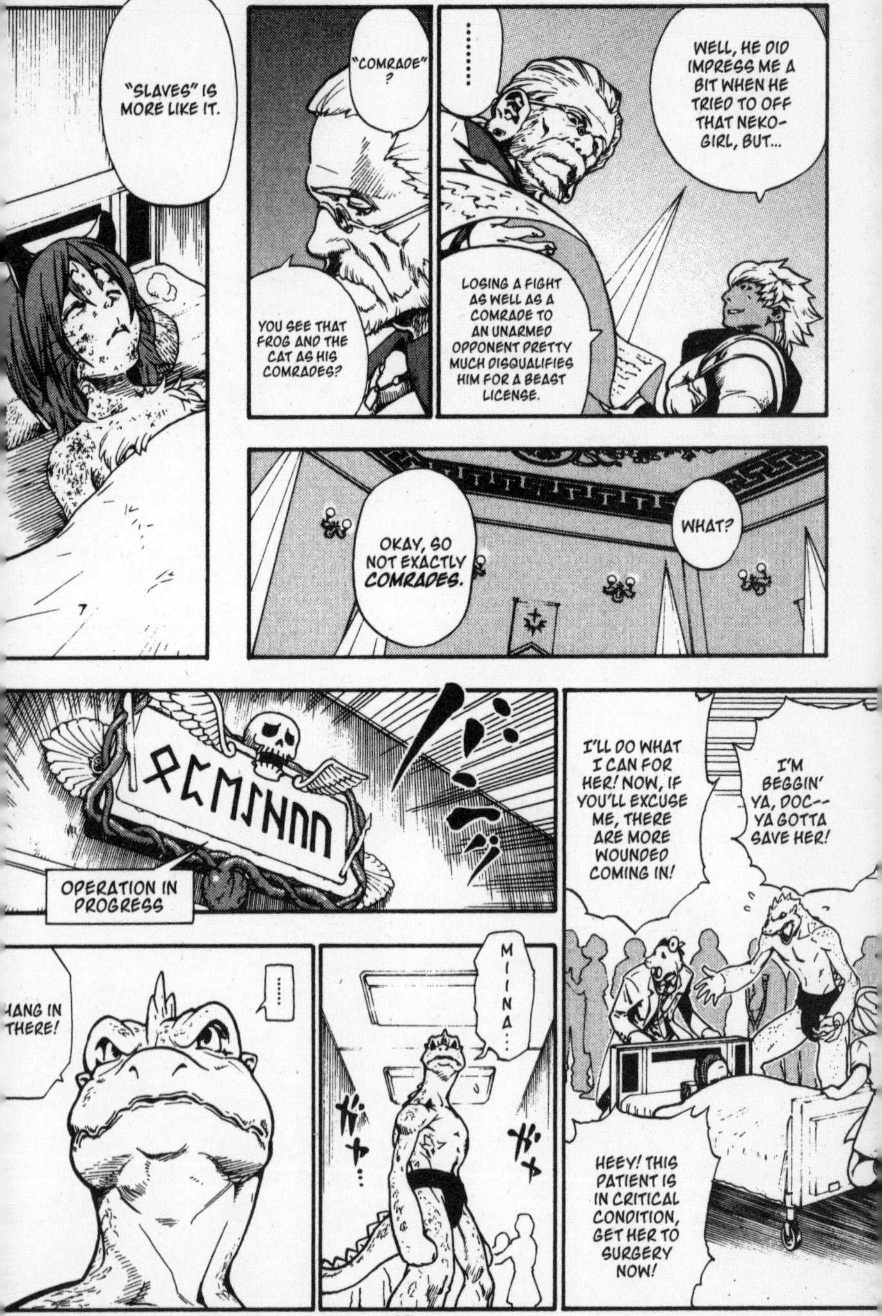
WELL, HE DID IMPRESS ME A BIT WHEN HE TRIED TO OFF THAT NEKO-GIRL, BUT...
......
LOSING A FIGHT AS WELL AS A COMRADE TO AN UNARMED OPPONENT PRETTY MUCH DISQUALIFIES HIM FOR A BEAST LICENSE.
"COMRADE"?
YOU SEE THAT FROG AND THE CAT AS HIS COMRADES?
"SLAVES" IS MORE LIKE IT.
WHAT?
OKAY, SO NOT EXACTLY COMRADES.
I'M BEGGIN' YA, DOC-- YA GOTTA SAVE HER!
I'LL DO WHAT I CAN FOR HER! NOW, IF YOU'LL EXCUSE ME, THERE ARE MORE WOUNDED COMING IN!
HEEY! THIS PATIENT IS IN CRITICAL CONDITION, GET HER TO SURGERY NOW!
OPERATION IN PROGRESS
MIINA...
......
HANG IN THERE!

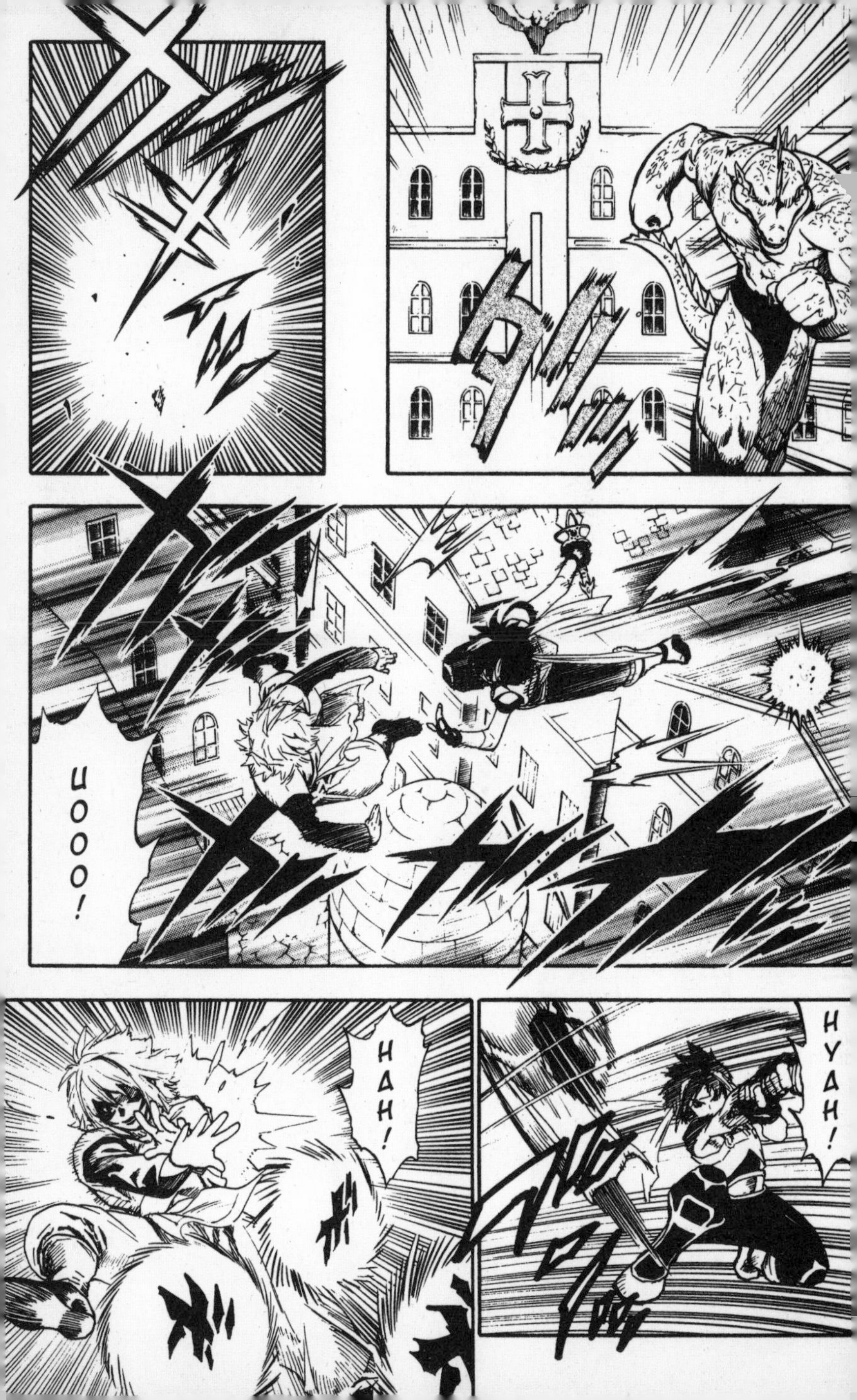
UOOOO!
HYAH!
HAH!

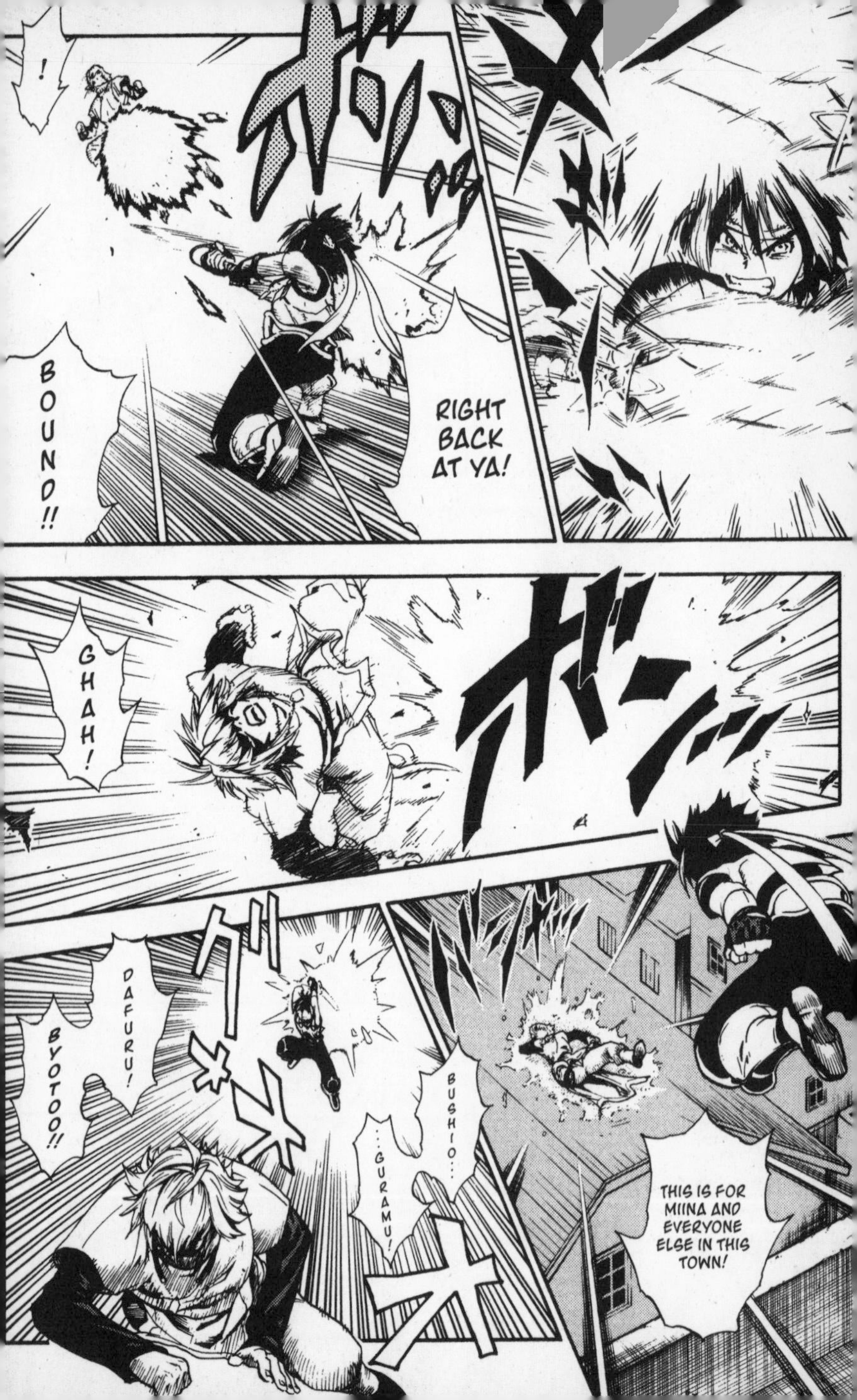
!
RIGHT BACK AT YA!
BOUNDO!!
GHAH!
THIS IS FOR MIINA AND EVERYONE ELSE IN THIS TOWN!
BUSHIO...
...GURAMU!
DAFURU!
BYOTOO!!

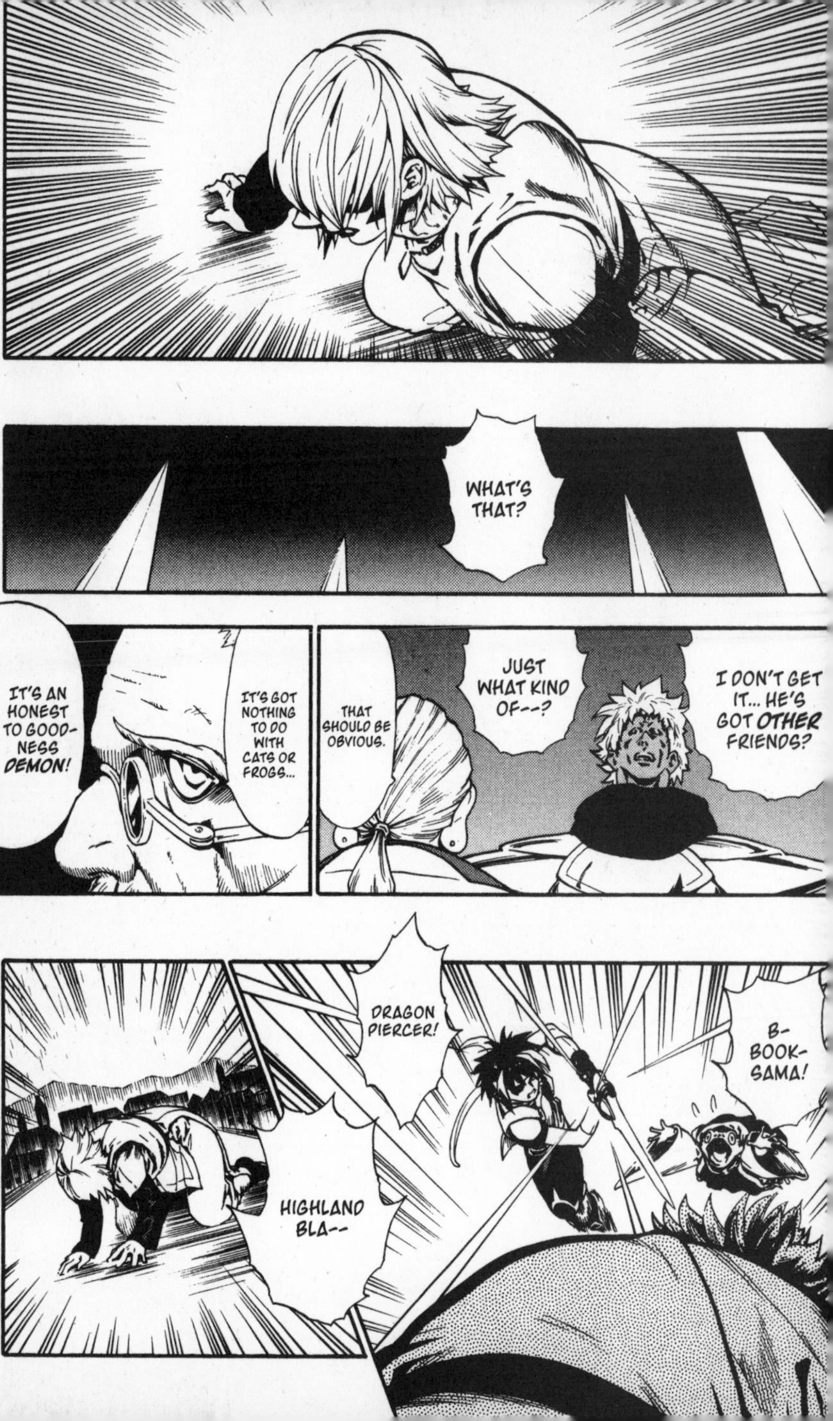
WHAT'S THAT?
I DON'T GET IT... HE'S GOT OTHER FRIENDS?
JUST WHAT KIND OF--?
THAT SHOULD BE OBVIOUS.
IT'S GOT NOTHING TO DO WITH CATS OR FROGS...
IT'S AN HONEST TO GOOD-NESS DEMON!
B-BOOK-SAMA!
DRAGON PIERCER!
HIGHLAND BLA--

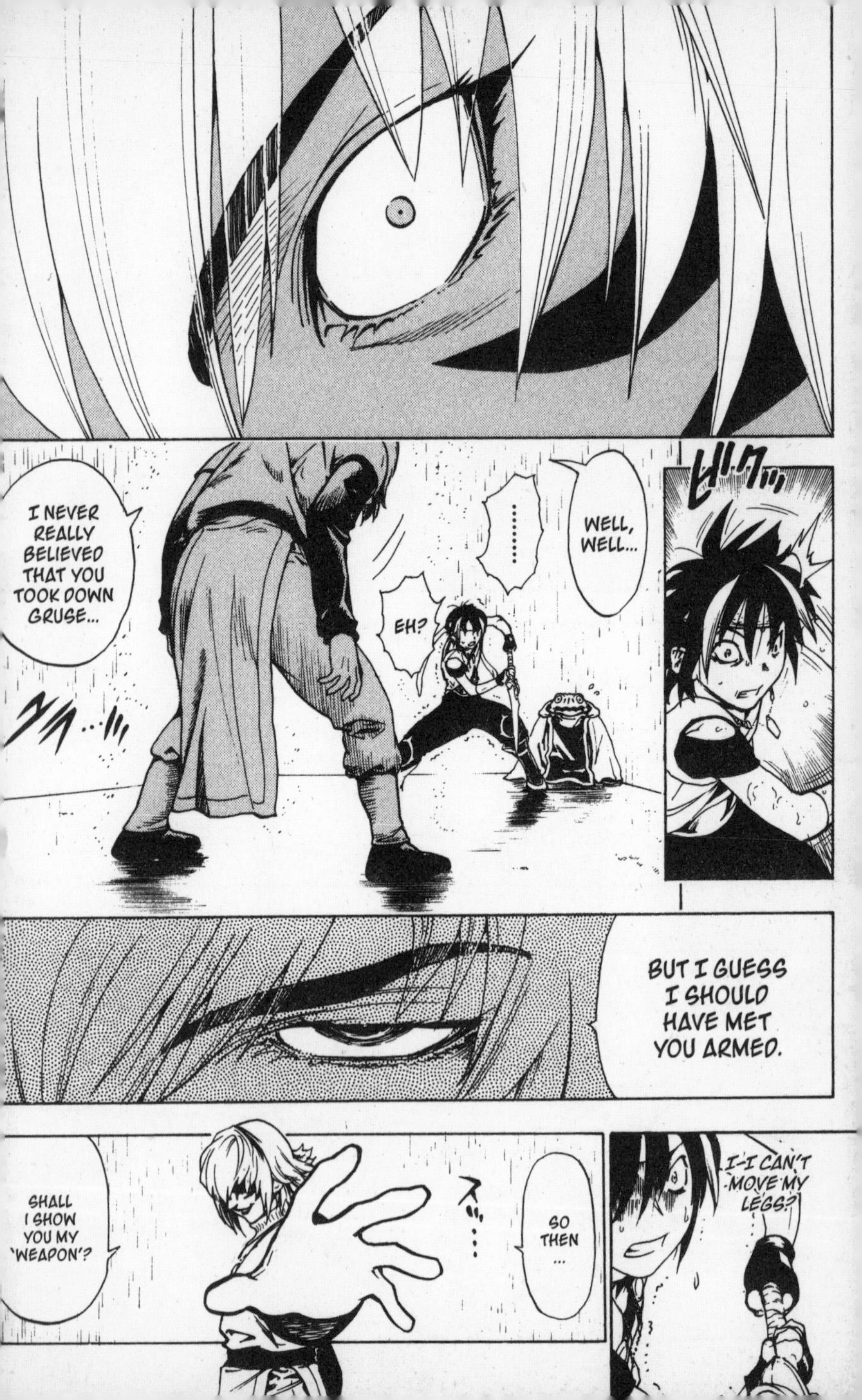
WELL, WELL...
......
EH?
I NEVER REALLY BELIEVED THAT YOU TOOK DOWN GRUSE...
BUT I GUESS I SHOULD HAVE MET YOU ARMED.
I-I CAN'T MOVE MY LEGS?
SO THEN ...
SHALL I SHOW YOU MY 'WEAPON'?

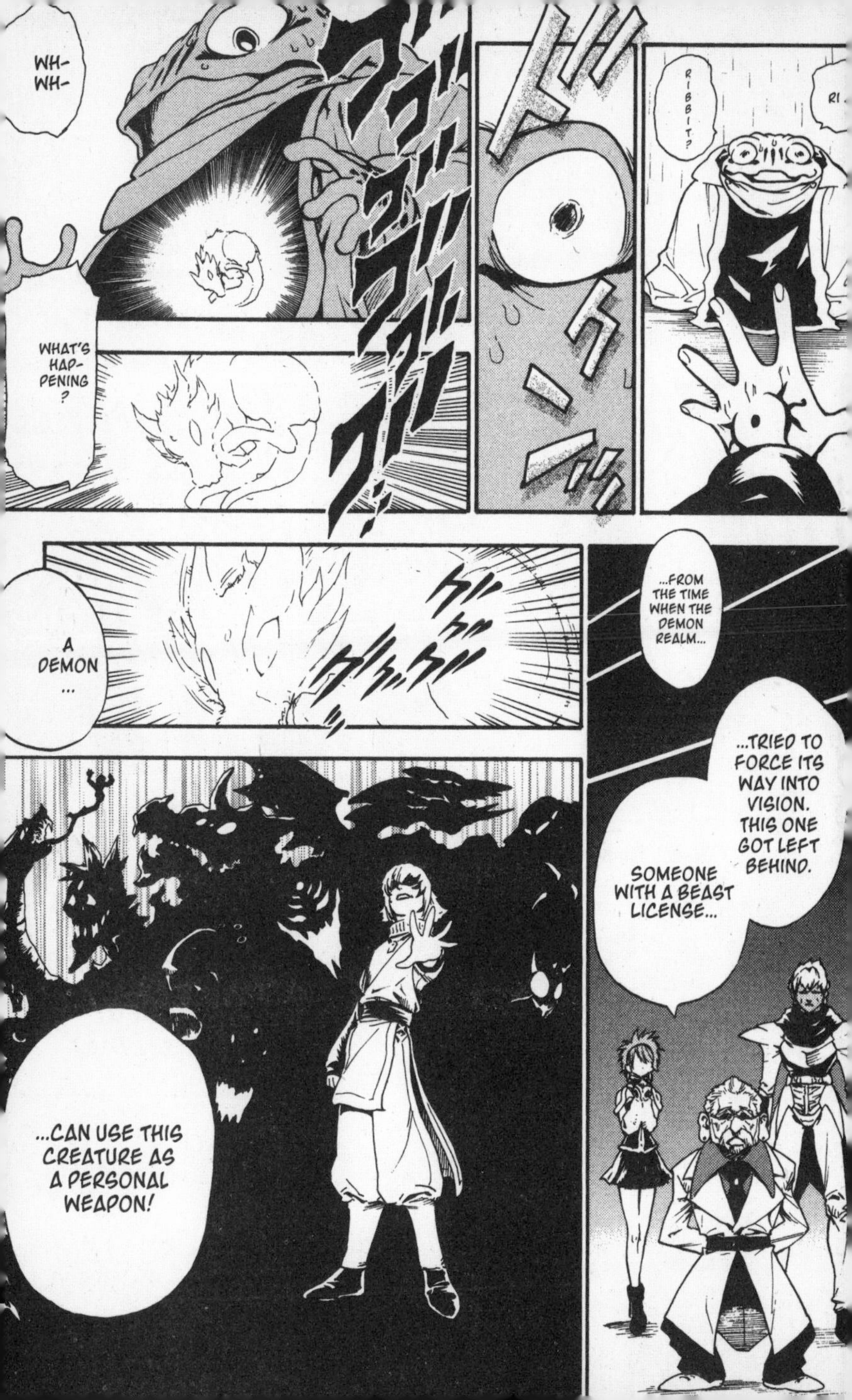
RI
RIBBIT?
WH- WH-
WHAT'S HAP-PENING?
...FROM THE TIME WHEN THE DEMON REALM...
...TRIED TO FORCE ITS WAY INTO VISION. THIS ONE GOT LEFT BEHIND.
SOMEONE WITH A BEAST LICENSE...
A DEMON...
...CAN USE THIS CREATURE AS A PERSONAL WEAPON!

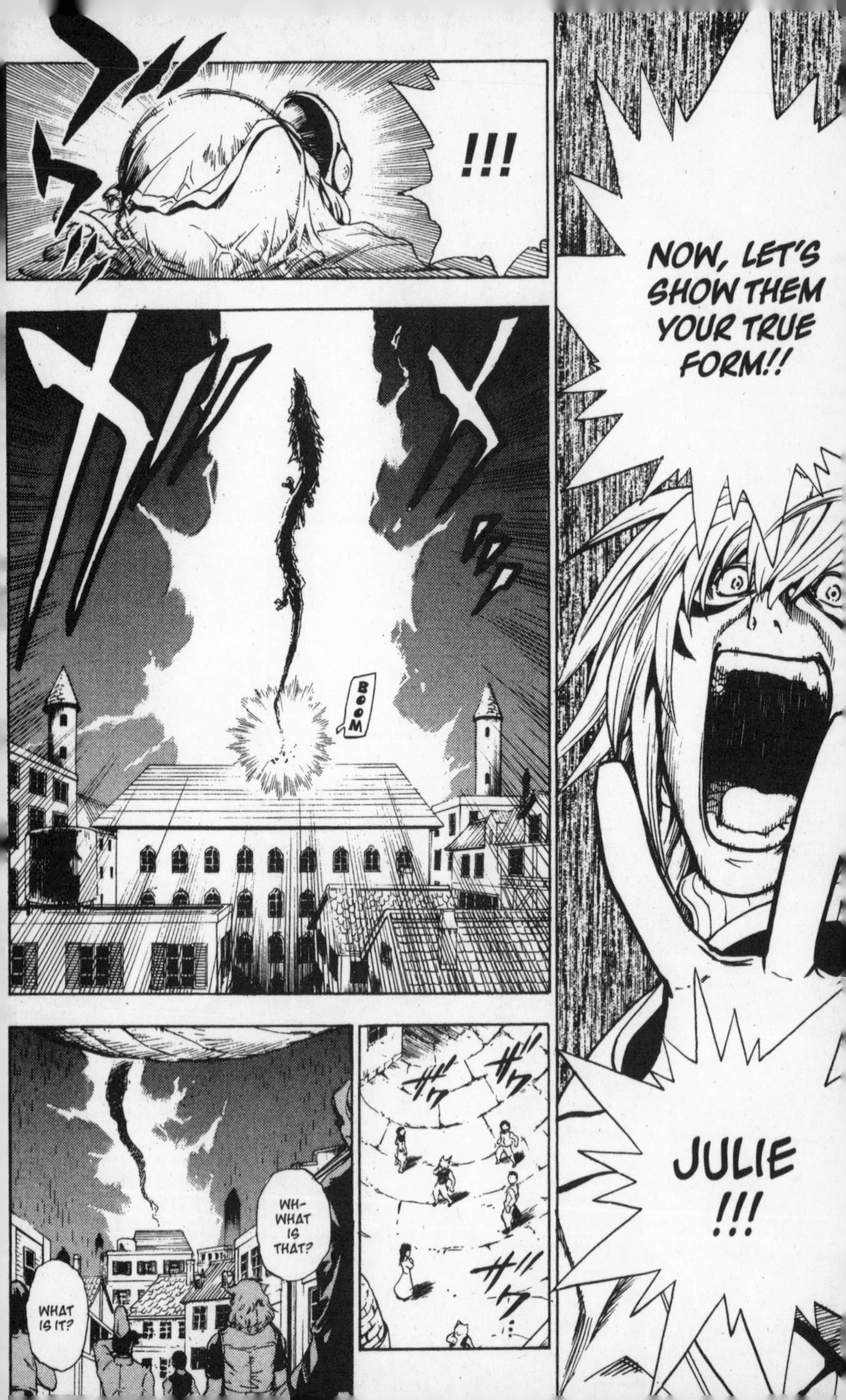
NOW, LET'S SHOW THEM YOUR TRUE FORM!!
JULIE !!!
!!!
BOOM
WH- WHAT IS THAT?
WHAT IS IT?

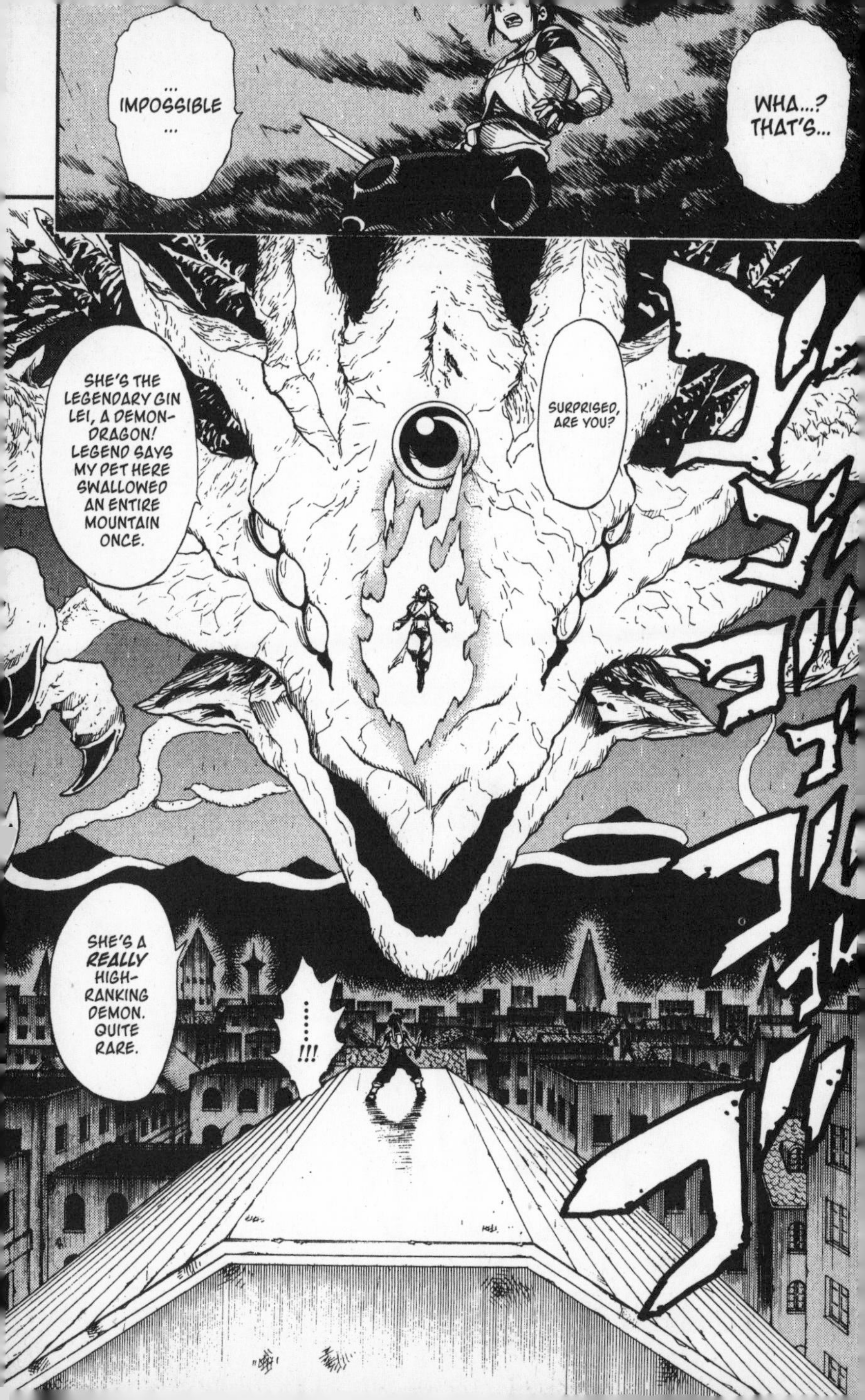
WHA...? THAT'S...
... IMPOSSIBLE ...
SURPRISED, ARE YOU?
SHE'S THE LEGENDARY GIN LEI, A DEMON-DRAGON! LEGEND SAYS MY PET HERE SWALLOWED AN ENTIRE MOUNTAIN ONCE.
SHE'S A REALLY HIGH-RANKING DEMON. QUITE RARE.
......!!!

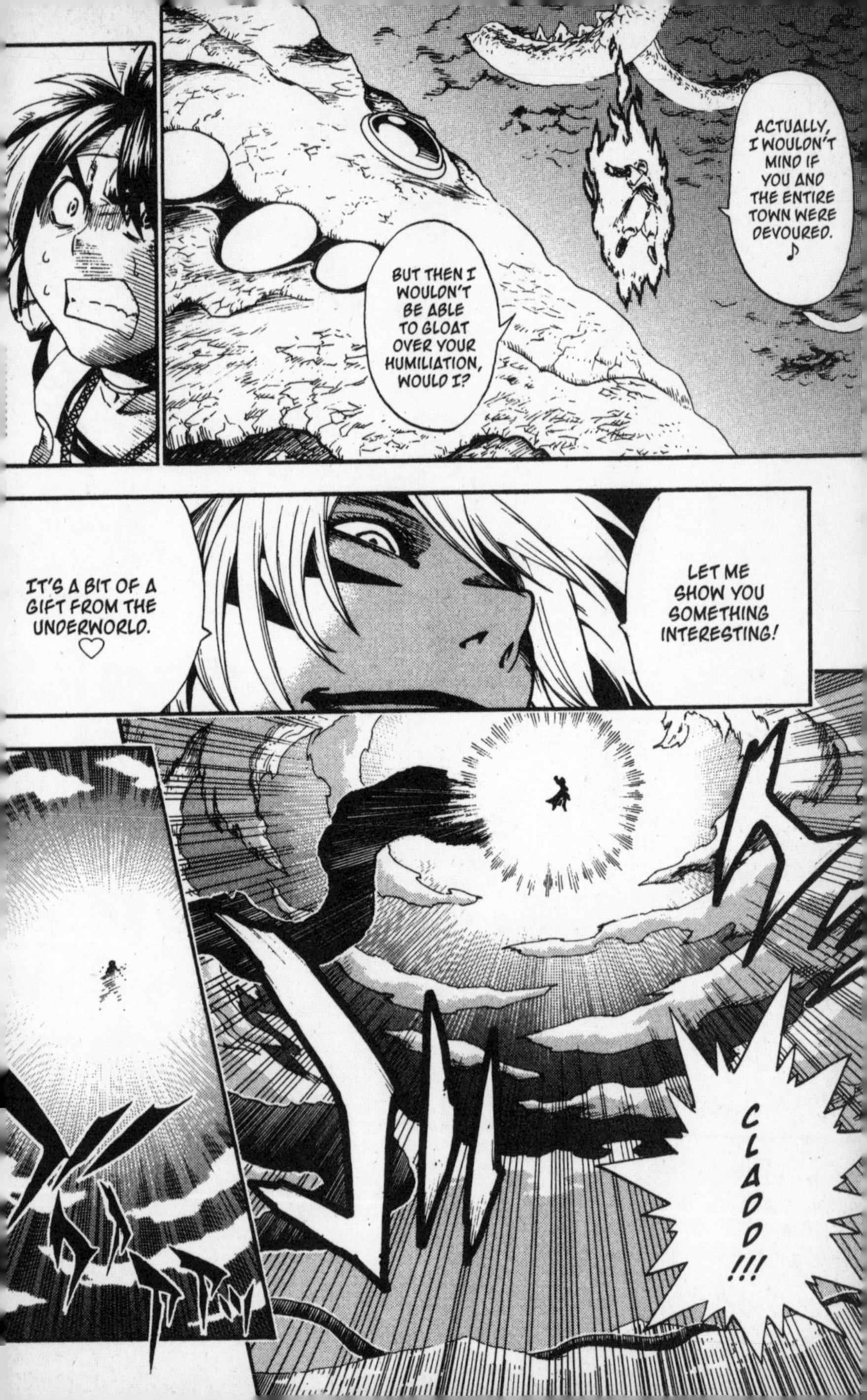
ACTUALLY, I WOULDN'T MIND IF YOU AND THE ENTIRE TOWN WERE DEVOURED. ♪
BUT THEN I WOULDN'T BE ABLE TO GLOAT OVER YOUR HUMILIATION, WOULD I?
LET ME SHOW YOU SOMETHING INTERESTING!
IT'S A BIT OF A GIFT FROM THE UNDERWORLD. ♡
CLADD!!!

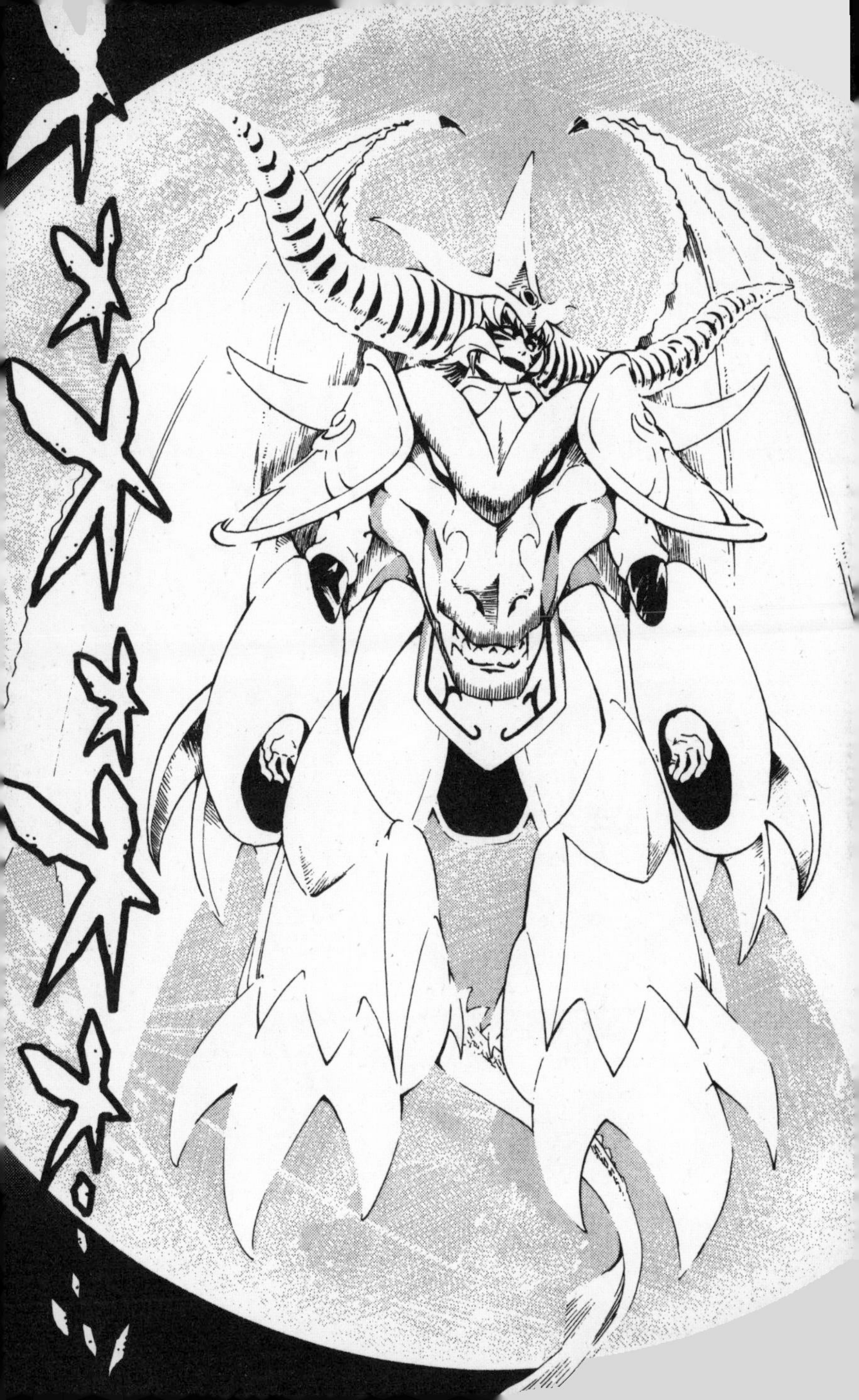

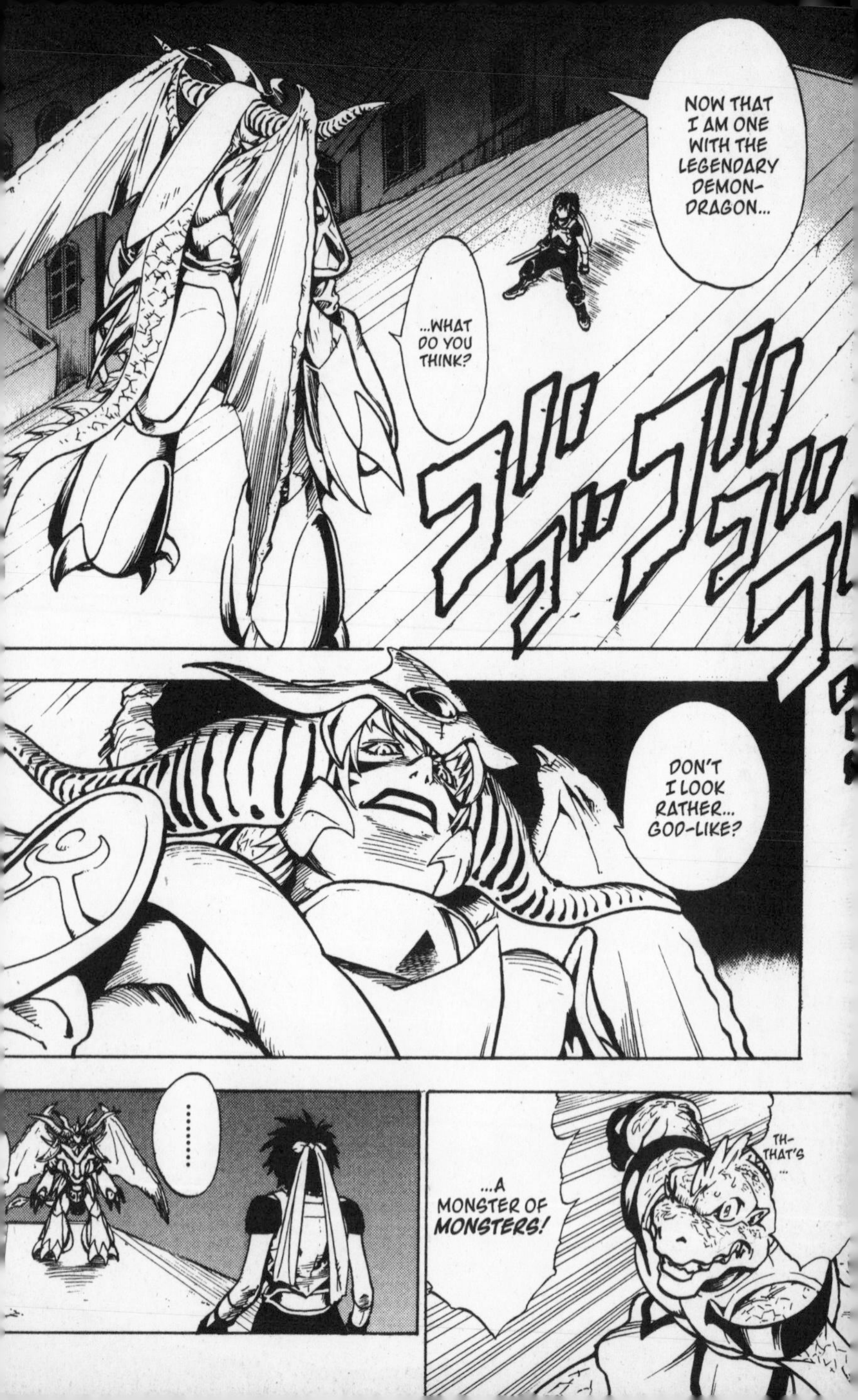
NOW THAT I AM ONE WITH THE LEGENDARY DEMON-DRAGON...
...WHAT DO YOU THINK?
DON'T I LOOK RATHER... GOD-LIKE?
TH-THAT'S...
...A MONSTER OF MONSTERS!
......

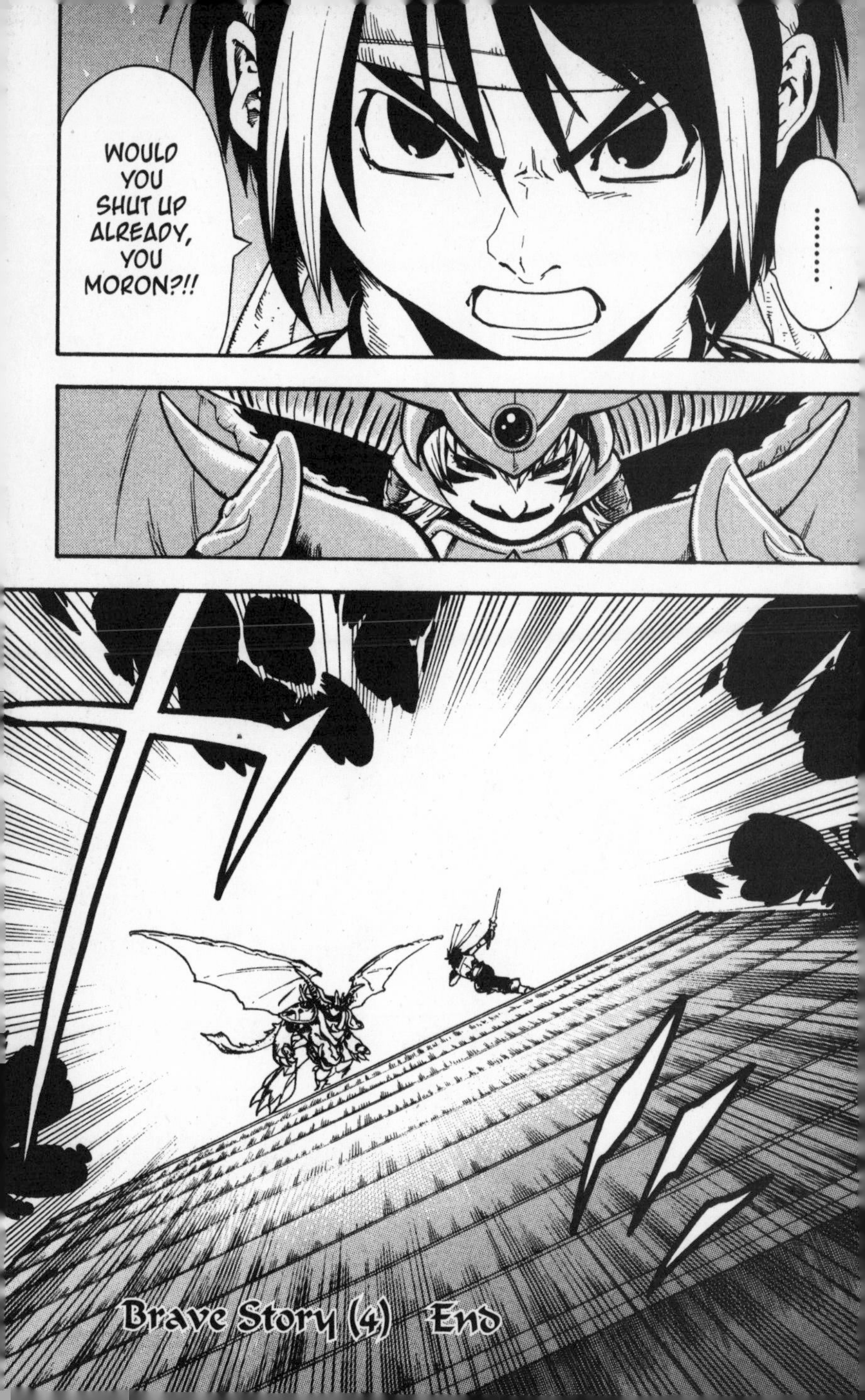

......
WOULD YOU SHUT UP ALREADY, YOU MORON?!!
Brave Story (4) End

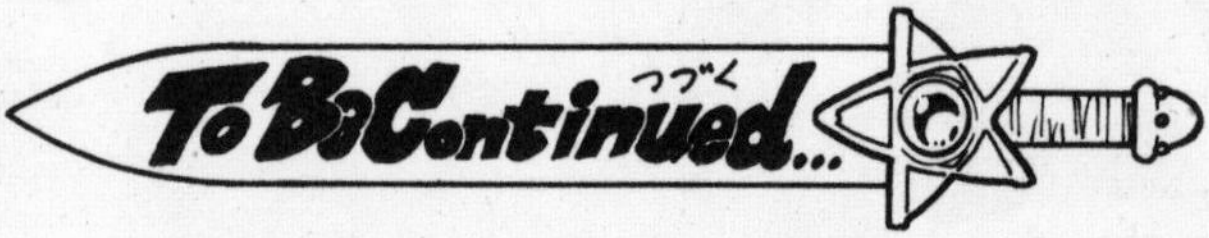
つづく
To Be Continued...

BRASTO SAGA ~5~

All Kinds of Questions Box #2

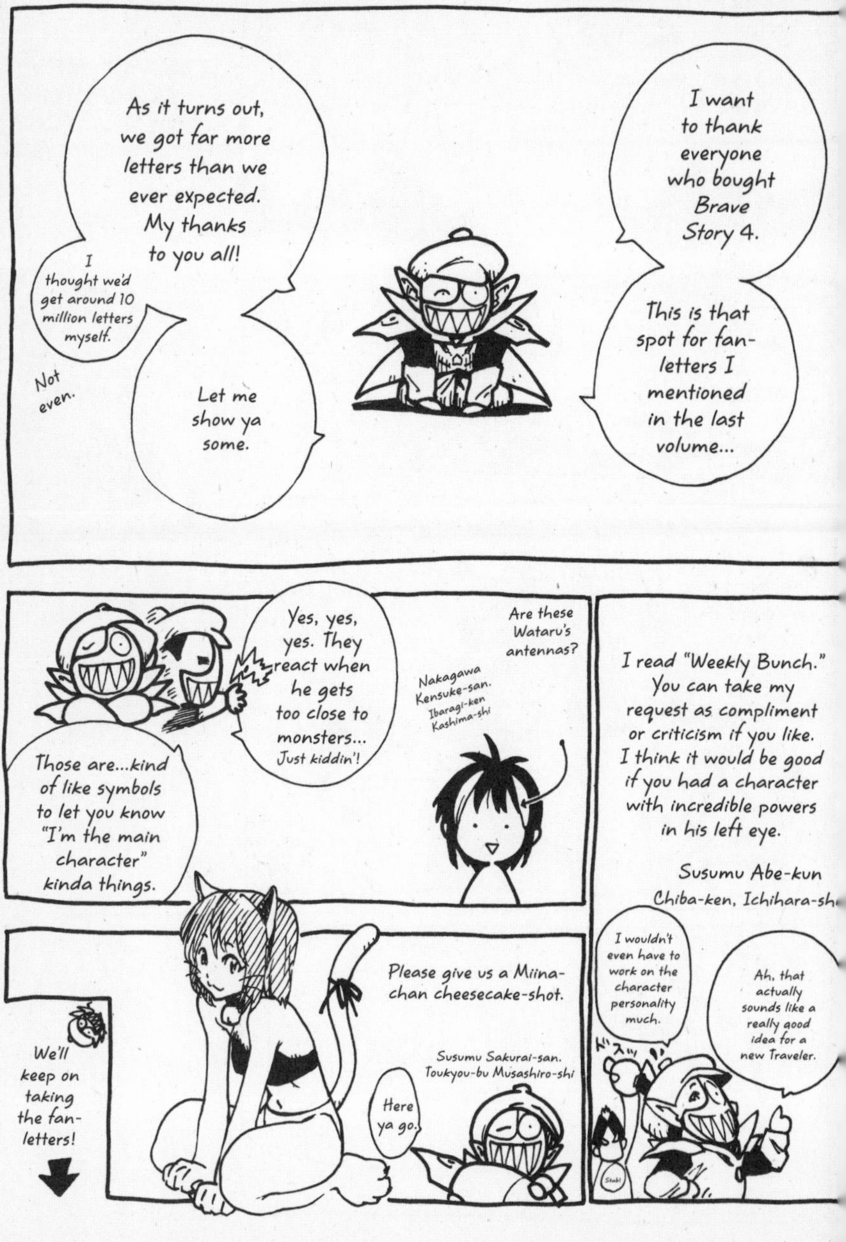

I want to thank everyone who bought Brave Story 4.
This is that spot for fan-letters I mentioned in the last volume...
As it turns out, we got far more letters than we ever expected. My thanks to you all!
I thought we'd get around 10 million letters myself.
Not even.
Let me show ya some.
I read "Weekly Bunch." You can take my request as compliment or criticism if you like. I think it would be good if you had a character with incredible powers in his left eye.
Susumu Abe-kun
Chiba-ken, Ichihara-shi
Ah, that actually sounds like a really good idea for a new Traveler.
I wouldn't even have to work on the character personality much.
ドスッ
Stab!
Are these Wataru's antennas?
Nakagawa Kensuke-san. Ibaragi-ken Kashima-shi
Yes, yes, yes. They react when he gets too close to monsters... Just kiddin'!
Those are...kind of like symbols to let you know "I'm the main character" kinda things.
Please give us a Miina-chan cheesecake-shot.
Susumu Sakurai-san. Toukyou-bu Musashiro-shi
Here ya go.
We'll keep on taking the fan-letters!

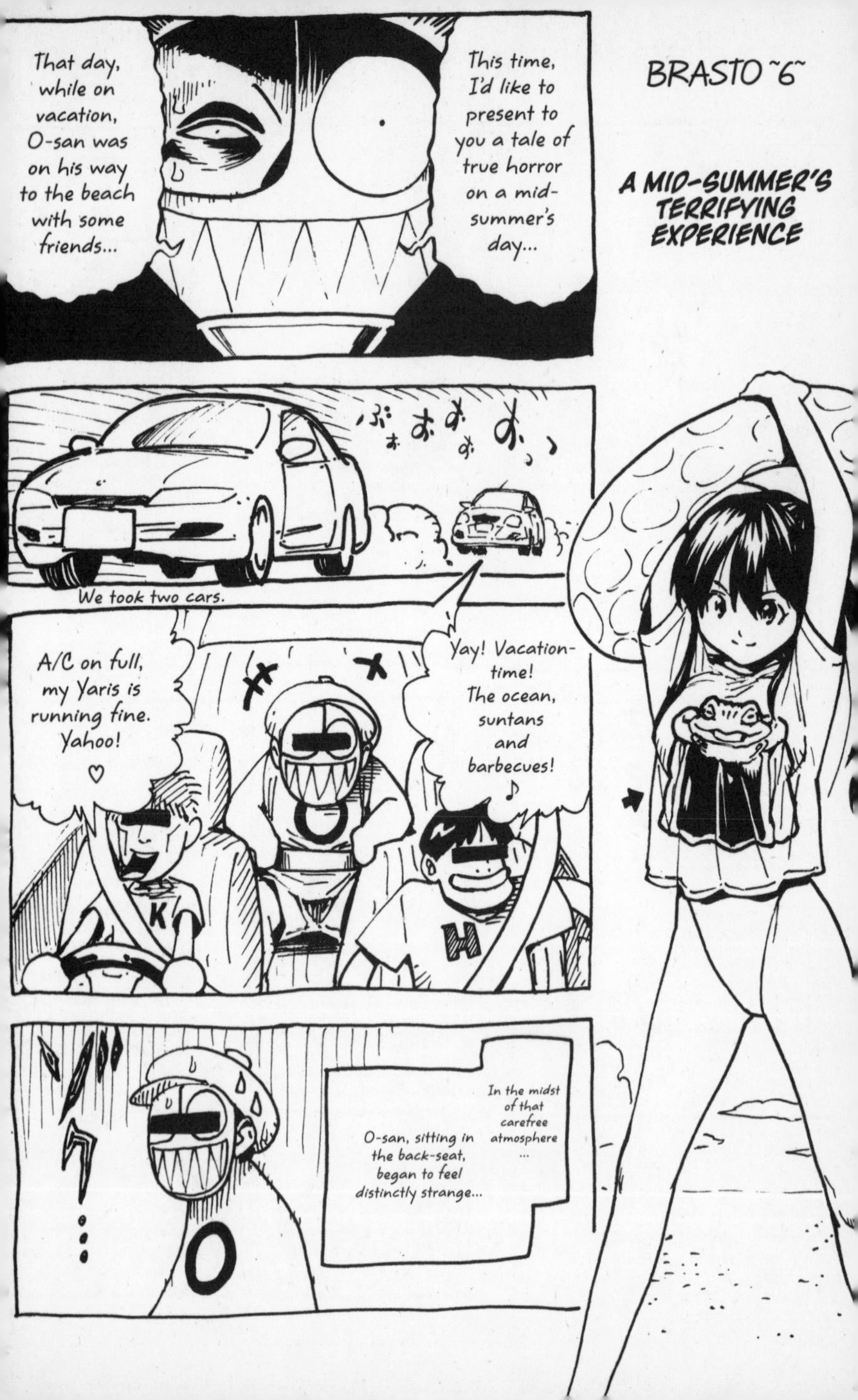
BRASTO ~6~
A MID-SUMMER'S TERRIFYING EXPERIENCE
This time, I'd like to present to you a tale of true horror on a mid-summer's day...
That day, while on vacation, O-san was on his way to the beach with some friends...
We took two cars.
Yay! Vacation-time! The ocean, suntans and barbecues! ♪
A/C on full, my Yaris is running fine. Yahoo! ♡
In the midst of that carefree atmosphere ...
O-san, sitting in the back-seat, began to feel distinctly strange...

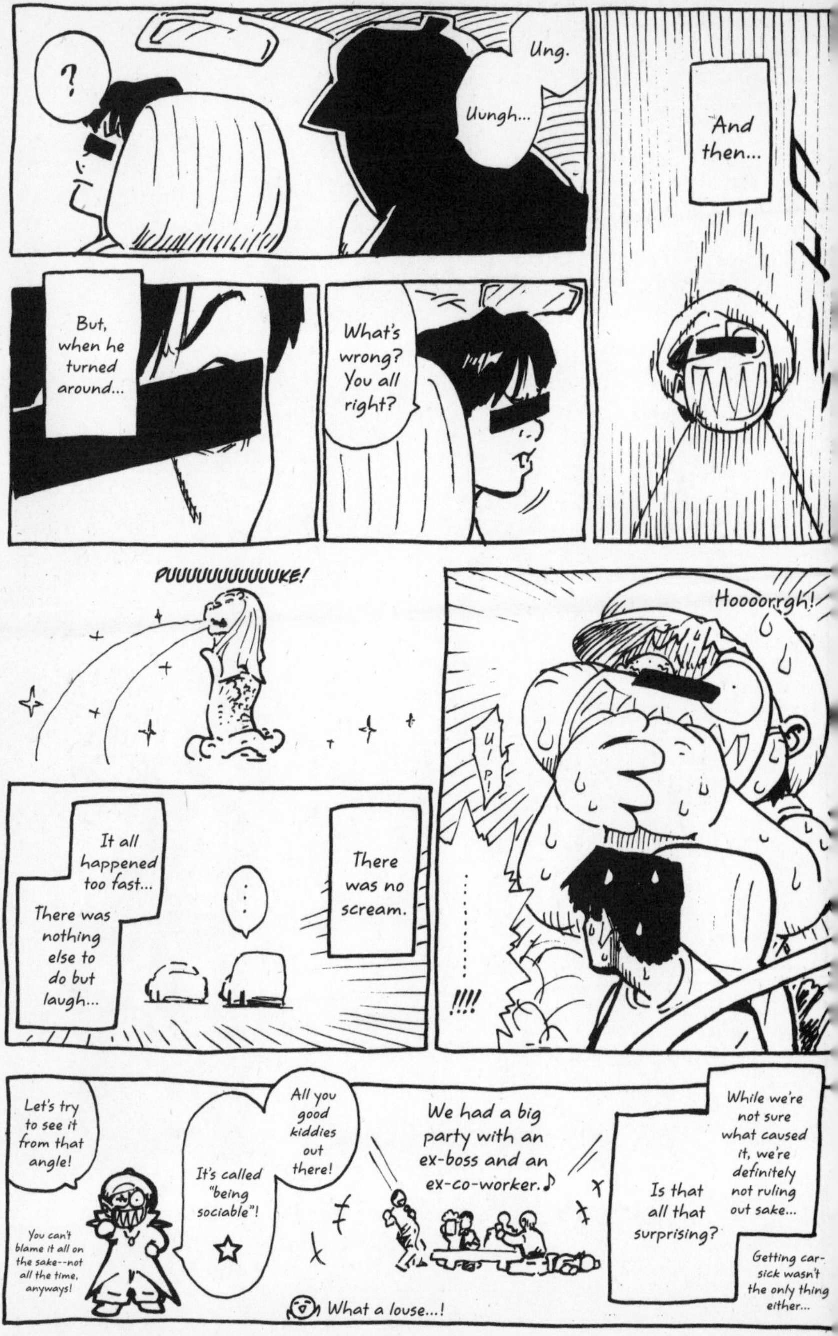
And then...
?
Ung.
Uungh...
What's wrong? You all right?
But, when he turned around...
Hoooorrgh!
UP!
......
!!!!
PUUUUUUUUUUUKE!
There was no scream.
...
It all happened too fast...
There was nothing else to do but laugh...
While we're not sure what caused it, we're definitely not ruling out sake...
Getting car-sick wasn't the only thing either...
Is that all that surprising?
We had a big party with an ex-boss and an ex-co-worker.♪
What a louse...!
All you good kiddies out there!
It's called "being sociable"! ☆
Let's try to see it from that angle!
You can't blame it all on the sake--not all the time, anyways!

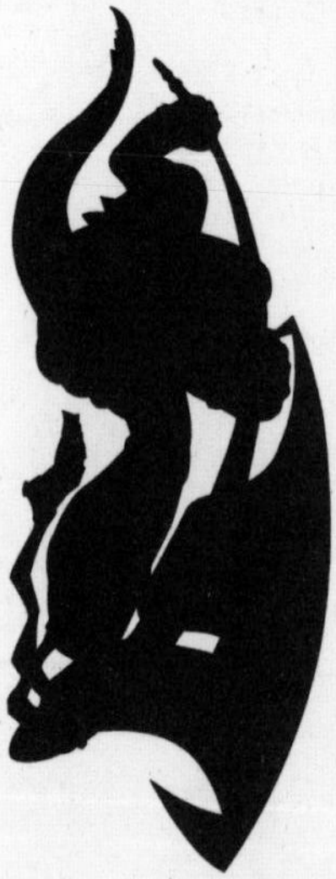

A Retelling of a Classic

BRAVE STORY

In the next volume of...

A Retelling of a Classic
BRAVE STORY

THE BATTLE BETWEEN WATARU AND BOOK OF THE
SHIGORA INTENSIFIES AS THE ANCIENT DRAGON JULIE
UNLEASHES ITS MIGHTY POWERS! WHILE THAT DUEL
IS BEING FOUGHT, UNBEKNOWNST TO WATARU AND
CREW, KAORI IS FINALLY FOUND! BUT SHE DOESN'T
QUITE SEEM TO BE IN FULL CONTROL OF HERSELF
WHEN A BRANCH PATROL TEAM FINDS HER...
THEN THE NORTHERN EMPIRE'S EVIL PLAN TO INVADE THE
SOUTHERN FEDERATION IS REVEALED! ALTHOUGH THE
SCHTENGEL KNIGHTS OF THE FEDERATION PREPARE TO
WELCOME THEIR INVADERS WITH THEIR SHARPEST AND
DEADLIEST WEAPONS IN HAND, IS THE NORTHERN EMPIRE
ARMY TOO STRONG FOR THE KNIGHTS TO TAKE ON?

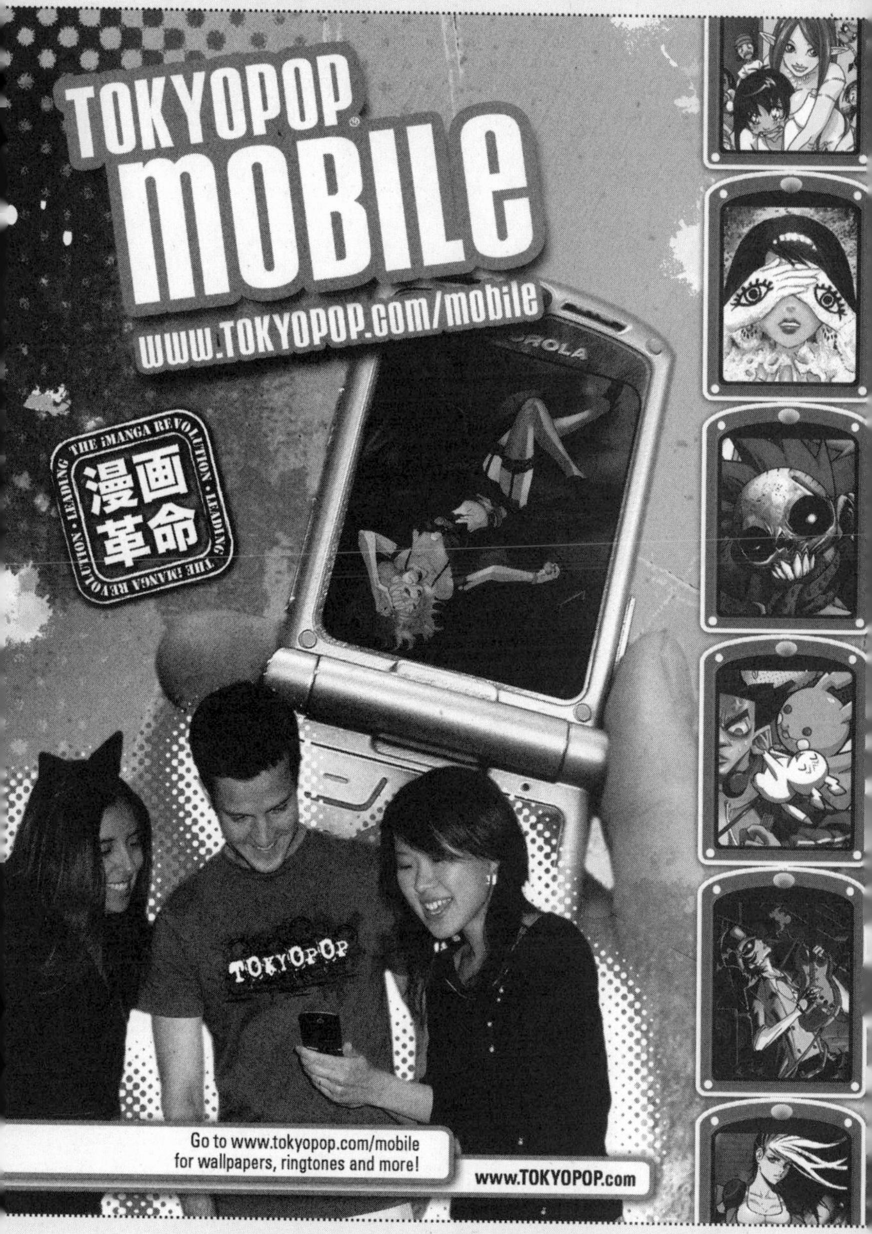
TOKYOPOP® MOBILE
www.TOKYOPOP.com/mobile
THE iMANGA REVOLUTION · LEADING · THE iMANGA REVOLUTION · LEADING
漫画革命
TOKYOPOP
Go to www.tokyopop.com/mobile
for wallpapers, ringtones and more!
www.TOKYOPOP.com

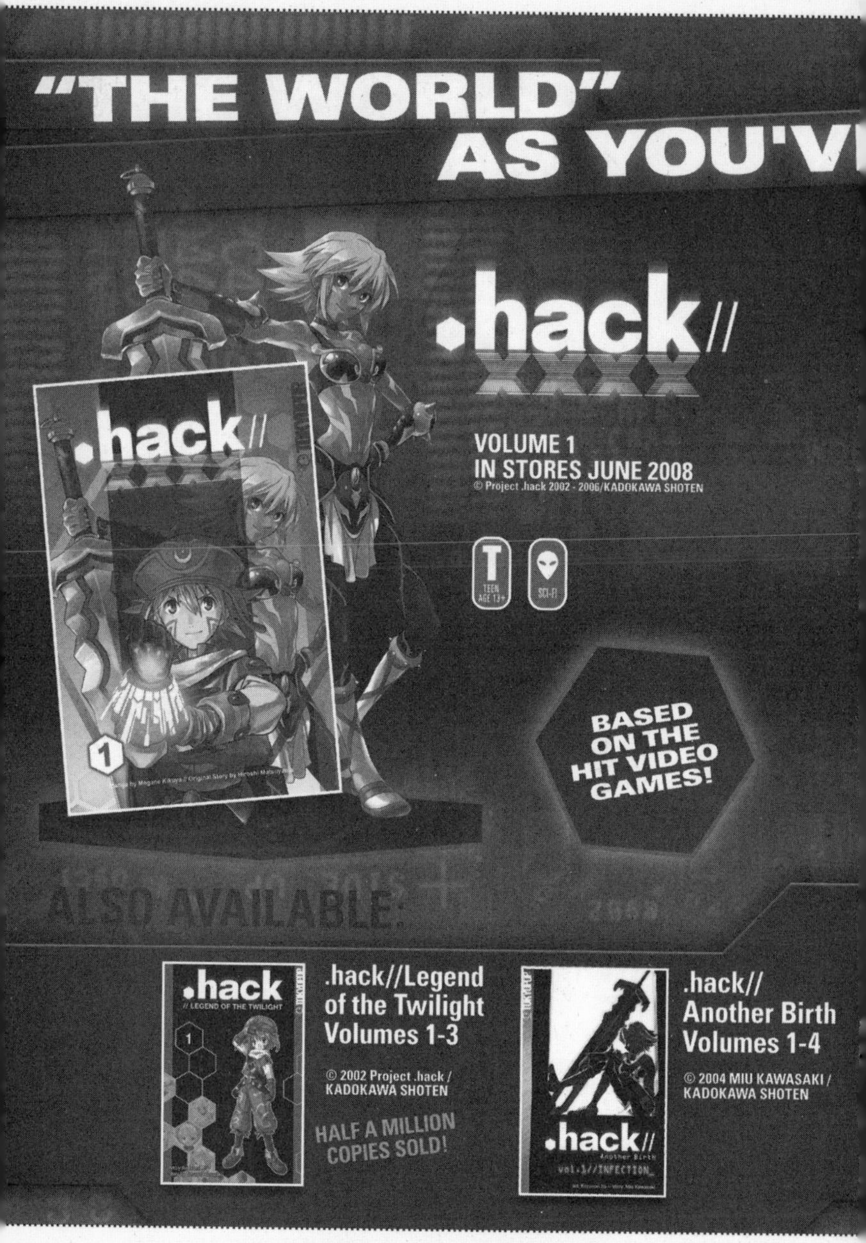
"THE WORLD"
AS YOU'V
.hack//
XXXX
VOLUME 1
IN STORES JUNE 2008
© Project .hack 2002 - 2006/KADOKAWA SHOTEN
T
TEEN AGE 13+
SCI-FI
.hack//
1
BASED ON THE HIT VIDEO GAMES!
ALSO AVAILABLE:
.hack
// LEGEND OF THE TWILIGHT
1
.hack//Legend of the Twilight Volumes 1-3
© 2002 Project .hack / KADOKAWA SHOTEN
HALF A MILLION COPIES SOLD!
.hack//
Another Birth
vol.1//INFECTION_
.hack// Another Birth Volumes 1-4
© 2004 MIU KAWASAKI / KADOKAWA SHOTEN

FOR MORE INFORMATION VISIT:

STOP!

This is the back of the book.
You wouldn't want to spoil a great ending!

FEB 1 5 2011

This book is printed "manga-style," in the authentic Japanese right-to-left format. Since none of the artwork has been flipped or altered, readers get to experience the story just as the creator intended. You've been asking for it, so TOKYOPOP® delivered: authentic, hot-off-the-press, and far more fun!

DIRECTIONS

If this is your first time reading manga-style, here's a quick guide to help you understand how it works.

It's easy... just start in the top right panel and follow the numbers. Have fun, and look for more 100% authentic manga from TOKYOPOP®!